SPORTS TALK RADIO IS A WASTE OF TIME

(And so is This Book)

A Common Sense Look At the
Sports World Past and Present

TIM HOLLAND

iUniverse, Inc.
New York   Bloomington

Sports Talk Radio Is A Waste of Time (And so is This Book)
A Common Sense Look At the Sports World Past and Present

iUniverse books may be ordered through booksellers or by contacting:

iUniverse
1663 Liberty Drive
Bloomington, IN 47403
www.iuniverse.com
1-800-Authors (1-800-288-4677)

ISBN: 978-1-4502-5330-7 (pbk)
ISBN: 978-1-4502-5331-4 (cloth)
ISBN: 978-1-4502-5332-1 (ebk)

Printed in the United States of America

iUniverse rev. date: 10/04/2010

A Few Scenarios:

Joe Q. Athlete comes to the plate in the World Series. It's the bottom of the ninth and his team trails 6-3. There are two outs and the bases are loaded. Joe Q. is no ordinary ballplayer. He is a .300 hitter with power and speed. He's a Gold Glove fielder. He's a perennial all-star. He's just the man his team wants at the plate this moment.

The confrontation between pitcher and hitter commences as Joe Q. steps into the box. As he takes the first pitch for a strike, the T.V. cameras cut to the stands. The audience sees a young man sitting in the box seats with the player's wives and girlfriends. The announcer says that he is Joe Q.'s boyfriend. "Boy, he must be dying with every pitch," says the color commentator. This goes on throughout the at bat. Joe Q. battles. The T.V. camera shows his boyfriend. All the way up to a full count of 3-2.

Now, the World Series rides on one pitch. A quick cut to Joe Q.'s boyfriend. Then back to Joe. Q. Then the pitch. Joe Q. crushes it to deep centerfield over the 400 foot sign for a grand slam home run to win the Series. As he rounds the bases, the stadium goes nuts. The T.V. cameras cut to Joe. Q.'s boyfriend who is being hugged by the other players wives (maybe) and mobbed by other fans around him (maybe). Joe Q. crosses home plate and is hoisted to the shoulders of his teammates. He celebrates with them for a while then goes over to the stands to find his boyfriend. They embrace on camera (maybe) and kiss each other on the lips. They look into each other's eyes and say "I love you." Then embrace.

Scenario II

It is the Super Bowl. Johnny Touchdown is one of the best quarterbacks in the league. He has led his team to their first Super Bowl appearance winning every award imaginable along the way. He is a perennial all-pro. During the course of his career, he has set records for touchdown passes in a season and thrown for over 5,000 yards. He was an All-American in college. Now, he is on the verge of his first pro football title.

In the Super Bowl, Johnny Touchdown plays one of the best games in pro football history. Throwing touchdown passes left and right while shredding the enemy defense. After each touchdown he throws, we are shown a young man in the stands. The fans know who he is, because the network just did a ten minute segment on him and Johnny during the pre game show. How they have been together for ten years and are in the middle of trying to adopt a child. They are not married, because same sex marriage is not legal in their state, but live together.

Johnny's live in boyfriend shows little emotion after every score. He leaves that to Mr. Touchdown. Mr. Touchdown celebrates each score with the enthusiasm of a child. After each one, he points to a section in the stands where his boyfriend sits. The fans around the boyfriend know who Johnny is pointing to and pat their neighbor on the back (maybe) and high five him (maybe).

After the game, as the confetti falls and Johnny gets the Super Bowl Trophy and MVP award, the boyfriend makes his way down to the field. He and Johnny embrace then hold up the MVP award. The TV cameras along with NFL Films, captures it all. Johnny and the boyfriend hold hands as they walk off of the field together. Later in his press conference Johnny Touchdown says that he couldn't have done it without his boyfriend.

Scenario III

Jumpin' Jack Jones plays basketball in New York City. Like Joe Q. and Johnny Touchdown he is a star. All-star, All-Pro, Dream Team you name it. He's been on championship teams in New York and seems to be a surefire hall of famer.

Jumpin' Jack loves the nightlife. However, unlike his teammates and peers, Jack likes to frequent the gay bars and clubs. It is known throughout the sport that Jumpin' Jack hangs out with men after hours from coast to coast and he is very open about it. He is followed by paparazzi, because this is big news. It doesn't bother him one bit.

Open a magazine and you will find Jumpin' Jack with gay celebrities from all walks of life. Musicians, actors, businessmen and artists. He names San Francisco as his favorite place to hang out when on the road. The gay community eats it up and he is a fan favorite from coast to coast. They hold up signs with their phone numbers asking him out for dates. Groupies follow him and hang out in the hotel lobbies where the team stays. Talk shows invite him on to talk as he's very bright, very articulate and very funny. What's not to like about him? He's a good young man. He's never in trouble with the law. He's always courteous to everyone. He signs autographs (if anyone wants them). He comes from a good home with two God fearing parents. Graduated from college with a degree in Psychology. He is the All-American boy.

Scenario IV

"Slapshot" Sullivan is one of the best hockey players in the game. He can score, defend, pass, skate you name it. He always seems to be one or two steps ahead of the opposition when he has the puck on his stick. His teammates love him for his work ethic, knowledge of the game and ability to play with pain. Like many scorers, he is poetry in motion.

Unlike many scorers, he is as tough as nails and willing to drop the gloves with anyone. Messing with Slapshot is putting your life in your hands, because he learned how to fight as a street tough in Montreal and knows how to use his fists. Slapshot has scored more knockouts than some heavyweight boxing champions.

His following of gay fans know this. No one on the ice will call Slapshot out on his manhood even though everyone knows he's gay. His teammates don't mind when Slapshot comes to their defense, because they know anytime he roughs up an opponent it completely demoralizes the rest of their team. Hockey fans across the league tried to get Slapshot's goat early in his career, but found that he was as tough, if not tougher, than anyone on their team and could beat them on the ice as well.

Scenario V

Campus, USA. The top teams in the conference and bitter rivals are playing to decide who's got the best basketball team. The home team is known for being some of the most rowdy and creative fans in all of college basketball. Tonight would be no exception.

Their opponent is led by the man considered the best player in the conference. Being that the two schools reside in the same state, everyone knows everything about both clubs players. And everyone knows that BMOC is not only the best player in the conference, but the only openly gay player. This is all of the ammunition the home team's fans need.

As BMOC enters the arena, he is met with taunts and jeers from the home crowd. Fans dress in drag with shirts displaying his number. Signs are held up ridiculing him and his teammates. When his name is called over the P.A. he is roundly booed.

As the game progresses, the crowd gets louder and more intense. It is a nip and tuck affair and BMOC more than holds his own. It is obvious that this one is going to come down to the wire with BMOC more than likely having the ball in his hands to win the game.

Sure enough, the home team leads by two with less than ten seconds to play. BMOC's team has the ball. After a time out, the ball is inbounded to BMOC who dribbles across the half court line towards the top of the key. Every fan in the arena is on their feet many of them calling out insults to BMOC. As the clock winds down, BMOC studies his opponent and dribbles it down to two seconds. With both feet behind the three point line, he rises and with a flick of the wrist takes the shot. It's straight and true heading right for the basket. The horn sounds as the ball swishes through the hoop giving BMOC's team the victory and the conference championship while silencing the fans. As BMOC and his happy teammates run off the court to the locker room, the home fans look on in stunned silence and BMOC blows them a kiss goodbye.

Scenario VI

It is the big game. The game of the week watched from coast to coast. Fans everywhere have gathered in front of their television sets alone and in groups to see who will win this titanic clash.

During the break, an ad for a well known beer company comes on. In it, we see Joe Q., Johnny Touchdown and Jumpin' Jack Jones at the bar. They are holding bottles of said beer and tell us that it's the one for them. There are no women in the bar, only men. Dancing and singing with their arms around one another.

The next commercial shows Jumpin' Jack driving to the basket and slam dunking on some poor soul. The camera pans to his shoes and tells us how they make Jack jump higher, run faster and shoot better. A Rap jingle is played and Jack is high fived by his friends as he heads back up court and a crowd of men in the stands goes crazy.

Then we get a commercial of Joe Q. playing left field. Behind him are a group of adoring male fans holding up signs and all wearing some form of clothing with Joe's number on it. The batter crushes a ball to left field and Joe takes off toward the stands. It's obvious that this ball is gone unless Joe can get to the wall, leap and pull it back. Running as fast as he can, Joe times his leap, goes up over the wall and makes the catch. He tumbles into the stands as his adoring fans go crazy. They pick him up so that he can show the umpire he's made the catch then mob him. We get a close up of the glove that Joe wears and are told it's what makes him an all-star.

The next commercial is, of course, Johnny Touchdown joined by his boyfriend. It is for an electronics companies HDTV. The two of them are shown sitting on a couch together sharing a bowl of popcorn and watching a movie. They both comment on the television's picture and sound quality along with all of its other features. Needless to say, they tell the public it's the HDTV for them.

Of course, these are all hypothetical situations. The question is, "Are we ready for this?" Are we ready for an openly gay superstar? Not an openly gay player.

But an openly gay player who is a superstar?

And more important, should we be?

IT'S NOT YOU. IT'S ME

I have a confession to make. Though I try, with the exception of track and field I just can't watch women's sports. Not basketball. Not softball. Not soccer. Not hockey. Not volleyball. Not lacrosse.

Before I explain myself let me give you a little of my past.

I come from a very athletic family of eight, five girls and three boys. Growing up, we played everything. Pickup games in the backyard whenever the weather allowed. Three of my sisters played competitive sports. One just played softball though she could run like the wind. Another played softball and ran track. And the third played softball and was very good at basketball. Yes, I lost to them a few times. My excuse is that they were older. The other two didn't play team competitive sports, but were good athletes too. When people see pictures of my family they comment on how athletic my sisters look. I was very proud of them all.

I went to college at the same time that Cheryl Miller was dominating the women's game at USC. Whenever she and the Trojans came on TV we dropped everything to watch. I can remember being in the middle of some of the most competitive pickup basketball games you'll ever see when someone would ask what time it was. If it was time for Cheryl Miller, that game was over.

Since then, I have only watched women's college basketball sporadically. I know how good the Tennessee and Connecticut women have been over the years and watched Maryland's team win it all in 2006. I have a lot of respect for them and how they play the game. The only time I'll sit and watch a game, however, is if it's the Final Four.

When the WNBA began, I watched. It was right after the women had won Olympic gold in 1996 and there was a rush to cash in on their success. I can remember a friend of mine telling me that the women's game would surpass the men's game in popularity. This was a man who was ten years older than me which came as a surprise. I told him no way. They would be a niche sport at best. I knew why I said that the point of which I'll get at shortly.

I had no interest in women's soccer during their World Cup run. It was nice as far as country, but it didn't raise my interest in the game one bit. It was a moment in time nothing more.

Even though they are not as good, I will watch high school sports, before watching professional women. I watch, because there is always a chance of seeing someone who may make it to the college and pro level. Knowing that these athletes have the potential to get better and a higher goal to be obtained makes me want to watch. It's like watching a child grow up. With the women I know that they are at their peak, which is very good, and not going to get much better.

During the last Winter Olympics, a woman asked if I had been watching the USA women's hockey team. I told her no and I probably wouldn't. She asked me if I liked hockey and I said yes. Then she followed up with how come I wasn't watching the women.

I had to be honest with her and with myself. The truth was, I wasn't watching, because of my own male chauvinism. I could not enjoy the women's accomplishment's because I was too busy comparing them to the men. In essence I was saying that I wasn't watching, because I didn't think that they were good enough for me to pay attention to. How lame.

As I said earlier with the exception of track and field, I don't watch women's sports. If I watch a basketball game I lose interest, because they can't dunk or put on the moves the men can. If I watch a soccer game I find myself saying that they run too slow. If I watch softball, they don't hit the ball as far. If I watch hockey, they don't skate as fast or hit the puck as hard. And I'll never watch a women's football game.

Another reason is that when I watch a sporting event I want to be entertained. I want to see Kobe or Lebron score 40. I want to see

Beckham bend it (the few times I watch soccer). I want to see Alex Ovechkin get a hat trick. I want to see Ryan Howard hit the ball 500 feet. In other words, I want to see something that I've never seen before and there always seems to be more of a chance with that in the men's game than in the women's.

It all gets back to the men with me and that's not right. These women are very good athletes in their own right. They are hard workers who could probably run circles around me in their sport. And there are plenty of stars past and present. Mia Hamm in soccer. The Houston Comets team, Chamique Holdsclaw, Sue Bird and Dawn Staley in the WNBA. Jenny Finch in softball. All terrific athletes. Just as good in their game as any man is in his (there I go again).

They will play their games with very little interest from me. I will watch if it's an event like the Final Four, the Olympics or the World Cup. Other than that if it's not on the track I won't be watching and it's not their fault.

The bottom line is that the problem is not with them. It's with me.

ELEVATING THE MADNESS

The Golden Age of NCAA men's basketball is over. It covered the years from 1981-82 to 1998-99. During that time we had four year players, All-Americans, great teams, great players, great coaches, great games, great rivalries, great conference tournaments, great tournament games, great Final Fours and great championships. It seemed as though every night the ACC, Big East, Big Ten, SEC and Pac 10 conferences had a game on that was must see TV. It was worth taking the first two days off from work to watch the NCAA tournament, better known as "March Madness". Final Four Saturday was must see and the Monday night championship never seemed to disappoint. You knew the players even the freshman, because you had read about them in the preseason preview magazines.

Then in the late nineties it all began to change. The biggest change was players deciding to skip out early for the pros. It was one thing when the sophomores and juniors left early. It became another when the Kobe Bryants, Kevin Garnetts and Tracy McGradys of the world decided to skip college all together. This caused a trickled down effect in the talent pool and teams became not as good, because talent that should have been going to smaller schools was now going to the bigger ones. And the revolving door of talent made it hard to keep up with who was who. Couple that with the fact that the NCAA tournament made the regular season and conference tournaments basically meaningless and the Golden Age was done. And that's too bad, because college basketball at its best is as exciting as anything in sports.

Then there was talk about expanding the tournament field from 65 teams, which most people think is perfect, to 96 against most fans wishes. If the regular season wasn't already meaningless it would really be with a 96 team field. And most fans would be apathetic towards another round with teams they feel are not going to have a chance to make the Final Four. The NCAA may go to 96 teams, but not at the moment. The decision was made to add three more teams for a field of 68. Instead of having one play in game between teams number 64 and 65 there will be four with the lowest seeded teams playing one another. And we get further away from the Golden Age.

There is a way to bring another Golden Age of college basketball. A way to make the regular season more relevant than it's ever been. A way to make the conference tournaments must see TV. And a way to make "March Madness" better than it already is, maybe even the most watched television event this side of the Super Bowl.

How about a 32 team Tournament of Champions? Only the teams who win their regular season or conference tournament would be allowed in the field. Take the top two teams from the top eight conferences and one team each from the sixteen conferences considered the next best. Here is how it would work.

Let's say for the sake of argument the top eight conferences in the nation are the ACC, Big East, Big Ten, Big XII, SEC, Pac Ten, Conference USA and Atlantic 10. These are where most of the top 25 and Final Four teams come from anyway so let's go with them. The winner of the regular season would get the automatic bid to the NCAA tournament, as they should, and the winner of the conference tournament would get the other bid. If there is a tie during the regular season the winner of the head to head matchup would get the automatic bid. If they split their head to head matchups, the team which goes the furthest in the conference tournament gets it. If they get eliminated in the same round then they would have a play in game before the conference tournament championship. If the team which wins the regular season wins the conference tournament, than the team which finished second in the regular season gets the second NCAA tournament bid. Then take the next 16 conferences which we call mid-majors and have the winner of the conference tournament get their automatic bid which is already the case. That gets us to our 32.

Sure we would lose the first Thursday and Friday of the 68 team tournament, but look at it this way. We would have meaningful basketball all season long. From the opening of the conference regular season to the last regular season game the drama would unfold. Then we would have three days of conference tournaments where, because everyone who didn't win the regular season would have a second chance, the coaches of the teams still trying to get in would be pulling their hair out. And the players, especially the seniors, would be playing as if it were their last game because it just might be. Then we would go right into the round of 32 with all of them being of championship caliber, no team any less than second best in their conference.

The best part of having a tournament of champions is that the competition committee would only have to seed the teams, because they would have all earned their way in. As much as people talk about the Bowl Championship Series (BCS) and how bad it is for college football think of this. The NCAA tournament seeds are decided by the competition committee. They take into account strength of schedule, strength of conference, overall record, conference record and final rankings by the media and coaches. Isn't this the same method that the BCS uses to decide who plays for the football National Championship? And doesn't the committee end up leaving out some deserving teams just as the BCS does. The point is that the NCAA basketball tournament is organized the same way as the football national championship. By human beings in a boardroom or at a news outlet or on a college campus by a head coach who hasn't seen most of the teams he's voting on. A tournament of champions would eliminate all of this, because every team would earn their way into it by winning either the regular season or conference tournament. Everything would be decided on the court.

And what happens to the 36 teams who would normally be in the tournament field? Why the National Invitational Tournament, of course. Which would be more entertaining, because it would have better, more well known teams and it would have controversy, because of the teams who would feel "wronged" in not making it to the big dance while someone with a lesser record does. It would also teach the players on these teams that basketball, like life, is sometimes unfair. What you may work hard for just might not come to fruition. If the worst thing to happen to them in their lives would be not making the NCAA tournament, then their lives will be pretty good.

Of course, this will never happen for obvious reasons. First being the reason the NCAA wants to expand to 96 teams anyway. They know that the regular season is meaningless so why not add another round of meaningful playoff games academics be damned. They would rather have the extra TV money while looking at half full arenas from coast to coast during the first three days of the tournament. All one has to do now is look at the half empty arenas at the neutral sites where the first two days of the tournament are played. Most hardcore basketball fans will tell you that the first two rounds are nothing more than a weeding out process and the tournament doesn't really start until it gets to 16 teams.

I say to this, what about having full arenas all year from coast to coast, because of the meaning brought back to the regular season? Even the out of conference matchups at the beginning of the season would draw fans who want to see how their team stacks up nationally against teams from other conferences. Then the conference tournament venues would be standing room only as the teams scratched and clawed for one tournament bid. And, believe me, the television networks would buy into it. They would be fools not to take advantage of having all of the extra viewers during the regular season and conference tournaments to sell commercial air time. This would help bring in more revenue all around for college basketball.

Second, the coaches would never stand for it. They feel as though they have enough pressure on them as it is. True, cutting the tournament field from 68 to 32 would make it harder to win a National Championship. And maybe there would be more pressure to field the best team no matter how it's done. But it seems to me that most college athletic directors are worried more about raising money than winning championships. If they aren't their bosses, the university presidents, are. So if anything the money brought in from the regular season and conference tournaments should lessen the pressure on them to win it all. Just make a run every year with a few trips to the tournament and things should be fine. Of course, that wouldn't be the case at schools like Kentucky, North Carolina, Kansas and Duke.

Third, there is no way that the tournament field would be contracted. Most people felt that the 65 team field wasn't broken so why did they have to fix that. There has never been a time where the playoff field has been reduced. Once you expand, contracting seems out of the question.

So I'm pretty sure that the Tournament of Champions will never take place. Thus there will never be another Golden Age of men's college basketball. That's too bad, because it really could be so much better.

TOO MUCH OF A GOOD THING

Once you could not find sports of any kind on your television or radio most of the week. There was no ESPN, Fox Sports or regional cable sports stations. During the spring and summer, if the local baseball team was on the road they might be on TV. If they were at home forget it. It was the same with college and pro basketball and hockey. Home blackouts were the norm in all sports so you might have seen the local team live no more than half the season. Talk radio was local and only on the AM wavelength. High school athletics were covered locally if at all. The only children's sport that was broadcast was the Little League World Series though where I grew up we had the "Marriot Super Bowl" of youth football games every Saturday.

As for highlights, well there was the six and eleven o'clock news. They gave you all of the local sports and whatever the major national story was. That lasted three to six minutes. On Monday night, the pro football team would do a studio show with highlights of Sunday's game. On weekends, the leagues would have their own highlight shows like "This Week in Pro Football" or "This Week in Baseball." This was a chance to see the out of market teams and players. The NFL would show highlights of other games at halftime or in the postgame show. That was it.

There was no Sunday night anything. A lot of cities had curfews on Sunday afternoon. Nothing was played after maybe 5:00 p.m. In the fall, the NFL's second game would end at 7:00 p.m. eastern time and you were done. After Monday Night Football you got nothing until the Saturday afternoon college game of the week. Colleges had rules on how many times each team could be on national television. Notre Dame was the only team to have all of their football and basketball games televised with them shown on tape delay every Sunday morning. In the winter, you got a pro basketball and hockey game on Saturday or Sunday. College basketball games were shown on Saturday and Sunday afternoon. In the summer there was the Saturday afternoon baseball game of the week and later a Monday night contest. ABC shows like "Wide World of Sports", "the American Sportsmen" and "The Superstars" along with CBS "Sports Spectacular" and NBC's "Sports World" filled the rest of the void. Boxing was huge and there were championship fights galore on regular TV no less.

Christmas and Easter were off limits. The NFL played playoff games on Christmas Day in 1971. When Christmas fell on a Sunday in 1977 they moved the NFC first round to Monday afternoon. The Blue-Gray college all-star football game was all there was on December 25.

Then along came the Major League Baseball Championship Series. It was the first event that I can remember being played on a Sunday night. Pro football soon followed with Thursday and Sunday night regular season games. The Fiesta Bowl was played on Christmas Day. The Big East conference was created and we got college basketball on Monday and Friday nights, the Atlantic Coast Conference on Wednesdays. The landscape of televised sports was changing.

In 1979 ESPN was born. Starting out showing anything and everything the network grew into what it is today while spawning other national and local sports cable channels along with league owned networks. All of a sudden, blackouts were lifted and the home team was accessible on TV almost every night. Sunday through Saturday became the sports fans delight with game after game and highlights 24 hours a day seven days a week. Then talk radio went from local to national and to television. Now, we are bombarded with sports programming and no day or sport is off limits.

The question is, "How much is too much?" Do we need to have football, baseball, basketball and hockey news around the clock year round? Do we need games on TV every night of the week? Do we need 24 hours of highlights? Do we need to know every high school athlete in the country before they sign their letter of intent? Heck, do we need to know them before they even get to high school? Do we need one hour pregame shows before everything? Do we need 24 hour sports talk radio? Do we need up close and personal stories about everyone involved in the sport?

It all seems to be a little much. One basketball game blends with another and another. Baseball games seem to get slower and slower. Even football can become a little monotonous at times. If you miss anything it will be shown a hundred times during the week if not totally replayed. The respective seasons overlap one another and we are beaten down with highlights. After a while, all of the players, teams and games start to look the same. The joy of a buzzer beater, walk off home run, game winning goal or "Hail Mary" touchdown is almost lost, because five minutes later it seems someone else does it and we see it again. Players and fans hamming it up for the cameras has become the norm. Part of the joy of watching sports in the past was that we were always left wanting more. All we got was a taste on weekends and the occasional weeknight baseball, basketball or hockey game.

I cannot remember the last time there were no sports programming on TV. Never in my life did I think I'd get weary of it, but I have. Mainly the highlight shows. The games are still worth watching, but the highlight shows are not. Too many talking heads, music clips and show business glitz. NFL Network had a good one when it first began in which they only showed narrated highlights and postgame interviews on Sunday night through Monday morning, nothing else. Then they made it a studio show just like all of the others. Call me old school, but I liked the first version better.

Though weary of it, I must admit that if things went back to the way they were it wouldn't be good. Like all addicts, we cannot get enough of a good thing myself included. If a sports channel is taken away from me, I want it back. If someone else's cable company can get something that I can't, I want it. If sports talk radio disappeared I would have nothing to listen to when there is no good music in my car. If there were no highlight shows, even the one on the "worldwide leader in sports", to turn to I'd be lost. The problem is that the networks know this so they can dictate how, when and what they want to show us. Like sheep, we follow, but if something is on TV or radio that I don't want to watch or listen to (which is 75 to 80 per cent of the junk they show and air) I'm out of there.

The one thing that I wish they would cut back on is the national coverage of high school and youth sports. Those should be covered by local media, because they belong to the community. Other than that, I'm glad we are able to pick and choose our programming.

So back to the question, "Is it too much of a good thing?"

Yes, it is. But it's nice to have it readily available.

UPSET? DON'T THINK SO

I don't believe in upsets. To me, if two opponents square off one of them has to win. And if the one with the lesser record wins it's because they were better that day. That's the only day that matters.

We tend to throw the word upset around a little too much. How can a nine seed beating an eight in the NCAA tournament be an upset? How can a three-point underdog winning a football game be an upset? How can any team winning a championship game or series be considered an upset? And how can there ever be an upset in college sports when 18 to 22 year old athletes are involved? No one knows what we're going to get from them, because they're not mature enough to be consistent.

The point is, anytime the team or player that is not favored wins everyone is quick to say that it shouldn't have happened regardless of the situation. Never mind the fact that point spreads are set up by human beings only for the sole purpose of evening out the betting money.

If you look back at all of the so called "upsets" in sports history there are common threads. Usually the underdog is either playing at home or on a neutral site. Many times, the opponents have already met earlier in the season. The favorite could have an injured player who is less effective or doesn't play at all. Sometimes it's just the law of averages. The winner has won so much that they are due for a letdown or it's a new season and there has been a major turnover in the roster. The head coach of the underdog may have been a former assistant for the favorite and knows their personnel. Or maybe, just maybe, the team that we think is going to win isn't as good as we think they are and the underdog isn't as bad.

Let's look at a few "upsets" in my lifetime and you will see what I mean.

The first that comes to mind is Super Bowl III in 1969 between the NFL champion Baltimore Colts and the AFL champion New York Jets. The Jets were 18 point underdogs in a championship game played at a neutral site. And their head coach, Weeb Ewbank, had come from Baltimore five years earlier. The key words are championship game, neutral site and former head coach. New York 16, Baltimore 7. The next year the AFL's Kansas City Chiefs were 14 point underdogs to the NFL's Minnesota Vikings under similar circumstances the only exception being that none of the Chiefs coaches had any ties to the Vikings. Kansas City dominated and when looking back at Minnesota's Super Bowl history of 0-4 we know this not to be an upset at all.

Later in the 1969 sports year, the New York Mets faced the Baltimore Orioles in the World Series. The so called "Miracle Mets" beat the Orioles four games to one. The Mets won 100 games in 1969 and swept the Braves in the National League Championship Series. That's pretty darn good. Then they won three of their Series games at home.

When the Notre Dame basketball team defeated UCLA to end the Bruins 88 game winning streak where was the game played? In South Bend, Indiana that's where. And has anyone else even come close to winning 88 straight? The fact that 18 to 22 year olds did it with the roster changing yearly makes the streak even more remarkable.

The great undefeated Ohio State football team of 1969 was beaten by Michigan in a rivalry game played at Ann Arbor. And the head coach of Michigan was none other than former OSU assistant Bo Schembechler who had been a Buckeye assistant the year before.

The NCAA's "March Madness" is known for its "upsets" or so it seems. Once again, we get back to the neutral site and 18 to 22 year old young men. Let's take a few of these games a step further.

North Carolina State defeated Houston at a neutral site in 1983. The Wolfpack of N.C. State was not chopped liver as they were Atlantic Coast Conference Tournament champions loaded with four year seniors. And Houston's weakness was free throw shooting. Their failure to make them down the stretch opened the door for N.C. State's last second victory.

Villanova's victory over defending champion Georgetown in 1985 is far from an upset. The teams were from the same conference, the Big East, so they played each other twice a year. Both of their regular season games had been close with Georgetown winning the second one in overtime, but this is never mentioned. There was plenty of familiarity for Villanova. And when Georgetown guard Reggie Williams twisted his ankle against St. Johns in the national semifinals two nights earlier, this brought the teams even closer.

Kansas' victory over Oklahoma in 1988 was a mirror of Villanova-Georgetown. Both the Jayhawks and Sooners were from the Big Eight conference and had already met twice. The game was played in Kansas City, Missouri. It was the perfect setup for Kansas.

UNLV was undefeated in 1991 when they met Duke in the semifinals. The Blue Devils won and went on to win their first National Championship. The two teams had met the season before in the finals with UNLV winning by 30. Duke didn't forget and UNLV, as young men are known to do, came in overconfident.

Back to college football, Miami, playing at home, defeated undefeated Nebraska in the 1984 Orange Bowl game to win the National Championship. Then they went out to Tempe, Arizona and in a matchup of unbeaten teams lost the 1987 Fiesta Bowl to Penn State for the National Championship. It didn't help the Hurricanes that their quarterback Vinnie Testaverde injured himself in a moped accident before the game. In 1993, this act was repeated as Miami lost the 1993 Sugar Bowl in New Orleans, Louisiana to Alabama which was simply a better team.

Ohio State's Fiesta Bowl victory over Miami in the 2003 Fiesta Bowl was a neutral site game. It was also a game played between two undefeated teams. Texas over Southern Cal in the 2006 Rose Bowl was another case of undefeated teams along with USC not having lost in three years and the Trojans being just a little overrated.

In baseball, the 1988 Los Angeles Dodgers defeated the Oakland A's. The A's had a good team, but L.A. had to beat a very good New

York Mets team to get to the World Series. Then the Dodgers were fortunate in that the first two games of the Series were in Los Angeles. They won them and Oakland never recovered. Cincinnati did the same to Oakland two years later.

I really cannot think of a pro football upset. The Denver Broncos were underrated when they beat the Green Bay Packers in Super Bowl XXXII. The New England Patriots had already played the St. Louis Rams in the regular season, losing by only six points, when they met in Super Bowl XXXVI. And the New York Giants played the Patriots in the last game of the 2007 season, losing by three, before facing them in Super Bowl XLII. If any, it would be the Jacksonville Jaguars defeating the Broncos in the 1996 playoffs, but in a one game playoff anything can happen.

Then we get to the 1980 USA hockey team. The winners of the "Miracle on Ice" game against the Soviet Union. I'm not buying it. The two teams had met before so it wasn't like the U.S. team didn't know anything about the Russians. And where was the game played? In Lake Placid, New York that's where. Last I checked my world atlas that is in the United States of America. The 1980 "Miracle on Ice" was also history repeating itself. It had been done just 20 years earlier in the 1960 Olympics.

No.

There is only one event that I even consider when it comes to upsets. It is the 1990 heavyweight championship boxing match between Mike Tyson and Buster Douglass. It was the perfect storm in that Tyson was ripe for the picking and Douglass was motivated by the death of his mother. Tyson was undefeated and had never been knocked down much less knocked out. Douglass knocked him out to win the belt. The only reason I even consider this one was that no one believed it after it happened. My nephews didn't believe me when I called them with the news. The news services wouldn't confirm it. It was crazy. Then again, the guy whose house we watched it at predicted that Tyson would lose before the fighters even entered the ring. He didn't consider it an upset at all.

I know that many people will disagree with me and that's fine. If the "underdog" didn't win every now and then sports wouldn't be worth watching.

I just feel like as long as the game is played by fallible human beings, it's anybody's ballgame. Though there have been undefeated teams and players, there has never been a perfect team or a perfect player. And there will never be.

WHAT HAPPENED TO BASEBALL?

Major League Baseball Commissioner Bud Selig tells the public how baseball's popularity has never been greater. We keep hearing how attendance and revenue are up across the board. New retro ballparks have sprung up from coast to coast since the opening of Baltimore's Oriole Park at Camden Yards in 1992. All of this is true, but the question to be asked is this. Why is it when I look out at baseball fields in the spring and summer where I live all of them are empty? No players. No fans. Not even softball and Little League. If no one is playing a sport that everyone used to play how is it more popular?

Why do people buy into what Commissioner Selig is saying? Maybe because baseball is the National Pastime and nostalgia gets in the way.

First off, the reason baseball's attendance figures are up is twofold. When I began watching the game, there were only 24 teams, 12 in both the American and National Leagues. Now, there are 30. That's six new teams. That's six new stadiums to fill. Wouldn't that raise attendance?

Second, baseball used to total attendance only by the number of people who came through the turnstiles. So if the box score said 13,953 then that was the number of fans who were at the game. Now they go by paid attendance which is the number of tickets sold. With many teams selling these tickets weeks in advance the attendance numbers are going to be inflated. So the Florida Marlins can announce a paid attendance of 23,000 and only have 5,000 people in the stadium. Telling people that you had a season total paid attendance of 2,000,000 people sounds much better than saying you had an actual attendance of 1,200,000. That's just good market strategy.

The increase in revenue does not come from just paid attendance. Almost every team has a cable TV contract now where in the past it was local TV and radio which paid the freight. And MLB merchandise is much more prevalent now than it used to be just as in all sports. Internet revenue helps also.

Now just because you make more money doesn't mean you are drawing more fans to your sport. Maybe the fact that ticket prices have skyrocketed has something to do with it also. If fans are paying the same amount for one ticket as they used to for four then you're going to make more money. Inflation is a part of sports just like everything else.

No, to me, the measure of a sport's popularity is the number of people who are playing it and talking about it. Where I live, an area with two baseball teams thirty miles apart no less, there are nights where you could fit the actual attendance from both in the same stadium and still have empty seats. And once the season is over it's over.

This was not always the case. There was a time where baseball ruled. Growing up I can recall every father in town was a baseball fan and a lot of the moms. And so were the kids. The hot stove league was literally that as men would talk about the game during the winter. Once spring training commenced, it was all baseball from March to the end of the World Series in October. Summer days were baseball or softball. You played one or the other whether male or female. Adults and kids had their leagues. As kids, we didn't need a league just a place to play. There were times where we literally played in the horse pasture. Everyone had a ball and a glove with bats readily available. The sound of summer was the sound of baseball on the radio or TV. Everyone knew their teams and the others around the league. Collecting baseball cards was part of being a kid. That changed in the early 1990's and it really took effect after the 1994 baseball strike which canceled the end of the regular season and postseason.

For me personally, it wasn't just the 1994 strike which began to push me away from baseball it's what the sport did when it came back. In 1996 baseball decided to split the American and National League into three divisions instead of two and double the number of postseason teams in each to four adding a wildcard team. This, in effect, killed the most exciting part of the baseball season for me, late August and September when teams were fighting to win their division pennant.

There was nothing better than watching two or more teams fight it out down the stretch for one playoff spot. Would the frontrunner hold on or be caught? Would a team come out of nowhere down the stretch picking up game after game on the leader until they caught or passed them? Would two teams go into the last game of the season tied for first place or, better yet, have to play a one game playoff to decide it all? To me Bucky Dent's home run for the Yankees that helped beat the Red sox in a one game playoff in 1978 was much more memorable than Aaron Boone's shot which did the same in game seven of the 2003 American League Championship Series, because the chances of playing a game seven in a playoff are much greater than having two teams play 162 games and finish with the same record.

It was great seeing a team ride the hot pitcher or hitter to the pennant. If it wasn't your team, it was great seeing a team which had been in first place suddenly lose their momentum and begin to press as they look at the scoreboard and see someone gaining on them in the standings. Many times, August and September was where league MVP awards were won as a player like Carl Yasztremski for the Red Sox in 1967 would just put a team on his back willing them to victory day after day.

Give me a month and a half of scoreboard watching drama over one week of wildcard games any day.

I'm not the only person that baseball has lost of course, but am part of a major segment of the population which has lost its passion for the game. The African-American player and fan. Black people of all ages used to love baseball at every level, pro and amateur. And we played it in some form all of the time. I can remember some of the fiercest sports arguments being about baseball. One of the teams blacks loved were the "Swingin' A's" of Oakland who won three straight world's championships from 1972 to 1974. My mother is not a sports fan but she loved that team. She remembers the names Catfish Hunter, Vida Blue, Rollie Fingers and Reggie Jackson. They are the only team I can ever remember her openly rooting for. When the A's lost in 1975 to the Boston Red Sox there were a lot of disappointed black people.

This passion was reflected on the diamond as well. There were black stars everywhere especially in the National League and they were the team we rooted for in the all-star game even though the Baltimore Orioles of the American League were our home team. Whatever position you played as a kid there was a black superstar to identify yourself with.

My generation was starting to find other sports besides baseball to root for and play. Basketball and football didn't take long to rank with baseball in our lives. It was only a matter of time before those sports which were faster paced and becoming to look more like us began taking away from baseball's popularity. Then along came the thing that really turned the African-American fan away. All of those black faces that we were used to seeing started to disappear and were replaced by Latin American ballplayers. And the powers that be in baseball didn't care.

Why did this happen? That's an easy one to answer. Baseball stopped scouting black talent. Instead of spending money in the black communities they went down south to the poorer Latin countries where they could find talent on the cheap and weed it out. When I grew up, baseball teams would send scouts and coaches into black communities and hold clinics. They would donate equipment to the local leagues and send scouts out to coach the teams. That started to disappear in the 1980's when I played high school and summer league.

I couldn't figure out why until I went to college. There I talked to players from Latin American countries who were on ours and other school's baseball teams and almost to a man all of them had been scouted and offered contracts by the age of 15 or 16. They had decided to go to school, but many of their friends had gone off to the minors. All of them said that they hadn't been offered much, but a contract is a contract. It's more than anyone that I knew had been offered. After talking to these young men, it all became clear. It was cheap labor and killed two birds with one stone in minority hiring by having Latin American ballplayers of color replace African American ballplayers of color. It was that simple. It was good for the Latin ballplayer, but bad for the African American.

Baseball gave it another try in the early nineties with black fans though not the players. The only reason for that was nostalgia. It was the sudden popularity of the old Negro Leagues which existed back in the early and mid part of the century. Baseball wanted to cash in on this just as they did with those old timers days and baseball cards during the same period. This would have been the time to go after young black ballplayers too, because they were caught up in it as well and had returned to the diamond, but they didn't. Once that passed, black fans and players were neglected again despite programs like Reviving Baseball in Inner Cities (RBI).

And it's not just blacks who have stopped playing the game. White people have turned to other things besides baseball as well. When I say that ball fields are empty, I mean they are everywhere. Some of the ball fields that were around when I was growing up no longer exist. Many kids have turned to playing soccer and lacrosse. The rest, along with adults, just stay indoors out of the sun and in the air conditioned comfort of home or go to the pool.

All of this has contributed to the dying of interest in baseball in the United States. Has the Latin American fan and player made up for all of the black and white fans and players lost?

I know that Commissioner Selig and everyone in and around baseball will disagree with me on this so I've got one more theory as to why I believe the game isn't as popular. Contraction.

If the game is so popular why did MLB want to contract the Montreal Expos in the early 2000's before finally moving them to Washington D.C.? Maybe it's because the sport has too many teams that lack fan support. Are Miami and Tampa, Florida baseball cities? How about Pittsburgh (yes, but they can't afford to compete).

It seems to me that if the game was as popular as we are lead to believe contraction wouldn't have even been an issue.

If people stop dancing and listening to a Top Ten song, then doesn't its popularity decrease?

IS IT SPORT OR COMPETITION

There is a difference. Some of the things that are presented as sport are really competitions. People don't like to hear that what they are doing is not a sport, but does it really matter as long as you are active and having fun?

Many of the events that we see on TV presented by ESPN, like the X Games, are competitions. Many of the events that we see in the Olympics are as well. For the sake of argument, here's what separates sport from competition.

If it's head to head, that's a sport. If you have to score your own points, it's a sport. If it's being timed and the best time wins, it's a sport.

If a judge's score determines who wins or loses (with the exception of boxing where you are actually trying to knock out your opponent first), then it's a competition.

To eliminate things like chess and checkers anything where you have to use only your brain is a game.

Here's what are sport and what is competition.

Of course anything where two or more teams go at it head to head is a sport. That includes the obvious like football, basketball, baseball and hockey. When two teams compete at separate times and their performances are judged, that's competition. Figure skating, gymnastics and synchronized swimming come to mind.

When individuals go at it head to head, that's sport. Wrestling, boxing, tennis, golf, track and, yes, auto racing. When individuals go at it separately and they have to score their own points, jump higher or do it the fastest, that's also a sport. You are controlling your own fate. When individuals go at it separately and a judge scores their performance, then that's competition. Again figure skating along with gymnastics, skateboarding and bodybuilding fall into this category.

What do you mean I'm not playing a sport? That's what I hear all of the time. Is hunting a sport? You shoot at a defenseless animal that doesn't have a weapon. Is it a competition, the animal runs off and you try and catch it. It's a sport (though many think a cruel one), because your reward is in what you catch and that's in the fate of the hunter.

How about fishing? You sit all day to catch a few fish that either come up to your line or not. Well, you have to set the bait, catch the fish and reel them in. Yes, that's a sport.

Bowling? They keep score, right?

Bull Riding? They are timed and must stay on that bull in order to advance. It's a sport.

The luge, bobsled and skiing are sports.

What about diving? Well they go at it individually and a judge scores each dive. That's competition.

I know a lot of work goes into bodybuilding, just as it does in most competitions, but it's still judged which makes it a competition. Now weightlifting? That's definitely a sport.

Snowboarding, dunk contests and motorcycle stunt contests. All competitions.

When you think about it, it's quite simple. If you can control your own fate physically, it's a sport. If your fate is left in the hands of judges, it's a competition, because you are trying to impress physically. That's all.

Let me make this clear. There is nothing wrong with either. And one is not better than the other. As long as you are doing something physical that you like, God bless you.

As for things like eating the most hot dogs in a certain amount of time?

Well those are contests.

SILLY SUPERSTITIONS

Yes, I admit that I'm superstitious. I am trying to break the habit, but can't. I know that what I do has no effect on the outcome of games, but do it anyway. I'm not alone in this superstition thing at all.

Maybe part of it is that I played baseball growing up where there's plenty of superstition. From Little League threw high school I had to have my lucky sweatshirt or undershirt to wear in warm-ups. It changed from year to year, but once I found it there was no changing. Unlike some people, I did wash mine. However, if I took a shower before a game I couldn't hit my way out of a paper bag. I said this once on the bench and my coach who was as old school as it gets told me it was a bunch of crap. He was probably right, but no shower for me before games.

Our star pitcher in high school always ate alone at the same pizza parlor the night before he pitched. The year that we won the state championship, he let the whole team eat with him once and the next day suffered his first loss of the season. From then on, he ate alone and didn't lose another game. That same season, our manager would not wash his truck despite people scribbling "Wash me," on the back window of the camper. Did this help us win it all? I can't say that, because of what I did myself. I always thought that black cleats were bad luck for me so I wore white for most of the season. However, in the state playoffs I switched to black and we still won. Either I tempted fate or we were just good enough to win it no matter what any of our superstitions were. Also, there was one particular fan that whenever he showed up we lost. He showed up for most of our playoff games and after we survived the first one with him there, I knew that there was no way we'd lose.

The next season with the exception of our pitcher who had graduated we had the same team back. The coach still didn't wash his truck and I went back to the white cleats. We got to the state championship and lost. Just as most of us thought we would. The karma just wasn't right and we could sense it.

In summer league there was a friend of mine that whenever he came to our games we lost. The team started to call the poor boy a jinx as young men, me included, can be quite cruel. We finally won one with him there and he couldn't wait to let us know about it. Years later, my nephew felt the same about my brother who is his uncle. Whenever my brother showed up to one of my nephew's games you could bet the ranch they would lose. My nephew would give his uncle bogus times and dates of games so my brother couldn't make it.

Yes, there were a few black cat crossings the day of or night before games. Yes, guys had to have their lucky number, hats, socks, towels and T shirts. Yes guys had to chew gum or eat sunflower seeds. Even relationships were dictated by baseball. If you were going with a girl and playing well she stayed all summer. If you went into a slump then it was time to dump her and find another, no kidding.

The only thing that I carried over to football was my cleats and undershirt. Oh and my number which the team didn't order my senior year. This was just great. I ended up with a separated shoulder in game four and appendicitis three weeks later.

As fans, many of us think that we can have an effect on what happens between the lines. How many of your friends have rituals that they have to adhere to before and during their favorite teams games? I know that I do and I'm not alone.

When you see me at a sporting event where my favorite team is involved I won't be wearing their colors. Whenever I do, whether it's during the week or on the day of the game, they lose. When football season starts, I put away all of my Pittsburgh Steelers stuff. I put away my shirts, towels, pictures, books, blankets and everything. When the season ends, I bring it back out. Yes, I've made mistakes and they have been costly.

In 2000, the Steelers lost their first three games including one to the Cleveland Browns when they couldn't get the field goal unit on in time. For the life of me I couldn't figure out why a team that was pretty good all of a sudden had trouble getting out of their own way. Then I looked in the back window of my car. Sitting there were my "Terrible Towel" and a little Steelers bear that my sister had given me. I immediately took them out and put them in a drawer. The Steelers won the next week and went on to win nine of their last thirteen. They missed the playoffs by one game. To this day I'm still kicking myself for being so stupid. How could I not check the car when putting everything away?

In 2004, I took a chance and left all of the Steelers gifts that I got for Christmas under the tree. The team was red hot then not having lost since week two of the season. They made it to the AFC title game and got crushed by the New England Patriots. I expected them to lose, but didn't help at all by leaving my Steelers Monopoly game out. During that game, my brother in law came by to pick up my nephew. The Steelers were struggling until he got there when they started to make a comeback. I wanted to beg him to stay, but didn't. As soon as he left, the Patriots put the game on ice. Of course, these things had nothing to do with it. Like I said, I thought the Patriots were going to win.

You may laugh, but remember this. The Steelers have done very well over the last two decades with three trips to the Super Bowl and two world's championships. You best believe that I will not wear black and gold or have anything of those colors around until Pittsburgh plays its last game of the season.

When our teams are winning, many of my friends and I have to watch the game at the place that the winning streak began. It may be at a friend's house. It may be at the bar. It may be at home. But it has to be with the same group of people. No outsiders. My father watched Super Bowl XXX in which the Cowboys beat the Steelers just long enough for Dallas to build a ten point lead. When he left the Steelers started to play better, but still ended up losing by those ten points. If you watched alone, then no one is allowed to watch the next week especially if it's a playoff game. If you are sitting in a certain position and things are going well stay in it blood circulation be damned. If the team is struggling and you're not doing them any good take the hit and change the channel or just leave the room. You're not doing them any good by watching them so don't.

My nephew's luck switched from one uncle, and again my brother, to another when it came to his support for the Oakland Raiders. Whenever he saw uncle number two, who is also a Raider fan, on the day of a game or even talked to him on the phone my nephew thought his boys were doomed. I'll never forget the look on his face when my brother walked into the house wearing his Raiders sweatshirt on the day of the 2000 AFC Championship game between the Baltimore Ravens and the Raiders. My nephew was 18 years old and though he didn't say the bad words out loud I could read lips. Of course, Tony Siragusa separated Rich Gannon's shoulder and the Raiders were done.

When we went to watch the Raiders play the Redskins in 2006 we had an extra ticket and my nephew would not let me give it to my brother. We took his cousin, uncle number one's son. Well uncle number one found out and called uncle number two. The phone rings while we are in the parking lot tailgating. You guessed it. It was uncle number two and he wasn't happy. My nephew didn't care. He cared even less when the Raiders won the game. In 2009 we watched the Raiders lose to the Cowboys on Thanksgiving Day and I swear every time uncle number two watched the Raiders played like crap. As soon as he left the room, they outplayed Dallas. My nephew's dinner did not sit well.

People's mouths can mess things up too. We were at a Maryland Terrapin-Virginia Cavaliers football game in 1999 where Terrapins running back Lamont Jordan ran for over 300 yards. The Terps were playing for a bowl bid and on Jordan's last long touchdown run one of my nephews said, "Well it looks like Maryland is going to a bowl game,". I told him not to say that, because there was still plenty of time. You guessed it. Maryland lost.

In the month before the 2006 Rose Bowl between the University of Texas and Southern Cal ESPN kept comparing the Trojans to all of the great teams of the past and asking what would be the score if they played. Being a USC fan, I couldn't believe it. How could they be comparing a team that wasn't even as good as the one that won the National Championship the year before to teams of the past? Especially since there was still one more game to play against a very good Texas team with probably the best player in the nation in quarterback Vince Young. After that, there was no way the Trojans were going to win. None. They lost it in the last seconds. The Patriots suffered the same fate in 2008 as they were undefeated and being anointed the greatest NFL team of all time before losing to the New York Giants in the Super Bowl.

Before the great meltdown of the Maryland basketball team in 2001 against Duke, ESPN showed updated Atlantic Coast Conference standings assuming the Terps had won. I groaned immediately. Sure enough the lead and game were gone in sixty seconds.

Now does any of this really have an effect on the outcome of games? The lucky towels, shirts, hats, underwear and socks. The non washing of vehicles and eating of certain foods? The rituals of watching games in the same spot and or sitting in the same position? The people that you surround yourself with? The pre ordaining of teams and players?

It probably does not. I know my Reverend doesn't think so. He calls it silly superstition. He believes in the supernatural not superstition and him being a man of God, I believe he's right.

I'm trying to break myself out of the habit. I'm trying to say that it doesn't matter whatever happens is going to regardless of what I do. And most of the time this is the case.

But I'm not going to change. I will do whatever it takes for my team to win and as long as the percentages are on my side I'll continue my silly superstitions.

COLLEGE BASKETBALL IS NOT BETTER THAN THE PROS

First off, this is not about whether college basketball players are better than the pros. The answer to that is pretty simple. Interns are not better than pros. The pros are better, period, or they would not be getting paid. This is whether or not the college game is better than the National Basketball Association. Here are the arguments for the college game and whether they hold up or not.

The College Players Care More:

It is impossible to be a great or even good NBA player if you don't care about the game. All of the great ones care. To be an NBA starter you have to not only be better physically than everyone else, but also have a better work ethic. I watched the best player at college my freshman year work his butt off to make it to the NBA and he did. I watched a player who was considered just as good, if not better, than him my sophomore year try to do it all on athletic ability. He was drafted in the first round no less and ate himself out of the league. The same work ethic he had in college, which he didn't need because of his talent, was the one he took into the pros and he washed out.

To be an NBA All-Star you have to be better physically and mentally than the best players in the world. You cannot do this if you don't care. Kobe Bryant, Lebron James, Dwayne Wade, Steve Nash, Tim Duncan, Carmelo Anthony, Paul Pierce, Kevin Garnett. These guys are the best, because they maximize their talents by working hard to hone their skills. The NBA is a full time job without the benefits of campus life. It's work and in order to be the big man in the pros it takes a lot more effort than it does to be big man on campus.

36

The College Players Play Harder:

Okay, here's the thing. The NBA players get a bum rap when it comes to the whole play hard thing. People turn on their TV's and they watch an NBA game and it looks as though the players are going through the motions until the last five minutes. The truth of the matter is that the NBA players make the game look so easy it seems as they are coasting. When on their game, they are mind numbingly good. The nets barely move when a jump shot goes through. Kareem Abdul-Jabbar made the hook shot look so easy they named it "Skyhook" for him. Some guys just can't be guarded when they are hot.

There are times when one NBA team dominates another and it looks as though the losing team shows no effort. There are reasons for this. The main one being that NBA players do a lot more traveling around the country than the college men do. Besides maybe a couple of early season tournaments, college teams hardly ever leave their time zone once the conference slate starts. At the end of the college season, how many times have we seen college players lose their legs during their conference tournaments when they have to play back to back nights? Or look fatigued during the NCAA tournament when they have to travel a couple of time zones and play two games in three days? Meanwhile, an NBA team can travel as far as three time zones and stay out west or east for as much as two weeks. The plane flight alone can zap your legs of their energy. Couple that with your body clock being screwed up and living out of a hotel room for days at a time, how can an NBA player stay fresh over an 82 game season?

Another thing is that the colleges only play two games a week. The pros can play as many as four. And most of the time one of the college games is at home. And as I mentioned in the last paragraph, the NBA plays 82 games compared to maybe 35 for college. It's easier to play harder when you know you don't have to pace yourself to get through the grind of an NBA season and have something left for the post season.

With all of that, most of the time NBA players still give you a good effort. They still play to win their individual matchups and the game. And in the post season they give us their maximum effort, but we'll get to that later.

College Players Care More about Their School
Than NBA Players Care About Their Team:

It depends. In the college game, the star players don't care about their school that much. The role players and benchwarmers might, but the ones with NBA dreams really don't. That's why so many of them leave early for the pros or transfer to another school. All they really care about is doing their time and getting a shot at making some money whether it's in the NBA or oversees.

It's not their fault. The business of basketball breeds this. The college player has been coddled for so long that when being recruited out of high school, he is looking for the school which best suits him as a basketball player, nothing more. Isn't that selfish? Once he gets there most of the great ones want to know what the school is going to do for them not the other way around. And it is the star players who we come to watch. Sure, there are more players who won't make it to the pros out of college than will, but all of them are there for selfish reasons. They have been brought up that way.

The NBA player has no choice over which team he gets to play for, so if he goes to a bad one where the organization is run like crap wouldn't it affect his play? Wouldn't that make him play selfishly to get other teams to look at him and hopefully bring a trade for his services?

Either way you slice it, the college player who is very good and the pro player who is great that wants to go to a better team play for the same reason, money.

College Players Are More Fundamentally Sound:

I've watched the college game for a long time. They are not more fundamentally sound than the pros. The pros are physically better as mentioned before. They pass better. They shoot better. They box out better. They run their plays better. This is because they practice it more. They have the time to do it.

College Players Play Better Defense:

It is easier to play defense in the college game than in the pros for this reason. There is no college team with more than three guys on it who can create their own shot. If you don't have to guard two guys, often three, it is easier to play zone or man and double team the men who can beat you. It is easier to take away dribble penetration and force jump shots. It is easier to take one or two players out of their rhythm than it is to take four or five.

Think about this for a second. Every team who has won the NCAA championship has won it because they have had the ability to outscore their opponent. The teams who have relied on strong defense and half court offense may get far in the tournament, but they don't win it. Because you can't find five guys who can guard five good scorers for an entire game.

This is the case in the NBA. They play good defense, especially in the post season. But you can't make it in the pros if you can't find a way to score unless you can keep the ball away from the other team by rebounding it.

A scorer will score no matter who guards him, because he knows where he is going and the defender does not. It takes more energy to chase so the offensive player will wear his defender down over time. Eventually, he will get his points. If nothing else, he will find a way to get to the free throw line.

The colleges look like they play better defense, because they have fewer players to guard.

The College Atmosphere Is Better Than the Pros:

Yes, there is nothing like a big college basketball game held on campus. The fans, cheerleaders, band and student section is electric. Well, they only have about sixteen games a year to do it, so each one means more to them. With a new student body every year, each big game experience is new to someone. The pros can't duplicate that except maybe in the postseason which leads us to.

March Madness is better than the NBA Playoffs

March Madness is cool. The so called "upsets" and buzzer beaters which lead up to the Final Four are exciting. The neutral site crowds getting behind the underdog is good theatre. And with all of that, nine times out of ten a number one or two seed wins it all. Even if a lower seeded team wins you can bet that it's a team from one of the major conferences. It's March Madness' dirty little secret. The first week is about entertainment the next two crowning a champion.

The NBA Playoffs are a nightly drama drawn out over seven games home and home. Sure they last too long, because of the down time between games, but after playing 82 in the regular season the players need some bounce back time.

The fans ratchet it up during the playoffs to a point where you can't hear yourself think. They are just as enthusiastic as any regular season college crowd and more so than a neutral site NCAA tournament one. For at least two games and, if the series goes seven, up to four.

But what makes the NBA Playoffs better are the performances by the players. It is where Magic Johnson, Larry Bird, Michael Jordan, Tim Duncan, Isaiah Thomas, Kobe Bryant and Shaquille O'Neal forge their legacies. Sure, they have played great during the regular season, but in the pros it's a whole new level. Whereas the team may pick up its game in college, the individual players do it in the pros.

And the NBA playoffs are not short on buzzer beaters. No way. Jordan, Magic, Bird, Lebron, Kobe, Reggie Miller, Robert Horry, Derek Fisher, Charles Barkley all could hit a big shot at the buzzer to win a game and did. Knick fans will never forget Miller scoring eight points in nine seconds to beat them in Game one of the 1995 Eastern Conference Semifinals and Pacer fans will not forget New York's Larry Johnson burning them with a three point-basket and free throw to beat them at the buzzer in 1999. How about Magic Johnson's "Junior Sky Hook" to beat Bird's Celtics in Game Four of the 1987 Finals. Or Birds steal and pass to Dennis Johnson in the Eastern Conference Finals to beat Detroit that same year. Horry did it so many times he got the nickname "Big Shot" Bob. No the college game has nothing on the NBA playoffs when it comes to great performances, drama and last minute heroics.

And there is nothing better than when a star player lives up to his hype or doesn't.

For these reasons, the college game is not better than the pros. Before I am accused of college bashing let me say there was a period when the college game was better than the pros. It was the period from 1994 to 2001.

During that time, the NBA game regressed big time. The game went away from free flowing offense to bullying defense with Pat Riley's Knicks and later Miami Heat leading the way. Fouls were not being called as they should and the game bogged down into a half court affair. On top of that, Michael Jordan retired for the first time after the 1993 season. When he came back in 1995 the Bulls did not win the championship, but they did the next three years. They won it partly because they were a good team and partly because the league was in a period of transition with stars retiring and being replaced by young players who didn't understand the meaning of being a professional and were only looking out for themselves. This was the whole being "The Man" syndrome.

The Bulls won it also, and more importantly, because, the rest of the league quit. They conceded the title to Michael Jordan before he stepped on the floor. Unlike Magic, Isaiah and Bird who conceded nothing to one another and whom Jordan had to conquer to get to where he was, this group of athletes kissed Michaels rings and worried more about making money and endorsements than winning titles. I don't know if Jordan is the greatest basketball player that ever played, but I do know this. He made an entire league quit. I can't think of another athlete in a team sport who can say that.

When Jordan retired for a second time after the 1998 season, this left a void. Then the players went on strike before the 1998-99 season and the game did not recover until the 2001-2002 season when the Los Angeles Lakers were in the midst of their three peat and newer, younger players had entered the league.

Meanwhile, the college game was flourishing. Even though the Final Fours were not as good as they were in the 1980's, the regular season and tournament games themselves were much better as the shot clock and three point shot were starting to take full effect. We had a full-fledged villain in the Duke Blue Devils whom you loved or hated. And players stayed in school for three and four years. We had personalities and storylines every season.

Then the Kevin Garnett's, Kobe Bryant's and Tracy McGrady's of the world started to skip college and go straight to the pros. And the men who did go to college left school earlier and earlier. The pros got their act together and regained the top spot they should have never lost.

The pro game is better, just as it is in football, baseball, hockey or any other sport. If people would open their eyes and not be blinded by March Madness they would see this. The truth of the matter is just because you like something more doesn't make it better.

But if you still think that the colleges play better basketball, than pay them. Because if you tell me that I am better at something than someone else or you like my product more, than I think I'm worth more than a college scholarship.

WHY SOCCER IS NOT OUR CUP OF TEA

Wasn't soccer supposed to be the most popular sport in America by now? If not the most popular sport wasn't it supposed to be at least one of them?

I can remember my boy's club football coach telling us how soccer was going to take kids away from football and baseball. "Pretty soon, there won't be anyone playing football anymore," he would say. "All the kids will be on the soccer field." This was in 1978 at a time when our clubs football participation was starting to go down. As an eleven year old I couldn't imagine anything taking the place of football, especially soccer.

This was also at a time when Major League Soccer was going semi strong. Pele had come over from Brazil to play for the New York Cosmos and Washington had their own team in the Diplomats. "Get your kicks with the Dips," was their slogan. They played at RFK Stadium and sold out every now and then. This was the start of the soccer revolution.

Thirty years later, we are still waiting for pro soccer to really take hold in this country. In one sense my coach was right. Soccer has taken kids away from football and baseball. Young people male and female are starting to play it as soon as they can run it seems. Adult leagues can also be found. There are soccer complexes all over and the game is being played year round. When the weather gets cold, the action is moved indoors. So, yes, there are lots of people playing soccer today.

Of course, I have a theory for that. It is my belief that parents turn their kids to soccer at an early age for a couple of reasons. The first is that the game is not as expensive or violent as football. Whereas in football you have to wear a ton of equipment, soccer only needs shorts, a jersey, socks and cleats. Football is a contact sport. You are taught to hit another person on every play. Aggression is encouraged. There is no such thing as play nice in football. Soccer is to be played under control with no pushing or shoving and as little contact as possible. The chances of getting hurt in football are much greater than they are in soccer, though you can get injured playing both.

Second, soccer is the politically correct sport. Boys and girls can play it separately or together. Either can be the star of their team. It allows the kids to run around under their parents supervision and helps make up for the exercise they don't get while playing video games indoors instead of pickup games and other things outdoors at home. Everyone gets to touch the ball whereas in football only six of eleven people on offense get to, seven if you count the center. The defense can only touch the ball if they can take it from the offense. So in soccer, everyone gets to see their kid be the center of attention even if it's only for a second or two.

So from a playing standpoint, youth soccer will be around for a while.

The question then is how come this has not translated into more well known American professional soccer players and, even more puzzling, fans? Maybe I can answer that. Or at least give an explanation.

The reason why soccer doesn't rate with the American sports fan is because it's too soft.

The American fan wants two things from their sport, speed and power. We've got to see our athletes show us something that we can't do or do it ten times better than us. Those of us who are fortunate to have our health can kick a soccer ball and run. Even if we can't do it now, we could at one time. So we are not going to sit and watch someone do something we don't think is that hard though at the highest level it is.

If we want to see people run there had better be a stopwatch to time them. Or there had better be a goal line to reach. Or there had better be a base to get to with a ball being thrown there to stop them. Or there had better be a ball being chased.

You can kick a soccer ball as hard as you want, but it will never replace seeing a field goal kicker in football blast a 50 yard field goal. It will never replace a batter hitting a baseball 500 feet. It will never replace a hockey player hitting a slap shot so hard that it's a blur going into the net or the goalies glove. It will never replace a basketball player throwing down a dunk so hard that it rattles the rim or blocking a shot and sending it into the third row of the stands. It will never replace a pitcher cutting loose a 100 mile per hour fastball right by an outmatched hitter. It will never replace a boxer knocking out an opponent. Golf has the tee shot, tennis the blurred serve which scorches the ground for an ace. Even bowling has an element of power with pins scattering when the ball hits them.

We have dunk contests in basketball where the most vicious ones win. We have home run contests to not only see who can hit the most, but who can hit them the farthest. We have a slap shot competition in hockey to see who can scream it into the net the fastest by hitting it hardest.

Everything in football is speed and power. In fact, players are taught the man who can build up the most momentum is the one who will hit the hardest. Couple this with the size and strength of the players and you get some hellacious collisions.

Then we get auto racing which also combines both elements. There is the thrill of seeing cars race around an oval or down a straightaway at speeds as high as 250 miles per hour. There is the power of hearing the engines roar. And there is the danger of seeing all that speed and power end in something disastrous.

Though soccer is a good game played by great athletes at all levels it just does not provide the element of power and speed the American sports fan is looking for. It will always be a good game for people of all ages to play and I would recommend it to kids instead of football.

However, it will always be a niche sport to Americans who will watch only during the World Cup. It may be the most popular sport in the world, but it's very unlikely it will be in America.

It's just too soft.

JUST GIVE ME THE GAME

Call me old school, but here goes.

I enjoyed half hour pregame shows on Sunday afternoons before the National Football League games started. Now, I get an hour during the regular season and a whole day it seems for the Super Bowl. Not to mention 24 hour coverage from the NFL Network, ESPN and Fox Sportsnet.

I enjoyed simple player introductions before the game. I enjoyed hearing the National Anthem played. I enjoyed the announcers lead in to the game. I enjoyed one minute breaks for commercials. I enjoyed not having sideline reporters. Here's what I'm getting at.

I don't need a pregame show that lasts more than a half hour. I don't care about feature stories. I don't need to know about the town the game is being played in. I don't need to know what some celebrity thinks about the game. I don't need funny skits. I don't need any music videos or sappy look backs. I don't need to know anything that doesn't pertain to what's going to happen on the field. Give me some strategy and a couple of interviews with the people involved and that's it. The actual game telecast should be nothing more than play by play, instant replays and analysis with only statistics that matter. Sideline reports should be only for injuries. Don't give me crowd shots of the player's wives and family members or some goofy fan covered in paint. Give me two thirty second commercials and get back to the game.

As for the event, I don't need to tailgate. I don't need a concert in the parking lot. I don't need a concert before the game. I don't need a concert at halftime of the game. I don't need a concert after the game. I don't need fireworks during the player introductions. I don't need a jet flyover. I don't need loud music piped into the speakers and crushing my eardrums. I don't need to be told how and when to cheer. I don't need piped in crowd noise. I don't need to be bombarded with advertisements during every break in the action. I don't need cheerleaders. That's right, I don't. I like end zone celebrations, but can live without them. I don't need tee shirts shot into the stands or dancing fools or crazy contests during every break. I don't need to sit in a skybox, especially with people who are not watching the game.

If it's football give me the kickoff, the action in between and the final score. If it's baseball, give me the first pitch, the action in between and the final out. If it's basketball, give me the opening tip, the action in between and the final buzzer. If it's hockey, give me the faceoff, the action in between and the final horn. If it's boxing, ring the bell, fight until someone gets knocked out or they go the distance and get out of the ring (actually boxing is pretty good at this).

Cut out the fat. Cut out the excess. If I want to k now someone's life story I'll read their book. If I want funny, I'll turn on Redd Foxx, Bill Cosby or Richard Pryor. If I want a party, I'll go to the club or someone's house. If I want a television show, I have plenty of channels to find one. If I want to hear people talk I'll watch "Face the Nation". If I want loud music I'll turn on the radio or stereo. If I want a concert, I'll find out when a group I like is in town and go see them. If I want fireworks, I'll go out on the Fourth of July and find them. I come to the game dressed so don't need a t-shirt. If I want to watch the game in a lounge chair indoors I'll stay at home and save gas. I like women that I actually know so I don't need cheerleaders. If I want to watch ordinary people dance I'll watch "Soul Train".

I don't care if they play it in the sandlot, the junkyard or the parking lot. I don't care if they play at one o'clock, five o'clock or nine o'clock.

Just give me the game. That's all I want.

LOVE THE GAME, HATE WHAT IT DOES

I have a love, hate relationship with football. Let me explain.

In my younger days, I participated in a football camp held in western Pennsylvania. The camp was run by a scout of an NFL team and the coaches were not only pro assistants, but former NFL players. Everything was run like a training camp with two a day practices and evening meetings. The NFL scout was the head coach and he ran the show all week.

During the team meetings, the head coach would ask the assistants to stand and say something inspirational to us players. For the assistants who had not been players and had no major physical hang ups, this was easy. For the former players, it was not.

The meetings were held in classrooms and everyone except the head coach sat in seats where the desk and chair were one piece. It's hard for any grown man to sit in a desk chair, but even more difficult for men who are over six feet and weigh anywhere from 200 to 275 pounds. Being a little guy I wasn't effected, but most of the people in the room were, especially the former players.

Whenever they were called on to speak, standing took great effort. Watching them get out of those chairs was like looking at a building being put together in sections. First, the legs had to be coaxed into straightening, because of bad ankles and knees. Then the arms would have to summon the strength to push up off the desk, because of worn out shoulders and bent fingers. Next, the back would have to be straightened very slowly due to years of spinal damage from blocking and tackling. And, finally, the head and neck would have to be raised in order to look at the audience. If they walked to the front of the room,

48

and most of them did not, it was slow and looked painful. Returning to their seats and sitting looked just the opposite of standing. The same way the body had been built up it was torn down as each man looked like a building collapsing into a heap.

No one commented on it that night, but you could see everyone in the room noticed how deliberately these men moved. It was confirmed the next morning at breakfast. My roommate who was a defensive tackle and I were sitting with a couple of other guys when he asked did we see how the coaches had moved the night before. All of us answered at the same time and guys at the tables nearby chimed in as well. "If that's the way I'm going to look, I don't know if I want to play pro ball," said my roommate. We agreed. None of us made it and we are all the better for it, because we had already done enough damage to ourselves in the past and that week.

A few years later, I was having a conversation with some coworkers at lunch. We were all former high school football players who were undersized and scrappy. The positions we played were varied from me being a quarterback to a guy who had played on the defensive line. The talk was not about how much we had enjoyed playing football, though we had, but all of the injuries that had been suffered and how they were effecting us. None of us had children at the time, but we all agreed that our sons would not be forced to play football. If they asked to play the game fine, but we weren't signing them up for it. We didn't care if they ever played a down.

I only played tackle football from the ages of 10 to 17 and I'm still paying for it. I suffered three sprained shoulders, one sprained knee, a compression fracture of the mid spine and worst of all three concussions. The first concussion occurred when I was knocked out cold and was so severe that I missed a week of school. I was eleven years old.

If all of this happened to me as a youth when my body couldn't generate the speed and power that an adult football player can generate than how much damage are the pros doing to themselves every time they play? We saw it at that football camp. We saw men walking with limps. We saw men with rings on their fingers that they couldn't take off, because their knuckles were too bent and calloused. We saw men who couldn't stand or sit for long periods of time. We saw men who were living with pain on a daily basis and I felt for them.

With all of that, their passion for the game had not died. They drove us hard and got right into drills if they could. The linemen and linebackers were yelled at by coaches who looked like if they could put the pads back on, they would.

That's the thing about football. If you love to play it, you will sacrifice everything to be good at it. The main thing that is sacrificed is the body. Even if it is by choice, it's still painful to watch.

No one loves football more than I do. And when it comes down to it, I'm as old school as it gets. I think today's game is too clean. Teams are playing in domed stadiums and on synthetic turf. Even the grass fields are nice. Every new stadium has skyboxes and Jumbotron video screens. I came up at a time when the game was played on fields that when it rained, they turned into mud bowls. When it snowed, the snow wasn't melted by a heated field. Stadiums like Baltimore's Memorial, Washington's D.C. and Cleveland's Municipal were old and junky which was fine by me. The more run down the stadium, the more the game looked like a battle of gladiators, especially when there was weather involved.

When I was growing up, the game on the field was more violent with fewer rules to protect the players. The clothesline tackle around the head and neck was legal. The head slap was legal. There were no penalties for leading with the crown of the helmet except for spearing when tackling a player on the ground. Quarterbacks were hit long after the ball had been thrown. It was so bad that I can remember teams and players actually being quoted in the papers on how they were going to try and knock an opponent out of Sunday's game and they would. It was almost expected. Even worse, players were literally dragged off of the field if they were hurt in order to save the team a timeout. This was the era that the men I've mentioned played in and they are paying for it now. The era before them was even rougher.

I know I'm contradicting myself, but the fact is the rules of the game had to be changed for the safety of the players. The game had become such that with the speed and size of the players increasing yearly under the old rules someone would have gotten killed. That's right, killed. An

NFL player would have been in court defending himself for murder and the league didn't need that. I may think it's too clean, but if it means cutting down on the risk of injury to the players I'm all for it. The human body can only take so much. Whether it's by choice or not, football player's bodies take a beating every time they make contact with an opponent who is just as big or bigger and moving just as fast or faster. If they don't pay for it immediately, they will the next day, the next week and the next year for the rest of their lives.

When I was little, I never gave a thought to what the game did to the players or me. As I grow older, I think about it more and more. Every time I see a big hit, I have mixed emotions. It's the way that I want to see the game played, but I feel bad when someone doesn't get up. Even if everyone does get up, I know that each person has taken another chink out of their armor. As the players get older, the wear and tear becomes more noticeable until their bodies just can't respond the way that they want and it's time to retire.

One of the reasons why I'm against any changes in the overtime rules is because I want the game to end sooner rather than later for the sake of the players. The longer teams play, the more worn down they become. The product may not be effected during that game, but it will be the next week or later on in the season. It's hard enough to keep players fresh over a long season already. Having longer games, and seasons if the league decides to add two more games, will only make things worse for them.

I know it's the nature of the game, but for me it's still painful to watch. After seeing what retired players are going through, I'm on their side in the fight to get legal benefits that I think they deserve. Even though it was by choice, these men's bodies helped make the league what it is today and it wouldn't hurt the league to help them with their medical bills.

Though my conscious tells me there is no place in society for football that the game is too violent, in my heart I still love the game. I love the build up to the big game. I love the strategy. I love to see great athletes do amazing things. I also love to see them make mistakes and look human. I love almost everything about the game. Especially the hitting.

But I hate what it does to the men who play it.

LET THEM PLAY

There are some things in life I thought I'd never see. I thought I'd never see water bottled and sold. I thought I'd never see a day when there were no fruit trees, berry patches and nut trees in the Southern Maryland area where I live. I thought I'd never see an African-American President. And I thought I'd never see recess and physical education taken out of our elementary, middle and high schools.

I turn on the NFL, MLB and NBA Networks and see commercials urging us to get our kids out for play. Sixty minutes a day, they say. Yet, schools around the country are eliminating recess and their gym programs. When I was growing up, we had 25 minutes for recess and three days a week of P.E. in elementary school. When the weather was nice late in the school year, our teachers would let us go outside at the end of the day if all of our work was complete. Sometimes two classes would get together and choose sides for kickball or dodge ball games. The upper classes, fifth and sixth grade, would meet to play each other in football and basketball during an extended P.E. And every year we had a class competition called Field Day or Play Day run by our P.E. teacher.

In junior high, we would have class intramurals in which captains were chosen by our gym teachers and they picked teams for whatever sport was in season. Sometimes, especially if it was coed, the teachers would pick teams themselves. Each class lasted 45 minutes with 35 of those for play. At the end of each classes "season" the first place team would play the winner of the class in their grade for the championship. I can remember playing championships eight times in eight different sports my eighth and ninth grade years and losing them all. The Buffalo

Bills of 1990 to '93 have nothing on me. I was finally on a winner in softball at the end of my ninth grade year and it felt good.

High school gym was optional after freshman year. I took it every semester except the second of my sophomore year, because I didn't fill out my schedule correctly. Every day without gym, I gnashed my teeth until baseball season started. The class was 55 minutes with 45 of those for play. We were tested in distance running and weightlifting each quarter and the rest was intramurals just like junior high.

So basically from the time I entered school to the time I graduated there was always at least 35 minutes of play time in school every day for everyone. That's more than half of the play time the pro leagues are asking of kids now. Couple that with all of the pickup games we played after school, on weekends and in the summer you get much more than an hour a day. Now, recesses have been shortened in elementary schools. Gym classes have been cut down to three times a week in junior and high schools. And kids are less inclined to play after school.

No one needed to make us play. Our parents would simply walk into the room and ask if you had anything to do. If you said no, they'd find some chore to occupy your time. The best thing to do was take their cue, get up and go outside or don't give them a chance to ask.

It was a different time then. Most homes only had one television with no cable channels which mom watched soap operas and dad watched westerns. Video games were in the future. Home computers were nowhere to be found. And not too many homes had air conditioning to keep us cool in the summer. All of this helps explain why kids in my generation got more exercise than today's youth. We had nothing else to do.

That's why kids today need recess and P.E. even more. For many of them, it's the only chance that they will participate in an exercise program. They have the television with cable in their rooms. They have the Playstation video games. They have the laptop computer which along with their cell phones allows them to communicate with friends without leaving home. They have air conditioning in their homes. The incentive to play has been taken away by luxuries we didn't have. So the time at school may be all they get to play.

It just makes sense to have recess and P.E. in school anyway. A healthy body helps to make a healthy mind. Kids need to get out and do. The more active they are outside, the better they are in the classroom. I know I was. These play periods also break up the monotony of the day. I look back and think "How in the world did I sit in one class all day in elementary school?" I liked to learn, but didn't like school. There is no way I could have made it without recess and P.E. All there would have been was lunch where you still sit at a table for half an hour. Sure I was wired after playing, but my mind was sharper and I was more alert too.

The games we learned at recess and P.E. were taken home and played after school. Everyone would do their homework then meet outside to play. We knew the rules, because they had just been taught to us. If we wanted, we made our own rules to compensate for smaller teams or field size restrictions.

Junior high was the most boring three years of my life in school. We didn't have extracurricular sports so it was go to school, get on the bus and go home. Gym class was the only thing that kept a lot of guys even interested. It also helped break down a lot of social barriers between students of different schools. We had six elementary schools merge into one junior high and there was tension between us entering the door. By ninth grade, all of that was gone and guys who had started out as sworn enemies became friends. I really feel those intramural teams in P.E. had a lot to do with it, because they gave us a chance to learn about each other.

High school gym was basically for the jocks and guys who wanted an easy A. This was just about every male in the building. That didn't matter. What did was the fact we were still participating in sports.

Giving kids a chance to play and stay fit are the obvious reasons for having gym and recess. However, there is another important factor especially with gym and that is the interaction between teacher and student.

Sometimes, kids like I was don't really respond to what their teachers are saying, because they see them more as an authority figure who is always trying to lecture them. A gym teacher can cut through this, because most of them are or were athletes themselves which makes them cool to their students. And they are in less structured settings than a classroom. By just allowing kids to do something they like a teacher can earn a lot of respect. This can be done easier in a gym class than in English.

Gym teachers get to see a kid's true personality. Whether they think a kid is good or bad, they'll always try to find a way to get through to them. I was a hothead growing up. Not a bad kid, but a hothead. My elementary and junior high gym teachers knew this. They would sit with me privately and talk one on one when they knew I was doing wrong. They wouldn't raise their voice just tell me I was wrong plain and simple. At first, I thought they were just picking on me. As I got older what they said made sense and I find myself telling young people today many of the things they told me. I am grateful that they thought enough of me to do this. If more young people could hear the message that I heard they would be much better off especially young men who don't have a father figure in their lives.

All of this should be taken into consideration when people start taking away kids play time in school. Recess and P.E. are essential for the health of our youth. It helps them mentally as well by giving their minds a break from the books for a good period. It also gives them some incentive for good behavior, because kids don't want their fun time taken away. And very importantly it creates productive relationships between gym teachers and students in a less formal setting than a classroom which allows for life lessons to be taught on and off the field.

So please, let them play. We are all the better for it.

DYNASTY

The first time I saw the word was while looking through the public library sports section as an eight year old. I grabbed a book with a Green Bay Packer helmet on the cover and read the title, "Packer Dynasty". I had no idea what the word meant, but being a football fan decided to check it out. At that age I wasn't much for reading just liked the pictures. To this day I have not read "Packer Dynasty."

I know what the word means now. The dictionary says dynasty means, "a family of rulers following one after another," or, "the period of time during which such a family rules." In sports, we take the word family and replace it with team. If we go by the dictionaries meaning, there haven't been many. If we go by the brief period that sports has existed as we know it, there are a few more. Everyone has criteria for what makes a dynasty. Here is what I think along with the teams that deserve consideration.

First, you must win a championship. Getting to the championship game or series multiple times without winning one does not make a dynasty. You can only be king if you are on top. You can only rule if you conquer all in front of you.

This eliminates the Buffalo Bills teams of the early 1990's. The Bills made it to four consecutive Super Bowls from 1990 to 1993, losing them all to three different teams. They may be one of the best teams to ever play football, but they're not a dynasty. Same with the Denver Broncos who lost three Super Bowls in four years in the 1980's and the Minnesota Vikings who went to four Super Bowls under head coach Bud Grant and lost them all. Like the Broncos, the Vikings lost three in four years in the 1970's.

The Los Angeles Lakers of the 1960's fall into this category in the NBA. They made it to the finals six times in eight years (seven out of nine of you count the 1969-70 season) and lost them all. It was their luck that the Boston Celtics were ruling the roost at that time. In hockey, the St. Louis Blues went to three straight Stanley Cup Finals at the end of the 1960's and lost them all.

Second, you must win more than one title and repeat as champions at least once. Repeating as champion is not as hard as we are lead to believe. Anyone can rule for a year. The truly great teams win back to back. This eliminates some really good teams.

Baseball has a few teams with one championship that are given dynasty consideration. The Atlanta Braves went to five World Series in the 1990's and won only one. The Brooklyn Dodgers went to six from 1947 to 1956 and won only one. The Baltimore Orioles went to three straight from 1969 to 1971 and won only one. The Oakland A's repeated this trick twenty years later from 1988 to 1990.

The New York Football Giants of the Sam Huff era, also, fall into this category. They won the championship in 1956 then claimed five Eastern Conference pennants from 1958 to 1963 in which they did not win a title. The Los Angeles Rams went to three straight NFL championship games from 1949 to 1951 winning one. The San Diego Chargers did the same in the American Football League from 1963 to 1965.

The Julius, "Dr. J.", Erving Philadelphia 76'ers went to four NBA Finals from 1977 to 1983 winning only one.

Even though you win two or more championships during a period of time, there has to be a repeat in there somewhere. The team that immediately comes to mind is the San Antonio Spurs from 1999 to 2006. They won four NBA titles during that time, but never repeated. That may be harsh, but somewhere along the line they should have been good enough to win back to back. The Boston Celtics of the 1980's won three titles from 1981 to 1986 without a repeat.

The Oakland/Los Angeles Raiders are another team that won multiple titles who never repeated. They won the Super bowl three times from 1976 to 1983, but couldn't put together back to back. The Dallas Cowboys of the 1970's went to five Super Bowls and won two with a six year gap between titles. The San Francisco 49'ers of the 1980's saved themselves from this category by winning the last two of their four titles in the 1980's back to back.

Many of these teams did not repeat, because of reason number three. You must be the best team of your era.

The Cowboys and Raiders had to play second fiddle to the Pittsburgh Steelers who won four titles during the 70's. They both got their shots at Pittsburgh in post season play (Dallas twice, Oakland five times) and came out on the short end more often than not. The Celtics of the 80's had to deal with the Los Angeles Lakers who beat them twice in three championship Finals and won five titles during the decade including back to back in 1987 and '88. The Spurs saw the Lakers three peat during their run winning it all in 2000, '01 and '02.

Now that we have eliminated the good teams, we get to the mini dynasties. By the dictionaries meaning there is no such thing, but their definition covers centuries while American sport is more like one century. To me, this is a team that has won three or more titles within a five year period with one repeat along the way. This is where most sports dynasties fall with a few exceptions.

In football you will only find mini dynasties, because it's so hard to keep a good team healthy for a long time and it's hard to replace good players when they move on. The Green Bay Packers have had two dynasties. The first was from 1929-1931 when they won three consecutive NFL championships. The second was from 1960 to 1967 when they played in six NFL championship games, won five, repeated in 1961-'62 and won three straight from 1965-'67. Along the way, they won the first two Super Bowls. The Chicago Bears won three titles in four years from 1940 to 1943 repeating in '40-'41. They won another in 1946 which gave them four in seven years.

Then there are the Cleveland Browns of the old All-American Football conference and NFL from 1946 to 1955. Four straight AAFC crowns from '46 to '49 followed by an NFL title in 1950 for five straight championships. In all, the Browns went to ten straight championship games winning seven and finishing by repeating in 1954-55. It became eleven championship games in twelve years when they won the Eastern Conference in 1957.

The Browns may have been the ultimate football dynasty, but for the argument that the Detroit Lions beat them three times from 1952 to 1957 and back to back in '52 and '53. The Lions are one of the exceptions as they won three titles in six years while playing for the championship four times in that period. Their problem was that they lost to the Browns along the way and had to share top billing with them.

The Pittsburgh Steelers of the '70's won four championships in six years. Along the way, they defeated the Raiders in the AFC and the Cowboys in the Super Bowl to cement their dynasty status. The 49'ers are an exception, because they won four championships in the decade of the 1980's and repeated once. The Dallas Cowboys were the dynasty of the 1990's with three titles in four years from 1992-94. And the New England Patriots the dynasty of the 2000's with three in four years from 2001-2004.

Basketball gives us the Minneapolis Lakers who won five titles in six years from 1949-54. The Los Angeles Lakers of the 1980's went to eight finals during the decade winning five titles with a repeat in 1987-88. Then there are the Chicago Bulls six championships in eight years during the 1990's as they won three straight from 1991-93 and 1996-98 and the Lakers three straight from 2000-02.

Baseball has the Philadelphia Athletics who won three out of four World Series from 1910-13 and the Boston Red Sox who did the same from 1915-18. The Oakland A's won three straight World Series from 1972-74 making them the only Major League team to do it besides the New York Yankees who we will get to later.

Hockey gives us the Toronto Maple Leafs who dominated the 1940's winning the Stanley Cup five times in the decade with three straight from 1947-49. From 1942 to 1952, the Leafs won six championships in ten years. Toronto won three straight from 1960-'62 as well. The New York Islanders won four straight from 1980-83 and the Edmonton Eskimos won five out of seven right after with back to back in 1984-85 and 1987-88.

In college sports, it's hard to quantify mini dynasties, especially in football, because there is no title game and different polls decide champions. Women's basketball gives us the Tennessee Volunteers who won three straight NCAA titles from 1996-98 and the Connecticut Huskies who won four titles during the 2000's and a fifth in 2010.

Now we get to the teams which define the word dynasty in sport.

The first is the UCLA men's basketball team from 1964-75. The Bruins won ten NCAA championships in twelve years with eleven trips to the Final Four. They won seven straight titles from 1967-73. The Bruins beat ten different teams in the Final game. UCLA put together the longest winning streak in NCAA men's basketball history by winning 88 straight games.

Then there are the Boston Celtics from 1957-69. The Celtics won eleven championships in thirteen seasons. Boston center Bill Russell has more championship rings than fingers. The Celtics won the title eight years in a row from 1959-66. They finished their run with a repeat in 1968-69.

The NHL has the Montreal Canadiens. The Canadiens have won twenty-three Stanley Cups. They have repeated as champions five times. They won the Cup five straight years from 1956-60 and four straight from 1976-79. They won the Cup in every decade of the 1900's.

And baseball gives us the king of dynasties, the New York Yankees winners of twenty-seven titles. World Series champions in every decade except the 1980's since moving to Yankee Stadium in 1923. The Yankees have played in the World Series in every decade since moving to Yankee Stadium. New York has repeated as World Series champions six times. They have won five in a row once, four in a row once and three in a row once. From 1947 to 1964, the Yankees played in sixteen World Series and won eleven with five straight from 1949-53. The four in a row came from 1936-39. The three in a row came from 1998-2000 in which they won it four times in five years. As of this writing, the Yankees are once again world champions having won the 2009 World Series.

The Bruins, Celtics, Canadiens and Yankees are as close to the dictionaries definition of dynasty as you can get. No one else comes close.

YES I WATCHED PROFESSIONAL WRESTLING

Yes, I watched pro wrestling. I watched from my youth to my late twenties. I wasn't as crazy about it as my older brother, my cousins and many of my friends, but I knew the names just as they did. I watched every Saturday when I could. I knew who all the champions were in the different organizations and the number one contenders. And I knew who was coming to town each month to compete at either the Capital Centre in Landover, Md. or the Baltimore Civic Center. And I enjoyed every minute of it.

I did not start out as a fan. At first, when my brothers and cousins would turn on wrestling I would leave the room, because I couldn't stand it. It seemed like the dumbest thing ever put on the air. The way it worked was we lived next door to my cousins and my uncle was a huge wrestling fan. The deal was that since wrestling and Soul Train came on at the same time my brothers went to my cousin's to watch the Worldwide Wrestling Federation while my female cousin came over to our house to watch Don Cornelius with my sisters. I hated both shows, so usually ended up going outside or to my room to play. To this day, I still get a sick feeling in my stomach at 5:00 p.m. every Saturday, because that's when both shows came on.

Then, wrestling got me. We were at my uncle's one day when the WWF was giving out the award for manager of the year. Most of the wrestlers had managers with many of them former grapplers. With the exception of one man, Arnold Skoland, they all represented bad guys. Each contestant stood in the middle of the ring while the voting was announced. Needless to say, the last men standing were Skoland, the good guy manager, and Captain Louis Albano considered the best of the bad guy leaders. And, of course, Skoland won to the delight of the crowd.

This did not please Captain Lou who proceeded to take this huge trophy that stood in the middle of the ring and bash it to pieces over Skoland's head repeatedly. No one came to Skoland's aid as his head turned into a bloody mess and the crowd shrieked in anger and fear. Everyone watching in my uncle's house was going crazy and for the first time so was I. On Monday, it was the talk on the bus and at school and I was hooked.

The wrestling of that era was basically the same as today' with the plot being good vs. evil, right vs. wrong, villain vs. hero, white hat vs. black hat. Each of the top wrestlers had a manager who was usually a former grappler and, if he was a bad guy, helped him cheat. Almost all of them had cool nicknames like Haystacks Calhoun, Chief Jay Strongbow, Jimmy "Superfly" Snuka, "The American Dream" Dusty Rhodes , "The Nature Boy" Ric Flair, Andre "The Giant" , Hulk Hogan, "Superstar" Billy Graham, Bobo Brazille, Junkyard Dog, "Killer" Kowalski and "The Living Legend" Bruno Samartino . If you followed the sport back then, you know who I'm talking about.

There was no Monday, Thursday or Friday night wrestling. Everything was taped during the week in some arena that they never named and showed on Saturday. Living in the upper northeast, we were in World Wrestling Federation (now WWE) country so that's what organization we got. Until WWE president Vince McMahon monopolized the sport, each organization had its territory, just like the mafia. The WWF had the northeast. The National Wrestling Alliance had the southeast. The American Wrestling Alliance had the southwest and there were certain states like Florida and Texas who had their own organizations. Wrestlers did not go from organization to organization unless their contracts ran out. None of the owners invaded anyone else's territory or signed someone's wrestlers.

The Saturday format was pretty simple. A few matches where a bad guy would kill some nobody in order to spark the wrath of the crowd and promote ticket sales for the upcoming local card. A few matches where the good guy would fight some no name bad guy, almost get beat and pull it out at the end. If the champion was a good guy, he never wrestled on TV. If he was a bad guy every now and then he would. Championship and marquee matches on television were rare and usually ended with the bad guy doing something illegal to get disqualified or the good guy getting jumped and hit over the head with a chair by some outsider who was friends with the good guy. The title NEVER changed hands on Saturday afternoon.

One thing I remember about those old WWF TV matches was that there was this fat guy who used to sit in the front row across from the cameras every week. He always wore the same outfit, a white tee shirt and jeans and never moved. The funny thing is none of the action outside the ring ever went near him or so it seemed.

After each match, the winner would come by the announcer's table and do a quick interview in which he'd tell everyone as loud as possible where to be that weekend so they could see him kick someone's butt. If it was a good guy, he was cheered. The bad guys got booed mercilessly and egged the crowd on. The wrestlers who did not perform on TV that week would do separate taped interviews promoting the upcoming Saturday night event in the arena before the fans were allowed to enter and these were played during the show. Most of these were adlibbed and worth an Oscar or two.

The northeast circuit worked like this, Washington, Baltimore, Philadelphia, New York. There was one event in each city each month. The same wrestlers would meet in all four of them. Their feud would last the entire month with neither man getting a clear cut victory, especially if they were fighting for the title, until the last card on the last Saturday of the month. This was usually held in New York's Madison Square Garden and that was the only place the title would ever switch hands. If you didn't have a ticket, you didn't see it. There was no live TV, no highlights shown later, no radio. You had to pay to watch. After a while, those of us who were smart figured the circuit out, but it still didn't stop the arenas from selling out or us from watching.

With it being year round, wrestling was talked about quite bit. And acted out as well. It was nothing for two guys to square off and put a few moves on each other. It was not unusual to have someone walk in on you and drop an elbow or "soup bone" as we called them on your head. Battle Royals were common. I can remember one day at baseball practice when I was a teen we were waiting for the high school team to finish so that we could practice. There were fourteen of us and the whole time we talked wrestling. Then out of the blue someone said, "Ding!" and guys immediately squared off with the person next to them and went to work with kicks, headlocks, soup bones, head butts, you name it. I can't imagine what our coach was thinking, but he probably suspected anything from us by then. That's how crazy we were about the "sport."

Later National Wrestling Alliance (NWA) wrestling was broadcast in our area and we thought we were in heaven. Now we had two shows to watch with two different sets of characters though the NWA did not have cards in our area until later. When this happened, Vince McMahon started to make his move and he built the WWE into what it is today. This was also when I gave it up, though I still know the characters who are involved now.

Today's wrestling is different than what we watched in that there is more of a soap opera aspect to it. The plot takes place more outside the ring than in it. Females were few and far between years ago with the Fabulous Moola being most recognizable. Now, women are everywhere inside and outside of the ring. McMahon has added sex to the mix along with a lot of other unsavory aspects which kids really shouldn't be watching. Also, many of today's wrestlers are so well known that they've gone national becoming TV and movie stars in their own right and there is nothing wrong with that.

Many of my friends still watch. I guess I just outgrew it. The plot gets old after a while. Pro wrestling will never go away, because what is old to some is new to someone else. Or as the old saying goes, "There's a sucker born every minute."

I was one of them hook, line and sinker and don't mind admitting it.

Yes, I watched wrestling. And enjoyed every minute of it when I did.

ALI-FRAZIER NO MORE

Ali-Frazier. Frazier-Ali. The names will forever be linked in boxing and sports history. The Muhammad Ali-Joe Frazier heavyweight trilogy is considered by many to be the best in boxing history. It had drama. It had social overtones. It had political overtones. It had suspense. It had violence. And it had some of the greatest boxing ever seen. To this day there is no middle ground. You are either an Ali man or a Frazier man. Even people who weren't born when they fought, but have read about it and seen the fights on film choose sides. I know, because I've argued with them.

I don't argue about it anymore. The Ali-Frazier trilogy occurred when I was a young boy and since my father was a Muhammad man that made me and my family one too. Frazier was the bad guy and always would be. Or so I thought. Now I have nothing but respect for Frazier and Ali and what they both put themselves through in those fights. But I will never watch them again and here is why.

Muhammad Ali and Joe Frazier started out as friends. They met in the late sixties when Ali was in boxing exile, having been stripped of the heavyweight championship in 1967, because he refused to register for the draft during the Vietnam War. Ali's reason for not registering was his religion. As a member of the Muslim faith, he did not believe that the war was just and did not think it right to fight in Vietnam.

It is forgotten by many that Frazier supported Ali during this time. After they met, Frazier was one of the men who lobbied for Ali to have his license renewed. He may not have totally agreed with Ali's beliefs, but felt that Muhammad deserved a chance to make a living. When Ali needed help financially, Frazier loaned him money.

None of this interfered with Frazier's boxing. While Ali sat and awaited his fate in court, Frazier was on his way up in the heavyweight division eventually winning the vacated title in 1970. Along the way, he had to listen to the naysayers who did not think that anyone was the champ except Ali. This had to be one of the motivations for him to help Ali. Frazier had to know that the only way he'd be recognized as the true heavyweight champion of the world was to beat Ali.

Ali won his battle in court and got his license renewed in 1970. With Frazier now entrenched as the champ, the way was clear for a match between the two unbeatens once Ali got a few tune-ups under his belt. They finally agreed to meet in March of 1971 at New York's Madison Square Garden. It was the beginning of a great trilogy and the end of a good friendship.

Immediately, as was the norm with him, Ali began to spout off about what he was going to do to Frazier. Ali always did this in order to promote his fights, but also, because he was supremely confident that he would win. He had done it when he beat Sonny Liston to win the title in 1964 and he would do it now to Frazier. Some of it was playful, but a good bit of it was personal and hurtful to Frazier like Ali calling him an Uncle Tom. How could a man whom he had befriended turn on him so? A man whom he had helped get back into boxing and loaned money to when he needed it. Instead of firing back verbally, Frazier's response was to train harder than ever and do his talking in the ring.

The fight was one of the most anticipated in boxing history and divided the country. Most of black America sided with Ali. Most young, white American's did as well. Everyone else rooted for Frazier. A win for Ali would be a victory for the rebellious. A win for Frazier would be a victory for the establishment even though Joe was as far removed from them as Ali if not more so. It was Frazier who had grown up a sharecropper's son and struggled to get where he was while Ali grew up on hard times too in Louisville, Kentucky.

Madison Square Garden brought out the A list in celebrity and they saw a great fight that went the distance with Frazier winning by decision. The most memorable moment was Frazier's picture perfect right hook packed with three years of pent up emotion which floored Ali in the fifteenth round. How Ali got up, no one knows. Both men left the ring battered and bruised and Frazier spent the next two weeks in the hospital. At one time there was a report that Frazier had died in the hospital to which Ali responded that if it was true he'd never fight again.

While Frazier lay in the hospital, Ali went public in telling people that he had won the fight. That he was the people's champion. Maybe this was to promote publicity for a rematch. Maybe it was the way he truly felt. Either way, this did not sit well with Frazier who decided he would give Ali a rematch later rather than sooner.

The second fight could not live up to the first. It was fought in 1973 after Frazier had lost the title to George Foreman. Both men needed a win in order to get a shot at Foreman, Frazier to win his title back, Ali to get the shot he'd lost when Foreman beat Frazier. Both were shadows of their former selves with Ali winning a fifteen round decision to even the score.

The stage was set for their final match after Ali defeated Foreman to win the title back in 1974. With the title in hand, Ali gave Frazier one more shot in what would be called the "Thrilla in Manila."

By now, it had gotten ugly. Ali continued to say hurtful things about Frazier. He still called Frazier an Uncle Tom and worse, a gorilla. Everyone who knows boxing history has seen the clip of Ali punching a toy gorilla and saying, "Come on gorilla. We're in Manila." Whether he was doing this to anger Frazier or promote the fight it was wrong. The fact that Ali, a black man, was doing this and that blacks thought it funny made it worse.

As for Frazier, he was now seething. His frustration boiled over in a memorable sit down on ABC's "Wide World of Sports" with Ali and Howard Cosell in which highlights of the first two fights were being shown. Frazier got into a wrestling match with Ali that saw both men wind up on the floor. Ali was joking while Frazier was very serious. By the time of the fight Frazier was literally out to kill Ali.

The "Thrilla in Manila" was a fight between two champions past their primes who summoned everything they had one last time. It was the most brutal fight I have ever seen. Ali jabbed Frazier to the point where both of Joe's eyes became swollen shut. Frazier, literally trying to kill his opponent, beat into Ali's body so violently that the champ said later it was the closest he had ever come to death. The heat in the ring was unmerciful and sapped energy from both men. After fourteen rounds, the gallant Frazier could no longer see Ali or the jabs that were being thrown at him. Frazier's manager, Eddie Futch, would not let him go out for the fifteenth and the fight was over with Ali winning by technical knockout. Immediately after the fight was called, Ali stood for a second with raised fists to acknowledge the crowd then slumped to the floor totally exhausted. The damage both men had inflicted on each other is still being felt by them today.

After the fight, Ali and Frazier had nothing but praise for one another, but as the years went by Frazier became a bitter man towards Ali with good reason. He had not only suffered two defeats to Ali, but public humiliation as well. As Ali's fame grew, Frazier became a footnote to Muhammad's legacy playing second fiddle to the self proclaimed "Greatest". No one remembered what Frazier had done to help Ali. The only thing that was recalled was the fights themselves and how, if you were an Ali fan, Frazier represented the establishment. This was not the picture that Frazier wanted history to paint of him, because it wasn't the truth.

Though he has been cordial to Ali in public, it is now Frazier who says bad things about Ali. It is Frazier through slurred speech of his own who says he's the one who brought on Ali's Alzheimer's with his punches. It is Frazier who says that God took Ali's speech and motor skills away from him for all of the evil that Muhammad did to Joe verbally. It is Frazier who believes that he won all three fights.

Muhammad Ali and Joe Frazier gave us three of the greatest fights of all time, but at what price? Looking at them now is painful to me and not just because of their physical state. It's painful, because I chose a side without knowing everything that was happening behind the scenes. It's painful, because I did not give a man, Joe Frazier, the respect I should have and gave another, Ali, more than he may have deserved. It is painful, because black America turned on one of our own who had worked hard to become successful and had done nothing but represented blacks in a positive way.

And most important, it's painful because we watched a good friendship come to an end and turn into hatred all in the name of sport. No sporting event should become such that it causes this to happen.

For these reasons, I will never watch the Ali-Frazier trilogy again.

KARMA

Yes, I believe in it. The dictionary defines it as the force generated by a person's actions held in Hinduism and Buddhism to perpetuate transmigration and its ethical consequences to determine his destiny in his next existence. Let's see how it determines a person or teams destiny in his present existence.

The first time I really gave karma a thought was while watching a 1986 NFC playoff game where the New York Giants hosted the San Francisco 49ers. Early in the game, San Francisco wide receiver Jerry Rice caught a perfect pass over the middle from quarterback Joe Montana and was gone. There was nothing but God's green Astroturf in front of him and, inexplicably, Rice fumbled the ball without being touched. Rice and the Giant defenders chased the football all of the way into the end zone where New York recovered. Game over. Giants 49, 49ers 3. I went outside at halftime to help my father fix a barn door and he asked me the score of the game. I told him the Giants were killing the Niners and he said that it was no surprise. "It's just the Giants year," he said.

The next week, New York played the Washington Redskins for the NFC championship on a windy day in the New Jersey Meadowlands. It was so bad that both teams decided if they won the coin toss they'd defend the goal line with their back to the wind. Washington being the visiting team got the choice of heads or tails, guessed wrong and the Giants took the wind. New York quickly scored 17 points and the rest of the day was nothing more than both teams getting painful exercise.

The Giants went on to win their first Super Bowl and I became a believer in karma.

Former major leaguer Lonnie Smith was a great example of karma. We used to say that if you want to win a World Series, sign Lonnie Smith. He won it all as a Philadelphia Phillie in 1980. It took the Phillies 28 years to win another. Smith was traded to the St. Louis Cardinals in 1982 and they won it all. It took the Cardinals 24 years to win another. They might have won it sooner, but they traded Smith who ended up with the Kansas City Royals in 1985. Kansas City faced St. Louis in the World Series that year and came back from a three games to one deficit to win it. Kansas City has not won a World Series, or been to one, since. Smith's karma finally ran out in 1991 when he joined an Atlanta Braves team which went from worst to first and won the National League pennant only to lose the World Series in seven games to the Minnesota Twins, but three out of four isn't bad.

Looking back, I see many examples of karma. In 2009 Brett Favre signed to play for the Minnesota Vikings after retiring from the New York Jets. This after signing with the Jets after retiring, or being forced out some would say, from the Green Bay Packers. Before signing with the Vikings, Favre sat out the whole offseason and most of training camp. After his signing with Minnesota, many Viking fans were torn as to whether or not they wanted to root for a man who had beaten them so many times while with Green Bay. This was not a good sign. Favre had a great year and led the Vikings to the NFC championship game. Then with the game on the line, he threw a killer interception and the Vikings lost to the New Orleans Saints in overtime. With Favre's past history of throwing big picks in important games and all which had led up to his signing with the Vikings there was no other way for this story to end. That script had been written in August.

As a Steelers fan, when I heard the report in 2006 that quarterback Ben Roethlisberger had been in a bad motorcycle accident my first thought was is he okay? My second thought was that the Steelers, who were the defending Super Bowl champions, were not going to repeat. Fortunately, Ben was okay, but the damage to him physically was such that he couldn't recover in time to be productive during the season. He had a terrible year and the Steelers went 8-8 missing the playoffs. Really, there was no use in the Steelers even playing that year. They were done in May.

Yes, I believe that the "Spygate" scandal was the reason for the New England Patriots losing their undefeated season in Super Bowl XLII to the Giants. The whole thing with the Patriots filming other team's practices and signals was wrong and they had to pay. It didn't matter who they played in the Super Bowl, they were going to lose. Think about it. They were less than a minute away from winning it all. Everyone remembers Giant quarterback Eli Manning's escape and pass that David Tyree made an unbelievable catch on. I remember the play before when New England's Asante Samuels had the game clinching interception go right through his hands.

The 1979 Pittsburgh Pirates had the karma. The "We Are Family" Bucs won any and every way possible led by their first baseman and team captain Willie "Pops" Stargell. Even though they were down three games to one in the World Series to the Baltimore Orioles with two games left on the road, Pittsburgh came back to win it all and Stargell hit the big home run to win game seven.

Stargell had only done what he'd seen his friend and former teammate Roberto Clemente do to the Orioles back in 1971. After years of being in the shadows of Willie Mays, Frank Robinson, Henry Aaron and Ernie Banks, Clemente finally got to show a national audience how great a ballplayer he was and he did winning World Series MVP while leading the Pirates to the title. It was his moment, well deserved, and he made the most of it as should have been expected.

Former heavyweight champion of the world Riddick Bowe did not lose his title in the ring that night in 1993 to Evander Holyfield Bowe lost the title when he and his manager Rock Newman threw one of their unified title belts, the WBC, in the trash when it was stripped of them for not taking on the number one contender. They disrespected the belt and paid for it by losing the other two to Holyfield.

The New York Knicks could not win the NBA title under Pat Riley, because they were not playing the game the right way. Their style of pushing and clutching and grabbing was against the rules and the league let them get away with it. You could bet that if the Knicks were at home and losing in the fourth quarter, they would get every call and come back to win. So their punishment was John Starks going cold as ice in game seven of the NBA Finals against the Houston Rockets in

1994. Their punishment was the Indiana Pacers Reggie Miller getting away with a push of his own in the Garden then shooting them down in game one of the 1995 Eastern Conference Semis. Their punishment was Charles Smith getting three shots blocked under the basket as time ran out by the Chicago Bulls Scottie Pippen, Michael Jordan and Horace Grant in 1993. Their punishment was Patrick Ewing missing a runner in the lane at the buzzer in a game seven loss to Miller's Pacers at the end of that 1995 playoff series. Riley's protégé Jeff Van Gundy who coached the Miami Heat and played the same style couldn't win it all either for the same reasons stated earlier. Riley did win it all when he went to Miami, but he did it with a scorer named Dwayne Wade and a future hall of fame center in Shaquille O'Neal. Not "Force Ball."

Philadelphia Eagle fans are desperate for a Super Bowl championship. They haven't won an NFL title since 1960 when everything that could go right for them did. They even beat Vince Lombardi's Green Bay Packers in the championship game. Every year, they lose and wonder why?

Maybe booing Santa Claus wasn't a good idea. Maybe fighting with every fan from the opposing team who shows up in their stadium is a bad idea. Maybe just being rowdy period is a bad idea. Maybe taking more pride in hurting the other team than winning is not a good idea. Philadelphia is a rough and tough crowd. I know, because I've been there. They take pride in it and there is nothing wrong with being tough. There is such thing as being too rough and maybe, just maybe, Philly fan is.

Major League Baseball's punishment for the so called "Steroids Era" was being exposed by the poster child for steroids Jose Canseco all because they didn't like him and wouldn't give him a chance to hit his 500th home run.

The Washington Redskins may turn it around one day, but I had a bad feeling about their fortunes from my first sighting of owner Daniel Snyder at training camp in 1999. I remember sitting in the bleachers at Frostburg State College with my best friend, Tom. When Snyder walked onto the field I told Tom that there was something I didn't like about him. Something just didn't seem right. I don't know why, but I just sensed that the Redskins fortunes were about to get worse. As of this writing, one would have to say that the bad vibes I had were warranted.

It was, and still is, nothing personal. Just a feel, a sense, that the karma wasn't right.

The Oakland Raiders had no chance of winning the Super Bowl in 2003 against the Tampa Bay Buccaneers. The Bucs were coached by Jon Gruden the man who had taken the Raiders to the playoffs in 2000 and 2001. Gruden had been allowed to sign with Tampa after Raiders owner Al Davis decided that Oakland could win without him. Gruden led the Bucs to the NFC championship while his replacement, Bill Callahan, led Oakland to the AFC title. Oakland had a good team, but their fate was sealed in the NFC championship game when the Bucs Ronde Barber intercepted Eagle quarterback Donovan McNabb and ran it back for the clinching touchdown. Once they were scheduled to play the coach who had built them and knew them inside out, the Raiders were done.

My final example is the lifting of the famous "Curse of the Bambino." We all know about how the Boston Red Sox seemed to be cursed, because they traded Babe Ruth, "The Bambino", to the New York Yankees back in 1920. While the Yankees went on to win 26 World Series from 1923 to 2000, the Red Sox didn't win any. Along the way, they were beaten out by the Yankees for the pennant in 1949, 1978 and 2003 in crushing fashion. When they made it to the series in 1946, 1964, 1975 and 1986 they lost all of them in seven games.

The Yankees were loaded again in 2004 after signing all-star shortstop Alex Rodriguez, who spurned an offer from Boston, from the Texas Rangers and moving him to third base. They were well on their way to another pennant and World Series at the expense of the Red Sox when they lead them three games to none in the League Championship Series. No team in baseball history had ever come back from a three games to none deficit to win a playoff series and it didn't seem as though Boston would be the first, especially with the last two games scheduled for Yankee Stadium.

Well, the Red Sox pulled it off. They ran the table on New York winning four straight and the American League title. Then they went on to win the World Series in four straight from the St. Louis Cardinals. The "Curse" was dead. Boston went on to win another championship in 2007.

Most people feel that the curse was killed in that series against New York, but it was not. The curse was officially killed back in July of that season. The Yankees were cruising along with a huge lead in the American League East and were in Boston for a three game weekend series from July 23 to 25. In the Saturday afternoon nationally televised game New York had a commanding lead late with Alex Rodriguez at the plate. The newest Yankee "Bambino" was hit by a pitch and got angry. Instead of simply heading to first base, Rodriguez decided to challenge Boston catcher Jason Varitek to a fight. It was a bad decision. Varitek roughed up A Rod, but more important the Yankee third baseman woke a sleeping giant. The Red Sox came back to win the game in extra innings, caught fire to win the American League wild card then won a first round playoff to set up their run to the famous come from behind victory over the Yankees.

No, the Yankees did not lose that pennant in October. If A Rod had just left Varitek alone, Boston may not have even made the playoffs. They were struggling that much in July. A Rod woke them up and karma did the rest. A Rod, an outsider to the whole Yankee-Red Sox rivalry, tried to force his will on it and Varitek wouldn't let him. This set the stage for everything that followed.

Yes, I believe in karma. Good and bad. As the old saying goes, "You reap what you sew."

SPORTS AND RELIGION

I've been watching the media and fans reaction to former Florida Gator Heisman Trophy winner Tim Tebow lately with greater interest. A lot of it has to do with the fact Tebow is a very religious young man who wears it on his sleeve and as of this writing, I am going through a spiritual awakening of my own.

Let me start by saying that I did not root for Tebow when he played for the Gators. It had nothing to do with him as a man. I think that he is a great football player and leader. I also think from what I've seen, heard and read about him that he is a great role model. I did not root for Tebow, because he played for Florida and I'm not a Gator fan.

However, I have always had respect for Tebow as a football player. Though I don't think that his style of play will translate into being a good National Football League quarterback, he's still enough of a player to make it in the pros somewhere. One of the reasons I respect Tebow is that he was willing to sacrifice his advancement as a player in order to help his team win games. The truth is Florida used Tim Tebow in ways that would help them win regardless of whether it helped make him a better quarterback. Tebow could have balked at this. He could have asked coach Urban Meyer to change the system for him. He could have transferred to another school, but didn't. It may cost him career wise and financially, but Tebow did what he thought was right by his teammates and I commend him for that. I doubt if many people, including myself, would have done the same.

What has puzzled me the last few months is the backlash Tebow seems to be getting for being so open about his religion. From what I have seen, the young man has not gone around preaching the gospel and saying that he is better than everyone. He has not gone around telling people that he is going to heaven and they are not. The only thing that I have seen him do is worship the Lord his way and to me there is nothing wrong with that.

The reason why people are so hard on Tebow is simple. He is too good to be true. He doesn't seem to have any flaws that we know of, though nobody is perfect, and this bothers us. People like Tebow come off as self righteous to us not because they are, but because they make us see ourselves as being the flawed humans we are. No one likes to be reminded by anyone that they are not perfect. No one likes to feel like they don't measure up. People like Tebow bring out these kind of emotions in us and we don't like it.

So the way to get back at them is to root against them. To hope that they fail. To tell them that we don't care about their religious beliefs and values. To try and find flaws in them. To try and tear them down after building them up. Let's face it there are many people who rejoice in the failures of others. These are the people who like nothing more than to see someone who was put on a pedestal do something that knocks themselves off of it. Our media coverage tells us that much. It is a flaw that humans have, the little green monster called jealousy.

Tebow is just one example of this. Pro football hall of famer Reggie White was another. Known as the "Minister of Defense," White got a lot of flack from people for saying such things as God told him to sign with the Green Bay Packers when he became a free agent and later the Carolina Panthers. He got flack for saying that God had healed him when he severely injured his hamstring in 1995 while playing for the Packers. He got flack for mentioning God in his interviews.

Personally, I don't have a problem with athletes worshipping the Lord. I don't have a problem with them pointing to the sky or dropping to one knee or crossing themselves. I don't have a problem with them wearing scripture on their eye black or speaking in tongues. I don't have a problem with them praising their God while giving an interview. I don't have a problem with them getting together with their opponents after games to pray. As long as they keep it in the proper perspective.

When athletes say that they or their team won, because God wanted them I find it hard to believe. God does not decide wins and losses in sports. He has more urgent things to do than that. Besides there are God fearing athletes on both teams so why would the God who loves us all equally, unconditional of whom we are, choose between one side or the other?

What God does do is give an athlete, all of us for that matter, a talent and a forum to use it. It is up to the athlete to make the most of it. Those who maximize their talents are successful while those who do not don't. If the talent on both sides is equal it is the actions of those talented people who decide wins and losses, not God. As the saying goes, "God helps those who help themselves." Athletes have to realize this before making the statement that it was God's will for what happened during the game.

The reason that I say this is, because many times we hear athletes thanking the Lord only when they do well. Many of them give him all of the credit and praise when things are going successfully. They don't give him the credit and the praise when things are going bad despite the fact he is still with them then. God is still allowing them to use their talent by keeping them healthy and giving them their platform to perform on. God is still allowing them to express themselves the best way they know how win or lose. God is still protecting their teammates and coaches. God is still protecting their family and friends. These are the times when they should give praise the most, because then they are telling God that they believe in Him unconditionally just as He believes in them.

I would be more inclined to listen to an athlete who prays through the good and bad times than one who does only when they win. I would be more inclined to listen to an athlete who thanks God for the opportunity despite coming up short than one who says that it was God's will. I would be more inclined to listen to an athlete who said that everything happens for a reason and that God was with them every step of the way even though they lost.

It would be nice to see more God fearing athletes in television feature stories, newspapers and magazines instead of those that are in trouble.

I don't have a problem with athletes using sports as a forum for their religious beliefs, as long as they are consistent with it win or lose. Because the good Lord cares for everyone who performs, not just the winners.

ENHANCING PERFORMANCE

Here is the thing. There is no "steroid era" in sports. Performance enhancing drugs have been around for so long, and still are, that we can't come up with a definitive time when they began. The only thing that we know is that they still exist and are being used today. That's the truth whether we like it or not.

They are used for many reasons. Some people use them to help with strength. Others use them to maintain endurance. Some use them just to look good or cut. And many athletes use them to bounce back from injury by speeding up the healing process.

Most people believe that steroids first came on the scene in the 1960's. They were mostly used by Olympic athletes especially those in East Germany. Here in the United States, bodybuilders, wrestlers and weightlifters were thought to be using them along with some football players. No one really knew the long term effects. They just knew that PED's made them run faster, jump higher and lift more. Since drug testing was not performed at that time and nothing was illegal, there is no way of knowing who used and who did not.

PED's did not become known to the professional sports world until the 1980's when NFL players were widely suspected of using them. As mentioned earlier, many football players had been using them since the sixties, but no one thought much of it, because again no one knew the long term effects. By now, the International Olympics Committee was testing for PED's with Canadian sprinter Ben Johnson being the first high profile gold medal winner to be stripped of his medal after a positive test in 1988. The NFL soon followed suit and implemented drug testing in the early 1990's.

Then baseball fans learned of their sports steroid use in the 2000's thanks to former major league outfielder Jose Canseco. His tell all book told of PED's being used as early as his rookie year of 1987. The period from the mid 1980's to 2006 is considered the "steroid era" by baseball experts.

Before steroids, athletes used amphetamines to get themselves ready to play. This was done in all of the major pro sports baseball, football, basketball and hockey. Football players used them to get emotionally high for their sixty minutes of violent hell. The athletes in the other three sports used them more to get through a game after traveling a few time zones or a day game after a night game. Either way it enhanced their performance, because it allowed them to summon energy they otherwise didn't have. New York Yankee pitcher Jim Bouton wrote about this in his famous book "Ball Four" and Dallas Cowboy split end Peter Gent did in a fictional football account called "North Dallas Forty."

Though it is not considered a performance enhancer, marijuana has been used by many athletes over the years. They are used more to relax them than anything else. Some would say that using marijuana would be detrimental to performance despite what we see from many musicians. Whether it hurts or helps is up for debate, but I for one have seen its effects first hand.

While playing basketball one hot summer day, a group of us decided to take a break under the recreation center canopy. We had just played three straight games and the team that I was on had won them all. The break was being taken in order to get out of the sun for a while and get something to drink. While relaxing we decided that the first team to four wins would be declared the winner on this day. Being up three games to none made that a pretty easy decision for the guys on my team. Just win one and we could go home.

While I sat drinking my Gatorade, someone lit a joint and passed it around. I had known every man there since childhood so wasn't surprised. They knew that I wasn't a smoker, but offered me a hit anyway which I declined. Only one other person besides me passed on a chance to take a smoke and he was a teammate. Everyone on the opposing team did.

When we returned to the court you could see that something had happened. Our opponents were all of a sudden unstoppable. Their point guard sliced through us like butter, passing and scoring at will. Their shooting guard was pulling up and hitting jumpers from everywhere. Everybody on the team seemed to be playing the game at a different level, a different speed. Not a fast one, but controlled. There was no wasted motion. Every movement was as smooth as a jazz musician playing his horn. I swear it seemed as if they were moving in suspended animation. It looked like they were leaving a vapor trail behind them as they ran, jumped and shot.

After their first two trips down the court, we knew that we were in trouble. I began to wonder if maybe I should have taken a hit after all.

Needless to say, they came back and swept us in four games. Not only did they sweep us, but they didn't even break a sweat in doing it. It was the greatest exhibition of basketball that I have ever seen on the playground and I've seen some of the best. No one had better basketball players than our area of Maryland except Baltimore City. Our high school held the state record for state championship won for a while.

Call it coincidence. Call it what you want. I'm here to tell you that from what I saw that day, marijuana was more of an enhancement than a detriment in my book.

I first learned of steroids while in high school during the early 1980's . It was mainly considered a problem in college football that was moving down to the prep level. The first person that I saw take them was a young man who played football and was a freshman my senior year. He was a skinny kid without much talent and looked like he'd never amount to much. A couple of years later, I came home from college and everyone was telling me how big he'd become. When I finally saw him it was unbelievable. He had gone from the skinny kid in the old Charles Atlas ad to the bully on the beach. I couldn't believe my eyes.

I didn't suspect much and had no idea that rumors were floating around about his use of steroids. When I went to a practice later that year there he was bigger than every player on the field. That's when I became suspicious. After seeing him play a game I became even more suspicious. The reason was that he showed me the first sign of 'roid rage. After a play in which he thought he'd recovered a fumble, he slammed the ball into the turf and swore at the referee earning a personal foul. The coach took him out, yelled at him and sent him to the bench.

My suspicions were confirmed the next spring when I came home and was told the young man had suffered a fit of 'roid rage and done bodily harm to some people. It was the first time I had seen the full effects of what PED's could do. This was 1987.

College was an eye opener, also. I can remember an outfielder on our baseball team who was just ripped. The problem was that he was always hurt, but when he did play he showed speed and especially strength. One night, he hit a ball clear over the light tower in left center field. Our left center power alley was 387 feet from home plate. The light tower was at least 40 feet high. It was a mammoth blow and I remember the buzz in the bleachers lasted all night. I never saw anything like it and never thought anything of it until Jose Canseco began playing for the Oakland Athletics. After watching Canseco, I finally put two and two together and figured our college ballplayer had been using.

He wasn't the only one. We had a Latino infielder who was not very big. He was in his senior year and desperate to make it to the pros. So he began to shoot up. Many of his friends on the team tried to talk him out of it, but he felt it was his only chance. Needless to say, he didn't make it.

Two years later, I was at a free agent football camp of players trying to make it to the pros. All week long we compared athletes with guys simply saying, "He's on it," and "He's not." We had a big fullback who was the star of the camp and his buddies who had played with him in college clued us in at breakfast that he was using. He and his brothers, who were older and not at the camp. They came onto campus later in the week and we just looked at them and shook our heads.

The most obvious user was a guy who played one of the least suspected positions for PED use. One of the quarterbacks in camp was using big time and admitted it to us. Every vein in his arms and legs seemed to jump out. You could see the blue blood. His eyes always had a far away glassy look to them. At times, he seemed hyper talking wildly and moving his hands quickly. In the cafeteria, guys started to move away from him. He usually sat alone though his table was near ours and we watched his act in amazement. He was something else.

On the field, though not very good, he played without fear. His jersey was ripped to shreds with shoulder pads hanging out. His pants were rolled up above the knee. He wore high top cleats with no socks. A character if ever there was one and a PED user.

When pro football player Lyle Alzado tried to make a comeback with the Los Angeles Raiders in 1990, it was horrible. I was at a friend's house when his brother and some other guys called us downstairs to watch a pre season game between the Raiders and Bears. "You gotta come see Alzado," they said. We went down and looked at the TV. There was Alzado wearing his old number 77 jersey. He was bigger than any football player I had ever seen. Every vein showed even the ones in his head. He looked grotesque. I can't lie, everyone in the room began to laugh and make comments about how bad he looked. When the ball was snapped and he tried to run, Alzado looked like a parking garage trying to chase the car that just left it. After a while we semi began to worry, because the thought crossed our minds that Alzado could die right there on the field. No one gave a thought to leaving this meaningless pre season game, because we all wanted to see what was going to happen to him. He survived thankfully, but gave up on the comeback some time later.

As I mentioned earlier, Canseco was the first baseball player that we suspected. We used to watch him at old Memorial Stadium and later Camden Yards in Baltimore and ask each other if Canseco was on the juice. To a man, we said yes. The only other player we suspected was Mark McGwire. I didn't really become suspicious of major league ballplayers until I began coaching youth ball myself during the mid 90's. This is when weight lifting was finally considered more help than harm in baseball and kids started to pump iron. So did the major leaguers. All of a sudden guys were walking onto the field looking bigger than linebackers in the NFL. Baseballs were being hit to the moon. The reason given was that the balls were juiced, pitching wasn't as good and ballparks were smaller. I thought otherwise.

My suspicions grew in 1996 when Baltimore Orioles outfielder Brady Anderson hit 51 home runs a record for leadoff hitters. From the beginning of the season to the end you could see a physical change in Anderson. Though it's never been proven that he did PED's, Anderson had never hit more than 19 home runs in a season before that year and never did again.

My suspicions also grew when Houston Astros third baseman Ken Caminiti came back from a torn rotator cuff before the 1996 season ended. A torn rotator cuff injury takes a long time to heal and usually is a season ender. When I heard the news of Caminiti's comeback, I looked at my nephew who was a Little Leaguer at the time and said, "You know how he was able to come back so soon don't you?" My nephew asked how and I told him steroids. There was no other way.

The Mark McGwire, Sammy Sosa race to break Roger Maris' single season home run record in 1998 should have been the red flag for everyone. Not only did they break a record that had stood for 37 years, they shattered it. Much the same way Ben Johnson had shattered the world record in the 100 meter dash at the 1988 Summer Olympics. Along the way, McGwire and Sosa hit home runs of mammoth proportions, never slowed down even in the dog days of August and flexed arms that looked far bigger than the ones on the bubble gum cards from their rookie years. No one said a word. When McGwire came to Washington D.C. for an exhibition game the following summer and hit balls on the roof of RFK Stadium I couldn't take it anymore.

When my boss walked into work the next day, he asked if I had seen McGwire's performance and I said with a laugh that I had. He asked me why I was laughing and I said, "Can't you tell. He's on the juice," Here was a lifelong baseball fan in his fifties and he looked incredulous. He asked me if I really thought so and I said yes. "You saw Frank Howard play with the Dodgers and Senators," I said. You know they have the seats that he hit homers into the upper deck at RFK colored. You know how big Howard was. And McGwire hit balls ten times as far. Come on, he's strong, but not that strong." My boss still couldn't believe it.

Nobody did until Jose Canseco wrote his book and Barry Bonds' quest for Henry Aaron's all-time home run record. And once they did, they became angry. Fans wanted the player's suspended, even banned for life. Writers and former players wanted asterisks put beside any records set at that time. There was and still is growing sentiment that no player during the era from 1990 to 2005 be allowed into the hall of fame.

Where was all of this outrage while steroid use was going on? If I was exposed to it in the mid 80's and many of the people that I knew were also, how could people who call themselves journalists not know about it ten years later? If everything that the pros do trickles down to the lower levels and high school kids were using how could the pros not be questioned?

The answer given is that they didn't know. The truth is that people looked the other way. Nothing that happens on a ballclub can be kept a secret for long. Eventually, someone talks and everyone finds out the truth from ownership down to the locker room attendants. The players knew. The managers knew. And the front office knew. How the media couldn't have known or suspected something is hard to say.

When Canseco first wrote his book everyone went after him guns blazing. He was jealous, because he didn't get the publicity that McGwire and Sosa got. He was mad because he thought he was blackballed and didn't get a chance to hit his 500th home run. He was a locker room snitch. He was a goofball who didn't know what he was talking about. Everyone went after the messenger hoping that the message would go away. Once many of the things Canseco wrote began to be proven correct than people wanted justice served with asterisks, hall of fame denial and bans from baseball.

The people in baseball want to have it both ways. They want to forget that they all benefitted from players using PED's from the commissioner to the owners to front office personnel to the managers to the players to television, radio and other media. All of them made money from ticket sales, merchandise, TV revenue, newspaper and magazine circulation and books that were written about the players. Now they want the men who helped make them rich punished. Why didn't anyone think of this while it was going on? Some did, but most didn't and the ones who did were told to clam up, because with no drug testing in baseball, they had no proof.

Baseball cannot keep these men out of the hall of fame without being hypocritical. They can't say to a player "You were wrong, but thanks for the money we made from it. Now you won't get my hall of fame vote." Or "You're banned from baseball for life." Especially since baseball has always been known for its cheaters with quite a few already in the hall.

As for the record book, they shouldn't be allowed to change that either or put asterisks beside any entry until they have drug tests which prove a player used. Even then, there were no suspensions of any player for PED's at that time so obviously baseball thought everything was okay. They thought it was okay all of the way to the bank.

Football took a while to catch up to steroids before implementing drug testing. Once they did, there was nothing done retroactive to the history of the game. The NFL knew that despite their suspicions there was no way of knowing who did what so why bother? Baseball needs to do the same. And truth be told, football drug testing leaves a few questions also. I say this, because with all of the NFL's testing how come there has never been a quarterback who tested positive? There have been positive tests at every position, except quarterback. Guess it's just blind luck.

The way baseball people reacted after Canseco's book reminds me of a time when I was playing basketball and the guy that I was guarding dribbled the ball and switched the ball from one hand to the other before dribbling again. He made his move and I called double dribble. He said it wasn't or I would have called it before he made his move. I told him it was and give up the ball. He said, "You fell asleep," and he was right. He had committed a double dribble, but I waited too long to call it. Baseball players did use PED's and the people in baseball waited too long to call them on it. Now they want them to pay for it. To quote my opponent, "You fell asleep." Deal with it.

If they would have asked us, we could have told them exactly what was going on with PED's in all sports. There are plenty of telltale signs to PED use.

If someone shatters a record that has stood for a long time or only been broken in small increments, check them out. If that shattered record is broken by someone else, check them out too.

If an athlete comes back quicker than normal from an injury which should keep them out for a while, check them out.

If an athlete's numbers skyrocket one year and never reach that level again, check them out.

If an athlete who looks like Jane all of a sudden looks like Tarzan and he's already had his growth spurt, check them out.

As for the future there will always be PED's. They can test all they want, but athletes and scientists will always find a way to beat it. The question is, "Do we as fans really care?" I think if we did, we'd ask for harder punishments for the athletes. Even if we did, the truth of the matter is anything short of actual prison time will not stop athletes from using performance enhancing drugs. To them, getting caught and suspended for a few games is no worse than getting a traffic ticket. Sometimes, taking away a person's freedom is the only way to get them to obey the law.

I can see a day when PED's are allowed in pro sports. The teams would hire trainers and doctors to monitor the players PED intake. They would be used for everything from strengthening to recovering from injury. This would make players less inclined to go out and find them on their own. This was the case in football before drug testing. One could make the case that they would still be in the pros if it hadn't trickled down to the lower levels with high school kids starting to die.

Before you get upset with what I'm saying, think of all of the PED's that people us today. Celebrities are getting bodywork done all of the time for no other reason than to look good on camera. Musicians have used drugs for years to get through concerts. What about hair transplants? And let's not forget all of the erectile dysfunction ads we see on TV. If that's not a PED, I don't know what is.

The funny thing about the erectile dysfunction drugs along with birth control for women is that they go against what once was considered as big a sin as there was, sex of any kind which did not lead to reproduction.

There was a time when people were told that if they had unwed sex they would go straight to hell. Then the sexual revolution brought on unwanted pregnancies which led to abortions. Instead of quoting the Bible on unwed sex, the powers that be said, "If you can't beat 'em, join 'em," and birth control and condoms became the answer. All for the express consent of allowing people to have sex despite what the Good Book said.

Then when older men became unable to perform sexually, they were treated to drugs which allowed them to overcome their erectile dysfunction. Drugs which allowed them to perform. Fifty years ago, this wouldn't have even been thought of, but the children of the sexual revolution had to have it.

If people can create drugs and defend their usage even when they go against the Holy Bible, why wouldn't they eventually allow athletes to use drugs to enhance their performance?

UH OH! AND OH NO!

What this chapter is about are moments which occur in sports which in my mind or someone else's foreshadow the future of a player or team. The best explanation I can give is that an "Uh-oh!" moment is one in which a team does something that changes the team in a positive way. An "Oh no!" moment is one that changes it in a negative way. Having said that, an "Oh no!" moment can be a negative in the eye of a sports fan if it's an "Uh oh!" or positive one for a team he roots against. It's probably easier to explain with a few examples.

The first "Uh oh!" moment that I can recall occurred in the summer of 1976. My older brother's and cousins were talking basketball and the same players name kept coming up. All I kept hearing about was "Dr. J., Dr. J." Being eight years old and not up to speed on my pro basketball, I finally said "Who's Dr. J.?"

Remember the scene in the movie "Sandlot" when Smalls asked who's Babe Ruth? If you do, then I don't have to tell you what happened next. To a man all of them looked at me as if I were an alien from another world. "You don't know who Dr. J. is?" they all said. "Man he's the greatest basketball player on the planet." They laughed and tried to explain to me who this guy was.

Finally, one of them said, "Do you remember the guy who played for the New York Nets and made the windmill dunk they kept showing on the end of the year highlights? That's Dr. J."

Immediately, I knew who he was talking about. Since I had always been a National Basketball Association (NBA) fan and knew nothing about the now defunct American Basketball Association (ABA) it took me a while to put two and two together. Dr. J. was Julius Erving. The guy who had performed the greatest dunk I'd ever seen by going baseline and bringing the ball in a windmill motion from his hip to slam it down. After the ABA disbanded, Erving had been traded by the Nets to the Philadelphia 76'ers one of the worst teams in the NBA. My first thought after figuring this out was "Uh oh. The Sixers are now a contender." In the next seven years, Philly went to four NBA Finals finally winning it in 1983 after experiencing another "Uh oh!" moment when they acquired all-star center Moses Malone from the Houston Rockets.

My first "Oh no!" moment came during the 1977 NFL draft. The Tampa Bay Buccaneers had the first pick that year. Defending NFC East champion and arch rival of the Washington Redskins, the Dallas Cowboys were in the number two spot after making a trade with the Seattle Seahawks. The two players expected to go first were Heisman Trophy winning halfback Tony Dorsett from the University of Pittsburgh and Southern Cal tailback Ricky Bell. Most experts thought that Dorsett would go first to Tampa, but the Bucs took Bell, a good back in his own right, instead. The main reason for the Bucs drafting Bell first was that their head coach, John McKay, had coached him at Southern Cal before taking the Tampa job. This left the door wide open for Dallas to take the one player they needed to fill the one weakness they had, Tony Dorsett. The groans heard around the D.C. metro area could be heard all of the way to Dallas, "Oh no!" The rest of the league and anyone who wasn't a Cowboy fan felt the same. Dallas went on to win the Super Bowl that year and the NFC title the next. Dorsett went on to a hall of fame career.

This scenario would be repeated with even more devastating effect in 1990 when the Cowboys were able to draft Florida Gator running back Emmitt Smith. Not everyone knew the ramifications, because Smith was not even a top ten pick, but I did. I had followed him since his days at Pensacola Escambia High in Florida and knew how good he was.

When Smith was recruited by the Gators in 1986 my college roommate's brother who was a big Florida fan kept talking up another recruit named Octavius Gould. I told him that after Emmitt Smith gets to Gainesville we'll never hear Octavius Gould's name again. When I got back to Maryland I kept bragging about Smith. In his first game against Alabama, Smith ran for over 200 yards. I was watching at home and said to my friends, "That's him. That's the guy I've been telling you about." They were impressed, but thought he was too slow for the NFL.

This was the conventional wisdom concerning Smith which led to him being available when the Cowboys pick in the first round came up. Dallas coach Jimmy Johnson knew about Smith from his days as head coach at the University of Miami when he and his staff had scouted all of the top Florida talent. They wasted no time in drafting Smith with the seventeenth pick of the first round and another Dallas Cowboy "Oh no!" moment was experienced by me. Only this time, I was the only one that I knew who felt this way.

The rest is history. Emmitt went on to lead Dallas to three world's championships and racked up more yards rushing than anyone in the history of the game.

Georgetown basketball's "Uh oh!" moment, and the Big East conference for that matter, came when they signed center Patrick Ewing to a scholarship in 1981. Ewing joined a team two years removed from a trip to the NCAA's final eight, but still relatively unknown. The Hoyas were second fiddle in their own town to the University of Maryland Terrapins and the Atlantic Coast Conference. With Ewing, the Hoyas got instant credibility and the landscape of college basketball changed immediately in the D.C. area and in the ACC and Big East.

Georgetown went on to become the first Big East team to reach the Final Four in Ewing's freshman year. They became the first to win it in his junior year. The Hoyas went to three Final Fours in four years. Georgetown and Big East basketball were here to stay.

Deion Sanders had an "Uh oh!" moment when he signed on to play cornerback for the San Francisco 49ers in 1994 and an "Oh no!" moment when he signed with their arch rivals the Dallas Cowboys the next season.

The Niners were struggling early in the 1994 season while Deion played baseball. San Francisco had lost consecutive NFC title games to Dallas and had made offseason free agent signings in order to catch up to the Cowboys. But the move which put them over the top was signing Deion. With him, they were able to overtake Dallas and win the Super Bowl.

After the season, Sanders became a free agent. Dallas owner Jerry Jones essentially said, "If you can't beat them let them join you," and signed Sanders not only for his team, but to keep him away from everyone else. "Oh no," Dallas had done it again. For 1995, it was worth it as Dallas went on to win its third Super Bowl in four year.

Two that slipped by everyone, and for good reason, were the Bears hiring of Mike Ditka as their coach in 1982 and the drafting of quarterback Jim McMahon the same year.

The Bears hadn't won anything in years so when owner George Halas picked his former tight end from the last championship Chicago team of 1963 not too many eyebrows were raised. To me, Ditka was the perfect fit. He knew the history of the Bears and the city of Chicago. Coming from Dallas where he had been an assistant coach for Tom Landry, Ditka had learned football and how to organize a team. And, most of all, he was a Bear plain and simple. "Uh oh! The Bears fortunes just changed," I thought.

I knew that they had changed when they drafted McMahon. Now they had the tough quarterback to go along with the coach. McMahon was perfect in that he had the right demeanor to put up with Ditka. And he was the type of hard-nosed quarterback Chicago fans loved. So to me for all of the talk of Buddy Ryan and the 46 defense the two moves that were "Uh oh," moments were bringing in Ditka and McMahon. In 1985, two years after Halas' death, the Bears won their first and only Super Bowl championship.

The Windy City would not see another championship until Michael Jordan joined the Bulls in 1984. In his first six seasons Jordan became the best scorer in the game and there were those who thought he was too selfish to win a championship. For many those doubts were not erased until the Bulls won it all in 1991.

Jordan erased those doubts with me on a night at the Capital Centre in Landover, MD during a game with the Washington Bullets. The Bullets were not even a playoff team and they beat Chicago easily. No one believes me when I tell them this, but Bullets guard Jeff Malone took Jordan out of the game in the second half by denying him the ball. The other Bulls could not pick up the slack. We had seats a few rows behind the Bulls bench, close enough to see the player's expressions.

Late in the game, Chicago called time out and the team headed towards the bench. The look on Jordan's face told it all. He was thoroughly disgusted. I had never seen an athlete that mad close up before. You could tell that he felt the Bulls had no business losing that game.

My first thought when I saw this was, "Uh oh. I don't know who it is that thinks this man doesn't want to win. And I have no idea why people think that he won't. Michael Jordan is going to make it to the winner's circle with or without the rest of these Bulls." As we all know, the rest is history.

Not much was thought of it when Southern Cal signed Pete Carroll as their new football coach in 2001. Most people thought of Carroll as an unsuccessful NFL coach and thought it would be much the same at USC. While talking to a gentleman who I used to coach high school football with, we agreed that USC was the perfect fit for Carroll. "Uh oh, USC football is officially back." All Carroll did in his 10 years is win two National Titles, finish runner up once and win the Pac Ten conference seven years in a row. In that time, he only lost one bowl game.

Around the same time, the Detroit Lions hired Matt Millen as their General Manager. Everyone hailed it as a great move. Millen was thought to be one of the sharpest minds in the game based on his work as a player and in television. If anyone can get things straight in Detroit, Millen could.

Millen's first mistake was holding out for retired running back Barry Sanders in hopes that he would come back to play. His second was an "Oh no," moment, signing Steve Mariucci as his head coach in 2003. Though Mariucci had done well in San Francisco what Millen forgot was that the 49ers were already built while the Lions were rebuilding. Mariucci had never been part of a rebuilding team and wasn't able to build the Lions. Millen eventually lost his job and the signing of Mariucci was the first and biggest mistake he made.

The New York Knicks suffered an "Oh no," moment which they brought on themselves while trying to beat the Chicago Bulls during the 1990's. After losing in the conference finals to Chicago in 1992, the Knicks decided that forward Xavier McDaniel, known as the "X Man", was not worth keeping. They let him get away to the Boston Celtics and brought in Charles Smith to replace him. This was an "Oh no," moment for the simple reason that if there was one man whom Bulls forward Scottie Pippen wanted no parts of it was Xavier McDaniel. Now with the X Man gone, Pippen could roam the floor with the freedom of knowing that McDaniel would not be there to rough him up. The Bulls did not have to worry about McDaniel hurting them on the boards, on defense and in the scoring column.

Sure enough, the very next year the two teams met in the playoffs again. How can anyone forget the end of game five in which Charles Smith got the ball under the basket late and had his shot blocked THREE times by Michael Jordan, Horace Grant and, yes, Scottie Pippen. The Bulls won the series and another NBA title. The Knicks are still looking for a championship that they haven't won since 1973. You would think that they would have learned their lesson after trading center Bill Cartwright to the Bulls in 1988 and losing to Chicago in 1991 and '92.

When New York Giant linebacker Lawrence Taylor was suspended for the first four games of the 1988 season, Redskin fans looked at the schedule to see who his first game would be against. Sure enough it would be against Washington. "Oh no, he's gonna be raring to go for that one." Then the week before the Redskins-Giant game, Washington lost their starting quarterback and Mark Rypien had to make his debut. So now, Lawrence Taylor was coming to town with a chip on his shoulder and the Redskins would be starting a second year quarterback. For Washington this was not good.

When the Giants defense took the field for the first play everyone watching where I was said "Uh oh, here we go." On the first play, Rypien went back to throw. Taylor blew by his man, hit Rypien from the blind side and caused a fumble that was picked up by Giant linebacker Harry Carson. The Giants offense scored shortly thereafter. Everyone's worst fears had come true and even though LT didn't do much else the rest of the game, that one play was enough to give the Giants an early lead which they held onto for the win.

Of all the players who came into the NFL from the United States Football League in 1986, there was one that I knew would change the fortunes of his franchise right away. At that time the Bills were one of the worst, if not the worst, team in the NFL. They had drafted defensive end Bruce Smith in 1985. The next big name had already been drafted back in 1983, but had gone to the USFL. When that league folded, quarterback Jim Kelly finally came to Buffalo and, "Uh oh," the Bills were on their way. He may not have been the final piece, but he was the one that got the ball rolling in the right direction. That direction was four straight Super Bowl appearances from 1990 to 1993.

Now, not every "Uh oh," moment pans out. One I remember is thinking "Uh oh'" when the Miami Dolphins hired Jimmie Johnson as their coach in 1996. I figured if Johnson could turn around the Dallas Cowboys as he had in the early 90's, he could definitely turn around the Dolphins who were much more talented.

What I failed to see was that in Dallas Jimmie had replaced the franchise icon in Cowboy head coach Tom Landry whom new owner Jerry Jones had fired. With the face of the franchise, Landry, replaced Johnson had nothing to stand between him and building the team that he wanted.

However, in Miami while replacing one icon in head coach Don Shula Johnson was not able to get rid of the other franchise icon, quarterback Dan Marino. Even if Johnson had wanted to trade Marino like he did his best player in Dallas, Herschel Walker, management would not allow it. Marino had been in Miami longer and was the one player whom the fans could identify with. Trading Marino would have been a public relations nightmare.

This caused a clash of wills between player and coach which neither man won. Marino knew that he wasn't going anywhere and felt that his way of doing things were the right way. Johnson knew that he couldn't build the team he wanted with Marino on board. As long as Marino was the quarterback Johnson had to win at that moment with little regard for building for long term success, because the quarterback was at the end of his career. The end for both came in a 62-7 playoff loss to the Jacksonville Jaguars in the 1999 playoffs.

Honestly, off of the top of my head the only other "Uh oh," moment that I can remember being wrong about was the Cleveland Browns hiring of Bill Belichick as head coach in 1991. I thought for sure that the former Giant defensive coordinator would do well in Cleveland. Belichick did get the Browns to the playoffs as a wildcard in 1994 even beating his former boss Bill Parcells and the New England Patriots. But in 1995, Browns owner Art Modell announced in mid season that the team was moving to Baltimore and everything fell apart. Belichick was fired after the season and did not get another head coaching job until 2000 with the Patriots.

I got a second chance on my "Uh oh," with Belichick in 2001 when the Patriots went into New York to play the Jets in a big game. The Jets were considered a playoff contender while the Patriots weren't being taken seriously by anyone at the time. New England went into New York and crushed the Jets. As a Steelers fan, I remember thinking to myself, "I hope this team doesn't play Pittsburgh in the playoffs, because they just turned the corner." Sure enough, in January the teams met in the AFC championship game at Pittsburgh and the Patriots won. New England went on to beat the Rams in the Super Bowl two weeks later and won two more championships in the next three years. To me, that win over the Jets was where it all started.

And an "Uh oh," moment which I thought had passed occurred with the St. Louis Rams of the late 90's. In 1997 Dick Vermeil took over as Rams head coach. The Rams were one of the worst teams in the league and most people thought that hiring Vermeil was a mistake, because he had not coached since 1983. Early in the season there was no reason to believe that St. Louis was on the verge of a turn around. Then the Rams went into Carolina and crushed the Panthers. They dominated from start to finish and I thought this team was on the way.

In 1998, I was looking for big things from the Rams and they disappointed. Not only did they not make the playoffs, they finished with a losing record. The main reason was the spotty play at quarterback. So in the offseason, St. Louis signed free agent quarterback Trent Green from the Washington Redskins and let incumbent Tony Banks go. The Rams went on to win the NFC West running away then advanced to the Super Bowl. This was the team that I saw in that late December game against Carolina.

The only surprise was that it wasn't Trent Green who led them, but 1998 scout team quarterback, Kurt Warner. Warner had one of the greatest seasons any player has had in NFL history winning league and Super Bowl MVP as the Rams won the title. I was right with my "Uh oh," Just a year off.

As of this writing, I haven't seen anything lately that could be categorized as an "Uh oh," or "Oh no," moment. These things spring up on me, they aren't studied or planned. It's just a feel, something that gets you to look more closely at a team or player.

I can't wait for the next one.

AN HONEST RATING

We think that we know it all when it comes to evaluating talented athletes and we know nothing. So when a player that we feel is a great talent doesn't do well he's called an underachiever or, even worse, a bust. When a player that we feel isn't gifted athletically does very well he's called an overachiever. It gets to the point where almost every athlete that we see falls into one category or the other.

Here is something to think about. Maybe the player that we think is great really isn't and never was. And maybe the player that we thought was not so great is and always was. Maybe there is no such thing as overachievers and underachievers. Maybe there is simply the guy who maxes out his talent and the guy who just never had the drive, desire or skill to be anything but average. Reasonably we would have to assume that if you can do something than you will. And if you can't, regardless of how much of an athlete you are, than you won't.

I've done a little bit of coaching in my day. At the high school level I remember coaches looking at certain players and pegging them for positions before they even put on a uniform. This was usually based on their body type. Then the player would get on the field, not perform to the coaches expectations and be considered an "underachiever". Often it had nothing to do with the player's failure, but the coaches for they had put the player in position to fail. Once the player was moved to a position that suited his physical skills not his body type he "achieved" what he was capable of.

On the flip side, I saw many times when a player who was not even considered good enough to play a position because of his body type was given a chance and did very well. This player was, of course, considered an "overachiever" when the truth of the matter was his skill set was perfect for the position though his body type was not.

Looking at some "overachievers" the first one that comes to mind is hall of fame split end Raymond Berry of the Baltimore Colts. Berry played 12 years in the NFL and when he retired had more catches than anyone in history. The son of a high school coach in Texas, he was drafted out of Southern Methodist University as a defensive end before being switched to offense by the Colts.

Berry was thought to be too slow and small to succeed in the NFL. He wore contact lenses when he played and glasses off the field. He had one leg which was shorter than the other. Most football people wrote him off, but not Colts head coach Weeb Ewbank. He paired Berry with quarterback John Unitas and the two of them went on to become one of the greatest passing combinations of all time.

All of Berry's physical attributes were not thought to be good for a hall of fame career, thus he is labeled an "overachiever." The reason why Berry is not an "overachiever" is that he maximized his physical skills, which he had to have in order to be successful, with hard work and the use of his mental skills. Working with Unitas day after day and working out on his own in the offseason, Berry honed his skills to perfection. His success was no accident, it was earned. It was Berry who came up with the quote, "Luck is when preparation meets opportunity and I must be prepared to create my own luck." For twelve seasons Raymond Berry did not create his own luck, he took advantage of his opportunities. This, to me, is a man who did not "overachieve" but achieved all that he was willing to work for.

The thing which brought basketball fans to Boston Celtic hall of famer Larry Bird is that many of them saw him as an "overachiever". Bird had come from the small town of French Lick, Indiana and played his college ball at Indiana State University. Indiana State was considered an afterthought to the Hoosiers of Indiana University until Bird got there. He led the Sycamores to the Final Four in his senior year in 1979 losing the championship game to Ervin "Magic" Johnson and Michigan State.

While with the Celtics, Bird was considered by many to be the best player in the NBA despite being thought of as a slow footed white boy.

Despite what people wanted to say, the reason that Bird became so popular was that he was a white man thought to be the best player in a sport dominated by blacks. Despite what our eyes showed us from a talent standpoint all anyone wanted to talk about was how much smarter Bird was than everyone else on the court. He wasn't the best athlete which meant that he shouldn't be the best player. The only way to explain it was that he was the smartest. His brains allowed him to "overachieve" on the basketball court.

Never mind the fact that Bird worked at his craft harder than anyone. Never mind the fact that Bird had the size to play three positions. Never mind the fact that Bird could shoot pass and defend, because he practiced these things. It all had to do with his smarts.

Well a man can be the smartest person on the planet, but if he doesn't have the skills no way does he have a career like Birds. People who are smart and have talent become all-star players. People who have smarts and no talent become coaches.

Baseball is famous for its "overachievers". They are usually little guys who play shortstop, second base, catcher or outfield. Like Bird they are called smart and always they are "scrappy". They have to be in order to make up for their supposed lack of talent.

Baseball is one of the hardest sports to play and master. There is no way a person can make it to the major leagues without having talent and a lot of it. He can be as smart and scrappy as he wants, but if he can't hit and field it doesn't matter. And just about every baseball player that I've been around has been a very good all around athlete, able to play any sport well. There is no such thing as an "overachiever" in baseball. The game is too hard for a person with marginal talent to make it.

Everyone who is short and slow is considered an "overachiever". Though a good big man will beat a good little man most of the time there are athletes who can compensate by knowing how to use their lack of size to their advantage. Whether it's by using their brains or use of body control, they can do it. And they have done it time after time. The lack of speed can be made up for with precise footwork, practice, knowledge of the playbook and thorough study of an opponent's strengths and weaknesses. Those athletes who have the focus to do this achieve their goals, but only if they have some other talent to compensate for lack of size and speed. We've seen enough of these types of athletes to know it can be done.

Then there is the non-drafted free agent who makes it. They are considered "overachievers," because of being overlooked. Most of the time, they come from small schools that aren't on the scout's radar. Many times, they are late bloomers who don't reach their full potential until after college. But many times, they are good players who scouts know that they can get without drafting them. The talent pool isn't as small as we think. There are always good players who stay under the radar that, if given the chance, can make it. The shame of it is that many of them don't get the chance, because their measurables don't label them as worth taking the chance.

Now, we move on to the "underachiever". The player with supposedly so much talent that anything less than what the scouting report says they should accomplish is considered a disappointment. We see this every time there is a draft or recruitment of a player.

How many times have fans been told about how great a high school player is in football or basketball only to see them not live up to their billing in college? Every big name player in high school is rated by the different recruiting websites and written media. The best used to be called "Blue Chippers," but now they are rated by a star system from one to five. The more stars by the athletes name, the better they are supposed to be.

This system is flawed, because it does not take into account many things. It doesn't take into account the level of competition a player goes against. It doesn't take into account whether that player goes to a private or public school which makes a difference. Private schools can recruit from all over while public schools can only use the students who live in their district. It doesn't take into account the type of coaching a player is getting. And it definitely doesn't take into account the type of kid being recruited. Whether he is a team player or individual. Whether he is coachable. Whether he is intelligent. What his family background is. And how motivated he is. These are the so called intangibles that can't be measured. If the people who scout don't know these things, than how can the rest of us?

All we get from the coaches are the player's measurables. Height, weight, speed, vertical leap and game statistics. That's it. Most of us haven't even seen these kids play then expect them to be the greatest thing since sliced bread, because some recruiting website says so.

Then they get to college and play against athletes who are just as big, just as fast and just as strong. Many times those stars have labeled them as better than they really are, but we only see them as "underachievers." How could this kid with five stars by his name not be able to shoot or throw a forward pass? Maybe the truth of the matter was that he never could, but someone thought so or didn't think it mattered. The skill set was there and he dominated limited athletes with his own limited skills, because he was just the best athlete on the field or court and it didn't translate to the next level.

This is no different in the pros at draft time. Everyone is happy on draft day. Every team gets the player that they wanted. All of the first round picks will be solid pros or have huge upsides. Then most of them never pan out. Once again, it has nothing to do with their lack of talent we are told. It has everything to do with their lack of intangibles. They didn't work hard enough. They weren't smart enough. They weren't team players. They weren't coachable.

To me if the athlete has that much physical talent and doesn't make it it's not because he's an "underachiever". This is simply a case of a guy who is not willing to achieve. And if the athlete is not willing to do what it takes to achieve than we cannot assume that they would have ever achieved in the first place. Potential means nothing. The United States of America has the potential to be the greatest country in the world, but has it accomplished everything that it is capable of? Probably not. Does that make us "underachievers" or a country just not willing to work together to achieve what's best for everyone?

The higher an athlete is drafted the more potential of being labeled a "bust" if he doesn't make it. All first round picks are supposed to become hall of famers. When they don't, everyone is disappointed. Especially if the player is the number one pick overall.

I feel as though, if an athlete is drafted in the first round he doesn't have to be a hall of famer, but should be a serviceable starter for a good part of his career. The only thing that should prevent this is injury. To me, no player whose career is cut short by injury should be considered an "underachiever" or "bust". As long as sports are played by humans there will be career altering or ending injuries. If a running back like Cincinnati Bengal Ki-Jana Carter tears up his knee in the preseason of his rookie year that doesn't make him a "bust" just a very unfortunate young man. These things happen. Sometimes they happen before a career is allowed to get off of the ground.

Other times they happen during the course of a career and we think what might have been. An example is hall of fame New York Yankee outfielder Mickey Mantle. Mantle had one of the greatest careers ever, but there are many who think that he could have been greater if not for all of the injuries he suffered during his career. My question would be wasn't he great enough? He won MVP awards. He won the Triple Crown in batting in 1956. He won numerous world championships. He hit more than 500 home runs. He hit more home runs in World Series play than anyone in history. He's in the hall of fame for crying out loud. What more do you want?

And what one person may consider an "underachiever" someone else may think of as "star-crossed". An example is former NFL running back Joe Don Looney. He was a first round draft pick of the New York Giants out of Oklahoma University in 1964. He had size, speed and strength. Looney was considered by many to be the greatest physical specimen at the running back position since the Cleveland Browns drafted Jim Brown in 1957. Scouts drooled over his potential.

If you've never heard of him it's for a good reason. Besides being a character, which the scouts knew about when he came out of college, Looney never really did much in the NFL. He clashed with players and coaches. He didn't practice or play hard. He was to the NFL what the diva wide receiver is considered today, but with less to show for it. To this day, all we ever hear is how great Looney could have been. But we never hear him called a "bust" though he is the definition of the term. He came from a big school, he had the physical skills and he was a first round draft pick. And he did almost nothing. If that's not a "bust" than what is?

But Looney gets a pass, because he was considered an eccentric. He was a character who gave people a lot of legends. There was always the chance that whoever signed him on their team would have to take the chance of him not panning out. The reason Looney is not considered a "bust" is because teams knew that he had flaws despite his talent. Well doesn't every draft pick? The truth is that Looney was just an athlete who didn't have the work ethic to achieve, because he didn't want to. He's not the only person in this world guilty of that.

Those without talent don't achieve. Those who have the talent and are willing to put in the work achieve. Those who have the talent and aren't willing to work don't. And those who have talent but suffer from serious injury are just unfortunate.

There are no "overachievers" or "underachievers". There are those who achieve and those who don't. In this way sports is no different than society.

SERVING OUR YOUTH

Youth and high school sports are a subject familiar to most people. Whether it be playing, coaching, parenting, officiating or just watching we have all had some experience with it. There are some who would say that youth and high school sports are not one and the same, but to me anything below the college level falls into this category.

We all know that there is good and bad with youth sports. I have been involved with it for over thirty years since the age of 10 as a player, coach, fan and official and seen a lot. I played on championship teams and terrible ones. I played for good coaches and bad. I played for teams which traveled, though not very far, and teams where I could ride my bike to the field. I've played against guys who have made it to the pros. I've coached a guy who has as well. I've coached teams with good athletes and not so good athletes. I've coached good kids and not so good ones. I've coached teams with resources and teams with little or none. And I've officiated at all youth levels.

So I think that I can speak somewhat knowledgeably on this subject. Though it has never been completely a utopia, I don't like where youth sports are today compared to my time. Needless to say, there are things that I would like to see addressed.

The very first thing that I would like to see changed in today's youth sports is the concentration of young athletes playing one sport. Many of them are doing it not because they want to, but because their parents and especially coaches want or make them.

There was no such thing as a coach suggesting that a youngster concentrate on only one sport when I was coming along. In fact, we were encouraged to play as many sports as we wanted just as our coaches had growing up. The only thing that they would tell us is to concentrate on the sport we were playing at that time. In other words, our baseball coach didn't want us playing basketball or football during baseball season. He always said that the size of the basketball and football would effect our throwing of the baseball, because they were bigger and heavier. Of course, we didn't listen and played both anyway. It wasn't like we were going to the major leagues anyway, so why not have fun doing something else.

There were coaches who would try to steer us into playing sports which they thought would benefit their teams when we came back in the fall, winter or summer. For example, the basketball coaches wanted their guys to run cross country for endurance. The football coaches wanted their guys to run track, especially skill position players, in order to learn form-running. Coaches would also try to steer us into playing certain positions. My assistant football coach hated the fact that I played catcher in baseball, because he wanted me to put on weight which was impossible in 90 degree heat and humidity with all that catching gear on. He wanted me to play the outfield or shortstop.

Now coaches almost demand that their kids concentrate on one sport. Their reasoning is that how can a kid reach their full potential if they don't play a sport year around? By practicing in the offseason, going to clinics and playing in offseason leagues they will be ready for the regular season. Coaches aren't really worried about players reaching their full potential as athletes. They want their kids to play a sport year round to make the coach's team better.

Though there is some truth to the fact that the more you do something the better you get is it really worth sacrificing the chance to play other sports at such a young age? I played whatever was in season and they all benefitted me in the other sports that I participated in. Baseball and basketball taught me hand eye coordination which I used in football. Soccer, which I only played in gym class, taught me foot eye coordination. Football and basketball taught me body control which I used in baseball. It all worked to make me a complete athlete not just a specialist.

The other reason that coaches suggest their players concentrate on one sport is it's easier to get a scholarship that way. Most of the youngsters who are serious about their sport play it not only out of love, but to move on to the college level. They don't really think that they are going to the professional ranks, but do know that college costs money. Getting an athletic scholarship guarantees them an education whereas having to pay out of pocket may be too costly. The parents know this too, so they are more willing to go along with the coach in this aspect.

Whoever came up with this idea is selling everyone a phony bill of goods. If an athlete is good enough, he can play any sport and still get a scholarship in the one that they want. Most college recruiters actually want to see athletes play other sports so that they can evaluate them in different settings. A quarterback's arm can be evaluated by watching him throw a baseball. A football player's speed can be evaluated against others by running track, his strength by watching him wrestle. A basketball player's leaping ability can be evaluated by watching them play volleyball. Recruiters don't mind if an athlete plays more than one sport in high school. For them specialization doesn't have to start until the athlete gets to their campus.

I know high school and youth coaches who will not let players come out for their teams if they don't participate in offseason workouts. To me this is wrong. In high school sports are an extracurricular activity just as the debate team or yearbook club is. The athlete does not owe the coach anything until the first day of practice. They are entitled to do whatever they want until that day. From the first practice to the last game the athlete has to be totally committed. After the uniforms are turned in they once again owe the coaches nothing. In other words, though the coaches don't like to hear this, high school and youth athletics belong to the students not the coach. Those who are eligible academically, in good standing with the school and pass the physical have to be allowed to try out regardless of what they do in the offseason.

Maybe this has already happened, but if I had been a player and one of my coaches wouldn't let me play another sport or try out for the team he coached because I didn't participate in the offseason I would have sued him and the school or league. And I would have won. If more parents did this we would see less of kids concentrating on one sport. There would be many parents and coaches upset at the time of the lawsuit, but in the long run everyone would benefit in my opinion, especially the kids who youth sports are supposed to be for anyway.

Change number two would be a reduction in the number of traveling teams and tournaments. To me traveling to another league, region or state should be a privilege that a player earns by being one of the best at what they do over a season in a local league than being picked in a tryout for the sole purpose of playing around the country. Youth sports should always start out on the local level first. Let all of the kids who are eligible try out for the team. Those that make it play the season. The ones who have earned it make the all-star team and travel. This is the model that Little League baseball has been based on for years. Somehow everyone, including Little League, has gotten away from this.

Now teams are specifically organized for travel. They are called select teams and they play outside of their local leagues and high schools. Some baseball leagues have been known to pick their all-star teams before the season ends, play them in a select league, then enter into the Little League all-star tournament. This is all done to win the tournament there is no other reason.

Many kids play on both local and select teams. Many times this keeps them on the field or court seven days a week which is too much at the youth level. The body and mind need time to rest and playing every day doesn't allow for this. And kids need to do other things with other kids than just play sports.

I would get rid of travel teams that aren't an all-star unit altogether. No more select teams as well. A player would have to earn his seat on the bus, plane or train by their performance in the local league. The Little League way, when adhered to, is the best in my opinion.

As for high schools traveling here is a thought on that. Just like youth sports, I think that high school athletics should be a local thing not a national one. I think that teams should only play schools that are in their area which is usually the case in most areas. Win the league and advance to the regional playoffs. Win the region and advance to the states. This is the way that the public schools have been doing it for years with few exceptions one of those being a team which needs money to fund its program traveling to a school which guarantees them a certain payout for coming.

Private schools on the other hand travel often and sometimes great distances. Of course, private schools have played by a different set of rules forever. And once television came along to offer them a bigger stage private schools jumped at the chance to compete nationally.

High schools travel for the same reason that coaches tell their kids to play the same sport year around. Exposure to college and in the case of baseball pro scouts. Once again it gets back to getting that opportunity whether it be a college scholarship or pro contract. High school sports are now a minor league in itself.

The third change that I would make has to do more with high school than youth and this is no more rankings nationally or locally. I know that it creates interest, but is it necessary? Even if it is are the rankings accurate and can they be?

Once again I get back to the point that high school should be about the community. The interest should be local not national. High school sports should be kids playing on the field and their classmates, faculty members, parents, alumni and town folk watching them. It should be the band playing the school fight song and performing at halftime. It should be cheerleaders and pom pons performing their routines. It should be covered by the local media.

It shouldn't be about who the press thinks is the number one team in the state or country. It should be about winning the league, city or state title nothing more or less. Half of the time the rankings are unfair anyway, because they rank public schools with private ones despite the fact the latter can recruit while the former cannot.

When rankings are involved it makes schools and coaches do things that they would be less inclined to if they were not. Many public schools recruit also though not openly like the private schools for public school kids have to go to the school in their district. And kids who want to go to a public school power only need to find a relative who lives in the district of that school, use their address and enroll.

What's wrong with that? Well the whole concept of districts is to allow each school to have a chance somewhere along the line to win. The theory is that there will be no dominant team and each group of freshman who come in can stay together and build towards a championship run in their junior and senior years. If players are allowed to cross districts, the same teams will be good every year and the schools that lose players will also lose interest in their sport which may lead to the school dropping it altogether. That's not a good thing.

I saw this happen first hand to high school baseball in the county where I went to school. Though it wasn't a public school, but a private one which took all of the talent it still happened. Before this private school program came along, our county was as good as anyone in baseball. We boasted two state championship teams in the highest classes my junior year one of them being my own. There were always good teams and our all-star teams in the summer were some of the best.

Then this private school began to recruit kids from all over the county and Southern Maryland. Before you knew it they were ranked number one in the area and everyone with baseball aspirations wanted to go there. They had three different varsity teams and the best one traveled across the country. The coaches recruiting pitch was that by playing for him kids would get college scholarships and pro contracts though not many of them did. Not only did he have the kids buying into it, but the parents as well.

Meanwhile, public school baseball slowly died in our county. Fewer and fewer kids came out for the team leading to some schools not fielding teams at all. The ones who did want to play would transfer to the aforementioned private school or another in order to just get a chance to play games. Now, there are hardly any high school baseball teams in our county and the ones that exist aren't very good. Baseball lost an entire generation of kids.

As for the private school well they had their run and it's done. Only a handful of their players got a chance at the pros and none made it to the majors. And interest in baseball has waned there as well. It seems to me as you would want more teams good and bad playing than one great team or no teams at all.

No, I'm not a fan of rankings. Not at all.

Next, we get to adult conduct. Adult conduct in youth and high school sports is not all bad, but is a problem. From coaches to parents to fans it seems as though there is a disconnect to the reality of what youth and high school sports should be, what they are and what they are not.

First, youth and high school sports should always be about the kids. The younger the athlete the more this should be. Let them play. Let them have fun. Teach them the rules and make them play by them. There is nothing wrong with discipline through team rules as long as everyone abides by them and there is a lesson attached. Teach them how to play the game the right way. And play games to play them not to win them. If things are done right, the winning will take care of itself whether it's on the scoreboard or in the lessons learned through playing.

As athletes get older and move on to high school there is nothing wrong with making things more competitive. At the high school level, the best of the best should make the team and play, because this teaches kids the lesson that as you get into the real world things have to be earned through hard work. Once a team is built then it gets back to the same concepts as mentioned in the last chapter.

It seems that many adults forget this. They look at youth and high school sports as what they should be to them, not the kids. One can go to any youth and high school sports event and see parents acting as if every game is for the championship of the free world. They yell at their kids and their teammates. They yell at the coaches. They yell at the officials. They yell at the other team and their fans. They complain about how the coach does things. They treat a youth or high school sporting event the same way they treat a professional game that they watch on television or attend. It's crazy. And the funny thing is that many of the parents and adults who do this have never played a minute of the sport that they know so much about.

Then there are the coaches. They yell at players, though not nearly as much as when I played. They argue with officials. They bend the rules when it comes to picking their teams by going after players that are ineligible especially in high school. Many of them, especially at the youth level, are volunteers and though they mean well really don't know how to coach. They let the best players on their teams get away with breaking rules that others have to adhere to. And as mentioned earlier, they try to steer young athletes into only playing the sport that they coach.

Because of this, youth and high school sports have become a place where the kids don't have fun, because of the pressure put on them to win. They have become a place where adults take out their anger on the people involved from players to coaches to officials. They have become a place where coaches care more about winning games than obeying the rules or doing right by the kids. This didn't just happen yesterday. It's been around for as long as I can remember. Sad to say, I don't see it changing anytime soon.

What we all have to remember about youth and high school sports is that they are not the pros or even college. The games are not broadcast on television and ESPN won't show the highlights on SportsCenter. They are not a breeding ground for future All-Americans or pro hall of famers. They are not a place for parents to live precariously through their children's success or failures. They are not a place for coaches to build a resume as coaching legends.

How do we get from where we are with youth and high school sports to where we should be? How do we get to where the kids have fun, the adults attend to have a good time and enjoy the contest for what it is and the coaches do the right thing?

Go back to rule number one. The games are to be played for fun no matter what level. The more fun they are, the more likely kids are to stick with them. The thing that has to be remembered is that the reason most kids play youth and high school sports is because their friends do not because they have aspirations for the pros or college. It's just a way for them to get together for fun outside of school.

I have learned that a good way to gauge how much a kid wants to play a sport is to not ask them to or sign them up for it. A parent should let their child come to them and ask if they can play. This shows that they are interested. I don't know how many kids I have seen from childhood to now who never reached their full potential or got the most out of playing, because their parents signed them up when they didn't want to play and they lost interest.

Before giving the child permission, a parent should explain to them the commitment that will have to be made as far as practices and games. The child should also be told that he should only play for fun and when the game is no longer fun than they don't have to play it anymore. If the child still wants to play sign them up.

Once the parent gives the child permission to play they should set a good example by supporting them, the other kids on their team and their coaches. They should also show sportsmanship towards officials, members of the other team and their parents. Volunteer to help with their time in some way. Not everyone has the time to coach, but most have time to go to the games and some practices. Give a hand when you can to help the coaches, players and other parents in some way.

And remember, not all adults are cut out to be coaches. Some will be good, some bad, but as long as they do right by the kids support them. They are taking time out to help your child. If a parent doesn't think that the coach is good enough volunteer to do it themselves. If a parent does not do this, than they have to live with the coaches decisions as long as they are fair.

Coaches need to simply do right by the kids and play by the rules. Always keep the game fun. Always be fair to every child who plays. Set a good example by abiding by the rules and showing good sportsmanship on and off of the field. Make everyone on the team from assistant coaches to the equipment managers do the same. Forget about rankings and play the games to play them. Don't worry about how people feel about their coaching methods as long as it helps to bring out the best in the kids. And coaches should not be allowed to dictate to kids what sports they can and cannot play. That should be a parent/child decision.

Adult fans should go to youth and high school sports to support the teams and have fun. Enjoy the games for what they are not what the fan may think it should be. Be courteous to the players, coaches and officials. And, like the parents, fans should look for opportunities to volunteer their time to the local leagues and schools even if it's nothing more than officiating or buying uniforms and equipment.

These are the guidelines that have always seemed to work in youth and high school sports from what I have experienced. Every person that I have known that has abided by them has been successful in getting the most out of the youth and high school experience. There will always be good and bad in youth sports. There just doesn't seem to be a reason why the bad should outweigh the good. The only way to avoid this is to have cooperation at all levels from parents down to the kids who play.

If this can't be accomplished than maybe the kids are better off just playing pickup games in the backyard. No parental supervision, no pressure to win, no crowds to watch, the kids making their own rules and just playing for love of the game. They may not reach their full potential from a fundamental standpoint, but at least they'd be playing for all of the right reasons.

DO AFRICAN AMERICANS CARE ABOUT HOCKEY AND DOES THE NHL CARE ABOUT THEM

When I was about four or five years old, I watched every sport under the sun. Football was my favorite, followed by baseball. My third favorite was not basketball, but hockey. This made me an aberration among young black boys, but I never gave it a thought. To me, hockey was cooler than basketball and I watched the National Hockey League game of the week on Sunday's whenever I could on CBS which wasn't often, because my family wanted to watch the NBA on ABC. If I recall, there was even a hockey highlight show that used to come on every Saturday.

I didn't know many of the players, but was a Boston Bruins fan. My favorite player of course was Bobby Orr. I used to go out and grab any kind of bent stick that I could find along with a can or ball and play my cousin in one on one. Once, I even stumbled and jammed the stick into my stomach which was my first experience with getting the wind knocked out of me.

Then, when I was about seven or eight, the NHL disappeared from network television. CBS decided to replace it with the NBA and ABC did not pick it up. Since we didn't have a local team at the time, my interest turned to the sport that I could watch which was basketball. Though the first sporting event that I ever went to was a Washington Capitals game, my interest in hockey waned. Despite the fact that I knew the Stanley Cup winners, I did not become truly interested again until Wayne Gretzky joined the Edmonton Eskimos. With no place to watch him, because we couldn't get cable I didn't really go out of my way to keep up with the game.

Another reason why I didn't watch hockey was that there weren't any African-Americans playing it. Football, baseball and basketball had many African-American faces. Hockey did not. With no one to relate to on the ice, the thought of becoming an NHL player never crossed my mind though it did many of my white friends.

The only time that I can remember hockey making inroads with African-Americans was during the early 1990's when the proliferation of TV was bringing new fans to all sports. It was nothing to turn on the television or open a magazine and see a famous African-American actor or musician sporting a hockey sweater. Even if it was just because they liked the colors or logo it helped the sport to have people of color wearing their merchandise. This would have been the perfect time for hockey to go into African-American communities to develop young talent. Then the NHL went on strike, lost their TV contract nationally and with ESPN and what chance there was to gain the African-American youth was gone just as it had when I was a kid.

The shame of it is that when it comes to hockey many African-Americans are of the same mindset as me. We don't watch, because there aren't too many people who look like us on the ice or in the stands. So we turn to sports which we find African-American faces in the winter, mainly basketball. Some of us, like me, watch the Stanley Cup playoffs, but most don't.

Those who don't may be missing out, because hockey is a great game. Though I don't get to as many games as I used to it's my favorite sport to attend. There is nothing like the sound of skates gliding across the ice. Seeing a player getting hammered into the boards is pretty intense. The roar of the crowd as the intensity increases especially in the playoffs. Watching a great player use fancy stick work to score or seeing a goaltender making a save of a hard slap shot. Even without the fighting, it's a great game to watch. There is even something nice in watching the Zamboni clean the ice between periods.

So why aren't there more African-American hockey fans? Will there ever be more African-American hockey fans? And does the NHL really care if African-Americans show up or not?

We have already partly answered the first question. African-Americans don't follow hockey, because there aren't that many of us to root for. Though there are more African-Americans in hockey than ever the only star that I can recall was Edmonton goalie Grant Fuhr. Most African-American hockey players have been good players, but not all-stars.

People come out to watch their own. They also come out to watch stars that look like them. When Jackie Robinson broke the color line in baseball, African-Americans began to leave the Negro Leagues to watch the Major Leagues. When Arthur Ashe won Wimbledon, blacks began to watch tennis. When Tiger Woods began winning major tournaments in golf, blacks began to watch. If hockey were to come up with a few black stars, African-Americans would begin to watch.

It's the same theory used in boxing with the whole notion of the "Great White Hope" heavyweight champion. Every time a white heavyweight boxer becomes good interest in the sport from whites increases. The most watched pay per view boxing match of all time is the Gerry Cooney-Larry Holmes heavyweight title fight of 1983. Holmes defeated Cooney and boxing did not see another white challenger except the fictional Rocky Balboa until Tommy "The Duke" Morrison came along. I didn't think much of Morrison or the hype as I was no longer a big boxing fan.

That was until I was outside a store on the day of a Morrison fight and there were some white men going into the liquor store next door. One asked the other if he was going to watch the Tommy Morrison fight that night and he said yes. Then they gave each other a high five and started shadow boxing. Other white men joined in the conversation and you could see the excitement the fight was generating among them. I had no clue Morrison was fighting that night, but after seeing this decided to watch. "The Duke" was knocked out and all I could think of was "What was all of the hype for?"

The truth was the hype stemmed from the "Great White Hope" that Tommy Morrison represented, nothing else. White people had finally found their man and thought sure he would be the one to rest the crown. Though Morrison did go on to win a part of the heavyweight crown, he never became undisputed champion and the search for the "Great White Hope" continued.

Though African-Americans are not looking for a "Great Black Hope" in hockey just as they did not in golf or tennis it would help bring more of us to the NHL if they had a few black stars. Especially if those stars were born and raised in the United States of America. Even better if they came from cities like New York, Chicago, Detroit or Philadephia. Home grown African-American talent from cities with major television markets would boost interest among blacks.

But how can a sport like hockey create African-American talent when there are very few of us playing or watching the game? Like everything else, hockey has to go to the people and not expect the people to come to them. Is this easier said than done? I don't know, but it's worked in other sports so why not hockey? If nothing else it's worth a try.

African-American communities have always gotten support from sports like football, basketball, baseball, boxing and even soccer. There is not an African-American community in the USA where you can go and not find kids playing these sports mainly football and basketball. Baseball lost a good bit of their African-American fans when they stopped going into the inner city and the southern states to scout talent and conduct clinics. They are trying to make up for that with the Renewing Baseball in Inner Cities (RBI) program.

Hockey needs to do something similar. There are hockey teams in every major city in the United States. And most of them have ice or inline skating rinks. Even if there isn't a rink available as is the case in many African-American communities, a gym floor that can be used with a plastic puck and plastic sticks could work just as well. That's what we used in elementary school. Then send players and coaches into the communities to introduce themselves and the game through classroom visits and clinics.

The main thing is to find a way to get kids to play. Once they play, then they become interested. Once they become interested, then it's time to work on finding ice time and equipment. Once you find ice time and equipment, then it's time to work on forming leagues. When leagues are formed, then you start nurturing the talent.

This would not create star players or new fans overnight, but it would be a start. Once young African-Americans begin playing, they and their parents would be more inclined to watch and attend games. This would benefit everyone from the pros down the kids. It would give the pros another place to mine talent and the kids another sport to participate in.

What is stopping this from happening? Well here is a guess. Hockey doesn't really care, because it's a sport played globally so they figure they don't need to create a bigger talent pool. And African-Americans don't really care because we are too busy limiting our sports options by steering our kids to basketball. If hockey doesn't want us, than why should we care? Also, African-Americans have so many more options in sports and life than they did years ago when football, basketball and baseball came calling which is a good thing. The truth is that hockey could bring in African-Americans but they are not going to go out of their way to find them. And African-Americans aren't going to go begging them to do it.

It's that simple.

DAYS AND MOMENTS I'D LIKE TO FORGET

As I write this, the Washington Capitals are one day removed from probably the worst playoff loss in franchise history after losing game seven of their first round series to the Montreal Canadiens. The Caps became the first team in National Hockey League history to lose in the first round of the Stanley Cup playoffs as a number one seed to a number eight after leading the series 3-1. Hockey fans in the D.C. metropolitan area are devastated. Though I'm not a big hockey fan, I feel their pain.

All of us as sports fans have had days and moments that happened to our favorite teams and players that we'd like to forget. Moments that ruined our day, week and year. Moments that are so bad that we refuse to read the paper or watch the highlights the next day. Moments that we never want to experience again. Moments that are so bad that we look the other way whenever we see the highlights on television. Moment that we refuse to talk about if someone brings them up. Here are a few of mine and some from people that I know. Many of them are famous to others, but not to us. Remember one man's highlight is another man's lowlight.

The first sporting moment that I can remember and would like to forget happened in the 1975 National Basketball Association Finals between the home town Washington Bullets and the Golden State Warriors. The Bullets had Elvin Hayes, Phil Chenier, Kevin Porter, Mike Riordan and Wes Unseld to name a few. Golden State had Rick Barry and no one else as far as Bullets fans were concerned. After all those years of losing to the Boston Celtics and New York Knicks as both the Washington and Baltimore Bullets it seemed as if our team's time had come.

121

Not only did the Bullets lose, they got swept four games to none. Everything that could go wrong did. After losing game one at home, the Bullets had to go out to Oakland for the next two which they promptly lost. Game four was a mere formality. The Bullets got up early and Warrior coach Al Attles was tossed from the game, but it didn't matter. The old Capital Centre sounded like a tomb when the buzzer sounded to end the game and series. We were devastated. And so was Bullets owner Abe Pollin as he fired head coach K.C. Jones later that summer.

The next was when the Washington Redskins went into Dallas to play the Cowboys in the last game of the 1979 National Football League season with the NFC Eastern Division title on the line. The Redskins began the day as a playoff team as they held the wildcard tiebreaker over the Chicago Bears. The Bears played early that Sunday and needing to defeat the St. Louis Cardinals by more than 33 points scored a 40-6 victory. The win gave the Bears the last wildcard spot if Washington lost. So the Redskins were stuck with having to win the division or go home.

Washington led 34-21 with four minutes left in the game only to see Roger Staubach bring the Cowboys back to win 35-34. It was a crushing defeat. Especially since the Redskins began the day as a virtual playoff lock only to end it with nothing. It didn't help that a division rival in St. Louis laid down to the Bears and that the arch rival Cowboys were the team which beat them for the division title.

To add insult to injury, the league scheduled Dallas and Washington to meet again on opening day 1980. The game was even broadcast on Monday Night Football. With Staubach retired and Danny White the new Cowboy quarterback everyone in Washington thought sure the Redskins would get their revenge. Dallas dominated and no one wanted to get out of bed on Tuesday morning. Except for all of the Cowboy fans in the area.

I remember how devastated people were in Baltimore when the Orioles blew a three games to one lead to the "We Are Family" Pittsburgh Pirates of Willie Stargell fame in the 1979 World Series. The Orioles had thrilled fans all year with their come from behind victories on the way to the American League pennant. When they went into Pittsburgh and won game four it seemed that with two of the last three games in Baltimore the Orioles were going to win it. Not so. Pittsburgh won game five then went back to Baltimore to win games six and seven. "We Are Family" might be a favorite song in Pittsburgh, but it isn't in Baltimore.

Baltimore fans have history of these moments. The main two on the field both happened in 1969. The first was losing Super Bowl III to the New York Jets in the game that many call the biggest upset in NFL history. The second was losing the World Series to the New York Mets later in the year in what many call the greatest World Series upset in history. How can one city suffer two such devastating losses in the same year?

I am too young to remember 1969, but know a lot of people who do. I had a boss who was a big Colts fan and can remember talking to him one day. He seemed to still be in shock twenty years after the fact. It was almost like he was talking about a death or tragedy in his own family as he barely spoke above a whisper. My cousin who was a huge Orioles fan never talked about the '69 World Series and we didn't bring it up.

I am here to say that if you ever go to Baltimore or talk to a Baltimore sports fan don't mention the year 1969 unless you want to get punched in the face. They can mention it and talk about it, but you can't.

Of course the most devastating moment in Baltimore sports history was watching the Colts move from Baltimore to Indianapolis in March of 1984. I saw it first hand and it was one of the saddest sights ever. Watching people's hearts just taken from them as their beloved Colts left under the cover of darkness. The city mourned for 12 years until the Cleveland Browns moved to Baltimore and became the Ravens. The Ravens are beloved by the city, but the older generation of Baltimore football fans will always be fans of the Baltimore Colts first.

When the Pittsburgh Steelers dynasty came to an end in 1980 it was in a Thursday night loss to the Houston Oilers. As a Steelers fan used to them always winning the big games this was a dark day. Not only did the Steelers lose, but they were shut out. After winning four Super Bowls in six years the king was dead and everyone knew it. I didn't want to go to school the next day, but had no choice. It was a long day of being teased by my classmates I'll tell you that.

I'd like to forget Georgetown Hoyas basketball's loss to the North Carolina Tar Heels in the 1982 NCAA championship game, 63-62. I'll watch it from time to time, but it still hurts to see Carolina's James Worthy dominate the game and Michael Jordan hit the winning shot. And it definitely hurts to watch Georgetown guard Freddie Brown pass the ball to Worthy by mistake as time ran out. At the time when Georgetown coach John Thompson was interviewed after the game he said, "It hurts right now, but I'll get over it." Maybe he has, but many Georgetown fans have not.

Three years later the Hoyas suffered a more devastating loss to the Villanova Wildcats in the 1985 finals. The Hoyas had been ranked number one almost the entire year and entered the game being hailed as one of the greatest if not the greatest college basketball teams of all time. Villanova shot 80 percent from the field and beat Georgetown 66-64. It may be a great moment in college basketball history to most fans, but to Hoya fans it's a day we'd like to forget.

The most devastating loss that I can think of for Washington sports fans in my lifetime was the 38-9 thumping the Redskins took from the Los Angeles Raiders in Super Bowl XVIII. The Redskins were defending world's champions and came into the game with a record of 16-2. They had already beaten the Raiders during the regular season 37-35 and many were ready to anoint them as one of the best teams ever. The Raiders weren't chopped liver so many billed this Super Bowl as having the potential to be the best of all time.

It didn't work out that way. The Raiders dominated from beginning to end and Washington D.C. went into mourning. I was a junior in high school and remember going in the next day. Everyone filed into the building in almost complete silence. Finally a couple of guys started singing "Hail to the Redskins" in a slow tempo almost like a funeral march. There was snow on the ground outside which was appropriate, because it was a long cold winter after that loss.

When I was a Los Angeles Lakers fan and they lost to the Boston Celtics in the 1984 NBA Finals I was angry. It was bad enough that the Celtics had Larry Bird and were my best friend's favorite team. What made matters worse was that my favorite player, Lakers guard Magic Johnson, had the worst playoff series of his life and I blamed him for the loss. All summer long, whenever my best friend and I got together he gloated and I kept saying Magic blew it. Sure the Lakers came back to beat the Celtics in 1985 and 1987 and Magic more than made up for his poor play in '84, but it still doesn't take away the sting of that first meeting and never will.

I got a break for a while until the Steelers went to the AFC championship game in 1994. Pittsburgh had gone 12-4 that season and had a devastating defense. They were on the verge of their first trip to the Super Bowl since 1979 when the San Diego Chargers came to town and beat them, 17-13. The defense gave up two long touchdown passes. I remember almost throwing the remote control through the TV when Charger wide receiver Tony Martin beat Steelers defensive back Tim McKyer on the second one. To this day, I have no idea why he was left in man coverage. The Steelers drove to the three yard line late and the game and missed on a fourth down pass into the end zone. No championship, no Super Bowl.

This started a trend of Steelers postseason disappointment. The next season, they made it all of the way to the Super Bowl only to lose 27-17 to Dallas. To this day, it is the one game that I wish the Steelers could replay. Not only did they lose, but they lost to the team I dislike the most. Most fans blame Steelers quarterback Neil O'Donnell for the loss, because of the two interceptions he threw in the second half, but there was plenty of blame to go around. When the highlight film comes on I watch until the Steelers score to cut Dallas' lead to 20-17 then I change the channel. I have a copy of the broadcast, but hardly ever watch it. It's just too painful.

The AFC championship games of 1997 and 2001 aren't quite as bad as the Super Bowl loss, but pretty close. Losing to the Broncos in '97 and the Patriots in '01 at home was no fun especially after both teams went on to win the Super Bowl. These are two games that I refuse to watch also.

The reason why I no longer watch college basketball is because of the Maryland Terrapins collapse against the Duke Blue Devils in the 2001 Final Four. Maryland had lost before, but not in such a big game nor in a worse way as they blew a 25 point first half lead. I saw the Maryland meltdown and thought that it was aided by some favorable calls for the Blue Devils. When the buzzer sounded and the Terps were defeated I swore off college basketball. For the first time in my life as a college basketball fan I did not watch the championship game. And to this day, if Maryland or Georgetown isn't playing, I only watch college basketball sparingly. The tournament is television background noise now. Depending on who's in it, I'll watch the Final Four and that's it.

The last devastating loss that I suffered as a fan was the 2006 Rose Bowl between my favorite college football team, the University of Southern California Trojans, and the Texas Longhorns. The teams came into the game ranked one and two respectively with the Trojans as defending national champions. USC boasted the 2004 and '05 Heisman Trophy winners in quarterback Matt Lienart and halfback Reggie Bush while the Longhorns had that season's runner up in quarterback Vince Young. The game had been anticipated for an entire year and I knew the Longhorns would be tough. I knew that there was a good chance that the Trojans could lose.

The Trojans did lose. They lost on a fourth and goal touchdown run by Vince Young with only seconds to play. The Trojans quest for back to back undefeated seasons and undisputed national championships went right out the window. They had played well enough to win and led for most if not all of the game only to lose it at the end.

When the game ended I turned off the television and sat in the dark. As much as I tried, I couldn't bring myself to get up off of the couch and go to bed. I stared into the darkness until sleep finally overtook me and woke up on the couch the next morning. To this day, I consider the 2006 Rose Bowl the best college football game I have ever seen, but will not watch it again.

I'm getting older now and don't take losses as hard, though Maryland's last second loss to Michigan State in this year's NCAA basketball tournament was crushing. Maybe it's because most of the teams I mentioned eventually came back to win a championship somewhere along the line. Maybe it's because I think even more than I used to that there are more important things than who wins and loses in sports. I don't know, but the losses don't bother me as much.

I'm sure there will be another time where one of my teams loses and I'll stare at a blank television screen in the dark. Though I think that I've already had my fair share of these moments I'd like to forget and I'm sure there will be a few more. I hope that they are few and far between.

For when we suffer from defeats it means that we care about the outcome. Once we stop suffering we stop caring and then it's time to turn in our fan card.

TOYS IN THE ATTIC

This chapter is written for fun as is the rest of the book. It's not about current or historical sports events. It's not about famous moments or games. It's not about the men who wrote sports history with their thoughts and actions. It's not about on the field or off the field issues.

This chapter is about us. It's about things collected at one time or another in my childhood that I would like to share with the reader to see if they were a part of theirs as well and if they remember. It's also about the way sports were presented to us at that time on television and radio. And how we went about playing them ourselves. Mainly it's just a hodgepodge of childhood memories that I would like to share. It's called "Toys in the Attic", because most of the collectibles I no longer have and many of them no longer exist, but they do in the cluttered attic of my mind. So here goes. Hope it's enjoyable.

We all collected trading cards growing up. Of course, baseball cards were the most popular. Topps and Fleer were the companies which sold them. Topps sold them in those small packs with the stick of gum that fell apart when you tried to chew it and left a sugary smell on the cards which lasted for some time. The hardcore fan bought the triple pack of 33 cards which came in three plastic packs perforated together and had no gum. Then there were the football cards, which were my favorite, along with basketball and hockey. The hockey cards had the coolest pictures, because the uniform colors were so bright and it always seemed as if the players pictured were skating in a deep freezer.

The football cards were interesting, because the helmet logos were removed. Apparently Topps did not have a contract with the National

Football League so they were not allowed to put helmets with logos on their cards until 1981. The only, exception for whatever reason, were the Los Angeles Rams. I can remember in their pictures the helmets had the team logo on them.

Another thing that I remember about the football cards was that the Wonder Bread Company used to put three Topps cards in their loaves. This was where I collected my first cards. The company also made Hostess snack cakes that used to come in boxes with cutout baseball cards on the back. There were three of these just as in the loaf of bread.

The Kellogg's Cereal Company had a unique baseball card that they put in boxes in the early seventies. They were 3-D baseball cards, one to a box. The picture cards had a 3-D background and were not much bigger than your hand. It seemed as every box we bought had a card of Los Angeles Dodger first baseman Steve Garvey announcing him as the 1974 All-Star game MVP.

Another cool card was produced by Sugar Day candy. The caramel sucker, which seemed to last all day, put a small caricature card inside each package. The cartoon picture would feature a famous athlete with a normal body and an exaggerated head. Usually, the player's nickname would be on the card. They were very small so hard to store and most of them got lost within a week.

We all categorized our cards in certain ways whether it was in alphabetical order, team order or whatever. I categorized mine by individual position ranking each player from best to worst. The all-pros and all-stars went on top and everyone else underneath in the order that I thought they ranked. I would lay the cards out on my bed by position. Baseball cards were placed on an imaginary diamond, basketball a court. Football cards were placed in the two back, two receivers pro set on offense and the standard four linemen, three linebackers, four defensive back set on defense. This made it easy for me to find a card, but hard for anyone else which cut down on the chances of having one stolen.

Old dart boards used to have a baseball diamond on the back and many guys used to take the cards of their favorite teams to play it. You would bring your team to a friend's house set your lineup and toss away. In 1978, Topps had a full baseball game on the back of their cards. Each player would have the result of an at bat listed on the back of the card, things like home run, triple, base hit, walk, strikeout, fly out and double play. In order to keep it random, each player had to shuffle their deck when they got to the bottom. The thing of it was that nobody ever memorized what was on the back of the cards. Why, I have no idea. It seems as if a person had a George Brett card with "home run" on the back he would remember it. Maybe they put different things on the back of each person's card, I'm not sure. The shuffling helped to fog the memory also as we never used two of the same person's card in any game. Of course, no one knew that one day the cards would be worth anything so we transported them in old cardboard shoe boxes.

Sticking with baseball, there was the candy bar which cost a nickel more than any other. It was the Reggie Bar named after New York Yankee outfielder Reggie Jackson. When he arrived in New York, Jackson said that he would become so famous that they would name a candy bar after him and they did. It was a peanut, caramel cluster that sold itself on its name, because it wasn't very good. Where I lived, candy bars at that time cost twenty cents. The Reggie Bar cost twenty-five and the joke was that Jackson got the nickel. I can't lie. I stole a Reggie Bar or two. Had to make up for that extra nickel.

I don't know if the Oh Henry candy bar was really named after Atlanta Braves outfielder and former home run king Henry Aaron, but I do know that after he broke the record there was a commercial with him endorsing it. And heavyweight champion of the world Muhammad Ali had Champ Chocolate Chip cookies. There was a family owned garage in my neighborhood that had an old painting of boxer Sugar Ray Robinson endorsing Coca Cola. I would have done anything to get my hands on it, but am sure it's a distant memory now.

I was in Little League when Big League Chew came out. It was a bag of shredded chewing gum sold in a pouch like those used to sell chewing tobacco. Every Little Leaguer had to have it and no one thought that it was the next step to buying actual chewing tobacco. That came later.

I wasn't into card games like Strato-matic baseball or football, but did play them from time to time. There was, also, a "Monday

Night Football" card game with a little record that you would put in to announce the play by play.

One of my best friends had a game called electronic football. It was not a hand held game, but a board game with a field above a grid of offensive plays on top and defensive plays on the side that had numbered results between them. Under the field and beside the grid was a bank of lights. Behind the lights were buttons, one black that each player would push on every play along with a choice of five white ones one of which was to be pushed at the same time as the black. The offensive and defensive plays were called by putting a dot on the name of the play you wanted to run. Then each player would press their buttons and a light would flash. Wherever the light flashed on the grid that was the result of the play. The way we tracked our progress was by taking a bread wrapper and putting it on the corresponding yard-line all of the way to the end zone. It was a guessing game. You had to outthink your opponent and guess what buttons he was going to push. Not exactly Madden, but it kept us amused.

So did another game called "NFL Quarterback." My neighbor and good friend had this one and we wore it out. It was a game with offensive and defensive cards. The offensive cards had results on them by different colors and the defensive cards were hole-punched. The offensive player put his card on the board and the defensive player covered it with his. There was a spinning wheel set up percentage wise by the same colors as on the offensive cards with the most likely result of the play having a larger color and the least likely the smaller. The trick was for the player on offense to spin the dial so that the arrow landed in the color which gave him the best result. The defense could not spin unless it was a kickoff or punt return. This was where I first learned the names of different offensive and defensive plays as most of them came right out of NFL playbooks. We used to play that game for hours and both of us hated losing at it.

Supertoe was another favorite. He was a field goal kicking doll that was about a foot high which came with a football and goalpost to kick through. There was also a tape measure set up by yards to measure the distance of the kick. What you did was set the ball in front of Supertoe then whack him on the head as hard as possible to make him kick. Supertoe was what we call a straight on kicker which probably explains why the toy doesn't exist today, because all of the kickers we see now are soccer style specialists. Whoever made that toy was an engineering genius, because we used to slam Supertoe's head as hard as we could and it never broke.

The only toy that I could think of which was tougher is the Evel Knievel motorcycle and action figure. There are many toys advertised that don't live up to the hype, but this one did. It was a motorcycle with a handheld crank that you wound up to give it a boost. The harder you cranked the faster and more powerful the motorcycle was and the better stunt you would get. It did somersaults, wheelies and jumped over anything. You could run it into walls and it would bounce back. That motorcycle was so tough that the crank broke before it did. There was a smaller scale motorcycle that went along with a van, sky cycle and jet propelled bike, but the original was the best.

Then there was one of the few things that I still have, the Super Bowl electric football game. The game with the plastic men shaped in different poses which moved on a vibrating field. I got my first one when I was eight. The two teams were the Miami Dolphins and Minnesota Vikings. I ended up with ten different teams and played it until I went to high school. My cousin was my opponent and we always said that no matter how many times we played there was always one play which unfolded just as it would in a real game. He beat me most of the time until I learned how to pass. Once I learned that, there was no stopping me.

When the handheld electronic football games came out I was in the sixth grade, but they did not become the rage until the next year. This was the first toy that I could recall that everyone had to have. Christmas 1979 saw every toy store in the country bombarded with requests for this game. They couldn't keep them on the shelves. I wasn't able to get one myself until two weeks after Christmas.

A friend of mine had a deck of football cards with play results on them, kind of similar to what the old Topps baseball cards had, but without the player's pictures on the front. We formed a lunch league one year with the cards and I made it all of the way to the Super Bowl only to lose.

But the real lunch time game was paper football. Simply put, you took a piece of paper, formed it into a triangle and took turns tapping it with your hand across a table. The object was to make any part of the football hang over the far edge of the table for a touchdown. Downs were counted by knocking the ball off of the edge. Anytime you or your opponent knocked the football off of the table three times before someone scored a touchdown the other person got to try a field goal through goal post made by placing the side of the palms on the table, pointing the index fingers toward each other until they met and raising the thumbs. This was a game that could be played anywhere at any time.

I had a good time playing it and was usually assigned with making the footballs, because not everyone could do it. The tighter the triangle, the better. If you were on the road, which was the opponent's classroom or house, then you had to use their football and everyone had one. Everyone knew my footballs, because they had the NFL logo and then Commissioner Pete Rozelle's signature written on them just as a regular pro football would.

Two more lunch break staples were penny soccer and penny basketball. Penny soccer used three coins. It started with a break like in pool and then you had to push one coin between the other two all of the way down the field until you scored into the goal set up on the end of the table between the opponents index and pinky fingers. In basketball, you spun the coin down to the end of the table and shot it into a basket made by cupping the hands. Pretty simple, but it kept us occupied.

Baseball and basketball could never really come up with a board game as good as electric football, though baseball tried the electric route, but hockey did. The table hockey game with the steel puck surrounded by rubber with the rods at each end which controlled the players. The players did nothing more than move maybe two inches each way and slap the puck, but it was great.

There was an O.J. Simpson doll. Yes there was. It came with an O.J. action figure in football uniform. Because O.J. ran track at the University of Southern California a track suit came with it as well. I always wanted one, but never got it for Christmas. It was one of the few things that I didn't get. There was also a football cleat made by Spotbilt called the "Juicemaker", because they were worn by O.J.

Growing up, bobble headed dolls were not very prevalent. Very few people that I knew had them. More of us had the little plastic football helmets that came out of the bubble gum machines. In fact a friend and I used to make our weekly football picks by taking the helmets of the teams playing that week and knocking them together. Whichever helmet fell backwards was the loser. The whole set of helmets could be bought by division along with a goal post to hang them by their place in the standings. They used to even sell little helmet buggies.

Remember the helmet buggy? It used to have the home team's logo and sit on the sideline during NFL games though no one knew what it was used for. At least in major league baseball we knew that the bullpen car was used to bring out the relief pitcher. As long as baseball games last today maybe they need to bring the bullpen car back.

Then we move to the games that we played. They were no different than what everyone else did we just had our own rules to accommodate for field size, time and number of players.

In baseball, there was pitcher's paradise in which we used no first baseman, but if the fielder got the ball back to the pitcher on the mound before you got to the next base on a force play you were out. And the right or left field rule in which all right handed hit's to right field and all left handed hits to left were automatic outs. And the five or ten run rule where if you scored five or ten runs before there were three outs in an inning the teams switched at bats.

We all played wiffleball and if we could find a place to play stickball. Those of us in the country would take an old stick and use it to hit rocks. Living on a tobacco farm, I had plenty of room, plenty of rocks and plenty of sticks to use. I broke many tobacco sticks trying to find just the right bat. My father knew this and would tell me to stop, because the sticks weren't cheap, but that never stopped me. He would even give me broken sticks in hopes that I would use them instead, but like a personal baseball glove one couldn't just use any stick to hit rocks. If I hit them too close to the house my father's booming voice would come out of nowhere, "Hey! Stop batting them stones!" We would pair off and play one on one using major league teams and their lineups.

By rule, you had to bat on the same side of the plate as the player who was up on your team. So everyone had to switch hit. After a while, we challenged ourselves by actually throwing the rocks and trying to hit them which are much harder than hitting a baseball. This was for the ones of us who couldn't afford or didn't want the Baseball Kid, a short baseball player who would pitch plastic baseballs to you.

Football brought the permanent quarterback when teams were uneven which we later changed to permanent offense. This was one player who always played on offense for whichever team had the ball. If the teams were even than you could rush the passer after counting a few Mississippi's or thousands. If the teams were not, than it wasn't a smart idea. You were allowed one blitz with no count per four downs. The team which gave up a touchdown had to walk to the other end of the field for the kickoff, though usually we threw the ball instead of kicked it. Two or three completions were a first down with only those that crossed the line of scrimmage in the air counting.

We had a pretty neat thing in organized football called the "Marriott Super Bowl". It was a series of televised youth games on local station 5 sponsored by the Marriott Hotel chain. The games came on every Saturday morning and would showcase two different boys and girls clubs playing in different weight classes. The players would introduce themselves before their game. The Marriott stopped showing these games just before I started playing.

When teams weren't picked then we played "Smear the Queer" or tackle the man with the ball. Whoever got the ball had to run threw everyone else all the way to the goal line. If he was tackled then he threw the ball into the air and whoever caught it was the next runner to be smeared. Some guys came up with a game called knee football which we played on our knees, but it just wasn't the same.

Basketball rules never changed, just the number of players. Maybe the basket was lowered so that we could dunk or there would be a take back line after missed baskets were rebounded by the defense, but nothing else. The main thing with basketball was that if there were a lot of guys at the same court winners stayed on until they lost and everyone else had to wait their turn. When you were at someone's house this usually worked pretty well, because everyone who was going to play was there when you started and each of us shot for teams then waited our turn. At the playground there was always the chance of someone really good showing up and taking your spot so you had to get what we called "downs" or first pick of players for the next game to guarantee a spot.

One year at the recreation center where I lived we actually had boxing matches in the parking lot. A guy brought in a set of gloves and people would sign up to fight each other in three round bouts. It was mostly the older kids so I never got a chance to do it and really didn't want to. Talk about a lawsuit waiting to happen, but you have to remember this was the 1970's and times were different then.

And since we are in the seventies and early eighties, let's not forget the baseball uniforms at the time. Thanks to teams like the Oakland Athletics, Houston Astros and Pittsburgh Pirates the traditional gray road and white home uniform went out the window. The first baseball team I played on had the traditional white uniforms, but after that it was ugly city. Our all-star uniforms were orange with blue lettering. In senior league we wore blue jerseys with white pants and those red, white and blue caps that the Montreal Expos wore at that time. Then we went to gold jerseys and black pants similar to the Pirates. In Babe Ruth League we wore light blue uniforms similar to those worn by the Kansas City Royals. This was par for the course when I played and we thought those uniforms were sharp at the time. Looking back, they were an ugly product of the disco era. At least our high school uniforms were the traditional gray.

Moving on to television and media, the first thing that I remember is there was a Willie Mays cartoon which came on ABC in the early seventies. It didn't last long, maybe one episode, and I doubt if you can find it on YouTube, but I remember it. It was called "Willie Mays and The Say-Hey Kid."

The Globetrotters had a lot of things including a cartoon which aired from 1970 to 1972 . Then they appeared as "guest" co-stars on the "Scooby Doo" show. The Globetrotters also had a Saturday morning children's show in 1974. Of course, we all remember them on ABC's "Wide World of Sports" as they were a Saturday afternoon staple along with stuntman Evel Knievel in the seventies. When these two were on everyone watched whether they were sports fans or not and they never disappointed.

Cincinnati Reds catcher Johnny Bench hosted the "Baseball Bunch" television show at the end of his career. Every week they would have different players come on to give tips on playing the game. Los Angeles Dodger manager Tommy La would give us some words of wisdom. And we would get highlights and bloopers from major league games. This show usually came on right before "This Week in Baseball."

The local football teams had their own weekly shows during the season. In Washington, there was a Redskin pregame show on Sunday then "Redskins Sideline" at 7:30 p.m. Monday night which showed highlights of Sunday's game and had a couple of players on as guests. Both of these shows were done from the studio of the CBS affiliate channel 9. I can still recall going out on Halloween one Monday night and every house we stopped at the man of the house was watching "Redskins Sideline". I was torn between going out for more candy or sitting and watching with them. I compromised by getting my candy last so that I could catch bits and pieces of it.

CBS had a neat little halftime football segment called Playbook hosted by former Colts quarterback John Unitas. And, yes, I remember when the home blackout rule was in effect regardless of whether the home team sold out or not. So if you didn't have season tickets the only time that you saw the locals was when they were on the road. This covered the regular season and playoffs.

I used to collect all of the preseason football and baseball magazines that I could get my hands on. The main two were by "Peterson's" and "Street and "Smith's". Those of us who were lucky enough knew someone who subscribed to "Sports Illustrated" or "Sport" magazine. Being a football man, my favorite was the NFL's "Pro" magazine which was the official game day program sold at the stadium. One could get a monthly subscription if they liked, but I could never afford it. Fortunately, a friend of mine did subscribe and he would bring them to school for me to read. Every once in a while he would give me one.

By the time that I left for college, I had a pretty good stash of things. Unfortunately, they all perished in the great house cleaning that took place while I was away. I lost almost everything including a couple of Super Bowl game programs and, worst of all, a 1953 Washington Redskins press guide. After that, I vowed to put everything in boxes and label them. I've only lost maybe one or two things since.

As you can probably tell, I had a pretty good childhood. How else to explain some of the things here that I remember?

Indeed it was and hopefully so was this chapter. Hopefully, it brought back childhood memories to the reader as well some similar to the ones mentioned and some of your own. Maybe it will make you call an old friend and say, "Remember this or that?"

And hopefully your attic is as cluttered, in a good way mind you, as mine. Hopefully, you can reach into it and pull out a few things of your own.

CHEATING

It is as old as sports itself. And taxes. Cheating, simply put, is breaking a rule and getting away with it. I am willing to bet that everyone who has ever played competitive sports besides professional golf, whether organized or not, has either cheated, benefitted from cheating or been cheated. It is never right, but it's okay when it benefits us or the team that we root for, but wrong when it benefits our opponent. Either way, it is a part of the games we play and watch whether we are for it or against it and I'm not sure if sports fans care whether it happens or not.

What led me to this chapter was something that I remember seeing while playing baseball as a kid. We were in the dugout and a friend of mine nudged me and said, "Look." On the dugout wall was this drawing of a man wearing a military hard hat and smoking a cigar which looked like the actor Carroll O'Conner in the movie "Kelly's Heroes." Written in a bubble beside him was this quote. "Fight the American way. CHEAT!" My friend and I laughed so hard that we were almost in tears. And both of us agreed that it was true. We were 15 years old.

I have seen people cheat at many things from football to card games. I have to admit, I've cheated a time or two, myself, though nothing that would get me put on probation or get me kicked out of a game or league. Actually most, if not all, of my cheating took place in games that did not count. In organized sports, I got away with a call or two, but that's not cheating. That's just the breaks going my way.

My first experience with cheating came in first grade recess when the kids from our class used to play the kids from the other in kickball. We would get them out and they would just keep running the bases

139

laughing at us all of the way. They would spend the whole recess at the plate while we would fume. We couldn't fight them and going to the teachers was equivalent to squealing. So we just stopped playing them and moved on to something else.

Our physical education teachers were sticklers on the rules and sportsmanship, so not much cheating went on in their class or you didn't play. The honor code was used when they weren't around and no one wanted to win by cheating. As kids we ruled ourselves and the gym teachers made sure of it. As students, we would cheat on an exam before we cheated in gym class.

They were better than some of the coaches that we had in organized sports. In Little League baseball, there always seemed to be a team that used an illegal bat or two. In some cases, they used illegal players. This usually happened at all-star time and though our league never did it, I know of at least one which did, because the man who cheated told me himself.

He and I were on the same all-star team together when we were seventeen whereas growing up this same guy was always a year behind us when we played them. His uncle was the coach of the thirteen year old Senior Little League team that he played for and brought him from out of another district to play. My teammate made the all-star team along with another very good pitcher and their team went on to win the thirteen year old Senior League World Series. I played against him the next four years and never gave it a thought.

Until one day one day when we were teammates it dawned on me that we were both the same age. I said, "Wait a minute. Weren't you on that thirteen year old team that won the World Series that year? How could you be seventeen now if you were 13 then?"

He looked at me, laughed and said, "We cheated." Then he explained how his uncle was the coach and had changed his and the other pitcher's birth certificates. There was no shame in his voice at all. As far as he was concerned, if they didn't get caught, then too bad.

Youth league baseball is famous for this, because anyone can change a birth certificate. My father swore for years that the Taiwanese dominated the Little League World Series, because they used older players. Eventually it was proven that he may have been right as the Taiwanese and Chinese were both caught using illegal players. Many people felt that the first American Little Leaguer to cheat was the New York pitcher Danny Almonte who pitched at age 14, two years over the limit, for the Bronx back in 2001, but they are being naïve. If you don't believe me, ask my friend. Birth certificates have been changed for years.

The cheating in youth league football where I live got so bad that the pregame rules had to be changed. When I played, teams were weighed only once at the beginning of the year and only had to weigh in again if they played in the championship game. The only thing that had to be done before the game was that each of us had a picture id card and the commissioners of the league would check us in while we warmed up. The smart teams would get an older, heavier player and use his little brother's id to check them in. Then the older player would play in the game. Another way to get around the picture identification was to have older players change uniforms with younger players at halftime. The referees hardly paid attention and most home teams left to some secret place at halftime anyway.

So the rules were changed. Now along with the picture identification each team's players must weigh in before every game. Any player who is over their required weight is disqualified for that game. And no team is allowed to leave the field at halftime. They must either go to one end zone or the other. This allows everyone to keep an eye on them.

Sometimes teams don't have enough players to field a team. So what they will do is bring in a kid from the neighborhood to take his place. If the opposition doesn't know your players than you simply call the replacement player by the name of whoever's place he took on the roster. I've been on teams that have done it. The excuse used is rather than have everyone suffer by one team forfeiting let them benefit by playing the game so that the kids on both sides don't lose any playing time. Most coaches and parents don't really believe this. They just don't want to lose by forfeit. The truth is that it should be a forfeit, because if the kids on the team which is shorthanded aren't dedicated enough to show up than they deserve to lose. If some outside circumstances come up which may force a team not to have all of its players, most leagues will try to find a way to accommodate them as long as they find out in advance so that forfeits are avoided.

High school sports teams around the country don't cheat as much as they "bend the rules," especially when it comes to eligibility. It seems as though every good public school team where I live has one or two players on the roster who are not registered in their district, use a false address or use the address of a relative who lives in the district. Every now and then a team will use a player whose eligibility has run out. Since it is up to the schools to police themselves, it is very rare that sanctions are handed down. As long as no one talks everyone deals with it. The reason being that if you are an athlete and want to win or earn a scholarship to college than it's best to go to one of these schools and play for their coach.

But when one talks, everyone does. A couple of years ago, there was a widespread cheating scandal in the county where I live. Almost every good football team was ruled ineligible for post season play, because they were using players who did not live in their district. An assistant coach at one of the schools turned in his alma mater of all teams, a school where he had played on a state championship team. They had stolen his younger brother from the team that he was coaching and he went to the authorities. This started a domino effect as everyone began to sing. Teams had to forfeit games left and right, but the assistant coach didn't lose out. In fact he came out ahead, because it was too late to prove that the coaches had cheated while he was a player so they couldn't take that title away. And by turning in his alma mater he got them and all of the other rule breakers to forfeit enough games so that his current team could make the playoffs. There have been many basketball teams who have been alleged doing the same, but no one has turned them in yet.

In almost every case that I've mentioned, there was an adult involved who condoned the action. How can we expect our youth to think that cheating is bad when their adult role models blatantly do it in front of them? And how can a coach administer discipline to the player when they break a rule on the field if the coaches themselves are breaking them off of it.

Players know this so they take their cheating to the field. I don't know how many pitchers I caught, hit against or coached against who cheated. It was easy, because only three or four baseballs were used in a game. One of my buddies that I played against in school loved major leaguer Gaylord Perry who was known for doctoring the baseball. This friend would put the sandpaper in his glove and emery board in his waistband to scuff the ball. Most of the guys simply put Vaseline on the bill of their caps. Others cut the ball with their belt buckle. Everything was very subtle. As far as us hitters, we used aluminum bats so there was no corking of the barrel as the pros were known to do.

In football, there were a few linemen who would throw dirt or mud in their opponent's eyes. Or there were offensive lineman who would put grease on their jerseys so when the defender tried to grab them their hands would slide off. Teams were and still are famous in high school for bringing in certain footballs just to kickoff with. When I played youth league, there were some teams who would have the people holding the chains signal to their defense whether the play called was a run or pass and which direction it was going. One game when I was a high school assistant coach we were down by two points and had fourth and inches in the fourth quarter. We ran a quarterback sneak. The home team had a group of junior varsity players holding the chains and after the play they moved the sticks up a foot. We caught them doing it on film. The referees missed it and when they measured we were six inches short of the first down. We never got the ball back and lost. The lost may have cost us a playoff spot.

In basketball, everyone that can get away with it travels. I've seen it at the pro, college and high school level. I've seen guys take the ball from the top of the key, hold it over their head and take three steps to the basket. I've seen guys change pivot feet before traveling. I was at a high school game where a player who was letting the clock run down before taking the final shot picked up one foot to wipe his hand off then picked up the other foot to do the same and the refs called nothing. The jump stop, when a player stops his dribble and takes a hop before shooting, is traveling. Once a player picks up the ball with both hands after dribbling and both feet leave the floor, he must pass or shoot. At least that's what I was taught. This has led to the Lebron James crab dribble where he takes a hop before putting the ball on the floor. That, too, is traveling. It is being called now, but for a good while players were getting away with "crossover" dribbles in which they would put their hand on the side of or under the ball then bounce it from one hand to the other. Even worse was when guard Walt Williams played for the University of Maryland and used to put his hand completely under the ball whenever he dribbled. Williams was a special case in that I think the referees let him get away with it, because the Terps were on probation and so bad at then if they stopped him from dribbling illegally Maryland would have never scored.

Most of the cheating at the college and pro levels is done behind the scenes, though I do know of a couple of cases that I heard of and witnessed in high school. Since many of the guys who played football knew the players on other teams from growing up together they still kept in touch and hung out from time to time. So the week of a game, especially a big one between two schools that were close to each other, coaches would have one of their players go to the house of one of the opponent's and try to steal the game plan. From what I've heard, their success rate was pretty high.

The recent "Spygate" scouting episode with the New England Patriots also reminded me of a time when I was an assistant and we were scouting an upcoming opponent. I was filming the game and the head coach asked me to try and film the opponent's defensive coach's signals. I was to get the sign, then switch to the field when the players broke the huddle in order to film the formation and the play. But we couldn't get the timing down and ditched the plan in the middle of the fourth quarter.

Scouting the opponent before a game is prevalent with cheating stories. I never thought much of what we had done when trying to film our opponent's signals until the "Spygate" situation with the Patriots in 2008. The Patriots were accused of filming the coaches of their opponents during games while they were giving signals to players. Then taking a copy of the coach's film and matching it with the play that was run on the field. This was the same thing that we had tried to do 13 years earlier. The Patriots were also accused of filming teams walk through practices the day before games in order to know the opponent's game plan. Patriots head coach Bill Belichick and his staff was turned in by one of his former assistants New York Jets head coach Eric Mangini. Belichick and the Patriots were fined, but the coach was not suspended.

The truth is that spying on the opponent had been going on in the NFL for years. The story goes that the week before the famous 1958 championship game between the Baltimore Colts and New York Giants, the Colts got the jump on New York by spying on their practices. Because the Giants were tied with the Cleveland Browns for the Eastern Division title, the two teams had to meet in a winner take all playoff at the end of the season while the Colts had the week off. So Baltimore sent a scout to New York who stood on a hotel rooftop which overlooked the Giants practice site, Yankee Stadium. From his vantage point, the scout was able to study the Giants and get a thorough scouting report which the Colts used the next week in their victory.

Hall of fame coach George Allen was well known for sending spies to watch the upcoming opponent's practices and was paranoid that teams were doing the same to his teams. Allen, and many other coaches, would also bring in players released by teams that they were about to play and put them on the roster for that week just to get information from them on their opponent. Then let the player go right after the game. Oakland Raiders owner and general manager Al Davis was accused of putting microphones in the opponent's locker room at the old Alameda Coliseum in order to hear what they were up to. And many teams would take their time exchanging films with the upcoming opponent or send a bad copy.

College football and basketball history cannot be written without including a chapter on recruiting violations which have been going on since the NCAA began. From giving recruits and their families gifts and cash to keeping them eligible by having someone else do their work the rules have been abused. At some schools the players didn't even go to class. I went to a small college with a Division I basketball team, but no football. This made basketball the big sport on campus and the players knew that. In one of my speech classes was a starter on the team who was not getting his work done. Our professor, who was in her first year, tried to get him to do his work, but he wouldn't. Somehow it got around to the basketball coaches and they had a talk with her.

I don't know what happened, but she never bothered him again and after the semester resigned from her post. And he continued to play as if nothing had happened.

Though things have gotten better the rules are still being bent, mostly in the recruitment of players. Although entrance standards are higher and high school transcripts are being monitored more closely there are still ways for coaches to break the rules. The main rule that is broken is contacting players outside of the legal time when they can be recruited and signed. This is usually done through a high school or amateur coach of the player that they are trying to recruit. By keeping in touch with the coach, they are able to keep in touch with the kid and monitor where they stand in the pecking order with other schools and what they have to do in order to become the top choice. Coaches will also go to summer basketball camps where they can't have any verbal contact with the players, but they can with the coaches. In football, they host high school players at speed and conditioning non-contact camps. All of this is considered okay, because everyone else does it, but it's really another form of cheating.

The thing that makes college cheating so bad is that the coaches who do it and are successful on the court or field can always get a job. They may get their school put on probation, but that doesn't stop them from getting another job somewhere else where some of them break the rules again. It is almost as if schools are forced by alumni to make a decision. Do you want to win with a coach that has a reputation for breaking the rules or do you want to lose with a coach who graduates his players at a ninety percent rate? Many take the former, because graduation rates don't bring in revenue and recognition while bowl games and NCAA tournament berths do. It is the business side of college sports that we have learned to live with, hypocrisy and all.

And that's the thing with cheating. We have learned to accept it in all of its forms. If the team isn't caught spying, then it is okay. If a team isn't caught changing a birth certificate, then it is okay. If a team uses an ineligible player or a player not on the roster and doesn't get caught, it is okay. If a player uses steroids and doesn't get caught, it is okay. If a player doctors a baseball or bat and gets away with it, it is okay.

They say that sport is a mirror of society. The cheating element is no exception from taxes, to rigging the ballot in an election it is there. "Fight the American way. CHEAT!" has been a motto that many people have lived by or been involved with and I'm no exception.

And that's too bad, because it's not right.

RIVALRIES

There is nothing like a good rivalry, especially when the athletes and people involved are winning. When you participate or one of the teams is a favorite of yours it is even better. And the bigger the stakes, the more intense the rivalry becomes between those involved on the field or in the stands. Victories are always nice, but wins over rivals are the best. They count double. If it's a playoff game, triple. And the losses are the worst, because as a player or fan you brood until your team gets another shot.

Rivalries are born in many ways. Geography has a big role in who becomes a rival. So does being in the same league, conference or division. The people involved help to make a rivalry what it is, also. And, as mentioned earlier, so does the success of the teams involved.

Playing in rivalry games is great. The games that I remember most from high school are the ones against our rivals who were about five miles east and north of us. There was nothing like the week or days before playing a rival with all of the buildup from the student body, teachers, alumni and community. If both teams were winning you knew that the crowd would be huge and the local press would be there to cover it. Since the schools were so close and many of us had grown up together, there was a lot of trash talk when people would see each other during the week. There was a lot at stake from bragging rights, to playoff spots to who would get the girl.

We weren't very good at football, but one thing that I remember is we beat both of our rivals my senior year. That means as long as we live all of us who were seniors can rub it in our friends from those schools face if we want and there is nothing they can do about it. In fact, in the six games that we played against them from my sophomore to senior year we only lost once, to the northern rival, and avenged it the next year. On their home field. It was sweet.

As for the eastern rival after we swept them our school lost to them fourteen straight times. Being as it was the school that my dad attended I had to hear it every year. One year, I thought for sure we would win. I was so confident that I didn't even go to the game. The next day I picked up the paper and saw that my school had lost for the eighth straight time. My father looked at my face while I was reading and said, "What happened? Did we beat you again?" Then he laughed until I thought his sides would burst.

In baseball we had a championship team. We played our rivals twice a year and never swept them. One beat us out of the county championship my sophomore year and tied us the next before we swept them with three wins when I was a senior. But my two biggest heartbreak losses, besides losing in the state championship game as a senior, were to those rival schools. One was a 1-0 loss to the team which we tied for the county when I was a junior. I can still remember coming up with runners on second and third with two outs and feeling the bat twist in my hand when I got a perfect fastball. I popped it up and we went on to lose.

The other was a loss to our eastern rival where my best friend on their team pitched and beat us. Again, I came up with a chance to win it and hit a ball which drove the centerfielder to the wall where he caught it. When I went out to the mound to shake my friend's hand, I told him good game, but why did he have to beat us? Being the competitor that he is, he never said a word or cracked a smile. He just gave me a look which said, "You know why." We had beaten him the year before and rubbed it in. Then we had beaten him that fall in football. This was his last chance to get revenge and he did. Yes, I knew exactly why.

As for me, I would rather play or coach in a rivalry game than watch it when my team is involved. Even if I think that they are going to win, I will not be satisfied until the game ends and the scoreboard has my team on top. Being unable to control the outcome makes it even harder.

Unlike most fans, I really don't have a team that I hate. I'm not a fan of the Dallas Cowboys or New York Yankees, but I don't hate them. As a Pittsburgh Steelers fan who lives in Maryland I don't root for the Baltimore Ravens, but respect them and love it when the two teams play. The reason why I don't hate the Ravens or their fans is because I saw the Colts move from Baltimore in the middle of the night when I was sixteen and remember how devastated the city was. Though I felt bad for the city of Cleveland, because it was the Browns who moved to Baltimore and became the Ravens, it was nice to see the city get a team again in 1995.

Also, the Ravens are a lot like the Steelers in the way that they run their organization and their style of play. Both teams are tough and physical. When they play each other you know that it will be the team that is most physical who will win. Every possession is vital and every yard earned. Most of the games come down to the fourth quarter with quite a few going into overtime.

So victories over the Ravens mean more than victories over anyone else in football for me. And the best year of the rivalry for me and all Steelers fans was 2008. That was the year Baltimore and Pittsburgh met three times and the Steelers won them all on their way to a world's championship. All year long I had to listen to Ravens fan calling the Steelers lucky and hoping to get another shot at them in the playoffs. When the playoffs started everyone kept telling me that the Steelers didn't want to play the Ravens again. "You don't want to see the Ravens," was all I heard. It didn't matter to me who the Steelers played. As far as I was concerned, no one was going to beat them, especially Baltimore. Not with a rookie quarterback in Joe Flacco.

The two teams met in the AFC championship game. It was one of the most physical games that I have ever seen and Pittsburgh won. I didn't gloat. There was no need. The victory spoke for itself and as I said, I respect the Ravens. But I did listen to Ravens fans commiserate on local sports radio and television. And I read the Monday Baltimore Sun sports section from front to back. I couldn't help myself. The best part is that no matter how long they play the game of football Baltimore can never outdo Pittsburgh in a season series. They can tie the Steelers by beating them three times in one year, but they can never do better. Pittsburgh Steelers fans always have 2008 on Baltimore.

To me, Pittsburgh and Baltimore is one of the best rivalries going today, but it's not the best in sports or NFL history. Most people feel as though the Boston Red Sox-New York Yankees rivalry is the best. I think it's up there, but it is not the same since the Red Sox finally broke the supposed "Curse of the Bambino" by winning the 2004 World Series. Along the way, Boston became the first team in baseball post season history to come back from a three games to none deficit to win as they did this to the Yankees of all teams in the American League Championship Series. Part of the charm of the rivalry was watching the Red Sox find a way to lose every time it mattered to the Yankees. From Bucky Dent's homer in 1978 to Aaron Boone's in 2003, it just seemed as though Boston was really cursed. Then when the Sox won it again in 2007, all the mystique of the rivalry was gone for me.

The only other baseball rivalry that most fans would know about is Dodgers-Giants. They have been battling it out over 3,000 miles as it began in New York with the Brooklyn Dodgers and New York Giants and relocated to California in 1958 as the Los Angeles Dodgers and San Francisco Giants. The rivalry is best known for the "Shot Heard 'Round the World," home run hit by the Giants Bobby Thompson that beat the Dodgers out of a pennant in 1951. And for an ugly incident where Giants pitcher Juan Marichal hit Dodgers catcher John Roseboro over the head with a bat in 1962.

The best rivalry in sports when I was growing up was the Dallas Cowboys against the Washington Redskins. The two teams began playing each other in 1960, but the Cowboys became so good and the Redskins so bad in the late sixties that there was nothing to make their games compelling. Then George Allen came along to coach the Redskins in 1971 and brought along a healthy hatred of the Cowboys and their coach Tom Landry. The next seven years would see the two teams meet in some memorable battles which could fill another book. The early eighties were just as exciting as things became so intense that I can remember people in Washington not scheduling anything on the Sunday that the two teams would meet. My mother would ask me before the season started what days the Redskins and Cowboys were playing so that she could tell her Elks Lodge and church not to schedule anything on those days, because no one would be there.

My first vivid memory of the Dallas-Washington rivalry was the Redskins crushing the Cowboys in the 1972 NFC championship game 26-3 which really set the whole thing off. Not only did the Redskins win the game, they physically manhandled the Cowboys. I had never seen so many players limp off of the field in one game. With all of the success that Washington had under head Coach Joe Gibbs, for Redskin fans who saw it nothing ranks with that '72 title game win.

From then on the two teams battled twice a year and when they were both good battled for playoff spots. The best way to explain it would be that Dallas was always the glamour team with a lot of talent while Washington was the gritty team with role players who always played with a chip on their shoulder. The Redskins would beat the Cowboys often in the seventies, but never, it seemed, when it counted. The roles were reversed in the early eighties until the Redskins became really bad the next decade and Dallas began to beat them regularly. The fact that neither team has really been a threat to win the Super Bowl since the mid nineties has tempered the rivalry as well.

One could make a case that in professional sports football has the best rivalries, because of the way divisions are set up by geography and the limited number of games teams play. Teams in the division only play each other twice during the season once at home and on the road. This magnifies each contest. So rivalries like Packers-Bear, Eagles-Giants, Saints-Falcons, Raiders-Chiefs, Cowboys-Redskins, Patriots-Jets, Browns-Bengals and Ravens-Steelers mean more, because we get less. I have seen fans come to blows in the stands during games between the Redskins and any of their Eastern Conference rivals, the New York Giants, Dallas Cowboys and Philadelphia Eagles. I have felt the hatred of Raven fan for the Steelers. I have seen Eagle and Giant fans go right at each other once they found out that they were rivals. After a Redskin loss to Dallas, one of my cousins hit his brother over the head with a beer bottle slicing his forehead open.

Pro basketball has nothing like this. For whatever the reason, basketball has a hard time sustaining rivalries. Maybe it's because it is so hard to keep a good team together for a long time. Maybe it's because the season, like baseball, is so long and every team plays against each other. Maybe the playoffs are too long. Basketball just doesn't seem to quicken the pulse when it comes to teams.

Basketball rivalries are based more on the individuals who play than the teams. Wilt Chamberlain versus Bill Russell. Wilt versus Willis Reed. Jerry West versus Walt Frazier. Kareem Abdul-Jabbar versus Moses Malone. Patrick Ewing versus Hakeem Olajuwon. Tim Duncan versus Shaquille O'Neal. And the best of my generation, Larry Bird versus Ervin "Magic" Johnson. Basketball is the most individual of team sports and it's the stars that we turn out to see. When we get two great ones against each other, it ratchets up the importance of the game.

I was a Magic Johnson man and Los Angeles Lakers fan while my best friend was Larry Bird and Boston Celtics all of the way. For what it's worth, I'm African-American and he's Irish. The truth is that I didn't root for Magic until he joined the Lakers. When the two met in the 1979 NCAA basketball finals I rooted for Bird and Indiana State not Magic and Michigan State, so race had nothing to do with it for me.

Even though the history books say that the Celtics and Lakers have been rivals since the 1960's the decade of the eighties was more about Magic and Bird than the two teams. They only met three times in the NBA Finals with Bird and the Celtics winning the first in 1984 and Magic and L.A. winning the next two in 1985 and 1987. But the rivalry between Bird and Magic was one of the few in team sports that existed even when they didn't play against each other. There was no in between. You were either for Bird or Magic. For 82 regular season games, fans would follow them on television and through box scores to see who outdid whom just as the two players were themselves. When they met everything stopped just as if it were a heavyweight boxing match. If my best friend and I watched the game together, it was as if we were playing and the man whose team lost brooded the rest of the day. There was literally a hatred for the opponent. Magic fans wanted nothing more than to see the Celtics lose and Bird fans felt the same for the Lakers. The 1980's may have been the ten best years in the history of the NBA and Magic and Bird were responsible. The league has not had anything like it since.

I am sure that hockey has some great rivalries, built mainly on post season play. Here in Washington D.C. there is no love lost for the Pittsburgh Penguins who have beaten the Capitals every time it has seemed to matter in the Stanley Cup playoffs from the days of Mario Lemieux to Sidney Crosby. Philadelphia and New York are rivals in everything and hockey is no different. There are others, but I'm not at liberty to elaborate because of my limited knowledge of hockey.

Then there are the great boxing rivalries. Because it is an individual sport where the fighters careers last only so long and they meet so infrequently, there has been nothing to match a title fight between two rivals. From Jim Tunney-Jack Dempsey to Evander Holyfield-Mike Tyson we have been drawn to the great title fight. Most of these rivalries become trilogies with each fighter usually splitting the first two fights then deciding it all in a third. Even when they only fight twice, the rematch is remembered just as much as the first fight. Though boxing rivalries are becoming a thing of the past at one time they may have been the best that professional sports had to offer and I miss them.

Then there are the college sports rivalries. These are where the fans passions run deepest. The difference between college sports rivalries and the high schools is that there is a national fan base, because of college alumni spread out across the country, whereas prep sports are more local. The difference between the colleges and the pros is that the alumni of a college feels like they are more a part of the team than professional fans do. The college alum has worn the same colors, been on the same campus and taken the same classes as the athletes they are rooting for while the pro fan hasn't done anything with anyone on their favorite team. The colleges are also more about state and regional pride compared to the civic pride of the pros.

Growing up in Atlantic Coast and Big East Conference country, I have seen some of the best college basketball rivalries of all time. And, unlike pro basketball, these rivalries are about the teams involved not the players. The Atlantic Coast Conference has four of its teams in the state of North Carolina. They are the North Carolina Tar Heels, Duke Blue Devils, Wake Forrest Demon Deacons and North Carolina State Wolfpack and when they play each other forget it. The arenas are going to be packed and the games are fiercely played, especially North Carolina-Duke. I've seen enough of them to know this. And every team in the ACC, especially my favorite team the University of Maryland, considers the Tar Heels and Blue Devils as their rival. The conference may have made a mistake by expanding from nine teams who played each other home and home every year to twelve teams with a rotating schedule, but the core rivalries are still there.

The Big East started out with seven small east coast schools and now has sixteen. It is considered one of the best conferences in the country, but expansion has hurt the rivalries in conference as well. There was a time when a ticket to see Georgetown play Syracuse at the old Capital Centre or Carrier Dome was impossible to come by. The same if either team was playing Villanova or St. Johns. It was crazy stuff with true hatred. I can still remember the ugly chants from Syracuse fans toward Georgetown center Patrick Ewing in which they said "Patrick can't read." And an incident where the fans were throwing fruit on the floor at the Hoyas. Like North Carolina and Duke in the ACC, Georgetown was the main rival of everyone in the Big East for years and the Hoyas relished it.

Every conference has its basketball rivalries for sure, but the football rivalries are the more well known. From the Southeastern Conference to the Pacific Ten every school has an in conference rival with many of them boarder or in state battles. Many teams have out of conference rivals as well that may be in a different conference, but not too far away. If I could afford it, I would jump on a plane at least three times a year to catch a rivalry game until I'd seen them all. The ones at the top of my list are Texas-Oklahoma, Notre Dame-Southern Cal, Florida-Georgia, Alabama-Auburn, Michigan-Ohio State, Southern Cal-UCLA, Stanford-California, Harvard-Yale, Army-Navy, Southern-Grambling St. and Mississippi-Louisiana State.

College football coined the expression "Big Game." The fans take this literally. For the colleges involved, there is nothing in the world more important and it's not just the week of the game, but year around. This is where the records of the teams truly do not matter. You can be a successful coach at Ohio State like Earl Bruce, but if you don't beat Michigan you are gone. Whereas you can have a poor season as Michigan's Lloyd Carr did in 1996 and save your job by beating Ohio State.

The Army-Navy game transcends the brotherhood of the armed forces. For 51 weeks of the year, the two units are one in protecting our country, but for one week in December they are bitter rivals. For a serviceman, losing to Army or Navy is like losing a war without the casualties. And it stays with them forever. The Army-Navy rivalry may not be the greatest on the field, but for pageantry and aura nothing beats watching the soldiers and cadets walking into the stadium in full uniform on a crisp autumn day. Then there is nothing more moving in all of sports than when the two academies stand as one to sing their school songs after the game. If there is one sporting event that should be shown live on national television every year it's the Army-Navy football game.

Most college rivalries are bitter. I remember my freshman year at college in Jacksonville, Florida where the Florida-Georgia game, known as the "World's Biggest Outdoor Cocktail Party" is played annually. Our gym teacher warned us the Friday morning before the game to be careful if we went out that weekend, because the town would be full of Gator and Bulldog fans loaded on alcohol. We were told to wear neutral colors, no Florida blue and orange or Georgia red and black in order to stay out of trouble. I had always thought that Redskins-Cowboys was crazy, but these people were nuts.

Florida was going into the game as the number one team in the country and there was talk that if the Gators won they would be allowed to tear down the goalposts while if Georgia did they would not. This came from the mayor of Jacksonville himself who should have known better, but was blinded by hometown loyalty. Georgia fans felt as though because the game was being played at a neutral site than they should be able to tear the goalposts down if they won. The mayor said no and Georgia fans countered with, "We'll see."

Wouldn't you know it? The Bulldogs came out and dominated the Gators winning 24-3. This was the worst case scenario for the Gator Bowl and Jacksonville police, because Georgia fans had been burning all week about the mayor's comments and rushed the field when the game ended. A riot broke out with police trying to protect the goalpost and Georgia fans determined to get to them. Bulldog fans were arrested and beaten to the ground by the police and security. I had never seen anything like it and remember thinking, "Now this is a rivalry. These people actually think that they are fighting the Civil War." This is the way that I have viewed SEC football ever since. As long as the conference exists, the Civil War will never die.

Even if the battle is between two teams in the same state. I was working for a company that had offices spread out all over the country. One of them was located in Mobile, Alabama and the agent used to call me every morning to start up his computer system. One year during the week of the Alabama-Auburn game I asked him who he was rooting for and will never forget what he told me. He said, "I wouldn't root for Auburn if they were playing the Russians." Now all of us who remember the Cold War know how strong of a statement that was. In the United States, we didn't root for the Soviet Union in anything. But in Mobile, Alabama the fans of the Crimson Tide would root for the Reds against the Auburn Tigers.

Southeastern Conference football is no joke. The media may tell you that Michigan-Ohio State football is the best rivalry in college sports, but I'm not buying it. I'll put Auburn-Alabama, Florida-Georgia, Alabama-Tennessee and just about any other SEC rivalry up against Michigan-OSU anytime. I'll put these rivalries up against any rivalries in all of sports anytime.

The colleges have every element that makes rivalries great, especially college football. Regional interest, national interest and ties to teams through alumni and state pride. Add to this the history of the rivalries passed down from generation to generation and you get emotions which run deeper and deeper with time. While rivalries in the pros may last for a little while and fade, those in college never do.

Just like a good old family feud, this is how it should be.

I WISH THAT I COULD HAVE BEEN THERE

As a sports historian, I have read up on great games and moments since the age of seven. Since I was born in 1967, many of them happened before my lifetime or early in my youth when my memory was not as clear as it is now.

To me, all of the history books and accounts in the world cannot replace actually being at an event. So this chapter is about going back in time. It is about the moments in sports that if I were put into a time machine I'd dial up the date so that I could be there in person along with reasons why I would want to. Maybe I was at some of them in a former life seeing as my birth date is the day that the St. Louis Cardinals won game seven of the 1967 World Series, but I doubt it. So here they are in no particular order.

I wish that I had been in the arena when Jack Johnson became the first African-American to win the heavyweight championship of the world by beating Tommy Burns on December 26, 1908 in Sydney, Australia. Because I want to know what the times were like, how much hatred there really was for African-Americans like myself. What was being said about Johnson and African-Americans before and after the fight? How much did Johnson care about representing black people? How much pride did blacks take in the victory and how much despair did whites? How much backlash was there from the white population? And when did the search for the "Great White Hope" begin?

I wish that I had been at the 1912 Stockholm Olympics when Jim Thorpe became the only man to win the Decathlon and Pentathlon. Because I want to know how great of an athlete Thorpe was. I want to know if it is true that Thorpe didn't bother to practice on the ship over to Sweden. I want to know what his Anglo-Saxon teammates felt about this Native American. Were they happy that he was representing their country (which was really his)? Were they happy that he won? Did Thorpe really say, "Thanks, King," when King Gustav said that he was the greatest athlete of all time? And how was Thorpe treated when he returned to America?

I wish that I had been at the 1919 World Series between the Cincinnati Reds and Chicago White Sox. This, of course, is the one in which the White Sox were accused of fixing the series by taking bribes to lose on purpose to Cincinnati. The players were acquitted in a court of law, but suspended by Commissioner Kennesaw Mountain Landis from baseball for life. I want to know why the so called "Black Sox" did it. Was it because they felt like they were underpaid by their owner? Was it because other teams or players were or had been doing it? How many players really knew? How many people inside of baseball and in the media knew? Why were they acquitted and was there ever a chance that they would be found guilty? And how good was that 1919 White Sox team? Were they that much better than Cincinnati where there was basically no way outside of a fix that the Reds could have won?

I wish that I could have been at both Max Schmeling-Joe Louis heavyweight championship fights. I want to know how invincible did people think that Louis was before the first fight? I want to know when was it that Schmeling actually thought that he could win. I want to know how much did the Nazi party and Adolph Hitler really back Schmeling before he won the first fight in 1936 and what were Schmeling's feelings towards the Nazis? I want to know how white America really felt about Louis while he was the champion. I doubt if everyone was really in Louis' corner. I'm sure that there were some white Americans who wanted him to lose in both fights. I want to know how Louis took losing to Schmeling in the first fight and was he worried about losing the second. I want to know which fighter, if either, bought into the political propaganda spewed by both the American press and Nazi Germany. I want to know if Hitler really turned off the radio when Schmeling went down for the count in the first round of the rematch in 1938. And I want to know how much of white America's attitude really did change about African-Americans after Louis won the second fight?

Then there are the 1936 Berlin Olympics. Just as with Jim Thorpe and Joe Louis, I want to know how track star Jesse Owens' teammates felt about him. I want to know if there were any white Americans who wanted Owens to go to Berlin and fall flat on his face. I want to know why German long jumper Lutz Long befriended Owens, his chief rival. Like Max Schmeling, how much did Long buy into the politics of Adolph Hitler? Did Hitler acknowledge Owens at all or did he walk out of the stadium as history says he did? How long did it take before Owens heroics were forgotten in the United States and he became just another Negro? And an almost forgotten part of the 1936 Olympics, why were the Jewish runners on the United States four by 100 hundred-yard relay team, Marty Glickman and Sam Stoller, replaced and why didn't Owens, one of the replacements, stand up for them by not running in the race, though he did protest the decision?

I wish that I could have been at Yankee Stadium in 1928 when Notre Dame football coach Knute Rockne gave the famous "Win one for the Gipper" speech at halftime of the Army game. George Gipp was a former Notre Dame halfback who had died of pneumonia and legend has it told Rockne on his dying bed to one day ask the boys to win one for him. I wonder if Gipp really did? And if so, I want to know if Rockne, who did not have one of his better teams that season, had planned all along to use the speech that day or if it were spur of the moment. I want to know how many of the players bought into it and knew who George Gipp was.

I wish that I had been there for every game of Joe DiMaggio's 56 game hitting streak in the summer of 1941. I want to know how many games he came close to not getting a hit. I want to know how many of those hits were bloopers or infield singles. And most of all, I want to know how many of those hits bounced off of a fielder or two's gloves and could have been ruled errors but were ruled hits.

I wish that I could have been around for the entire ten years of the American Football League from 1960 to 1969. I want to know why the league's founder, Lamar Hunt, thought that he could pull it off. I want to know what the National Football League tried to do to stop Hunt and destroy the AFL. I want to know what the sporting public really thought of the AFL compared to the NFL. I want to know if living in an NFL territory, I would have felt that the AFL was inferior to the NFL. I want to know which AFL teams I would have rooted for. I want to know if I would have watched more AFL football, because of the number of African-American stars they had compared to the NFL. I wish that I had been around for the espionage that the two leagues used trying to get players signed with their league. I want to know how AFL Commissioner Al Davis really felt when the two leagues merged behind his back in 1966. I wish that I could have been around for the weeks leading up to each of the four Super Bowls between the two leagues. Would I have bought into the NFL propaganda and picked the Baltimore Colts over the New York Jets in Super Bowl III and been as stunned as everyone else? Or would I have believed that the AFL had finally caught up to the NFL and could beat them? And would I have sided with the Kansas City Chiefs in Super Bowl IV against the Minnesota Vikings or stayed with the NFL again.

I wish that I could have been in Mexico City, Mexico for the 1968 Summer Olympics when United States sprinters John Carlos and Tommy Smith raised black fisted gloves on the victory stand during the National Anthem. I want to know how much of it was planned before the Olympics and how much at the actual time of the event. I want to know what the reaction of the fans inside the stadium, media and International Olympic Committee were when Smith and Carlos raised their hands. I want to know whose idea it really was. I want to know who was reluctant to do it and who wasn't. I want to know why other African-American athletes on the U.S. Olympic team did not back Carlos and Smith or do something on their own. I want to know how much influence Dr. Harry Edwards really had on Carlos and Smith. I want to know which members of the media were for Carlos and Smith and which were not. And I want to know what the rest of the world, including the athletes in the Olympic village, thought of Carlos and Smith's actions, the IOC's actions and the reaction of the American press.

I wish that I could have been there for the famous "Sudden Death" NFL championship game between the Baltimore Colts and New York Giants in 1958. I want to know why Yankee Stadium, the site of the game, did not sell out. I want to know what it was really like in Baltimore the day of the game. I want to know if the Giants, who won the championship in 1956, really thought that the Colts could beat them. I want to know how many football fans had even heard of Colts quarterback John Unitas before that game. I want to know how the fans and players felt after regulation when the score was still tied. Besides the referees did anyone know that there was an overtime rule in professional football? I want to know whether it was true that Unitas went for the touchdown instead of the field goal in overtime, because Baltimore owner Carroll Rosenbloom had money on the game and the team needed to cover the point spread in order for him to win. And I want to know what the immediate reaction was of the sporting public after watching the game. Did the game create more fans or was it the birth of the American Football League in the 1960's and the growth of television?

I wish that I could have been in New York City in 1951 to see the Brooklyn Dodgers and New York Giants battle it out for the National League pennant. The season which ended with the Giants Bobby Thompson hitting the "Shot Heard 'Round the World" home run against Brooklyn that won the pennant for New York. I want to know what the feeling was like in town and around the country when the Dodgers jumped out to an early lead. I want to know if the Dodgers felt as if anyone could catch them. I want to know if the Giants thought that they had any chance to win the pennant after July fourth. I want to know when was it that the Dodgers and their fans felt like the Giants were a threat. I want to know when the Giants and their fans begin to believe that they could catch the Dodgers. I want to know what it was like in Brooklyn as the lead dwindled. I want to know what the rivalry was really like for the two teams. I want to know what the other team in town, the New York Yankees, and their fans felt about the whole thing. I wish that I could have been there to see and hear the bench jockeying between Giants manager Leo Durocher and Dodger second baseman Jackie Robinson. I want to know if the Giants really did cheat by stealing the other team's signs from a center field window at the Polo Grounds. I want to know what the deciding playoff game was like. Of course, I want to know what it was like the instant that Thompson swung and the ball headed for the left field bleachers at the Polo Grounds with the pennant on the line for both teams. And I want to know what it was like in the streets of New York when the game ended. The despair of Dodgers fans and players and the joy of the Giants and their followers. I want to know if Brooklyn fans even bothered to follow the World Series or just went into mourning.

I wish that I could have been there the night that Wilt Chamberlain scored 100 points in a game for the Philadelphia Warriors. Was it one of those nights when Wilt was just unstoppable or were the New York Knicks just a bad team. How many fans were in the arena that night? What was the buzz as Wilt got closer to the 100 point mark? Where was the Knicks defense? Did the game become a fiasco at the end, more about Wilt getting his 100 than the teams trying to make the game competitive?

I wish that I could have been at the 1967 NFL championship game between the Dallas Cowboys and Green Bay Packers known famously as the "Ice Bowl." Call me crazy, because I hate the cold, but I want to know how cold it really was at Green Bay's Lambeau Field. I want to know the Cowboys reaction when they woke up that morning and saw the temperature at minus fifteen degrees. I want to know if the Packers really felt as if they could handle the cold or were they just as worried as the Cowboys. I want to know what was the story behind Packer head coach Vince Lombardi's field heating system not working. I want to know why any fan would bother to go out in the freezing cold and sit in those stands for two and a half hours, local TV blackout or not. I want to know how much thought was really put into postponing the game. I want to know what the feeling was among Packer fans in the stands when their team trailing by three points with five minutes to go in the game got the ball back for the last time. Were they optimistic or did they think that it was the end for their team? I want to know why the referees did not call Packer guard Jerry Kramer for jumping the gun on the play in which he and center Ken Bowman's blocks opened the whole for quarterback Bart Starr to score the winning touchdown. I think that they were too cold. And I want to know how many people got frostbite and how long did it take for everyone to thaw out.

I wish that I could have been there for the trial of major league outfielder Curt Flood when he took baseball to court over the standard player's contract in 1970. What prompted Flood to challenge the system after being traded from the St. Louis Cardinals to the Philadelphia Phillies in 1969? How many players agreed or disagreed with Flood, but were afraid to say so? What was said behind closed doors by the Commissioner and the owners? What members of the press sided with Flood and which ones thought that he was wrong? What was the fans reaction? Did most of them feel as though Flood should just shut up and play the game? Was Flood blackballed from baseball after the trial? How did the pressure effect him during the trial and after? And after losing his case did Flood still think that it was worth it and would he have done it all again?

I would have liked to have been there when heavyweight champion Muhammad Ali refused to step forward and be inducted into the United States Military on April 28, 1967. I want to know what the reaction of the rank and file was when Ali, who said that he would not step forward, did not move. I want to know what the other young men who were there, black and white, felt about Ali's stand. I want to know who resented it and who thought that it was heroic. I want to know what the soldiers already in Vietnam thought of Ali's stance? I want to know how the American and national press treated Ali and the story. I want to know how African-Americans, especially those who were veterans of foreign wars, felt about it. Did they feel as though Ali was right or selfish? I want to know how much the Nation of Islam had to do with Ali's decision. I want to know if Ali would have gone to jail if he had lost his appeal.

I wish that I could have been there when Jackie Robinson signed a contract with the Brooklyn Dodgers becoming the first African-American in the twentieth century to join a major league baseball team. I want to know why Dodger General Manager Branch Rickey picked Robinson over Negro League stars Josh Gibson and Satchel Paige. I want to know what Rickey's motivations were for signing Robinson. I want to know how the owners and players of Negro League teams felt about the signing. I, also, want to know what their white Major League counterparts thought. Was there anyone in Major League baseball besides Cleveland Indians owner Bill Veeck who was happy with Rickey's signing of Robinson? Was Robinson really told by Rickey to turn the other cheek until he established himself as a great player? What did former Major Leaguers think of Robinson's signing and Negro League players in general? Did the Ku Klux Klan send any threatening letters to Robinson, his family, Rickey, the Dodger organization or any of the Brooklyn players? Who were the members of the St. Louis Cardinals that signed a petition saying that they wouldn't take the field if Robinson played? Who were the members of the Dodgers that didn't want to play with Robinson? What did the press think Robinson's chances of making it were? How long did it take for Robinson to win over the fans of Brooklyn and his teammates? And how much changed socially the moment that Robinson took the field on April 15, 1947?

MOMENTS THAT I WOULD HAVE
LIKE TO BEEN A PART OF

Just as there are moments that I would have liked to have witnessed there are those I'd like to have been a part of or performed myself. Unlike the moments that I wish that I could have witnessed, these include events that happened before and during my lifetime. And here they are.

I wish that I could have been a part of the 1955 World Series champion Brooklyn Dodgers. The team that finally brought Brooklyn a world's championship and put to rest the saying, "Wait 'til next year." The team that finally defeated the New York Yankees in the World Series after losing to them in 1941, '47, '49, '52 and '53. Can you imagine what it must have felt like for the players, coaches and front office of the Dodgers to finally win it all? To finally be able to tell the long suffering fans of Brooklyn that they were better than the Yankees? To experience the 2-0 game seven victory at Yankee Stadium? Then to be a part of the celebration that lasted well into the next morning. The main reason that I wished I were a part of that team is because with the Dodgers moving to Los Angeles three years later this would be the only Brooklyn team in history to ever win a championship. I, like the men who actually did it, would be part of something unique in all of sports.

Just like the undefeated 1972 NFL champion Miami Dolphins. The 17-0 Miami Dolphins of head coach Don Shula. The team whose players meet for a champagne toast every year after the last undefeated team loses. Some people don't like it when they do, but I hope that they get to toast until the last player passes away. Now I know that the Dolphins are not the only undefeated untied team in pro football history. I know that the 1948 Cleveland Browns went 15-0 in the All American Football

Conference. But the Dolphins are the team that I saw when I was five years old and they left an impression that has lasted to this day. In order to fully appreciate this accomplishment I would have had to be a member of the 1971 Dolphins who lost Super Bowl VI to the Dallas Cowboys 24-3. Then I would know better how every member of the team approached the season. When did going undefeated become a goal, during the regular season or post season when they had to win? Was there ever any pressure or did the team stay on an even keel for the entire season. Was there ever a game where the team felt that they would lose? How did the players react when their quarterback Bob Griese was injured in the fifth game of the season? What was it like during Super Bowl week with everyone asking about the undefeated season? How did Shula handle Super Bowl week and the moments leading up to the game? And what was the feeling when the game was won and the undefeated season complete? Was there more joy in winning the Super Bowl or going undefeated?

I would like to have been a part of the Texas Western basketball team which defeated the Kentucky Wildcats of Adolph Rupp in the 1966 NCAA basketball tournament. This was the first team to start five African-Americans in an NCAA championship game. I want to know if Texas Western head coach Clem Haskins gave any thought to what he was doing and the social ramifications of it. I want to know what the buzz was like at the University of Maryland's Cole Field House, site of the game, when Texas Western's starting five was introduced, especially the Kentucky fans. I want to know what it felt like to be part of a championship game in which your team has more to play for than just a university. And I want to know what it felt like to silence a crowd of Kentucky fans, who thought my people and I to be inferior to them, at the game they loved the most. I don't think that I would have gloated, but I would have been very happy.

I would have liked to have been the jockey who rode Secretariat to the Triple Crown in 1973. Just to see what it was like to ride a horse so dominant. Just to see how Secretariat handled himself on and off the track. Was the horse as confident as it was good? Did Secretariat understand what was going on and revel in the attention? How much work was required once the race started or did Secretariat pretty much know what he was doing? And what must it have felt like to look behind you at the Belmont Stakes and see the field nowhere near you? If it were me riding that horse in the picture it would be hanging on every wall in my house.

I would have liked to have been a part of the Negro National Baseball League and play in the East-West All Star game in Chicago. Sure I would have had to put up with segregation and racial prejudice, but it's not like I haven't had to deal with it in my own life. I would have loved to play with and against the Satchel Paiges, Josh Gibsons, Judy Johnsons, Monte Irvins and Cool Papa Bells of the world. I would have loved to hang out in the clubs with the African-American celebrities of the time. I would have loved to play in front of them and other African-Americans. And I would have loved to have played in some of the all star games against white major leaguers. This was a group of men who did something significant and, for a time, baseball was one of the biggest industries for African-Americans in the United States. Through necessity, they did something unique and will always hold a special place in the landscape of sports history.

I would have liked to have played for Grambling University football coach Eddie Robinson or Florida A@M coach Jake Gaither when Historically Black College Football was at its peak in the 1950's and sixties. Or any other HBCU at that time. It would have been an experience. Playing in programs with little or no money, not so great facilities and shabby equipment. Playing in relative obscurity to everyone who did not read Ebony or Jet magazine or the local black newspapers. Knowing that you and many of your teammates and opponents were every bit as good as anyone who went to Notre Dame, Nebraska, Texas or Alabama and just wanting the chance to prove it. If you don't believe me just look at the rosters of the top college football teams today. Playing in the Orange Blossom Classic in Miami or the Bayou Classic in Louisiana. Homecoming week and the bands playing at halftime. Just like the men who played in the Negro Leagues, these coaches and players did something out of necessity and made it work. No excuses, no explanations.

I'm not a soccer man, but wish that I could be a part of one team to win a World's Cup championship. To represent your country in the world's most popular sport can be many things from exhilarating to stressful. To do it on the sport's greatest stage has to be close to the ultimate experience. Then to win it all and become immortal in the history of the game, your country and the world? How do you top that? The only thing that I can think of in professional sports may have been being heavyweight boxing champion of the world when the sport was at its peak. If you score a goal you will be remembered forever. If you score the winning goal, as Deigo Maradona did for Argentina in 1986, you become a God. What athlete doesn't want to become a God whether they admit it or not?

If there was one athlete that I could have been for one game it would be Chicago Bears halfback Gale Sayers on December 12, 1965 when he scored six touchdowns against the San Francisco 49ers. Sayers was a rookie that season and went on to score a then league record 22 touchdowns. Can you imagine coming into the pros as a 22 year old and dominating the way he did? Then to score six touchdowns in one game on a muddy field no less has to make a player feel almost invincible. I mean there are many of us who know guys who have scored a bunch of touchdowns in youth league, high school or college games. How many of us know guys who have done it in the pros? Not many I can tell you that, because they can be counted on one hand. Can you imagine playing in a game in which you score touchdowns rushing, receiving and running back kicks? Then to have three of those scores come from more than fifty yards out? How about the fact that you could have scored more than that if you hadn't been benched in the fourth quarter, because your team was on its way to a 61-20 victory. I don't know. I may have been tempted to ask back in for a chance to break the record. But back in 1965 records in sports other than baseball really weren't that important. Like Sayers, I probably wouldn't have worried about it too much as being a rookie the thought would have been that there would be other games on other days.

I would not have had to be New York Jets quarterback Joe Namath on January 12, 1969 when he led his team to victory over the Baltimore Colts in Super Bowl III, but I would have liked to have been a player on that team. To go into the biggest game of the year as 18 point underdogs representing a league, the American Football League, which was only in its ninth year of existence, which had lost the first two Super Bowls by a combined score of 68-24 and win had to be an unbelievable feeling. This was one of the few cases in sports history where a team could truthfully say no one expected them to win. What was it like in the days leading up to the game? Were you confident going in? When did you feel as though you were in control of the game? What was it like as the clock ticked down to zero and you knew that you were going to win? How did it feel leaving the field and in the locker room after the game? And how much pride did you feel in representing an entire league and winning not only for you and your team, but for them as well?

I wish that I could have been Chicago Cubs pitcher Charlie Root in the 1932 World Series when New York Yankee outfielder Babe Ruth supposedly called his home run shot on me. Because if Ruth truly did point to the center field fence and say that was where he was going to hit the next pitch I would have drilled his fat butt in the ear.

I would love to have been a part of the world champion Oakland Athletics of 1972-'74. The "Swinging A's" they were called and I can't remember a more fun team to watch. Sure they were the team to usher in the ugly baseball uniforms of the 1970's and eighties, but they didn't have to look good to play good. To be a part of the only team other than the Yankee dynasty to win three straight World Series must have been something. Even if it meant putting up with team owner Charles O. Finley.

Another team of that era I would have liked to have been a part of was the 1974 Super Bowl champion Pittsburgh Steelers, the first of their six world's champions. After 42 years of losing, the Steelers finally won it all after a season which saw them draft four future hall of famers, endure a pre season players strike, go through three starting quarterbacks which included the rarity at that time of having one of them be African-American and being considered the third best team in the conference. The real reason why I would have liked to be a part of it would have been just being there when team owner Art Rooney, Sr. was given the Super Bowl game ball by linebacker Andy Russell and the Vince Lombardi Trophy by Commissioner Pete Rozelle. That moment alone would have made it all worth it.

And finally, the one moment that I would have liked to have been a part of was the Kansas City Chiefs ten year history in the AFL. I would have liked to have been a member of the Chiefs from their and the AFL's inception in 1960 as the Dallas Texans all of the way to the Super Bowl IV win against the Minnesota Vikings on January 11, 1970. To be a part of a team and league which was given no chance to succeed then be the last team to represent the league in a championship game would have been accomplishment enough. To be a part of the first team created for the AFL and play for the man, Chiefs owner Lamar Hunt, who came up with the idea to start the league and see it all of the way through is a script that no one could write. It must have been a great feeling for the Chiefs to beat the Vikings and give Hunt a Super Bowl victory which tied the series between AFL and NFL at two games each. It must have been great to avenge the Super Bowl I loss to the Green Bay Packers in which Packer head Coach Vince Lombardi stated that the Chiefs and their AFL brothers were not as good as their counterparts in the NFL. Above all, it had to be the sweetest feeing that any owner in any professional sport can have for Hunt. He had not only won the world's championship of professional football, but he had taken a league which was his baby from the beginning all of the way to equality with the more established NFL in ten years. I can't imagine any owner feeling more exhilaration than Hunt did on January 11, 1970.

PRO BASKETBALL AND FOOTBALL
NEED MINOR LEAGUES

For the most part, professional basketball and football get it right. They are usually ahead of the curve in making adjustments to their sports on and off of the field. If the fans want more scoring, they change rules to allow it. If the fans want players tested for drugs, they do it. It was the National Football League which invented the common player draft of college talent in 1936 which the NBA implemented in 1957, ten years after its birth.

But the one thing that professional hockey and baseball does that both basketball and football should do is have minor leagues where the players that are drafted begin their careers. In baseball and hockey players are eligible for the draft when they are in their late teens, which is the same age as the young men who go to college to play basketball and football. Once drafted, these young men sign contracts with their teams and head to whatever level of the minors the organization feels that they are ready for. They don't have to worry about going to class or breaking NCAA rules as they would if they had gone to college. And they are paid to play from day one with no repercussions as there are if a college athlete takes money, as they should.

Of course, pro basketball and football will never go to a minor league system as long as there are big time college programs in each. Why would anyone in their right mind pay for players to develop when they can get the colleges to do it for free and who can blame them? Do law firms have agencies where they teach up and coming lawyers and pay them while they learn? How about the medical field, do they pay their interns when they come in to work for them? Scientists don't say, "We will send you to this school of science, teach you and pay you along the way," do they? So why would pro football and basketball do the same? The system in place now is perfect for them just as it is for the colleges who make a ton of money off of the players and give them only a scholarship. Scholarships are nice, but they don't pay any bills that may arise while an athlete is in school.

I like college basketball and football, though basketball not as much as I used to. But I get tired of all of the NCAA rules and the way that they are enforced. A lot of the problems which come about in college sports are for three reasons.

First the student-athlete who is given a scholarship is not up to speed academically for the school they have chosen. This leads to athletes being steered towards certain classes and academic workloads which don't benefit them, but the team for it keeps them eligible to play. Many of them never graduate.

Second, the student-athlete basketball and football player feels more of a sense of entitlement which leads to off the field problems. Though I don't feel as though athletes cause any more trouble on campus than other students, their problems are just more public, I do think that they feel untouchable when it comes to being disciplined by their schools. This makes it more likely that a few of them will get into some kind of trouble whether it's under aged drinking, fighting or just plain poor public behavior.

Third, many of the student-athletes who attend colleges and universities come from families with little or no money and can't support themselves because of the hours that they have to devote to their sport and the classroom. This leads to players getting paid money and given gifts by boosters and sports agents who want them as clients. Heck, even the coach can't help a player in need if he's on his death bed.

All of these problems would decrease if there were a minor league for basketball and football, because the ones who aren't college qualified or don't want to go can now go pro and get on with their careers. I don't really know if this is true, but I have heard of many scandals in college basketball and football. I have heard of very few in baseball and hockey. Would the fact that many of the young men who aren't qualified for college or don't want to go opted for the minor leagues instead? I don't have the answer to that, but it doesn't seem like a stretch.

What I am trying to say is that a young man who plays basketball or football should have the same opportunity to choose whether he wants to be an amateur or pro right out of high school, just like they do in baseball and hockey. And the NFL and NBA should give them that option. I am not against a young man getting an athletic scholarship and going to school. I am all for education. I just think that the option of a minor league or school should be out there.

If a young man decides to go pro, just as in all other sports, he loses his college eligibility. So a player couldn't go to the pros for two years, find out that he doesn't like it and enroll in a school to play football in the fall.

And if a young man decides to go to college than he has to play by the rules of the NCAA. He has to go to class and keep a certain grade point average to stay eligible. He has to abide by the rules of the campus. And he and his family cannot take any money or gifts of any kind. Just like the rules are now. They would be easier to enforce and people would be more inclined to agree with the punishment if the student-athlete had the option of a minor league and chose school otherwise. I would also make the student-athlete stay on campus for at least three years after his graduation class just as the NFL does today. If you opt for school then you must stay in school.

So how do you go about making a minor league in baseball and football? You use the same blue print as baseball and hockey. Draft the best high school and college athletes who have reached their seventeenth birthday and assign them to a team. Then when you feel that they are advancing move them up until they reach the big time.

Of course, I doubt if this will ever happen. One, the pros don't want the cost of starting it up and running it. Second they don't want to bight the hands of the colleges who have fed them talent for years. Third, they won't be able to promote the athletes that they draft, because most would have played in relative obscurity.

To the first reason, I would say that the leagues could afford to do it, because they are multi- billion dollar industries. And they have tried to do it before. The NBA does have their Development League of minor leaguers, while the NFL had their version in the World League of American Football which folded in 2005.

The reason that the D League has not gained in popularity is that they have not been able to get the best young talent away from the colleges. The colleges play their games on national television and are covered by the national media. The D League has no major television contract and is no more than a blip on the radar screen when it comes to coverage. If the NBA would draft players out of high school and send them to the D League, than the latter would immediately become more relevant. This would give them a better chance of getting a national television contract. And once the TV money starts coming in the chances of sustaining any league become greater.

The NFL's World League of American Football (1991-2007) was good for the game because it helped teams to develop players that they would have otherwise have to release. The problem with it was that it was played overseas during the spring. Not playing in America and playing during basketball and early baseball season made it tough for the league to gain the popularity that it sought. Just as we Americans will never really embrace soccer, the Europeans will never really embrace our version of football.

If the NFL were to bring back a minor league they would have to do it in the fall. The only thing that they would have to do differently than basketball is have the class system that baseball has. You can't put young men straight out of high school on the same field as grown men that have used up their college eligibility. Their bodies aren't developed enough to take the punishment. So there would have to be college and pro age levels in the minors. If a college age level player seems ready for the pro age than move him up. Where would you have the teams and who would own them? It seems to me that there are a lot of rich people who wouldn't mind owning a pro sports team. And many of them are friends of NFL owners. Go and find them.

Of course, these leagues would be going after the same talent as the colleges who wouldn't like that at all. The basketball and football teams at many colleges and universities are their biggest revenue sports. They provide money not only for themselves, but to fund other sports on campus. If the pros took away their best players and their TV revenue than where would they be? I don't know where they would be, but I do know what they would be. The Ivy League, where football was deemphasized years ago.

The working relationship between the pros and colleges would probably not be as good if there were a minor league, because they would be in competition for the best players. Maybe college recruiting would ratchet upwards in order to keep the young men from going pro immediately. Maybe the pros would have to pay signing bonuses that they don't want to get the best players to skip school and turn pro. One thing for sure is that the colleges would not be as friendly when it came to pro scouts coming to watch their players as they are now.

To the last reason, promoting the players, I would say that having a minor league hasn't hurt baseball or hockey. In fact I think that it would help basketball and football, because fans would have an interest in their team's minor league prospects just as they do in baseball and hockey. The same way that people followed the careers of future hall of fame baseball players while they were in the minors they would follow their future quarterbacks, linebackers and running backs. It would be one more thing for sports talk radio to touch on.

"Let's go to Rick in Hoboken. Rick, you're on the air."

"Hey, Larry. I just want to say that the Giants might be bad now, but next year they're going to bring up Buckethead Jones to play left tackle and that will improve the offensive line immediately. Jones is better than the guy they've got there right now, Sam Sackgiver, and the team needs to bring him up in minicamp so that he can have a chance to win the starting job."

Or something along those lines. If you think that's farfetched, than you haven't been watching the NBA or NFL draft or followed the quest for free agents in each league the last few years.

The idea of minor leagues has been thrown around and tried for years with little success. I think that's by choice of the NBA and NFL and as I've said earlier who can blame them? However, that doesn't mean that it cannot work. The hardest part would be breaking the stranglehold of popularity that the colleges have. Getting the talent wouldn't be a problem. Neither would a television contract, because TV will show anything.

The only thing holding pro basketball and football back from forming minor leagues is the cost of getting started which neither wants to pay. So instead of getting the best of both worlds with young men who want to turn pro being allowed to do so and the NCAA being able to truly say that their sport is amateur, we get college athletes getting paid, recruiting violations, athletes not going to class and not graduating and the big business of Division-I sports.

Somehow, I think that giving these young men a choice as baseball and hockey does, would eliminate some of these problems.

OFFICIALS ARE HUMAN TOO

I think that everyone involved in sports should have to officiate at least once in their lives. I mean everyone from team owners, to management, to players, to fans, to media. And not just one game, but an entire season. They should have to start the year in the youth league, then go to high school, a local college and a local semi pro or adult league. And they would have to do it with no formal training. No classes, no rule book and no scrimmages. Just put them on the field or court and say, "It's your game, now run it."

I am willing to bet that every person who did this would gain a greater appreciation for what officials and umpires go through and how tough the job can be. Most people aren't cut out to be game officials. It's a thankless job where you have to take a lot of crap from a lot of people. The only time that anyone ever notices you is when you make a call that goes against their team. Most people can't handle the criticism that goes with it. I would bet that if everyone in sports was to try officiating from youth league to semi pro, ninety percent of them would quit before they got through youth league.

So why is it that we are so quick to criticize officials? Why is it that men who get the call right ninety-nine out of a hundred times at the highest levels of college and pro sports are always thought of as a necessary evil more than the men who enforce the rules so that both teams have a fair chance of winning? Why is it that when they do miss that one out of a hundred, everyone thinks that it is inexcusable? Why are officials not allowed to make mistakes while players and coaches are? Officials are human too and no human is infallible.

If this is spoken like a man who has done some officiating in his life, than that's because it is. I have been a high school football official for going on six years now and have some knowledge of the process that the men who have made it to the NFL have to go through. In fact, a couple of men from the organization that I officiate for are in the NFL and we have guys at the college level as well. Not all of us are great officials, but we hold ourselves accountable and are always looking for ways to improve.

I absolutely enjoy what I do. Football is my favorite sport, but I would umpire baseball if there were more teams around where I live and I had more time. Basketball is also an option, but around here I've seen too many officials have to be escorted out of gymnasiums after games. At least in football we are outside and can get away from the fans where in basketball there is no way out. I know this, because I've been in a game or two where we've had to get a police escort off of the field after the home team lost.

Before I became an official, I was just like every other fan. Quick to get on them when they made a call that I didn't like or when they missed one that seemed obvious to everyone but them. I tell everyone that the reason I am no longer a big college basketball fan is because of the poor job of officiating that I believe helped the Duke Blue Devils defeat the Maryland Terrapins in the 2001 NCAA Final Four. And even now, I find myself questioning an official's call with the only difference being that it doesn't matter if it's for or against the team I'm rooting for.

But I've always felt that officials are human just like everyone else involved in sports. I have never been an advocate of instant replay. It doesn't bother me that they use it in football and basketball, but I liked it better when the human eye was the judge. My problem with instant replay is that it has created too many gray areas in the rulebook. Is it a catch or isn't it? Did the quarterback fumble or was it the tuck rule? Did the ball break the plane of the goal line or didn't it? How much time was on the clock when that last shot was taken? Do we need to put more time on the clock after a timeout was called?

If people could officiate for one year in the sport of their choice they would gain a greater appreciation for what goes into it. Every official and umpire that you see on television has had to pay their dues to get where they are. Most of them start out in youth leagues where the players are smaller than the balls that they play with and the equipment they wear. Then they move up to the high school level where they begin with the freshman and junior varsity before moving up to varsity. The good ones get a shot at college, but not until they prove themselves in high school and attend various officiating clinics. Most start out at small Division II and III leagues before moving up to the D-I level. The best get a shot at the pros if they want, though many are satisfied with doing college. At every level, there are classes that have to be taken, rules that have to be learned and game mechanics that have to be perfected.

Most people think that they know the rules to their sport, but they don't. That includes players and coaches. In high school, almost every state in the country has annual pre season meetings where the coaches are invited to discuss the new rules and go over any of the old ones, but many of them don't attend. Each of the coaches are given rule books, but many never read them until after they think an official has blown a call. And the players are too busy concentrating on their jobs to know any of the rules. That doesn't mean officials can get away with things on the field. If anything it means that officials have to know more, because more than likely they are the only ones who DO know the rules. As it should be.

Every year, our organization has a pre season clinic in which new rules are emphasized and standards for advancing in the ranks are set. We have many college officials and they have a similar pre season meeting of their own. Then the week before the season begins, we take our National Federation of High School Football Rules Test. Then the season begins and we do our thing. For varsity games, we try to get to the field an hour before in order to go over mechanics and discuss any rules before taking the field to talk to the coaches and game management. In the offseason we have meetings by position on rules and mechanics where we study film. And every month from April to July we are given a 25 question open book online test to keep us sharp. This is just for high school.

The colleges have a much busier offseason than we do. They host clinics for prospective officials where rules are discussed and officials take the field during practice sessions of local college teams. They have meetings similar to the ones we have in high school. And there is a lot of networking. The small college officials have to get to their games three hours ahead of time. The major Division I officials have to get to their sight the night before. I haven't been exposed to the pro level, but can imagine what they have to go through to be as good as they are, because there are more rules and their game is much faster than high school and college.

So that's what we officials have to go through to make it to the top. Most of us aren't good enough to make it, but that doesn't mean we aren't good at what we do at our level. Just like a good high school player may not be a good college player. Some of us may never master the rule book others the mechanics. Some just like to work at a certain position and nowhere else. Everyone has their own standard just as in any other field.

However, just because an official knows the rulebook doesn't mean that he's good on the field. And just because he's not good on the field doesn't mean that he's not up on the rules. There are many who just don't test well, but if you ask them to explain a rule and apply it they can do it perfectly. And there are those who can get a perfect score on a test and can't apply it to game situations. Even so, most of the time the officials get it right.

Still not convinced that the job is hard? Okay, let's forget about rules and mechanics in order to focus on what happens during a game. What do officials have to put up with on the sidelines from the coaches and players? What must they look for during the course of play? What constitutes a foul and what doesn't? How do you handle a hostile crowd?

On the sideline, officials have to communicate with the head coach. They must answer any question he may have on a certain play or ruling. They have to be there if the coach wants to signal for a timeout especially at the end of each half. The official must make sure that the sideline is clear in case the play comes into that area and so that he can move freely from end to end. And he must keep an eye out for anything illegal that may go on during play or a time out. He, also, must be the voice of reason in any confrontation that may occur when a coach does not like what is happening on the field. It is up to the official to take the high road in these situations. As long as the coaches do not make it personal, the official must have a thick hide and let them vent. If it gets personal or someone tries to influence an official's call, then by rule the official can enforce a penalty.

During the course of play, the official has a designated area to cover. No matter what happens anywhere else his eye is trained on the player or players assigned to him. This is easier said than done and one of the hardest things to learn when officiating, because everyone has a tendency to follow the ball. And the job doesn't stop when the whistle blows or the call is made. Whenever there is a break in the action, officials must police their areas to make sure that nothing illegal happens. This is when words are exchanged and tempers may flair. The more that the players see or hear an official in their area the less likely they will be to do something illegal. During the dead ball period everyone must be on the same page whether it's what down it is, how many free throws are to be taken, what the count is on the batter or whatever. Officiating begins and continues nonstop from the time you take the field to the end of the game. In college and the pros it continues even after the game is over. A penalty log must be taken and given to both teams head coaches and the entire crew has to stay at least a half an hour after the game in order to be available if the coaches have any questions.

Then there is what constitutes a foul and what doesn't? Well the main thing is that a foul has to be something that can be seen on film. If it doesn't show up on film, then it should not be called. The second thing that must be considered is does the foul effect the play. A good example is everyone's favorite football penalty that's not called offensive holding. It is said that holding occurs on every play and that may be true. But does a hold by the tight end lined up on the right side of the formation effect a sweep run to the left? In high school we say no. The only time that a penalty like holding on a running play should be called is if it happens at the point of attack, because the defender is being restricted from making an attempt at a tackle.

The thing is that you don't let the players play, but you call the fouls that have a direct bearing on the play itself. The only time that you would call something away from the play is if it's a personal foul or there are safety issues involved. At least at the youth and high school levels. In college and the pros, you have to call just about everything, because these are the most skilled of players and they must play by the rules.

Now that you know the rules, how to enforce them, how to handle players and coaches and what to look for during the course of play we get to the one thing that drives most people away from officiating. That would be the people who watch the game. How do you handle a hostile crowd?

Well, the easiest way to handle a hostile crowd is to not pay attention to them. Let them yell whatever they want. Let them disagree with whatever call you make. As long as they aren't a physical threat to you or the people on the field, let them vent as much as they want. The only thing that acknowledging the crowd does for an official is distract him from what's going on in the game. No matter what call an official makes not everyone is going to agree with it. That's just the way it is.

All of the things that I mentioned are easier to do the more organization and professionalism involved in the sport. At the youth levels, the fans are usually on the sideline right next to the playing area and within earshot of the official. There is no way to avoid hearing them. At times, unfortunately, there is no way to avoid face to face confrontation. In high school, the fans must sit in the bleachers so it is the coaches and players that an official must deal with. And the colleges and pros have the luxury of performing in stadiums and arenas with security guards in case anything gets out of hand.

The one thing that gets fans riled is when they think that officials are one-sided in their calls. That is, they think that one team is getting more fouls called against them than another. Or that a call is made by an official, because he favors one team over the other. I am here to tell you that in all of the games I have officiated never have I been on a crew which sided with one team or another. As far as we are concerned there is team A and team B. Sure, we know what games involve good teams and bad. We know when a game is considered to be big. However, most of the officials that I have worked with don't really care who the teams are. All we want is a good, clean game whether it's for the championship or last place.

And when the game is over it's over. We don't care who won or who lost. I have officiated with men who have forgotten what game they had the very last week. It's not that the game didn't mean anything to them when they were officiating it it's just that they have moved on to the next assignment as a good official should.

But rowdy fans are not the only threat to officials. Angry players and coaches pose even more of a threat than the fans, because they are close enough to harm them verbally and physically. Just as with the fan security, the more organized and professional a league is, the less chance there is for verbal and physical abuse. In the youth leagues, coaches are just as likely to get into it with an official as the fans are. Many coaches will be egged on by their fans and some coaches encourage it. High school can have its problems also. And even the pros and colleges make a mistake every now and then by bumping an official or arguing a call until they are tossed from the game. Every official has felt the wrath of players, coaches and fans at one time or another even the best.

I've found that the worst when it comes to dealing with officials are men in amateur adult leagues. Most of them are good men and show respect, but there are always a few players and teams that feel they never lose it's always the officials fault. And they aren't afraid to say it. Instead of playing the game, they complain over every call which goes against them. In the flag football league where I officiate it is nothing to be threatened with bodily harm by the players and coaches when things aren't going their way.

And these guys are dead serious. I've seen them fight each other enough to know this. To them, every game is life or death and they really think that the officials care who wins or loses. There is no room for error. I don't know how many times I've been called every name in the book and physically threatened. Because of this, when our teams go to national tournaments everyone looks at them with a wary eye. We have gained a bad reputation, well earned I might add, because of the actions of a few teams. I don't know how many times players, fans and officials from other areas have come up to me and asked what is wrong with our teams. They are appalled by their conduct and always say that where they come from those teams would be kicked out of the league. I guarantee you, that I could cure every person who thinks that an official's job is easy after one day of dealing with these guys.

Having said that, I and the officials that I have worked with love what we do. We like being a part of the game, though we try not to be too much a part of it. We enjoy the relationships formed between ourselves and the people we work for. We do enjoy it when the games are close and come down to the wire. We do enjoy watching great athletes do their thing. All of this trumps whatever trouble we may have with players, coaches and fans or we wouldn't do it.

So remember that the next time you watch a game and vent your frustrations on the officials. We do it because we love it. No other reason. And we are human and do make mistakes though most of the time we get it right. If people can accept mistakes made by players and coaches, then they should be able to accept them from officials as well.

Don't knock it 'til you try it.

THROUGH THE EYES OF A CHILD

My 15 year old great nephew is a big fan of the Green Bay Packers and his favorite player quarterback Brett Favre. He had the number four Favre jersey and the cheese head. For Christmas one year, I bought him the "Favre4ever" biography which included a DVD chronicling his life. After he watched it, he couldn't wait to tell me about it.

When Favre retired from the Packers, my nephew was disappointed. He couldn't understand why Favre would retire after having one of his best years in 2007. It was a year in which Favre took the Packers all of the way to the NFC championship game, one victory short of playing in the Super Bowl. Though it is pretty well known that the Packers were ready to move on without Favre as far as my nephew was considered number four could quarterback the team forever.

Then the unthinkable happened. At least as far as my nephew was concerned. Favre signed to play for another team, the New York Jets.

The first time that I saw my nephew after Favre signed I looked at him and said, "So I see your boy signed with the Jets. Are you gonna root for him or the Packers?"

My nephew looked away and mumbled, "I don't want to talk about it."

I said, "What."

And he mumbled again, "I don't want to talk about it."

At first, I was going to rub salt in the wound by teasing him. Then I looked at him and saw that he was truly heartbroken by the fact his favorite Packer and player was going to play again with another team.

I immediately thought of how I would have felt if say Terry Bradshaw had retired from the Steelers then signed on to play with the Minnesota Vikings. So I backed off.

What I was reminded of by my nephew is that children look at sports through different eyes than adults. They are not as jaded as adults and see the games as a fun pastime and players as larger than life figures that can do no wrong. When things don't happen the way that a child feels they should there is a feeling of betrayal and it is devastating.

When I was growing up sports were king in our neighborhood. We played and watched everything under the sun when it was in season. We collected bubble gum cards and put posters on the wall of our favorite teams and players. When playing in the backyard there was always someone that you emulated. In baseball, I was Henry Aaron of the Atlanta Braves and in football, Lynn Swann of the Steelers. In basketball, I wanted to be Ervin "Magic" Johnson of the Los Angeles Lakers, but played more like Dennis Johnson of the Seattle Supersonics. And in hockey when I was really little, I was Bobby Orr.

In organized sports everyone wanted a certain number and when they got it were immediately linked to a pro who wore it in that sport. I always wanted number 12 in football, because it was the number that all of the best quarterbacks seemed to wear. I started out with three in baseball, but lost it to someone else and switched to number six which was what Los Angeles Dodger first baseman Steve Garvey wore. When I was 12, I got number 32 for football even though I didn't want it. Everyone in the room immediately started calling me Juice the nickname for the Buffalo Bills O.J. Simpson. The other halfback on our team got number 34 which was what Walter Payton of the Chicago Bears wore. He was thrilled.

The next year I got number 31 which was even worse, because no one wore that number. My running mate got number 20. He was not thrilled. This was the year that the Detroit Lions drafted halfback Billy Simms who wore number 20. Everyone in the room started calling my teammate Billy Simms. I'll never forget what he said, "Bleep, Billy Simms. I want Walter Payton." This from a fourteen year old kid. He didn't get number 34.

But that's how we thought. We definitely thought that we played better in certain numbers than in others. My best friend always had to have number 14 in football. He had it every year in youth ball until the last when he was given 45. He was crushed and had his worst season. He injured his leg early in the year and was never right. And the truth of the matter was he just didn't look right in number 45, the same way that Michael Jordan didn't when he wore it for the Chicago Bulls. I wore 14 the first year that we played high school together on junior varsity, but gladly gave it back to him the next year and took my number 12 on varsity.

No one wanted the number of a nobody. Like my number 31. The only person that I could think who wore it was former Green Bay hall of famer Jimmy Taylor, but none of my teammates knew who he was. Donny Shell wore it for the Steelers, but he was a defensive back not a running back so it didn't count.

Pro sports merchandise wasn't very popular then so it was very rare you would see someone wearing the jersey of their favorite team or player. At most, you would have a baseball cap for the summer and a wooly hat for the winter. Most of the clothing was tee shirts, jackets or coats with a team's logo on them. We wore all of these things with pride and if you had something with your team's logo everyone thought it was so cool.

When there was a big game on we all watched and if our team lost it was never because they weren't good enough. It was almost always, because the other team cheated. How could the Steelers lose to the Raiders? No way. The Raiders cheated. That field goal was no good, but the refs said it was. The Cowboys beat the Redskins by thirty, because they cheated. They fumbled twice and the refs said they didn't. The Celtics beat the Bullets, because they were getting all of the calls. The Orioles lost to the Yankees, because the umpire called that ball fair and everyone knows it was foul. We just couldn't accept the fact that our heroes were fallible.

And God forbid they lost to one of your buddy's favorite teams or your team was the one that everyone loved to hate. That was grounds for playing hooky from school the next day. The sun almost always seemed to come up four hours early on the morning after a loss when you had to go to school. And they would be waiting for you at the bus stop, on the bus and at school. Guys would be relentless with their teasing just waiting for you to crack. Some guys would come close to crying while others would fight back and get themselves into trouble with the teacher. Recess was the worst, because that's when everyone could tease and you had to take it. It was brutal.

However, when your team won or your favorite player had a great game there was no greater joy. You couldn't wait to get to school or the playground to talk about it with your friends. "Did you see the Steelers game? Man, Franco Harris had 142 yards and scored three touchdowns. Mean Joe Greene knocked the quarterback out of the game. They're going to the Super Bowl this year." And there was never a time where we associated ourselves with our teams. It was always they not we. Win or lose. We weren't playing so how could we consider ourselves a part of the team. That was what the adults said not us. The first time that I remember saying the chant, "We're number one!" for a team was in my sophomore year of high school when our basketball team won the state semifinals at the buzzer.

No, sports were a fantasy world where we could only look, but not touch. Rarely did any of us get to go to games and no one had season tickets to anything. When we did go, we didn't want to leave. We wanted to take it all in, because there was no guarantee that we'd come back. Being in the stadium was like a dream. I never went to a football or basketball game when I was little and only one hockey game so my memories are from baseball. "Is that really Jim Palmer out there shagging flies during batting practice?" "Hey, there's Earl Weaver taking out the lineup card." "Wow, these guys are huge!" "I just got an autograph from Julio Cruz!" "These guys really are real. They talk and everything." To us it was the greatest thing in the world.

Our parents would try to take us on the days when teams had promotions like "Bat Day" or "Hat Day" or "Glove Day". The items usually weren't of the best quality, but you couldn't wait to get home and show them to your friends. It meant that you had really been to the game, not just watched it on TV. You were the envy of the neighborhood.

We listened to everything that the athletes and coaches told us and believed it. If Redskins head coach George Allen said "Don't smoke," we didn't. If boxer Sugar Ray Leonard told us to drink Seven Up, we did. If the Raiders said that they were going to get Lynn Swann on Sunday we knew that they would. Just as kids in the next generation wanted to be like Michael Jordan, we wanted to be like O.J. Simpson, Reggie Jackson, Joe Namath and Julius Erving. The press could not sway us. They could say anything bad about our heroes and we weren't buying it. They were all good guys to us.

Actually meeting an athlete was a dream, come true for us. It didn't matter if it was the third string tackle on the Baltimore Colts, if he was a player we were in awe of him. He was living the dream that many of us would have liked to, but never would. Their autograph may not have been worth much to a collector, but to us it was pure gold. And we followed and rooted for that player the rest of his career whether he stayed with our team or not.

I remembered all of this when I talked to my nephew that day. So I completely understood how he felt and where he was coming from. As adults, we should think about this whenever we talk to our kids about sports. They are still wide-eyed and in awe of the events and men involved unlike those of us who have grown jaded over the years from player's strikes, to franchise moves, to free agency, to college scandals, to the oversaturation of sports on TV. To them sports is still the last bastion of fair play and hero worship. We need to remember this when we see them at sporting events or wearing their favorite team and players apparel and not get on them as we would an adult. And we should remember to conduct ourselves properly when watching sports around our kids whether at the game or watching it on TV.

And the people involved in sports need to remember this, also. Though sport is a multibillion dollar industry those involved still owe something to the young people who watch for they are the fans and participants of the future. No matter what an athlete's attitude is towards the fans and media, they should never take it out on the kids. If they can't sign an autograph at least acknowledge the young person's presence. If the youngster waves and calls his name, at least wave back. Go to the schools, the hospitals, the churches and the parks where the young people are and talk to them about the game and life. Remember that what they say and do is emulated by many young people so carry themselves like professionals. Remember how much of an inspiration you are to the youth. Remember that you were once a kid yourself.

The owners need to think of this when they raise ticket prices so high that the middle class and poor can't bring their families to the games. They should think about how they are depriving young people of an opportunity to see that the athletes they watch on TV and read about in the press really do exist. They should think about this when they schedule games for nine o'clock on a weeknight when most kids go to bed no later than ten. Even if a kid is allowed to stay up late to watch or go to a game most of them will be too tired by the end or suffer from lack of sleep which effects them in the classroom. They should think of this when they promote their events by speaking to the kids as well as the adults, because maybe the youngster's parents are not sports fans and need to be persuaded by them to go to a game. Like the players, remember that you were once a kid yourself.

It goes without saying that today's youth sports fan is tomorrow's season ticket holder. In time, they will grow up to become just as jaded as the adults whom they watch games with. Until that day, let them enjoy sports as they see them not as we do.

NUMBED BY THE NUMBERS

I am not big on statistics. I used to be. To this day, I can tell you exactly how many yards Cleveland Browns fullback Jim Brown gained in his career, 12,312. I have no idea how many the reigning all-time rushing leader, Emmitt Smith, has. I can tell you that Buffalo Bills halfback O.J. Simpson ran for 2,003 yards in 1973. I think Eric Dickerson broke his record with 2,105 with the Los Angeles Rams in 1984, but am not sure. I have no idea how many touchdown passes Miami Dolphins quarterback Dan Marino threw for or yards, but I know that John Unitas threw touchdown passes in 47 consecutive games with the Baltimore Colts. You would have to tell me how many strikeouts hall of fame pitcher Nolan Ryan has. I am a Barry Bonds fan and have no idea how many home runs he hit, but know that Henry Aaron hit 755, Babe Ruth 714 and Willie Mays 660. I know that Lou Gehrig played in 2,130 consecutive games for the New York Yankees, but have no idea how many Baltimore Orioles shortstop and new Ironman of baseball Cal Ripken finished with. Nor do I know how many points Kareem Abdul-Jabbar scored during his NBA career or Wayne Gretzky in the NHL.

When I was growing up, we weren't bombarded with numbers and to be honest there weren't that many. The only numbers that I remember being important in baseball were the triple crown numbers for hitters, batting average, home runs and runs batted in along with stolen bases. The pitching numbers that mattered were wins and losses, earned run average, strikeouts, walks and saves. No one cared how many hits you got or your on base percentage. Doubles and triples were nice, but not really mentioned much. Defensive statistics weren't even considered. Sure they gave out the Gold Glove for the best fielder by percentage at each position, but most people just assumed that the player who made the all-star team got that.

The first change to the statistical landscape that I recall was the game winning run batted in. This was a stat which was incorporated to show how many times a player drove in a run which gave his team the lead late in a ballgame which eventually led to a win. The problem was and is when do you consider it a game winning RBI? Does a two run homer which gives your team a 2-1 lead in the bottom of the first inning of a game you win 3-1 count? No, it doesn't even though it is the game winner. The logic is that there is still a lot of baseball to be played and if the other team can't come back they lost the game, you didn't win it.

Then we got all kinds of crazy stats. Batting average with runners in scoring position. Batting average in day games and night games. Batting average on the road and at home. Batting average on turf and on grass. Batting average on the east coast and the west coast. Batting average in the last twenty, thirty or forty at bats. Batting average against left and right handed pitchers. Stolen bases against left and right handed pitchers. Grounded into a double play.

Then there are the pitchers. What is the left and right handed opponent's batting average against them? What is the percentage of runners who steal bases on them? What is their strikeout to walk ratio? How many pitches have they thrown? What is their ground ball to fly ball ratio? How many quality starts do they have (whatever that is)? How many called strikeouts do they have and how many swinging? What is their record on three days of rest compared to four?

All of this is nice for the manager of these teams to know, but not for me. All I care about is what the pitcher, hitter and base runner do in that moment. I don't want to know what the numbers say the future holds. Just let me have the moment and I'll take what they give me.

Football followed suit with baseball starting in the early eighties. I can recall having no idea who led the NFL in any statistic except rushing yards. Even if a running back gained more than 1,000 yards which was and still is the benchmark for a single season if he wasn't on my favorite team or led the league I had no idea how many yards they finished with. I was better at game statistics not season numbers. Football was always thought of as a team game and team statistics were put above all else. So most people had no idea until someone got close to a season or career record how many of anything anyone had.

I didn't know that Minnesota Viking quarterback Fran Tarkenton was anywhere near John Unitas' record of 290 career touchdown passes until he broke it. I had no idea that O.J. Simpson and Minnesota running back Chuck Foreman were close to breaking Gale Sayers' record of 22 touchdowns in a season until Simpson broke it and Foreman tied it in the last game of the 1975 season. The same game in which Tarkenton broke Unitas ' record. I had no idea that Washington Redskin wide receiver Charlie Taylor was on the verge of breaking the all-time record for passes caught set by New York Jet Don Maynard until the game he broke it in 1975. Maybe it was big news and I just didn't know it at the time.

The NFL didn't record quarterback sacks as an official statistic until 1981. So many players like hall of famers Deacon Jones, Merlin Olsen, Joe Greene, Doug Atkins, and Willie Davis never got true credit for the things that they did on the field while they did them. We didn't need the numbers to know how great they were. All that we needed to know was that when the opposing teams quarterback was on the ground most of the time one of them was in the area. The only defensive stat that was kept was interceptions. Now we have tackles, fumble recoveries, assists, passes defensed, turnovers, tackles for a loss and red zone defense (how many touchdowns or field goals a team gives up inside their own twenty yard line).

And the offense has their share, of course. Quarterbacks still get fifty yards added to their statistics when they complete a pass of five yards, but the receivers are now being credited with yards after the catch or YAC. Running backs are being credited with yards after initial contact. Barry Sanders was the first back that I remember whose carries for negative yards were recorded. We have come from behind victories for quarterbacks. Offensive linemen will never have a statistic to show their true worth so all we have are pancake blocks for them. Every rushing, passing and receiving yard is recorded now and documented extensively. Yards per passing and rushing attempt are given to us. And if anyone can explain the quarterback rating system to me I will be truly grateful.

Basketball really hasn't changed much. It's still points, assists and rebounds, known as the triple double. Blocked shots have been added to the mix and steals are more recognized. Rebounds have been broken down into offensive and defensive. Offensive rebounds lead to second chance points and defensive the fast break. Now we have points in the paint and three point shooting percentage. Heck, college basketball has quality wins and non quality whatever those are for ranking the NCAA tournament field. This is based on strength of schedule, another stat that we really can't trust.

And hockey hasn't changed much either with goals, assists and saves.

Why am I not a statistics man? Because I learned long ago that you can take a statistic and use it as a positive or a negative. And I've seen enough to know that some players pad their stats. There is nothing more meaningless than the home run hit in the bottom of the ninth when your team trails by ten runs and the opponent has a relief pitcher in that should be in the AAA minor leagues. Or the touchdown scored with thirty seconds left against a team with a twenty point lead playing a prevent defense. When I was in college our star basketball player went to Chapel Hill, North Carolina and scored like 34 points against the Tar Heels. We lost by thirty and most of those points were scored against Carolina's scrubs.

Which leads me to records. The truth of the matter is most records are set against bums. By bums, I mean bad teams or players. Check the record books and I'm willing to bet that most of the great games that players had in seasons that they set records were against lousy teams or players. O.J. Simpson ran for 2,003 yards in 1973. He got many of those yards against two lousy teams the New England Patriots and New York Jets. He got little or nothing in two games against the Miami Dolphins "No Name" defense that only went on to win the Super Bowl that year. When Peyton Manning threw for 49 touchdowns in 2005, he could have had 60 easily if the Colts had let him stay in games which Indianapolis played their NFC North opponents the Chicago Bears, Green Bay Packers, Detroit Lions and Minnesota Vikings. He could have thrown for ten touchdowns alone on Thanksgiving Day against the Lions.

That brings me to the point of how important is the record or statistic to the player or team. I can remember watching Cincinnati Bengals running back Corey Dillon going for close to 200 yards in the first half of a game against the Tennessee Oilers. He could have easily broken the single game record then held by Walter Payton of 275, but the Bengals took him out in the third quarter with 246, because the game was out of reach. The record has been broken three times over since then.

I mentioned Manning in the last chapter and use him in this one to prove that though Tom Brady threw for fifty touchdowns in 2007 he got the record only because the Patriots of that season cared more about it than the Colts did in 2005. Remember, the Pats played many blowouts that year where Brady stayed in while Manning sat out quite a bit of time in 2005.

Then there is the case of giving an opponent a record. How can we forget Brett Favre not telling his team that he was going to keep the ball on a running play and running straight into the arms of New York Giant defensive end Michael Strahan for a sack? This enabled Strahan to break the single season sack record. And Favre made a farce of the game. Not Strahan, because he was only doing his job. Favre did it. Strahan should have gotten the record on his own merits not because someone on the other team thought he deserved it.

As far as career records, we have all seen players past their prime stay in the game simply to break a record. Pete Rose did it when he chased Ty Cobb for the all-time hits lead in major league baseball. Bruce Smith did it when he continued to play for the Washington Redskins just to get the all-time sack record in the NFL. I'm not saying that either of them deserved or didn't deserve their records, but maybe their times had passed when they got to the mountain top.

How many hitters in baseball have sacrificed home runs for a simple sacrifice fly to drive in a run? How many batters have given themselves up which hurts their batting average in order to move a runner over by hitting to the opposite field? How many players did what Willie Mays said he used to do and hold up at first when he could have easily made it to second for a double in order to open a whole in the right side of the infield for left-handed hitter Willie McCovey? Remember what New York Yankee legend Mickey Mantle said when Oakland A's outfielder Jose Canseco became the first man to steal forty bases and hit forty home runs? Mantle said that if he had known it was such a big deal he would have done it long ago.

Don't even mention the rules changes. In basketball there is the three point line which came into the NBA in 1979 and college in 1986. And how many steps can a player take before he takes away an assist for his teammate? It used to be one or none. Sometimes it seems to me that if hockey could they'd give an assist to everyone who touched the puck on a goal. Baseball has the designated hitter and the mound has been lowered. And let's not forget the new baseball's that were brought in just when Ruth came along.

And then we get to football. From legalizing holding to not allowing defensive players to make contact with a receiver after five yards, football has done the most to open up their game. Holding is not really legal, but offensive linemen are now allowed to use their hands to block which was not the case prior to 1978. Then there is moving the hash marks in towards the middle of the field in 1972. Allowing the quarterbacks and defensive team captain to listen in on headsets to the coaches calling the plays upstairs. Domed stadiums which take the weather out of play. And the tackling zone being taken down a bit as players can no longer go to the head. Not to mention instant replay which has changed many a call that would have gone down in the books the other way.

All of the leagues have added more games and teams which mean more chances to put up numbers and more chances to do it against bad opponents. Even the post seasons have been expanded with extra teams and rounds.

And we can't look at the record books in almost any sport without making allowances for performance enhancing drugs. Baseball, football, track and field weightlifting and cycling are sports where PED's are considered to be widely used. We may not know everyone who used, but we do know that some of them have put up pretty good numbers and set records.

How come some records in some sports are considered more important than in others? For example why is it that Cal Ripken's consecutive game streak in baseball is considered important while Minnesota Viking defensive end Jim Marshall's streak in football is not? Marshall played at an all-pro level in football for nineteen years and never missed a game just as Ripken did. Marshall played on championship teams with the Vikings playing in four Super Bowls even though he was never on a winner. Marshall played with all kinds of injuries in a sport where men have been paralyzed and in rare occasions have died or come close to it. But he's never considered for the hall of fame. In his case, longevity doesn't count.

No, I'm not into statistics unless it is something unique. For instance, hall of fame Baltimore Colt Lenny Moore is the only player in NFL history with more than forty touchdowns rushing and receiving. That proves he was one of the most versatile players in football history. Oscar Robertson is the only player in NBA history to average a triple double of ten or more points, rebounds and assists in a single season. Now that's something. I'm not a Joe DiMaggio man, but hitting in 56 straight games is unbelievable.

No, the only stats that matter to me are points scored for and against when the game ends and wins and losses. Nothing else.

IT'S TOO HARD TO TELL

Everyone wants to weigh in on who is the greatest. Who is the greatest baseball player of all-time? Who is the greatest music group? Who is the greatest comedian? Who is the greatest President? Who is the greatest humanitarian? It is the bar room argument that will rage on forever.

When pressed, I'll weigh in with my two cents worth when it comes to sports, but for the most part believe that it's too hard to rank the all-time greats. There are just way too many variables to consider. What era did they play in? How good was the team around them? How good was the competition that they played? What were the rules at the time? Who was allowed to play and who wasn't?

Some experts say that you can only judge an athlete by how well he did during his time compared to others in his era. Others say that you have to ask the question, "Could the athlete have played in any era?" Then there are those like me who say that we can only judge the players that we have seen in our lifetime. All of these questions still leave any answer to who is the greatest open to conjecture. So for the sake of argument of course let's see how hard it really is to come up with the greatest of all-time in sports.

First, let's start with baseball. Most people who are baseball historians would say that George Herman "Babe" Ruth of the Boston Red Sox and New York Yankees in the early part of the twentieth century is the greatest of all-time. He ended his career as the all-time leader in home runs by far with 714 and was also a great pitcher with the Red Sox during their championship years of the 1910's. Ruth, also, held the record for most home runs in a season and most World Series homers when he retired. Funny thing is that when Ruth was playing there were many who thought that Detroit Tigers outfielder Ty Cobb was the best player in baseball and the greatest of all-time. Cobb finished his career with more stolen bases than anyone and his lifetime batting average of .367 still stands. As time has passed, many people who never saw either of them play have sided with Ruth. I guess it all depends on what you like. If you are into baseball strategy then Cobb is your man. If you are into the big bang, it's Ruth.

I'm sure that there were other players of that time who were considered good enough to be called the greatest. Cobb always swore that Shoeless Joe Jackson of the Chicago White Sox was the best he ever saw. Then there was Napolean Lajoie who played for many teams and Honus Wagner of the Pittsburgh Pirates. And Ruth had a teammate by the name of Lou Gehrig who was pretty good.

None of these men played during the era of desegregation which began when Jackie Robinson broke the color line in major league baseball in 1947. New York Yankee outfielder Joe DiMaggio bridged the gap having begun his career in 1936 and ending it in1951 and Boston Red Sox outfielder Ted Williams began in 1939 and ended in 1961. DiMaggio always considered himself the "Greatest Living Player of All-Time" until his death and Williams is considered by many including himself to be the greatest hitter of all-time as he is the last man to hit over .400 in a season. I didn't see either of them play, so don't know. Besides, there was a guy who played at that same time for the St. Louis Cardinals named Stan Musial who was pretty darned good himself. I just know that they played a good part of their careers in a segregated league. Whether they wanted to or not is another chapter.

After Jackie Robinson broke the color barrier, the league began to sign African-American ballplayers and you had best believe that they had to be ten times better than their white counterparts. Since then, we have gotten Willie Mays, Henry Aaron, Roberto Clemente, Frank Robinson, Mickey Mantle, Pete Rose, Barry Bonds, Rickey Henderson just to name a few. One could make a case for all of them in my book.

And how about pitchers? Of course before segregation there was Cy Young, Christy Mathewson, Walter Johnson, Lefty Grove and again Babe Ruth. After we have Sandy Koufax, Bob Gibson, Nolan Ryan, Juan Marichal, Steve Carlton, Greg Maddux and Roger Clemens.

How can anyone say that one of these guys is the best?

Moving to basketball, the immediate choice is Chicago Bulls and Washington Wizards guard Michael Jordan. Jordan won six NBA titles with the Bulls from 1991 to 1998 with a short sabbatical between titles to play baseball. He was a prolific scorer and defender. There may have been none better, but were probably some as good.

Boston Celtic center Bill Russell won eleven NBA championships during the late fifties and throughout the sixties in an era when another center by the name of Wilt Chamberlain was setting every offensive record in the book. They were both great players with Wilt winning the individual battles and Russell the team wars. Oscar Robertson may have been the best all-around player of that time. And Jerry West and Elgin Baylor weren't bad. Then Julius Erving came along in the American Basketball Association before joining the NBA. He played in the seventies along with Kareem Abdul-Jabbar. The eighties saw Ervin "Magic" Johnson and Larry Bird while the nineties had Hakeem Olajuwon. The 2,000's have seen Kobe Bryant and Tim Duncan.

Hockey has the man who is simply known as "The Great One" Wayne Gretzky. From a record book standpoint that's very hard to argue. From an intangible standpoint one could make a case for one of Gretzky's teammates Mark Messier who won championships with and without Gretzky. The old heads will give you Bobby Orr, Bobby Hull and Maurice "The Rocket" Richard. Someone with more knowledge of hockey would have to argue this for me.

Football has so many players at so many positions that it's impossible to come up with the greatest ever. Do you go with the players who played both ways, or "Ironman" football, in the first half of the twentieth century? Or do you go with the specialists who have been playing offense or defense since two platoon football took hold in the 1950's? Heck, it's even hard to come up with who was the best at each position. Football is the one game where you have to rely on teammates more than any other. How many good receivers haven't had a chance to showcase their talents, because they played with lousy quarterbacks? How many good running backs and quarterbacks have played behind terrible offensive lines? How many have had the benefit of playing with great players who make them look better? Who knows?

Boxing has brought us many greats at different weight classes so we use the term best "pound for pound." The rules of boxing haven't changed, but the level of competition has. Boxing has always been about the poor trying to make a better life for themselves, especially minorities and immigrants. But nowadays most of them have found other sports like basketball, baseball and football to get out of poverty. And with more and more fans turning away from boxing, because of its violent nature fewer men are taking it up as a profession.

That doesn't mean that there haven't been some great fighters. From Jack Johnson to Mike Tyson, there have been many. Joe Louis, Rocky Marciano, Gene Tunney, Jack Dempsey, Sugar Ray Robinson, Floyd Patterson, Muhammad Ali, Joe Frazier, Sugar Ray Leonard, Aaron Pryor, Marvin Hagler, Larry Holmes. The list is endless. You could put them all at the same weight and have them fight and get 99 different outcomes.

The talent pool is expanded so much in college sports that only a fool would try to come up with the greatest players in basketball and football. So many different conferences and teams to choose from. So many different styles of play.

ESPN did their fifty greatest athletes at the end of the twentieth century with the latest great Michael Jordan winning of course. Never mind that he had flamed out on the baseball diamond while other multi sport athletes like Jackie Robinson, Jim Brown, Jim Thorpe, Wilt Chamberlain and Bo Jackson had shown that they were more versatile. If it were the greatest athlete than maybe it should been the greatest all-around.

We haven't even gotten into the argument for greatest teams in sports. Do we go by one year? Do we go by a full decade? Do we go by the entire history of the game? It's interesting that NFL Films just did the "America's Game" series where they ranked the forty championship teams of the Super Bowl era. The team which won was the undefeated 1972 Miami Dolphins, but there are many who played for that team who believe that they were better in 1973 when they lost two games while repeating as champions. I was eight years old at the time and remember the consensus being that the '73 team was better as well. It's funny how history changes opinions.

Bill Russell's Celtics won eleven NBA championships, but in a recent poll the 1996-97 Chicago Bulls who became the first team to win 70 games in a season were voted the best team of all-time. The Los Angeles Lakers and Boston Celtics of the 1980's were probably just as good as both of those teams, but were so busy knocking each other off that they didn't win as many titles.

Which New York Yankee team was the greatest of all-time? Could any of them have beaten the Big Red Machine of Cincinnati that won titles in 1975 and '76? Or the Oakland A's of 1972 to '74? How about the 1984 Detroit Tigers? Who knows?

How many times have we seen players and teams about to be anointed the greatest of all-time only to go out and lose the next big game? Like University of Nebraska football in 1983 and Southern Cal football in 2005. Then there was Georgetown Hoya basketball in 1985 and University of Nevada Las Vegas in 1991. How about quarterback Brett Favre of the Packers going into Super Bowl XXXII, Kurt Warner before Super Bowl XXXVI, Tom Brady before Super Bowl XLII and Peyton Manning before Super Bowl XLIV? The Baltimore Orioles of 1969 and the Oakland A's of 1988. Then when it doesn't pan out we call them upsets.

But greatest anything is a popularity contest just like voting for student body president in school. It all depends on who you like. Some people go with the athletes who they feel set a standard for the sport which they played like Ruth or Green Bay Packer end Don Hutson or Chamberlain. Others go with whoever the most recent great player is feeling that the competition today is tougher. My argument to that is this.

Just because an athlete did something first doesn't mean they did it best. And just because an athlete did it last doesn't mean they did it better.

You won't get me to buy into it. I would rather appreciate greatness for what it is then single out one person or team. And wait until the season or career is over before making a judgment on how great someone is.

Besides, they won't need me to anoint them. They will do it themselves.

Which leads me to the next chapter.

THE HALL OF FAME

It is the ultimate honor that an athlete can obtain. Election to the hall of fame of their sport. It means that they left a lasting mark on the game. It means that they are not only considered the best of the best when they played, but of all time. It is their legacy for it remains long after they are gone.

But a case can be made that for every person who is elected to the hall of fame in some sports, there is one who may have been just as good who is left out. How can this happen? Easily. Everyone has their opinion on who should be a hall of famer and who shouldn't. It's hard enough to get people to agree in church so how can we expect the same from people voting on who should be in the hall of fame and who shouldn't.

I'm not intimate on what goes on in those rooms when they vote, but it seems to me it's pretty tough. Because no one wants to let a player in who is not deemed worthy in their eyes. And everyone wants all of the players that they deem worthy elected, especially ahead of the ones that they think are unworthy. Since only a select few are elected every year, this leaves a lot of very good people out. And the longer they go without being elected, the harder it is for them to get in.

Many people can't understand how a person can go from not being a hall of famer in their first five years of eligibility to suddenly being one in their sixth. Well, it depends on who is up for election when their time comes. Many times there are people who have been up for the hall of fame who have had to wait their turn, because there was someone else more deserving. Other times a sure fire first ballot hall of famer comes along who gets in ahead of them. There are times when many voters on the committee just don't think that the person is worthy of hall of fame selection. And let's face it some voters just may not like the person that they are voting for whatever the reason and won't vote for them. Remember, even Babe Ruth and Henry Aaron didn't get one hundred per cent of the vote when they were elected.

It is usually the writers who vote for hall of famers and many think that they don't know enough about the sports that they cover to do it. There is always a cry for people involved in the game and former hall of famers themselves to have the final say on who should get in and who shouldn't. Just from listening to those involved, I don't think that they could do any better than the writers, because of their loyalty to teammates and people that they played against which leads to bias. How many times have we heard a player on a championship team say that they believed their team was the greatest of all-time? Or heard a player say that his coach or teammate was the best? No, chances are there would be just as much if not more bias if the players did it instead of the writers.

And the players don't really know their history, so they would be more inclined to forget about the people who preceded them or know nothing of them at all. Most athletes are too busy playing the game themselves growing up to watch those who are in the professional ranks. And the ones they do watch are usually on their favorite team or is their favorite player. Once they leave the game, many do not follow it enough to know who is doing what.

Baseball pretty much has it right when it comes to voting by having the best of their writers and former hall of fame players elect their members. One could make a case that baseball voters have the easiest time, because they have certain milestones for players to reach statistically which separates them from the rest of the pack. If you bat over .300 for your career then you are probably going to get a call from the hall of fame. Former outfielder Al Oliver is the only lifetime .300 hitter that I know of who is not in the hall. He batted .301 for his career. Before the steroids era, 500 career home runs was a ticket to the hall. 3,000 lifetime hits or strikeouts punched your ticket. And for pitchers, 300 career victories get you over the top. These have been the standards for years.

And baseball rewards its career record breakers. If you set a record for home runs, batting average, hits, runs batted in, doubles, triples or stolen bases then you are going to the hall of fame. If you set a record for most wins or strikeouts then you are going to the hall of fame. Even a record like most consecutive games gets you in, though you have to have the statistics to go along with it.

The only thing that baseball, and most sports for that matter, doesn't really account for is defense. In baseball, if you win a Silver Slugger award for hitting you are more likely to get into the hall of fame than if you win a Gold Glove. Most voters don't understand how valuable defense is to the game of baseball. A great fielder can take away just as many runs as a great hitter can drive in during the course of a season. The men who are forgotten when it comes to hall of fame voting are those like shortstops Dave Concepcion of the Cincinnati Reds and Mark Belanger of the Baltimore Orioles. Two of the best who ever played their positions that don't get much consideration for the hall, because they didn't bat .300, despite the fact that they played on winning teams, championship teams. Hall of fame shortstop Ozzie Smith is the rare exception, but even he began to hit better towards the end of his career. Concepcion did the same, but probably will always be on the outside looking in.

Basketball and hockey aren't really that tough to grade either. Both sports look at the scorers first. If you score a lot of points then you are pretty much in. Basketball rewards the guys who rebound and pass the ball to their opponents so that they can score. And hockey rewards the goalies who stop the puck. Easy enough. These two sports also reward players who set career records

Football is where the real logjam is, because there are so many positions and factors involved. Think about this. In basketball only 10 men are on the court at one time. Hockey has twelve. Baseball is played nine to a side for eighteen. Of course all of these sports substitute, but not like football. When you take into consideration the fact that each unit on a football team consists of eleven men and there are offense, defense and special team that's 33 players at the least who are going to take the field during a game on each side. So a football game more than likely will have no less than 70 players take the field between the two teams. That's a lot of different people to look at. It's been that way since the 1950's. How in the world do you weed out a maximum of seven people a year for the pro football hall of fame from so many thousands of players over the last half century without leaving some very good ones out? You can't.

But football tries. They usually use statistics, but with the ever changing rulebook many of those who vote can't get a true reading on how great players of a bygone era were compared to today's because their statistics aren't as gaudy. Then there are all-pro and pro bowl selections, but many of them are based on popularity and name recognition. It's hard to make the all-pro or pro bowl team when you first get into the league, but once a player does he can make it strictly on what he's done in past seasons and many will admit this. And with players skipping the pro bowl so much now, we get second and third selections taking their spots which decrease the value of being chosen.

Some players are rewarded for longevity while others are not. If you are a wide receiver than you had better shatter a career record in order to get in on the first ballot. For running backs and quarterbacks just pass it no matter how long it takes. And some careers are considered so good that a short career doesn't matter, like Gale Sayers, while others are punished for getting injured in their prime, like Terrell Davis.

One way to get into the hall of fame in any sport without the stats or records is by being an integral part of a winning team. Especially if you play a key position like center field in baseball, center in basketball, goalie in hockey and quarterback in football. Most voters will look past lower individual numbers for the sake of championships, especially if the player performed well in the big games, but you still have to win. That's one of the reasons why Pittsburgh Steelers wide receiver Lynn Swann is in the football hall of fame and Dallas Cowboy Drew Pearson is not. Pearson was as good a big game receiver as Swann, but when the two teams met in the Super Bowl it was the Steelers who won not the Cowboys. And Swann outplayed Pearson in both games. So Swann gets in and Pearson does not.

Another way is to stay in the limelight. The quiet ones are forgotten. The writers always say that they want athletes to do nothing more than their job, but when they do all we hear is that they don't have a signature moment. The player may have had plenty of signature moments he just didn't toot his own horn about it or relive it for the next hundred years. Meanwhile, the guy who stood at home plate and watched his home runs go out or the guy who hung off the rim after every dunk or danced every time he scored a touchdown is the one they remember at voting time. That's one of the reasons why it took Washington Redskin wide receiver Art Monk so long to make it despite the fact he was the all-time leader in receptions when he retired. If Monk had been a showboat or simply talked to the media it wouldn't have taken him nearly as long to get elected to the hall.

The bigger the market that you play and do great things in, the easier it is to get elected, also. What's the old saying, "If you want to make all-pro, play well in New York," East coast players get more recognition than west coast, just like east coast teams do.

It used to bother me when certain players didn't make the hall in their respective sports. Art Monk's absence really bothered me, because I feel that if you set a career record in any sport than you have to be pretty good or teams wouldn't give you a chance to do it. But, now I just accept the fact that not everyone is going to get in, especially in football. So, like many people I have my own hall of fame of players that I keep. Some of them get in and some don't which is fine.

The hall of fame should be selective. That's what makes it so special.

ARE ATHLETES ROLE MODELS

It's the question that has been asked for years. Are athletes role models? There are many athletes who say that they are and those who say that they are not. For years, I believed the latter. But that's not the case anymore. The truth is that athletes are role models to young people whether they want to be or not. The problem is that we adults hold athletes to a higher standard which we shouldn't do. So when they disappoint us we are harsher on them than other people.

I say that athletes are role models to young people, because they were to me when I was growing up. I couldn't tell you who the Governor of Maryland was back then, but I could tell you that Bert Jones was the quarterback of the Baltimore Colts. I had no idea who The Reverend Jesse Jackson was, but I knew Muhammad Ali was heavyweight champion of the world. I had no idea that Washington D.C. had a mayor, but I knew that George Allen was coach of the Redskins. And, sad to say, I had no idea what my father did for a living other than knowing he worked for the federal government, but I could tell you that Charley Taylor played wide receiver for the Redskins. I'm not saying what any of the non- athletes did was unimportant, especially my father, but what the athletes were doing was more important to me. So they were the people that I looked up to and emulated.

When I got the football, I ran like O.J. Simpson or Larry Brown. When I threw it, I was Terry Bradshaw. When I caught it, I was Paul Warfield and later Lynn Swann. I can still remember spiking the ball in a youth league game, which was against the rules, because I saw Otis Taylor do it. In baseball I stole bases as Davey Lopes. I hit and played the outfield as Henry Aaron. When I threw rocks as a pitcher I was Jim Palmer. Hockey I was Bobby Orr. Sugar Ray Leonard was my man in boxing and that's who I was when I got into fisticuffs. I really didn't have a basketball player to emulate in the pros so usually went with whoever was the best on the University of Maryland Terrapins at that time. This could range from John Lucas to Ernie Graham to Albert King.

I collected baseball cards and magazines. I read everything that I could about any athlete. If Henry Aaron said, "Don't smoke," than I didn't. If Muhammad Ali said, "Don't drink," than I didn't. If Joe Namath used a certain shaving cream, than I wanted to use it too much to the chagrin of my father. It got to the point where if a teacher or adult wanted to get something across to me they would say something like, "Do you think that Larry Brown or Charley Taylor would do that?"

Back then we didn't hear about what athletes did off of the field. Not the negative things anyway. All we heard about them was that they were fine upstanding citizens in the community. Athletes didn't make nearly as much money back then as they do now so many of them had to get jobs in the offseason and live in the community which they played. They also had to look towards their future after retirement so had to conduct themselves accordingly.

All in all athletes were thought of as regular guys with a special talent and if they hung out with the fans anything they might have done which would be considered out of line was kept quiet and out of the news. The adults knew what the athletes were doing in a few cases, but not us kids. And if an athlete was accused of something like drunk driving or disturbing the peace it was more of a "boys will be boys," type of thing. Athletes dating women was just accepted as par for the course.

The only team I can remember being linked to partying and drugs back in the seventies were the Dallas Cowboys and that was just rumors I heard from the older boys. The only players were NBA basketball players. But we didn't know who did them, when or where. It just wasn't reported. That didn't stop the older boys from wanting to emulate those athletes in that way as well. Because it wasn't reported to be hurting the pros older boys that I knew got into drugs to be cool like their heroes. This was not just in sports, but acting and music as well. Even though this may have been the case I can never remember an adult saying an athlete was the reason why some kid had gone astray. Rock music was blamed more than sports.

Then the landscape changed. Athletes began to sign million dollar contracts and move away from where their blue collar fans were and into the high rent district. Television and radio started vying for headlines and everything began to become public. Athletes started to call more attention to themselves and fans wanted to know more and more about them off of the field just as they did with actors and musicians. The internet came along and today's news was yesterday's in no time flat. And there became a separation of athlete and fan.

This led to athletes being put on an even higher pedestal and held to a higher standard than they were in the past. All of this despite the fact that the athlete had not changed in one aspect. The great ones were still being coddled just as they had been before the money became huge and the fame greater. The only difference was they were being coddled at a much younger age, because everyone wanted a piece of the big money sports pie. And they were no longer one of the people if they made it big, because they were millionaires who didn't need to work in the offseason, worry about retirement or live in the same community as their blue collar fans.

Now when the millionaire athlete does something wrong it gets out more easily and everyone is up in arms after hearing about it. "How could Buck Brickhead be so dumb? Driving his car 110 miles an hour down the freeway like that. Doesn't he know that he's a bad role model for the kids?" Or "What is wrong with Chili Cheeseburger Childs, fighting in the club at 2:00 in the morning? He has no business being there anyway. Doesn't he know that he is setting a bad example for the kids?" I'm not saying that these athletes shouldn't be chastised for what they may have done. However, we never hear these things publicly when it's our neighbor, friend or family member who does the same and aren't they more visible to a child than Buck Brickhead or Chili Cheeseburger Childs?

The truth of the matter is that most athletes are young people trying to find their way just as we were when their age. The difference is that they have a special talent which allows them to earn a lot of fame and fortune. With fortune comes easy living which leads to plenty of free time. There is nothing more ripe with the potential for trouble than someone with too much time and money on their hands. And young athletes have plenty of it so many of them make mistakes. They feel that time is on their side and the money will be there forever. They have been told that they are invincible since the time their gift was discovered and come to believe it.

Some of them spend their money on material things like cars and houses, others on women. Still others go out to the clubs and party it all away. Unfortunately, many turn to drugs and alcohol. Many haven't been taught the value of a dollar and can't fathom ever running out when there are so many numbers on the left side of the decimal on their paychecks.

Even athletes who try to do the right thing often fail. How many athletes do we know who get married only to divorce later, because of the demands their sport places on them? Or they have extramarital affairs, because they are removed from their spouses for so long and can't resist temptations which sometimes lead to domestic violence.

I know what I was like when I was in my twenties. Believe me I wasn't an athlete and made stupid decisions. I know that if I had made it in athletics there are many things that I would have done wrong, also. I know that I would have been a womanizer which could have led to children out of wedlock. I know that I would have gone out on occasion. I know that I would have spent money on foolish things. I know that I would have been in situations where undesirables were around, because I grew up with a few and still consider them friends. I know that I would have driven my car a little too fast on occasion. I've never smoked, drank or done drugs so I'll draw the line there. So why should I be surprised when I read about young, rich people in all walks of life doing that now?

Of course, all of these things have been going on for years as I've already said. They just weren't reported as much and fans and media were more sympathetic to athletes who made mistakes, because they were still one of us. I'm not saying that was the right thing to do it's just the way it was. Not anymore.

The problem that I have is this. Why should we expect anymore from athletes than from ourselves? Why because a person can run faster, jump higher or throw farther than we can they all of a sudden become more of a role model for young people than those in our community who have regular jobs, go to church, raise their families and pay their bills? Why are their mistakes deemed to be worse than our own? Isn't my neighbor, coworker or myself drunk driving just as bad as an athlete doing the same? And why are athlete's triumphs greater? I mean don't people in everyday life do good things that benefit their communities more than a man putting a basketball through a hoop? They just don't do them in front of 20,000 fans which makes them more special to me, because they're not looking for recognition most of the time.

I know that I mentioned earlier that while growing up when I heard an athlete say something it was the Gospel to me, but here's the truth. When my father and mother told me to do something I did it also or paid the price. It may have taken a few whippings, but I did it. It was the same if a teacher or another adult told me as well. All of us were held accountable for our actions by the adults.

And it was my older brothers, cousins and their friends who had the most influence on me, because I saw the way that they lived their lives every day. I looked up to them and wanted to be like them. Fortunately, they had been brought up by good parents and were excellent role models for me. That doesn't mean they didn't do bad things. It means that I was able to learn from their good decisions and their mistakes.

And they would tell me when they had done wrong. They would also tell me what was good and bad for me whether I wanted to hear it or not. I don't know how many times I was told that I really didn't want to do something and would anyway only to have them come back and say, "I told you so." Those "I told you sos," add up.

In this way, I was no different than the athletes I grew up idolizing. All one has to do is read an autobiography written by a successful athlete and they will find every one of them had the same role models as most others. Their immediate family and the people in their neighborhoods that they grew up around.

I know that times have changed. I know that many young people don't have the family structure that we had growing up even in communities where opportunities for advancement have improved.

Thus, many of them look towards athletics as a way out and athletes as role models which are fine. It doesn't matter who they choose for a role model as long as they find one. But athletes shouldn't be the only role models and they shouldn't be blamed for the mistakes of our youth. Young people should be held accountable just as they were when I was growing up and the adults around them should be too.

Yes, athletes are role models. But you can't trust an image given on a television screen. It is the people in communities where young people live and grow up who have the biggest influence on them. It is time to stop denying that. It is time to stop using the actions of a few athletes who get into trouble as an excuse for things that our youth do wrong.

It is way past time for all of us to hold ourselves accountable.

WHAT HAVE I LEARNED FROM SPORTS?

Growing up I used to always get asked the same question. "Aren't you interested about anything other than sports?" "What are you going to learn about the real world if all you look at and read about is sports?" Well, let me say this. Sports got me through school. Not because I kept my grades up to stay eligible in high school, which I did. No, sports got me through school, because I applied it to my studies and used it to open levels of curiosity that I may have never thought of without it. So let me answer to those who asked what I learned with the help of sports.

The first, and most important, thing that I learned with the help of sports was how to read.

When I began school, I was very shy and not a good reader. In kindergarten and first grade, we never read much in the way of books. We usually got a few sentences to study and that was it. Then in second grade we were given our first reading books and placed into groups. Our teacher was as tough as they come and I remember early in the school year, she had each of us pick a story out of the book and read it aloud to the class. I picked the only story which had to do with sports. I stuttered and stammered through it and couldn't wait to finish. When I did, my teacher didn't mince any words. She told me that I had done a terrible job. For what seemed like forever she told me in front of everyone in the group how basically I couldn't read. Even though she told me that I could do much better, I was crushed. But I was also determined that I was going to do better the next time I read in front of that class. The problem was that I really wasn't interested in reading about anything other than sports.

Fortunately, I had a mother who was part time librarian at the school I attended. I don't know if the teacher, who lived down the street from us and went to school with my father, told my mother about my reading. I do know that my mother knew how crazy I was about sports. So all of a sudden these books began showing up at our house. Books which my mother told me were specifically for me to read. Every one of them was about sports.

Every week there was a children's biography in my mother's arms when she walked in the door. Books about, Willie Mays, Mickey Mantle, John Unitas, Henry Aaron, Jim Brown and Gale Sayers. I would grab them from her and look at the pictures first. Then I wanted to know what the words under the pictures were. Then I wanted to know what the words were being written about these athletes. Whenever I had questions about a word, I would ask my mother and she would help me to pronounce it. Then I would take the books to school and my friends and I would read them together helping each other with the words and names we couldn't pronounce.

As the year went on, my reading improved. Recently on Mother's Day, my sisters pulled out some old report cards that Mom had kept from elementary school. One of mine was from second grade. In the end of the year notes my teacher had written that I had improved greatly in reading. She wrote that if I continued to apply myself that I would get even better. I knew that she meant it, because as I said earlier this woman didn't mince words.

My third grade report card said that I was reading above grade level. By now, I was reading about a lot more than sports. And just as my second grade teacher had said I got better and better. By high school, I had to prove to some of my teachers that I was actually reading my assignments, because I'd finish so far ahead of my classmates.

To this day, I enjoy reading. I have two shelves full of books and magazines with plenty in boxes until I can buy a third. And I read about a lot more than sports. All because a mother was smart enough to see that her son had the ability to do something and just needed the right stimulus, sports, to accomplish it. I am forever grateful to her for that.

I first learned math from sports. From basketball, I learned how to add by two and in football by six and seven. I also, learned how to add by keeping the score of games as they were in progress. I learned how to first count to one hundred, because a football field was that many yards long and how to count backwards from fifty since that's what the announcers did once the team with the ball crossed midfield. I learned what feet were from baseball and yards from football. I'm sure that I'm not the only young boy who learned percentages and decimals from totaling his batting average which I thought was the neatest thing when I learned it.

I learned geography through sports.

When I was in seventh grade Social Studies we were talking about the American west and somehow the town of Palo Alto, California came up. The teacher asked what college was located in Palo Alto and no one raised their hand but me. She called on me and I told her Stanford University. I was a pretty intelligent kid, but in that Social Studies class if there were 35 students I was probably number 30 to 35. So it meant a lot to me knowing something that all of those brains didn't. And the only reason I knew was from reading about quarterback Jim Plunkett winning the Heisman Trophy while playing at Stanford in 1970.

The year before, our sixth grade teacher gave us a state to do an oral report on. Mine was Florida. I had no clue where Florida was on the map and the only thing that made me look was finding out it was where the Miami Dolphins played. So I looked in the encyclopedia and found out that Miami was at the very bottom of Florida. I also found out that Florida was the bottom state of the east in the United States. From then on, I knew where Florida was.

After this, I had to learn where every sports team in the US was on the map and did. I already knew what state they were in especially the California teams, because that's where I wanted to play. My favorite team may have been the Pittsburgh Steelers, but I wanted to play for the Los Angeles Rams, because they were in sunny California not cold Pennsylvania. After playing my college ball at the University of Southern Cal, of course.

Then I expanded to include colleges and bowl game sites. From there it was every major team in pro sports including the ones in

Canada. Why stop there? Why not learn where the athletes themselves were from? And let's go overseas to see where they are holding the Olympics. Better yet, when a certain country wins a medal let's go to the World Book Atlas and find out where it is. Before you know it, I'm spanning the globe just as they did on ABC's "Wide World of Sports."

I learned to appreciate classical music from sports.

My music teachers could have played all of the Bach, Brahms and Beethoven they wanted I wasn't going to listen. Why would I when there was James Brown, Stevie Wonder and Isaac Hayes.

But if you turned on the television and there was an NFL Films highlight show on then I was going to listen to the music of Sam Spence not knowing that he even existed. The music blended so well with the highlights that even one of my sisters once said the only reason I watched was to listen to it. There were times where she was right.

This led me to listen to classical music and instrumentals. To this day, I would rather listen to a good instrumental song than vocal track. And I'm very picky as to what I listen to.

I learned history from sports.

Every great sporting event happened on a certain date in a certain year. Babe Ruth hit 60 home runs in 1927. The Chicago Bears defeated the Washington Redskins in the NFL championship game 73-0 on December 8, 1940. The so called "Greatest Football Game Ever Played" between the Baltimore Colts and New York Giants was played on December 28, 1958. The St. Louis Cardinals won game seven of the 1967 World Series over the Boston Red Sox on October 12, 1967. These dates don't really mean much in the grand scheme of things. But what they did was give me a timeline for world and US events. And piqued my interest in finding out what the times and people were like in the era when they occurred.

I knew that Red Grange was called the "Galloping Ghost" while playing halfback for the University of Illinois in the era known as the "Roaring Twenties." And Babe Ruth was clouting home runs. And Jack Dempsey and Gene Tunney ruled the heavyweight boxing division. This led me to try and find out why this decade was called the "Roaring

Twenties?" What made it so great? Who was the President then? What were the advancements in science and technology? How were living conditions in the country and world then? I wanted to know the tenor of the times. This was not just for the "Roaring Twenties" but any decade or year in history.

Then I open a book and see a football game program from December 14, 1930 for a game between the Notre Dame All-Stars and New York Giants. At the top is a heading entitled "YOU CAN HELP SMASH THE BREAD LINE!"   What in the heck was a bread line I wondered? This led me to finding out about the "Great Depression" of the 1930's and early forties. I would have probably found out in a history class, but learned about it first in a football book.

While reading the story of track star Jesse Owens and his performance in the 1936 Summer Olympics at Berlin, Germany I learn that he and my people were not wanted by the Nazi party. Negroes were thought to be inferior by the leader of the Nazis a man by the name of Adolph Hitler. Who is Adolph Hitler and what was the Nazi party? Well, let's go to the history books and find out how terrible this man and his followers were.

This quest for historical knowledge still continues with me to this day. I began reading the World Book Encyclopedia yearbook as a boy just to find out which teams had won championships and which players awards for a given year. Then I began to read about wars, politics, inventions and world events that happened during the year I was interested in. One of the books I now have is a comprehensive day by day account of the 20th century.

I was always interested in sports history from day one. Once I learned how to read, I became interested in US and world history through sports. I'm glad I did.

These are the key things that I learned through my love of sports. All of them are important to me. I love to learn, but have never been much on formal education though I know how very important it is and recommend it to everyone. If I could not have applied sports to my studies then it wouldn't have been any fun. Thus, I would have been less motivated to learn. And an honor roll student may have wasted his potential.

So remember that the next time you tell a young person they will never learn anything useful from sports. Maybe, just maybe, they simply need someone to apply sports in some way to their studies for motivation. It doesn't matter how a person learns a subject as long as they do.

It worked for me.

MISSING THE POINT

There are many who believe that records in sports should not count before the games were integrated. For example, all major league baseball records should not count before Jackie Robinson broke the color line with the Brooklyn Dodgers in 1947. The reasoning is that because all of the best players were not playing in the majors we can't really say that the men who did play at that time would have put up the same statistics and set the same records. Also, we don't know if the players who were barred from the game could have done as well or better.

When this argument comes up those who defend the players from the pre 1947 era say it's not the white player's fault that others were not allowed to play. It was the rules of their time and they played under them. Then there are those who say that the players are not at fault for there not being any minorities in the game at that time, because they were innocent bystanders to the owners and Commissioner Kennesaw Mountain Landis' lockout of African-American talent. All that I know is the only people I heard who spoke up and said that they would sign or play with African-American players were New York Giants manager John McGraw, Boston Red Sox outfielder Ted Williams and Cleveland Indians owner Bill Veeck. Silence can be just as damning as actions.

Whether I believe the records should count or not doesn't matter, because they do just as the ones set during the last two decades. I'm not big on statistics and records so that really doesn't matter to me. And I'm not going to downgrade anyone who played before integration, because they did play under the rules of their times. I mean Ted Williams and Stan Musial were every bit as good after integration as they were before.

What I am here to explain is that maybe the statistics and records amassed after 1947 carry a little more weight than the ones set before. Here goes.

When the Dodgers signed Robinson from the Negro National Leagues to a contract for the 1946 season, there were those who felt he was not the best player black baseball had. There were many associated with the Negro Leagues who felt that Robinson was average in their league. But Dodgers General Manager Branch Rickey knew that he needed more than a good player to break the color line. He needed one who could handle everything that would be thrown at him from players, managers, fans and media who did not want a black man to integrate their sport. If that player failed on and off the field it would be a while before the next man got a chance.

In his first season with the Dodgers, 1947, Robinson helped lead them to the National League pennant. The Dodgers had a good team, but Robinson made them better immediately. We know that with him they won the pennant. We don't know if they would have won it without him.

That same season, Cleveland's Bill Veeck broke the color line in the American League by signing outfielder Larry Doby. Unlike Robinson who played minor league ball for a year in Montreal where he led them to the championship, Doby was called up during the season and struggled his first year. But in 1948 Doby found his stride. During the season, Veeck signed Negro League pitcher Leroy "Satchel" Paige. With the help of these men Cleveland won the World Series. We know that Cleveland won with them. We don't know if they would have won without them.

After signing Robinson, the Dodgers brought in catcher Roy Campanella and pitchers Don Newcombe and Dan Bankhead. Robinson brought a new style of play to baseball. A daring take no prisoners approach on the base paths and at the plate. And in 1949, two years after breaking the color line, the man who wasn't thought of as the best player in his old league won the National league most valuable player award.

For the next decade Brooklyn won six National League pennants and one world's championship. Campanella won three MVP awards in 1951, 1953 and 1955. Sure they lost to all white Yankee teams until 1956, but that's more because New York could afford to sing all of the best talent just as they do today. Would the Dodgers have made this run without those and other minority players like Joe Black, Jim Gilliam and Sandy Amoros? Maybe. But we do know that they became a better team with them. Better than all of the teams in the National League.

During this time, baseball was signing minority players, especially in the National League, but not at a fast pace. There was definitely a quota system in place and not too many teams were going to have more than four African-Americans on their team. So in order to even get a contract from a big league team the minority player had to be great. Not good, great. There were no spots on the bench for the utility player if he was a minority. Just take a look at the National League MVP's of the 1950's. There was Campanella along with Newcombe, Willie Mays, Ernie Banks and Henry Aaron. These players had to elevate their games which forced everyone else to do the same.

This quota system began to change during the 1960's as teams like the Dodgers, San Francisco Giants, St. Louis Cardinals and Pittsburgh Pirates started to sign more minority players and bring them up to the big leagues. Along with the signings in the fifties, the results were telling. From the first all-star game in 1933 to 1950, the American League won 12 out of 16 games. Starting in 1950 to 1987 the National League won 33 out of 41 games including streaks of eight from 1963 to 1970 and eleven from 1971 to 1982. A lot of this had to do with the fact that the National League had more minority all-stars than the American.

Once the quota system began to break down, the Yankee dynasty came to an end in the mid sixties. This was probably not a coincidence. This was the era when all of the best athletes were playing baseball so there was plenty of talent to go around. Teams began to build strong minor league systems able to compete with New York and the Yankees did not become dominant again until the age of free agency began in the late 1970's.

So one could make a case that baseball became more competitive and thus a better game than it was in 1947. With tougher competition maybe player's statistics should carry more weight.

Let's stray from baseball for a moment to a couple of other sports.

For years, African-Americans were not allowed to play college football at southern schools. They had to play at Historically Black Colleges and Universities or not play at all. When the pros opened the doors to these men from Grambling State, Southern, Prairie View, Morgan State, Florida A@M, Maryland State and the like they more than proved their worth. The American Football League was born in 1960 and in order to compete with the more established National had to sign players from wherever they could. By the end of the decade, the Kansas City Chiefs were the first team to have more African-Americans on their roster than whites and they won Super Bowl IV.

The south began to sign African-American players in the late 1960's and early 1970's. The old Southwest Conference and the Southeast began to sign players away from the HBCU's. Now, the Southwest's best teams belong to the Big XII. The Big XII and Southeast conferences are considered to be the two best in college football. We know that they are with minority talent. Do we know that they would be without it?

Then there is basketball. From the time of Wilt Chamberlain and Bill Russell to today, NBA basketball has been the sport where African-Americans have been pretty dominant for most of the league's existence. We do know that the Celtics won 11 championships in 13 years with Bill Russell. We don't know if they would have without him. We do know how good the Lakers were with Magic Johnson and Kareem Abdul-Jabbar. We don't know how good they would have been without them. And we know that the Bulls were good with Michael Jordan and Scottie Pippen. We don't know how good they would have been without them

My final argument would be this. In just about every state in this country public high schools are divided by class for interscholastic sports. The schools themselves get their students assigned to them by district and must choose from them for their athletic teams. The schools with the biggest enrollment play each other on down to the ones with the smallest. This is because the bigger schools have the advantage of more talent to choose from. Most of the time, if a bigger school plays a smaller one, the big school wins. In fairness the schools are separated for post season play so that the smaller schools have a chance to play for and win a championship. There aren't too many small schools that win championships that can compete with the bigger ones.

The private schools are different. They can recruit from anywhere and enroll anyone as long as they pay tuition. Thus they have a bigger area to sign players and can get the best of the best. Though the private schools don't always get the best players they usually find enough to be better than the public schools. It's just simple mathematics.

Here is my point. The fact is that records before integration should be looked at differently, because for better or worse not everyone was allowed to play at that time. It has nothing to do with race, but with the pool of talent that is available. If only a certain segment of the population is allowed to do something than how can we tell if they are the very best? And how can we tell if the people who are excluded can do as good or better? We can't. We have to actually see them compete just as we can't tell if Babe Ruth could have hit Bob Gibson, because they played in different eras. The truth is that society as a whole is better when everyone is allowed an opportunity to be successful not just a few.

One thing that we do know is that the level of competition improves when more people are allowed to compete. I have given some examples of that. The talent pool for athletes has always been there and still is today despite what is said. There is never a shortage of good players. What there is a shortage of is good owners, general managers and coaches. Always will be. But not talent. And the more talent to choose from, the more depth which can be amassed. We all know how important depth is to a team. A team with capable backups will sustain while one without will not. How many times have we heard that one team had numbers while the other didn't?

So there is a case that can be made that today's statistics mean more, because they were earned against tougher competition than the ones before integration.

It has nothing to do with race. It's just a simple case of numbers.

OH, THEN YOU'RE NOT A REAL FAN

Anyone who is interested in sports has their favorites. We have our favorite players, sports and teams. Some people root for a player who is from their home town. Others, because the player plays for their team. Some root for a player, because they went to the same college. And many, because they simply like the players style.

Some people root for the home team. Many do not. Some people root for out of town teams, because they are very good. Others because they may have parents or relatives who grew up or live in the city of their team. Some people root for a team, because their favorite player plays for them. Others may just like the way the team carries itself and plays the game.

There are many levels of fandom from the people who worship their teams like Gods to those who root and when the game is over, it's over. The ones who have bedroom shrines, season tickets and apparel call themselves real fans. Those who don't are considered casual fans who aren't serious enough about the game or their team. How many times have we heard a rabid fan say to someone less intense, "Oh you're not a real fan." And the person who is not considered a fan gets upset and tries to prove how loyal they are.

Well they don't have to. Just because one person has season tickets, a bedroom shrine and a whole wardrobe from their team doesn't make them anymore of a fan than the person who does not. It just means that they wear it on their sleeve more. There is nothing wrong with that.

So what is a real fan? And who can fans root for? How loyal should one be to the team or player that they root for? Where should there be a line drawn when it comes to rooting for a team or player and against an opponent? Can a fan drop his loyalty for a team or player and switch to another and under what circumstances? If they do drop their loyalty can they come back? Let's see if we can answer these questions.

First off what is a "real fan?" To me a real fan is anyone who roots for a team, no matter how zealous. As I mentioned earlier, there is the fan who is totally committed to their team whether it is on his own or has been handed down from generation to generation. This fan is the one who builds shrines in their homes either in a bedroom or recreation room or man cave. This shrine will see furniture in the team colors, memorabilia on the walls which may include autographed pictures and jerseys, game programs, pennants, clocks and calendars. This fan gives you a cup or glass with the team logo on it if you ask for a drink. This is the fan who wears the apparel of his team or player whether it be hats, caps, shirts, coats and especially jerseys.

These fans set their life schedules around their teams. Everything must be done by one o'clock Sunday or seven thirty Wednesday. And when those times come around and they're watching their teams you had better not bother them. When the team wins they win and are the first ones to say, "We're number 1!" even though they haven't done anything on the field, court or ice. When the team loses, their day and week is ruined, because, "We lost." They can tell you the third string tackle, third man off of the bench and middle reliever of their team.

And they remember games and players of the past as if it were yesterday. Any player who did well for their team is a God and the teams that won championships can never be replaced. As the years go by, even average players are looked at as hall of famers. Even average teams are looked at as great. These people take fandom to the max and there is absolutely nothing wrong with that. They are the reason why sports are so popular.

However, that does not mean the fan who doesn't have the shrine, memorabilia, apparel, memory, diehard attitude or worship for the team and player isn't a real fan. Far from it. For one, many fans can't afford to buy the things that the rabid fan does, especially tickets. Many of them are getting by the best they can and can't always be there to watch the team play in the arena or on television. And some of them just look at the games as a diversion, the home team that they root for because of civic pride.

I am a huge fan of all the teams I root for, but to a point. I am not into hero worship so will not wear the jersey of any player. I have a name given to me and like it, but am not going to put that on the back of a jersey either. However, I do wear the colors of my team, have memorabilia and know their history. When the team plays I'm front and center and you had better not bother me, but when it's, over it's over. It is time to move on. You will never hear me say "We won," or "We lost," unless they put me on the payroll. If I see the team's logo on a check with my name on it, I'll get a mouse in my pocket in no time and learn French. Until then, it's "They won," and "They lost." For me, sports is important, but not life or death.

I like sports period. That means even if my team isn't playing I'll watch and enjoy. I care about the entire history of the sport not just my teams. I probably know more about the history of some of the rabid fans teams than they do. That doesn't mean I'm more of a fan of their team than they are just more of a historian. Just like not making sports life or death doesn't mean you're not a real fan. It just means that you have other priorities.

To me as long as you know the rules of the sport, the name of your favorite team, what city they play in, the head coach, the main players and the teams colors you are a real fan.

Then who can fans root for? There are those who say you should only root for the home team and no one else. They represent your community and are a reflection of its core values. Some of them may live in your community. When they win it's great for everyone and when they don't it's not.

I think that this was more of the case before big money and free agency came into play. Yes, the players and coaches lived in the community and represented it. Most players, especially the all-stars, would play their entire careers in one city. Fans would get to know them and be more inclined to root for people they considered friends.

As the country evolves it becomes more transient. Now we are more likely to see fans who have been transplanted from their home town or state that still root for those teams. It's nothing to see New York, Boston or Chicago fans anywhere. Then there are those whose parents grew up in a certain city or went to a specific college and had to move, but kept their loyalties. Many times they pass this on to their children. So even though the child may have never set foot in the city or town where their parents are from this team becomes their favorite. In both cases mentioned this is completely accepted by most fans.

Another reason why fans may not root for the home team may be that they have a friend or relative who plays or coaches for someone else. It may be an old classmate or teammate from high school or college. It may be the son or daughter of a friend. Once again, there is nothing wrong with that.

Then we get to fans who root for teams simply because they like them or a certain player on the team with no regard for any of the things I just mentioned. They may root for them, because it's the cool thing to do like Dallas Cowboy fan. They may root for them simply because they win a lot like New York Yankee fan. Or they may like them, because of their style of play like me with the Pittsburgh Steelers. This is where the homer or player loyalist has a problem.

They think that these fans should root for the home team simply because they are local win or lose. They think that these fans are front runners who only likes winners. They think that these fans are bandwagoners who will jump ship as soon as the team starts losing and many times are right. Once again, they think that these fans are not "real fans."

I root for all of the home teams in my area but one, the Washington Redskins. That doesn't mean that I don't like them. I just like the Steelers more. Though I always rooted for the Steelers, I grew up supporting the Redskins also until the last decade. My not rooting for them now has nothing to do with their win-lose record, but with the way they run their organization. Yes I began rooting for the Steelers while they were winning titles in the seventies just as Cowboy fans did and Chicago Bulls fans when Michael Jordan was winning all of those titles in the 1990's. The difference between me and many of those fans is I stuck with my team even through the lean years of the eighties and into the nineties.

I have no problem with fans rooting for whoever they want so long as they do it in good times and bad. My response to the homer is that this is America, land of the free. We have the right to choose and if we want to root for someone other than the home team than that's our right.

So how loyal should fans be to the teams that they root for? I think that fans should be as loyal to the team as the organization is to them. If the organization is trying to win than the fan should stick with them through thick and thin. If the organization is only worried about a profit then the fan owes them nothing. If the players on the team are not fan friendly then the fan doesn't have to root for them. If the game day experience is not enjoyable then the fan doesn't have to go. It's up to the organization to accommodate the fan not the other way.

Speaking of the game day experience what is the line that has to be drawn when rooting for a team and against an opponent wherever you watch? Fans should root for their team and against the opponent, nothing else. They should not disparage an opponent or a fan of the opposition at any time. There is nothing wrong with a little trash talk as long as it's not personal and is in good taste. The game day experience should be fun for everyone.

Should the fans of the opposing team be allowed in the stadium? If they buy a ticket, yes. If they get that ticket from a fan of the local team it's not their fault. And if their team is playing than they can wear the colors though I wouldn't suggest this in Philadelphia or the Black Hole in Oakland. If their team is not playing than they can't wear the colors. Nothing drives me crazier than seeing a Dallas Cowboy fan with their jersey on at a Redskin-Eagles game. If you want to wear the jersey either go to Dallas or stay at home and watch the Cowboys on TV. Besides, it kind of seems foolish to me that fans like this would go to a game and give the enemy their hard earned money. And if the opponent wins their fans have every right to be as happy as the home team's fans would if they had won.

I went to a Redskin-Raiders game back in 2005 at FedEx Field with my 24 year old nephew who is an Oakland fan. He wore his colors of silver and black while I went neutral. The game was the return of former 'Skins coach Norv Turner who was in charge of the Raiders. Washington fans wanted nothing more than to win the game and rub it in Turner's face. My nephew and I wanted the Raiders to win and they did.

This did not make the people around us happy and as we walked out they began to give my nephew some mean looks. I told them that they were wasting their time being mad at my nephew. If they were mad at anyone it should be the 45 guys and coaches of the Washington Redskins not my nephew. They were the ones who lost the game and spoiled their day not my nephew. They didn't like hearing that and I didn't care, because I was right. And no one bothered my nephew.

Another situation was Fourth of July weekend 1999 when we went to Yankee Stadium to watch the Baltimore Orioles play the Yankees. My father had just gotten a new Oriole hat and was wearing it outside of the stadium. We told him that he couldn't wear it inside the stadium. My father looked at us and said, "I'm 63 years old. I'll wear whatever I want." And he did. The Yankee fans in his section let him have it and my father took it good naturedly.

I was sitting in another section and at one point looked up to see the fans in my father's section passing him a beer. Then I noticed that the man next to him was getting change and putting it in his pocket. My father began to drink his beer with a big smile on his face. After the game we asked my father what it was all about. He told us that he had won a bet with the fan next to him. Oriole designated hitter Harold Baines had come to the plate and my father had predicted he would hit a home run which he did. The fans were giving him the business and saying he was lucky when he said the next hitter, Albert Bell, would do the same. So the guy next to him decided that they should wager a beer on it. Bell hit the home run and my father got his beer. By the end of the day, my father and the fans had made peace and enjoyed a good afternoon at the ballpark. The Yankees came back to win and my father heard it on the way out, but no one bothered him and he was treated with respect. What more can you ask for?

Needless to say, neither of these scenarios would have played out in Philadelphia. In Philly they don't mess around. You are either for or against. If you are against it is at your own risk. There are many places where the home fans treat the opponent's fans poorly, but Philadelphia is the one place where you really do risk your life wearing enemy colors.

I don't know why they are so mad, but they are. It is alright to be passionate, but Philly fans take it too far. Now that their reputation is nationally known it will never change. It's a shame, because otherwise they are some of the best fans in the country.

I'm not one who hates an opponent. I may not like them, but there is no hate. And there is always respect. I'm a Steelers fan, but have respect for their rivals the Baltimore Ravens. I respect the New York Yankees though not a fan. I do not root for Duke University basketball, but have respect for their head coach Mike Krzyzewski. To me hate is too strong a word when sports are involved.

There should be more experiences between fans like the one my father had at Yankee Stadium than the one my nephew and I had and the ones that occur in Philly. Once again, it's sport not life or death.

Another thing that fans should not do is burn and loot when their team wins a big game. This usually happens on college campuses and it's not right. It's destruction of property and reckless endangerment. This is being way too loyal.

Now we get to a tricky one. Can someone drop their loyalty to a team or player for any reason and, if they do, become a fan again? There are those who say you should stay with a team or player no matter what through thick and thin. Once again, I say that you should be as loyal as the team or player you root for is to you.

If the team that you root for decides to put a terrible product on the field, than you can leave them. Why should you support a team that's not trying to win? Why should you support a team where the owner is only worried about making a profit off of you? You don't have to. Keep your money in your pocket. Don't go to the games. Don't buy their merchandise. It is up to them to win you back. If and when they put a decent product on the field, court or ice than you can and should go back to being a fan.

If the players on the team rub you the wrong way then you can leave. I was a Los Angeles Lakers fan for years. Not anymore. I root for the hometown Washington Wizards who are far worse than the Lakers. It was the whole Shaquille O'Neal versus Kobe Bryant thing that soured me on the Lakers. I thought both of them acted like children. I have never been a fan of Kobe Bryant, but respect him as a player and think he is one of the best of all-time just as with Michael Jordan. I am a fan of O'Neal. However, I think that they were both wrong and should have been more mature in handling the situation. Their feud turned me away from the Lakers and I doubt if I'll ever go back.

If you are a homer and the team moves than you can definitely stop rooting for them. The team has shown how loyal they are to its fans by moving. Why should the fans loyalty go with them?

Now if the team is trying to win and making an effort to put an entertaining product out there than you have to stick with them. Championships are hard to come by. Most people experience only one "Golden Age" from a team in their lifetime. When I did root for the Redskins I can remember looking at their head coach Joe Gibbs on the sideline and saying to myself, "We had better enjoy this now, because when that man leaves it will be a long time before the franchise has this much success." I was right. It's been almost twenty years since Washington has gone to the Super Bowl. To the fans credit they have still supported the team even though management has given them every reason to leave. Redskin fans are unique in that way. Many fans would have given up on the team long ago.

But fans have to understand that their teams cannot always win. There will be lean years and periods of rebuilding. As long as the organization is trying to improve than they must be given the benefit of the doubt.

It is during these times when we find out who the "real fans" are.

THERE IS NO LOYALTY

So now that we have a general idea of what fandom is about let's ask ourselves, "Is there loyalty in sports?" Is there loyalty between player and player, player and coach, player and team, player and owner, player and fan? Is there loyalty between coach and team, coach and owner, coach and fan? Is there loyalty between owner and fans? Or is all loyalty in sports strictly based on the bottom line of fame and fortune.

It is my opinion that there has never been any loyalty in sports from high school sports on up to the pros.

High school players transfer schools all of the time. They go to whatever school gives them the best chance to show off their talent in order to get a scholarship. There are coaches who go to schools which will allow them to break rules and recruit players. Then leave the school that they are coaching for another thus leaving their players in the lurch.

College has no loyalty as coaches recruit players then leave for other schools all of the time. The players are stuck with either having to play for another coach who didn't recruit them and wants to bring in his own players or transferring. Of course, if the coach leaves he can do his job at a new school immediately while the player has to sit out a year if he transfers.

The coaches who do stay have to win or lose their jobs. They can graduate their players at one hundred percent, but if the team doesn't compete for a championship or play in a New Years bowl game the coach is gone. So the coach is stuck between waiting to be fired or moving on to greener pastures financially. Either way he is going to get criticized so why should loyalty come into play?

Turning to the pros, think about all of the hall of fame players who have been traded by their teams after years of service, because they were thought to be too old or expensive or no longer good enough. A player may get resigned by his old team just so he can retire with them, but during their careers when the organization feels like they can't get any more from them physically or they can get someone of more value that player is shipped out.

Remember, Babe Ruth was traded at the end of his career from the Yankees to the Boston Braves one of the worst teams in baseball. He is only considered by many to be the greatest baseball player of all-time. Quarterback John Unitas of the Baltimore Colts was benched at the end of his career and received the news over the phone while in the locker room. Then he was traded the next year to the San Diego Chargers one of the worst teams in the NFL. Unitas is another who is considered by many to be the best of all time at his position.

Joe Montana finished his hall of fame career with the Kansas City Chiefs. Franco Harris with the Seattle Seahawks. Alan Page with the Chicago Bears. Patrick Ewing gave his heart and soul to the New York Knicks only to find himself in Seattle at the end of his career. Scottie Pippen went from the Bulls to the Portland Trailblazers. Wayne Gretzky may be the greatest hockey player of all-time and even he got traded twice during his career.

For the longest time the players had no leverage when it came to who they played for and where. The owners held all of the cards and could sign and trade as they liked. This kept salaries down and player options limited. The feeling was that ballplayers should be happy to just play. They weren't working a real job anyway so why should they get paid a lot. This caused distrust between players and management that still exists to this day. It was this distrust which led to the famed "Black Sox" scandal of 1919 when the Chicago White Sox allegedly threw the World Series against the Cincinnati Reds. The White Sox players were tired of being underpaid and took matters into their own hands by fixing the series. Once they were banned from baseball and Commissioner Kennesaw Mountain Landis came aboard the players were done.

Players were bought, traded and sold in all sports until free agency was allowed in baseball in the late 1970's. This led to free agency in other sports and what little loyalty there was between player and team was gone. It is very rare to see a player stay with one team for their entire career now. Either they decide to leave or the team trades or releases them. That loyalty bridge has been burned. It never really existed.

As far as loyalty between players, it has to exist in order to win. A team cannot win championships if the players are not totally committed to each other. The good teams understand this from the top of the organization to the bottom. The bad ones don't. Players have to be loyal to their teammates and coaches. They must do what the organization asks of them in order for the team to reach its potential. There is no other way.

The head coach is the one caught in the middle. He must be loyal to his players, because without them there is no chance of him being successful. They must trust that he will do right by them while they play for him. That he will put them in position to maximize their talents. That he will be fair and give everyone an opportunity to compete for a job. That he will take the best players and put them on the field regardless of where they were drafted or how much they make. That he will come up with a strategy for victory. That he will discipline each player equally and not play favorites. That he will be there for them off of the field as well as on it.

The coaches problem is that he has to think of the whole team not just one player. He has to win or the organization will let him go. So when the time comes for a coach to make a decision on a player no matter what they have done for the team, he has to decide what's best for the team. If that means letting a player go than he has to do it. Forget the championships that have been won. Forget the moments shared on and off of the field. Forget the fact that the player had a lot to do with the coach's success. If the coach feels that it's time to move on than it is.

Because if he doesn't and the team loses whatever loyalty there is between coach and owner is gone. The coach knows this. He knows that he will be the one to take the fall for losing, because it is easy to fire one coach than it is to fire a whole team of players. The coach may be a victim of poor management in the front office, but there is nothing they can do. History shows that there has never been loyalty when it comes to coaches and management. As the old saying goes, coaches are hired to be fired.

So we have come full circle back to owners. The men who always talk about how the team belongs to the fans. How much they care about the fans and would do anything for them. These are the men who are always asking the fans to support the team through thick and thin.

Then they come to the city hat in hand asking for new stadiums and practice facilities. Always threatening to move the team if they don't get what they want.

The bottom line is that owners own the teams and can do whatever they want with them despite what fans may or may not like. If they want the team to be terrible on the field, but make a profit than they can sign low priced talent and concentrate on stadium and memorabilia revenue. If they want the team to be really good than they can go out and spend whatever they want under the rules to bring in the right people to do it. They can hire and fire whoever they want. They can set ticket prices at whatever they want. They can set the price of parking to whatever they want.

And they can move the team whenever and wherever they want. If the Brooklyn Dodgers can move anyone can move. If the Baltimore Colts can move anyone can. If the Cleveland Browns can move anyone can. All of them had great fan bases and the owners left them.

If that doesn't tell you there is no loyalty, nothing will.

THE FIRST TIME EVER I SAW

This chapter is about first impressions. It is about the first time that I saw certain athletes in action not knowing who they were. Most of these impressions were forged while in college or the minor leagues while some in high school. A few were in the pros with most of these happening when I was a child. They left an immediate impact which made me keep an eye on them throughout their careers. All of them lived up to the potential greatness that they showed me that first time. Here they are.

The first athlete to make a lasting impression on me was actually already a great player. He was an NFL all-pro at middle linebacker with the Chicago Bears and his name is Dick Butkus. I was five years old back in 1972 and we had tuned in to watch the Washington Redskins play the New York Jets, but somehow the local station couldn't get the feed(Yes, this used to happen back then). So CBS gave us the Chicago Bears and Detroit Lions. I don't remember anything about the game, but Butkus. It seemed as though the announcers were saying his name on every other play. When it was over, the name Dick Butkus rang in my head all day. I had heard of Butkus from a Redskin-Bears game the year before in which he caught the winning extra point, but that's all I knew about him. I had no idea he was that great a player until that Lions game. It's over 35 years later and I still remember it.

Fast forward to 1976. The Bears again. This time they are playing the Redskins and CBS actually gives us the game. The Redskins have been a playoff team four of the previous five seasons with one trip to the Super Bowl in 1972. The Bears haven't won anything since winning the NFL championship in 1963. So most people around Washington felt that there was no way the 'Skins could lose.

Well, there was a way they could. The game begins and this little guy for the Bears keeps getting the football. He breaks tackles and fakes out defenders. He makes one touchdown run that has to be seen to be believed where he heads to the sideline, gets hit, somehow stays on his feet and gets to the corner. The Redskins were coached by George Allen who was known as a defensive genius and this little guy shreds them. Along the way, he leads the Bears to a romp.

Next day, the local sports anchors were raving about this little guy on the six o'clock news. I was at my cousin's house and when they showed the highlights my uncle called us into the room to watch. He was as excited as the anchors.

"Look at this guy," he was telling us. "Did you see that run? Three guys hit him and he still stayed on his feet." Then they showed the touchdown and my uncle went crazy. "Who is that guy? Where did he come from? Walter Payton? I've never heard of him."

Yes, that was my first impression of the great Walter Payton.

I'm not much of a college basketball fan at age 11. I watch the teams in the Atlantic Coast Conference and the Final Four, nothing else. So I tune into the 1979 Final Four to see who is in it. There is this team from Indiana State playing in the semifinals. Some guy wearing number 33 is just dominating the game. He shoots passes and rebounds better than anyone on the floor. The crowd is completely behind him and his team. I find out that Indiana State is undefeated, but have no idea who they have played and in what conference.

And I find out that the player who is dominating the game is Larry Bird. I knew a little about Ervin "Magic" Johnson and Michigan State University only because one of the local high schools had a player with the same name. After one game, I knew more about Bird and he was the one I rooted for in the famous championship between the two. His first performance came before Magic's and I never forgot it.

Later that year, I was watching a college football game on Christmas Day. I thought it odd, because usually the only football game on Christmas was the annual Blue-Gray all-star game. But here was some bowl game called the Fiesta on TV. I really don't remember much about the game except for who was playing quarterback.

The announcers kept talking about this freshman. How he had started for his team all year and shown a lot of potential. Then I watched him throw and what an arm. The release was quick and he was accurate. Being that it was college football in the late 1970's there was no such thing as a wide open offense outside of Brigham Young University so the coaches didn't let him throw that much. They let him throw enough for me to see what I had to.

They let him throw enough for me to find out that this freshman played for Pittsburgh University and his name was Dan Marino.

Not a bad gift on Christmas.

A year later we are watching the Gator Bowl between the University of South Carolina and Marino's Pitt Panthers. South Carolina boasts Heisman Trophy winning running back George Rodgers while Pitt has Marino and the man who many thought was really the best player in college football linebacker Hugh Green.

The Panthers have a pretty good team having lost only one game all year and they dominate South Carolina winning 37-9. Rodgers is held to little or nothing on the ground in part because of Green.

On this night, however, it is not Green nor Rodgers nor Marino who is the best player on the field. The Panthers boast a linebacker on the opposite side of Green who just dominates the game. He is a tackling machine as South Carolina tries to avoid Green by running away from him. They may have been better served running away from the other guy. By game's end the "other" linebacker is named most valuable player.

At school the next day, we were raving about this guy. All of us were saying that Green may have gotten all of the hype, but this guy was better. One of my friends was talking about him and trying to remember his name. He asked me who the guy was that had dominated the Gator Bowl.

I told him that it was Rickey Jackson.

The Washington Redskins are playing their second game of the 1981 NFL season. It is against an NFC East rival who they always beat. Washington has just come off of an opening day loss at home to their biggest rival the Dallas Cowboys. With a new head coach in Joe Gibbs this loss was not unexpected. A loss in week two, again at home, to this division opponent that they have beaten on a regular basis would be.

The game begins and Washington can't move the ball. The Giant defense which has always been their strength is everywhere led by middle linebacker Harry Carson. But it is another linebacker who catches my eye. He seems to be in the Redskin backfield on every play. He can't be blocked. He seems to be playing the game at a different speed.

Just as though it seems the Redskins are about to score and take the momentum this guy comes around end and hits quarterback Joe Theismann from the blindside as he's about to throw. The ball pops loose and New York recovers ending the threat and pretty much the game. RFK Stadium is stunned. So am I. I have not seen a linebacker dominate a game in this manner since Dick Butkus. I have to know who this man is.

This man wears number 56. His name is Lawrence Taylor.

The next impression did not come from seeing the player play, because his games weren't on network TV and cable only picked up on him later. The records that he set were thought to be misprints and the product of playing inferior college competition. I first heard of him from reading Jet and Ebony magazine. Every week during the football season these magazines would give the rankings for Historically Black College football. Then they would print the statistics of the players. No other magazine that I knew did so this was the only way to follow him and his quarterback.

Then a friend of mine went off to college. When he would come home for the summer people would ask him what school was he attending? His answer was Mississippi Valley State. Nine times out of ten if the person asking was white he would get a blank stare from them. So he would ask them this question.

"Have you heard of Jerry 'World' Rice? It's his school."

The answer was usually no.

"You will," he would say. "You will."

And we did.

There was one person who made it big in a sport other than the one I first saw him play. We were at a friend's house for a cookout when the Little League World Series came on in 1989. This was during the time when the Taiwanese team was dominating the tournament beating the American champion on a regular basis. This year seemed to be no different.

Little did we know, but the US team was pretty good. And confident. They outplayed the team from Taiwan and won. The victory made them celebrities not only in their hometown of Trumbull, Connecticut, but nationally. The person who stood out the most was the young man who had pitched and won the championship game.

The thing that I remember about him was that he was kind of chubby, but far from out of shape. It seemed to me that he had a bright future in baseball if he wanted to pursue it. But the young man liked another sport more. I made sure to keep his name in my head, because I thought that there was a chance he could make it.

A few years later I'm watching a college hockey game and the kids name comes up. There he is on the ice and he's good. Very good. National Hockey League good. This didn't surprise me at all. And it didn't surprise me that his team won the NCAA championship. It also didn't surprise me to see the young man holding up the Stanley Cup Trophy a few years later.

Chris Drury had the stuff from the time he took that mound in Williamsport, Pennsylvania.

Another great athlete came along in college basketball back in 1996. The University of Maryland had made it to the NCAA tournament and their first round opponent was a west coast team that Terrapin fans thought they could beat, but knew it would be tough. Maryland had a good team which was making its fifth straight tournament appearance, but we soon found out that the opponent had a great player.

From beginning to end this surfer looking dude just took over the game. There was nothing that Maryland could do to stop him. From the point guard position he handled the ball and controlled the tempo. He wasn't very big, but was quick and decisive. He slashed to the basket when he had to and either dished or scored. It was apparent early that if Maryland didn't stop this guy they were going to lose.

They didn't stop him and lost. They lost, because Santa Clara had a player that was just better than everyone else.

A guy by the name of Steve Nash.

Growing up in a baseball house it was hard not to know who the big names were coming up from the farm system. My father and cousin used to buy the pre season magazines which would list the potential rookies for the coming season and the top minor league prospects. So I pretty much knew about most players before they made it to the big leagues.

Then my passion for baseball began to ebb and I didn't keep up with the lower levels as much. The Orioles put a minor league club in Bowie, Maryland and for a while I went to a few games. Every time that I went to the park there would be one player who would catch my eye and more often than not he would end up in the majors shortly thereafter. Two recent names stand out.

The first I saw when Bowie hosted the Double A all-star game in 2005. This big kid who played first base. He didn't do much at the plate, but you could tell that there was power in those arms. Those arms would bring him up to the Philadelphia Phillies and Ryan Howard has been there ever since.

The second happened when my brother decided to give me a ticket to see the Baysox play on a Sunday afternoon which had a threat of rain in 2004. I went to the park not expecting much when the catcher of the opposing team came up and POW! A deep shot over the right field fence. Not much later he came up and POW! Another homer over the left field fence. With the game getting out of hand, the young man came up and doubled off of the fence before being replaced for a pinch runner.

I decided to look in my game program to see who this kid was. I really wasn't paying attention to the public address announcer so hadn't heard it called. When I saw the name it all made since. And I knew that we'd never see him play in Bowie again.

The name in the program said Joe Mauer.

I was a boy or young man when most of these moments occurred. I'm older now so not much gets by me when it comes to sports. Since the mid 1980's media coverage of athletes has become so intense that we know more about them when they come into the public than we did before. This makes it harder for one to have a first impression of our own.

And that's too bad. I like surprises.

WHEN SHOULD A PLAYER HANG IT UP

At this writing, there is one athlete who is polarizing to the public, because he strings everyone along with talk of whether or not he's going to play or retire. He has retired from two different teams only to come back. Now, he is with a good team that almost made it to the Super Bowl last year. Of course I'm talking about quarterback Brett Favre.

Though there are many, including me, who thought that Favre should have stayed retired after 2007, in 2009 he proved us all wrong by having one of his best years. Favre's year was so good that he took the Minnesota Vikings to a division title and the NFC championship game. Though he just turned 41, Favre will more than likely come back to play in 2010.

When it comes to retiring and coming out of retirement, Favre is more of the exception than the rule. When most athletes get to his age, they are no longer the players they once were. Today's players are more likely to be better at this stage than their predecessors, because of new methods of training, but are still noticeably a step or two slower.

Favre, however, is in a good position. He is playing for a championship caliber team whereas most times players are on teams in decline. He is playing for a coach who knows him and in the system he has always played in. He plays indoors at least nine times a year. Not a bad setup.

So, many of us were wrong about Favre. But often times we are right when guessing that a player is past his prime. It's pretty simple to tell. The films don't lie as they say. But it is not up to us to decide when an athlete retires at any time in their careers or whether they should play until they are 100. That's the athlete's decision. All we can ask is when should a player hang it up?

The first time that I remember seeing an athlete playing who was past his prime was in 1973. The Redskins were playing the San Diego Chargers on opening day. Quarterback John Unitas had been traded from the Baltimore Colts to the Chargers and started the game. Unitas had been a shell of his former self the year before in Baltimore and time had only added more rust. Playing for a bad team, with a bad arm and no legs Unitas had no chance and the Redskin won 38-0.

My cousin who was a huge Colts fan was at our house that Sunday. Unitas was his man and he was already hurt seeing him in another uniform. Seeing Unitas' performance made him feel even worse. I can remember him saying over and over, "That's not Unitas. That's not the Unitas I know." He said it softly with his head held a little low. I was five years old and still remember it to this day. Unitas would retire at the end of the season.

Then a few weeks later, there was New York Mets centerfielder Willie Mays falling down during the World Series. It had been 19 years since Mays had made his great over the shoulder catch of a Vic Wertz drive during the 1954 Series. For a six year old who had no concept of time, Mays falling meant nothing. For my father and his generation it was a sad end to a hall of fame career. Fate had conspired to put Mays there. He had already announced his retirement effective at the end of the season earlier that year not knowing the Mets would make it to the Series. Willie knew that it was his time even before the fall, but it didn't make it any less sad.

I saw my first real hero, Henry Aaron, finish his career as a designated hitter for the Milwaukee Brewers. It was the city of Milwaukee and the Brewers way of thanking Aaron for all of the good times he gave them while playing for the Milwaukee Braves. It was a nice gesture, but Aaron didn't look right in the uniform, especially in his token at bat during the 1975 all-star game.

Baltimore Oriole third baseman Brooks Robinson was benched at the end of his career and retired in midseason. San Francisco 49ers quarterback John Brodie retired with a sore arm. So did Pittsburgh's Terry Bradshaw. O.J. Simpson retired in San Francisco basically running on one leg. Many baseball players hung on by becoming designated hitters. Kareem Abdul-Jabbar was still productive when he retired, but not the dominant player he had been in his prime. It was the same with Dr. J., Julius Erving. Walter Payton stayed with the Bears a season or two too long. I remember the Canadian Olympic hockey team bypassing Wayne Gretzky for other players in a shootout against the Soviet Union in 1996.

Boxing is notorious for men staying past their prime. Who can forget Muhammad Ali making comeback after comeback leading to the sad sight of him being pummeled by heavyweight champion Larry Holmes? Holmes fell into the same trap himself later and was knocked out by Mike Tyson. Sugar Ray Leonard came back one time too many and was left beaten in the corner as Terry Norris pounded him for twelve rounds. Evander Holyfield is still trying to fight.

But we haven't answered the question of when should an athlete retire?

I would like to think that if I had made it to the pros my career would have been long and productive. And I would like to think that I would have known when it was time to give it up. To me, when an athlete gets around the tenth year of his career it's time to think about retirement. I'm not saying that they don't have anything left or should retire. I'm simply saying that they are on the downside of their careers and it's time to give it some thought.

Players of the pre free agency era had to play for as long as they could, because there were no big contracts and no major endorsements. So they kind of have to be given the benefit of the doubt for playing past their prime.

It's not like today's players can make more money after retirement than they do while playing, but the great ones make enough to where they should be set up pretty good financially after ten years. So the transition from playing to retirement should be easier. This does not seem to be the case. Many of them can't live without the game and the lifestyle that comes with it. Some of them are pressured from outside forces like agents, hangers on, spouses and the teams they play for or who might want them. Others may have financial obligations that can only be taken care of by playing. All of this has to be considered when we say to ourselves that an athlete should give it up or continue to play. Everyone's situation is different.

My answer to whether a player should hang on is this. If it is pride and legacy they are worried about than they should get out while they are ahead physically. If it is about hanging on to break a record than they should retire if the quest will take away from the team. If it's about hanging on to win a championship than, as with the record, don't stay if it will hurt the team or hold them back.

If it is about finances, than they should play as long as someone is willing to pay them. For those who say that athletes are cheating the game by doing this I say maybe the game owes them a little something for the years of sacrificing for the sport. Besides, if there is no place for them in the game than no one will sign them. If the sport wants to use them they will find a way to.

If the game is still fun and you can help a team in some capacity than play. The thing is that when you can no longer play it's over. There is no coming back. So have all of the fun you can and enjoy every minute until they push you kicking and screaming out the door. This may lead to some awkward moments at the end of a career, but so be it.

So I guess the answer to when do you hang it up depends on the individual and their situation.

I'm of the opinion that they should quit before their bodies give out on them. Quit while they are on top.

But the realist in me says that as long as someone is willing to put them on the payroll an athlete can play for as long as they want.

GRUDGING RESPECT

We hear and say it all of the time. "I hate that team," or "I hate that player." Usually the team or player we are talking about plays for a bitter rival. New York Giant and Philadelphia Eagle fans always say that they hate each other's team. Same with Boston Red Sox and New York Yankees, Michigan Wolverine and Ohio State Buckeyes, Boston Celtics and Los Angeles Lakers, Duke Blue Devils and North Carolina Tar Heels, Chicago and New York in anything.

Though I think that hate is too strong a word, it's alright to not like an opponent. And it's alright to not like a certain player or coach, but only in an athletic sense for we really don't know them and cannot unless we actually meet them. I used to use the word hate just as much as anyone. I hated the Cowboys, Celtics and Yankees. I hated Duke and North Carolina basketball. I hated Christian Laettner, Roger Clemens, Danny Ainge, Roberto Duran and Tommy Hearns. I hated Jim Boeheim, Mike Krzyzewski, Dean Smith, Tom Landry and Billy Martin. Now I only dislike.

Though I may dislike a team or player, one thing I will always do is give them the respect that they deserve. If they win a title, than they've got my respect. If they win an award that is deserved, than they've got my respect. If they make a great play during a game while it's still in the balance, than they get my respect. If they beat my team fair and square than they get my respect.

It has to be earned. There is no question about that. And it will always be given by me grudgingly. This chapter is about the players and teams who I don't like, but get my respect.

Grudging respect.

The Dallas Cowboys are the one team in sports that I dislike more than any other. Growing up in the seventies I can remember how Dallas was thought of as the greatest thing since sliced bread. They had the best coach, the best players, the best owner, the best stadium and the best cheerleaders. We were told this over and over until one would have thought the Cowboys invented the game of football. It finally culminated in the 1979 team highlight film when they were dubbed "America's Team." That was the last straw for me.

My main problem with the Cowboys though has always been their fans. The bandwagoners who are all over the team when they are winning then can't be found when they lose. The ones who wear Cowboy jerseys to Redskin-Giant games. The ones who always find an excuse when the Cowboys lose and act like every victory was supposed to happen. The ones who act like the league owes Dallas everything. The ones who still think that the Cowboys were as good as the Steelers during the seventies even though Pittsburgh beat them both times they played in the Super Bowl.

As for the team, I may not like them, but give them credit when it's deserved. Every Cowboy who is in the pro football hall of fame deserves it. They probably deserve a few more. Tom Landry was one of the greatest coaches who ever lived. And so is Jimmy Johnson who led Dallas to back to back titles in 1992-93. It is my belief that if Johnson had stayed for the 1994 season the Cowboys would have become the first team to win three straight Super Bowls. That's how much respect I have for him and that team. Grudging respect.

As a Los Angeles Lakers fan during the 1980's I hated the Boston Celtics, of course. I couldn't stand Larry Bird, Robert Parrish, Kevin McHale or Danny Ainge. Dennis Johnson was okay, because he had played for the Seattle Supersonics and Phoenix Suns before coming to Boston. And watching a Boston game with former Celtic Tommy Heinsohn announcing was like going to the dentist. Every time that the Celtics would win a title and team President Red Auerbach would light that victory cigar I wanted to shove it down his throat.

But I always had to give the Celtics their due. Without them, the Lakers would have had no real competition during the decade. Bird, Parrish and McHale formed one of the best front lines in NBA history.

The Boston Garden was one of the best home court advantages in the game. Every Lakers victory over the Celtics was sweet, because they were hard earned. Without Bird, there is no Magic Johnson really. Magic had to elevate his game to beat Bird and the Celtics and he did. The Celtics of the eighties were as good as anyone. I'm not afraid to admit that. Grudgingly, of course.

I've never been a New York Yankee fan and never will be. But the teams that they had at the end of the 1990's were some of the best in baseball history. They won four world's championships in five years from 1996 to 2000. In 1998 they won 114 games and crushed everyone in the post season. That team was so good they should have been crowned champions in May. As much as I disliked them they were beautiful to watch. They had great pitching. They never made a mistake in the field. Whenever they needed a big hit they got it. They played the game the right way and for that get my grudging respect.

Even when I was a Lakers fan, Kobe Bryant was not one of my favorites. I don't know him personally. He might be one of the nicest people on the planet and I hope that is the case. Either way what I think of Bryant as a person means nothing. Who am I to judge?

However, as a basketball player I consider him one of the best of all-time. When I rooted for the Lakers, Bryant was included. I wanted him to take the big shot. I wanted him to score 40 every night. I wanted him to do whatever was necessary for the Lakers to win. And I had no problem with him calling Shaquille O'Neal out on the court. One of my favorite moments was being at a Lakers-Wizards game when Michael Jordan was with Washington where Bryant took the ball coast to coast and slammed it home as His Airness could only watch.

Even though I don't root for the Lakers anymore and don't want Bryant to hit the game winner he still gets full credit from me. Now I don't want the ball in his hands at the end, because I know that he can beat the team I'm rooting for. But whenever he steps on the floor, I want to see Bryant go for 40. I fell asleep the night that he put up 81 and still regret it. It was basketball history and I missed it. He may not be one of my favorite people, but the man can play. Period. Bottom line. You have got to respect that.

As a Pittsburgh Steelers fan living in the state of Maryland, I am in Baltimore Raven country. The Ravens and Steelers are arch rivals and the fans hate each other though Pittsburgh fans feel as though Baltimore is the little brother that they have to keep in check. I work with plenty of Ravens fans and they never want to give the Steelers their due. Growing up as a Maryland basketball fan, I understand their makeup, because I am with them when it comes to Duke and North Carolina basketball. Every time that the Ravens beat the Steelers it's because they were the better team and tougher. Every time the Steelers win its luck or the officials did the Ravens wrong.

The Steelers fan sees it differently. The Steelers not only beat the Ravens because they are the better team and tougher. The Steelers win, because they are smarter. They don't make the unforced errors that Baltimore does. Though I know that every Steelers-Ravens game is going to be close there is never a doubt in my mind that if the two teams are equal, Baltimore will do something to give Pittsburgh the game.

Having said this I respect the Ravens immensely. First off, I remember what it was like when the Colts left Baltimore so can never really hate the Ravens. Second, the Ravens are a first rate organization very similar to the Steelers. They build their team through the draft. They play a tough style of football. They have a very nice, fan friendly stadium. And the players on the team know the pulse of their fans.

The truth of the matter is that Baltimore and Pittsburgh are similar in so many ways that you can't respect one and not the other. That's probably why they bring out the best in each other when they meet.

Track and field star Carl Lewis is another athlete I never rooted for. I thought that he was an excuse maker. It seemed as though when he lost in a sprint or the long jump the first thing that he did was accuse the winner of using performance enhancing drugs. He wouldn't come right out and say it, but everyone knew what he was getting at. Lewis was probably right more times than not for athletes know these things. But it still hinted at crying whenever he did it, because it seemed as though it was only when he lost.

But I would be a fool if I were to say that Carl Lewis is not one of the best athletes of all time. He was as fast as anyone in his day and could jump as far. He competed in three different Olympics medaling in all of them. He was the star of the 1984 Los Angeles games winning five gold medals. No matter what one thinks of Carl Lewis, he got it done.

And then there is Michael Jordan. I have always had a love-hate relationship for Jordan. The hate started first as I had to watch him sink the winning basket for the hated North Carolina Tar Heels in the 1982 NCAA championship against the hometown Georgetown Hoyas. Then came the first sign of respect as in his sophomore year, he brought the Tar Heels back from a huge deficit to beat Ralph Sampson and Virginia. This was the game in which Jordan's steal and dunk of an inbounds pass defeated the Cavaliers 64-63. That moment was when I knew Jordan wasn't all hype. There are those who say they were surprised Jordan became what he was in the pros. They must not have seen what he did that night against Virginia. That game alone should have made him the number one pick when he came out.

When he first got to the Chicago Bulls, I rooted for him, because he was going up against the Larry Bird led Celtics and the Bad Boy Detroit Pistons of Isaiah Thomas, Bill Laimbeer and Dennis Rodman. I can still remember him taking over playoff games against Detroit and willing his team to victory. Eventually, the Bulls hired Phil Jackson as their coach and surrounded Jordan with the players he needed to win. The Bulls beat the Lakers for the title in 1991 and won the next two for a three peat. I never rooted for them. I didn't want Jordan to outdo Magic. I didn't want the Bulls to win more titles than the Lakers of the eighties.

Then after the third title Jordan retired to play baseball. I didn't think that it would happen, but I missed him. When he announced that he was coming back during the 1995 season, I was very happy. And I wanted to see him take the Bulls to the championship. It would have been one of the greatest stories of all-time if he had, but the Bulls fell short.

The next season I went back to rooting against the Bulls and continued to until Jordan retired again in 1998 after another three peat. What bothered me most wasn't that the Bulls were winning titles, but the rest of the league seemed to have quit. None of the other teams thought they could beat Jordan. Not the Bulls, but Jordan. He was not the same player as before his retirement, but it didn't matter. The young men who were now in the league had idolized him as kids and thought of him as a God. Everyone knows that God always wins. So they went about making money instead of winning championships.

I've said this once and I'll say it again. I don't know if Michael Jordan was the greatest basketball player of all-time, but do know this. He made an entire league quit.

How can you not have ultimate respect for a man who does that?

ARE ALL STAR GAMES PASSE?

All star games in professional sports used to be showcase events. The major television networks paid for the rights to broadcast them. The season was split so that the games could be played at the midway point in every sport except football which scheduled its Pro Bowl a week after the championship game until 2009 when they moved it to the week before the Super Bowl. Every athlete who played a sport thought it an honor to be selected for the all-star team and took pride in playing in the game. The players were happy to be in the game, but none of them wanted to lose, because league or conference pride was at stake. Local news media would promote a player that they thought should make the team. And fans looked at players who were all-stars in a different light than those who weren't.

Though all star games are still events, they are not the showcase they once were. Today's all star games have much more of a festival atmosphere attached to them. Instead of being one day affairs they are now two and three days. This concept came not from the NBA of the 1990's, but the East-West Negro League baseball game back in the 1930's. Baseball and hockey have televised skills competitions the night before their games while basketball has a whole weekend of things to do inside and out of the arena with celebrities coming from all over the country. The NBA all star game is no longer shown on one of the major networks and the NFL was dropped for a few years until 2009.

Baseball was the first sport to let fans vote for all star teams and now everyone else does. This causes some ballot box stuffing at times, but most of the time fans vote for the players they want to see from all teams not just their own. This may leave a more deserving player who hasn't quite built a reputation yet from being elected as a starter, but they usually get a spot as a reserve.

The fan friendly aspect of all star games and weekends is good for the game. Putting a couple of days aside to not only celebrate the all stars, but the game is what it should be about. This should always be an all star game staple.

The problem with all star festivals, which is what they have become, is the main event itself. The all star games are not as good as they used to be. In some, like football and basketball, the players basically go through the motions trying not to get hurt. In baseball and hockey they play a little harder, but still try to avoid injury. The basketball all star game has turned into basically both teams trying to showcase the best player of the host city so that he can win the most valuable player award. Football's Pro Bowl has lost a lot, because many of the best players avoid it due to injury or indifference.

Before the games became two and three day festivals, they were single day events that were watched by every fan. Baseball was the model sport of the time and whatever it did everyone else followed. It was baseball which produced the first annual league sanctioned all star game in 1933. For years, the baseball all star game was the most popular. It was THE all star game. It recently has been challenged by basketball, but not surpassed.

With everything on one day, the focus was clearly on the games and the players knew it. They played hard and played to win. Who can forget Pete Rose of the Cincinnati Reds running over catcher Ray Fosse in the 1970 major league all star game to score the winning run separating Fosse's shoulder in the process? I can remember a Pro Bowl in which Terry Bradshaw was coming off of an MVP performance in the Super Bowl and threw an interception late in the game which cost the AFC the game and he was upset about it. These athletes knew that most of the country was watching and wanted to prove they belonged in the game. For many of them it was the only time all season that they would play on national TV as there were no cable sports stations at the time.

Of course, the difference between all stars of the past and today's is the money given to them. The all stars of the past had to play in the game so that they could get paid. Some of them had incentives in their contract for making the team so it would be two checks earned. The winners share was twice what the losers made and every penny counted to athletes at that time, because team owners weren't paying them much. The all star check could be used for anything from a new car to a down payment on a house which made winning matter.

Today's players make so much money that those selected to the all star games are usually taking a pay cut to play. Some of them earn more money for one game than the combined salary of many of the all star teams of the past. To them, the all star game is nothing more than a reward given by the fans or their peers. They get as caught up in the festival atmosphere as the fans and media and there is nothing wrong with that. The problem is that there is no incentive for them to play in the game or give maximum effort. Thus the fans get shortchanged.

Baseball has tried to make their all star game mean something to the players again by giving home field advantage in the World Series to the team whose league wins. Though I don't think that an exhibition game should decide the fate of two teams playing for a championship it does seem as though the players are putting more effort into the game now. Football moved its game to the week before the Super Bowl, but it seemed as though the players tried less.

Another reason why all star games have become less competitive is the movement of players from team to team through free agency. Where once players stayed with the same team or in the same league most of their careers for many reasons now they have the freedom to play wherever they want. This cuts down on loyalty to a certain league or conference and there is not the same dislike for the other. The players all know each other and many have played together. Most people don't try to beat their friends in an exhibition game, because they don't want to embarrass them and maybe hurt the friendship.

What is the answer? How do you get all star games back to the competitive level that they used to be? How do you get the players to care enough to want to show up and play? How do you get the fans to care about the games as they once did? How do you make it so that they are must see events once again with the major networks vying for the rights to show them?

The only way that I can think of would never be bought by anyone involved and may not change anything. Have the all star games be winner take all events. Have a winner's pot which the players would split and nothing for the losers. Then let's see how hard they play.

This will never happen. Players are not going to do anything extra for free. Even if they wanted to, the players union would not let them. And how much money would be enough to get them to play? Most of them would still be taking a pay cut to participate. Then there would be the risk of injury. Every athlete who got injured in a game in which they didn't get paid would be called a fool by everyone.

So the question remains are all star games passé?

As I mentioned earlier, the festivities surrounding the event are good for the game. Every sport should take time out to celebrate the game and those who are involved. Also, the fans deserve to see the best players in one setting once a year. And the players who earn all star selection deserve to have their moment.

But the games themselves have seen better days. They are necessary for planning the other events surrounding the festival, but if the players are not going to show up or play hard than the game has outlived its importance.

IT IS A MAN'S WORLD

Though women have come a long way, it is still a man's world. For better or worse, man has made the rules since the beginning of time which has allowed him to gain ultimate power. No movement can ever take place in society unless it benefits those in power. Change cannot occur unless there is a change in the thinking of men. Women can start a movement, but somewhere along the line men have to get on board for anything to be accomplished. Sport is no different. It may be worse.

Despite the fact we have had female professional leagues in basketball, soccer and softball along with boxing women still rate second. Despite the fact that the United States established Title IX for gender equity in education programs or activities receiving Federal financial assistance, women still rate second in sports. Despite the fact that women have proven they can do well in business, sports is still lacking in the hiring of females in front office and ownership positions. Despite the fact that there are more and more women sports anchors, we still have very few female game announcers and almost no color commentators.

Most men do not watch women's sports and I am guilty of that as stated elsewhere. We would rather watch the cheerleaders at pro basketball or football games than a women's basketball or football game. We will tune in sooner to watch an attractive female sideline reporter than a gifted golfer. Most men watch women's tennis only because the women wear skirts that aren't very long. To men, a good women's sport is beach volleyball, because the women wear two piece bikinis. Women's beach volleyball does nothing for me, but I know it does for other men, because I've been told this. And most men do not want to see women trying to compete against men in male sports such as auto racing, basketball, baseball or even tennis especially after Billie Jean King defeated Bobby Riggs in their famous match in 1973.

The only established women's professional sports leagues are offshoots of men's sports. They are the Ladies Pro Golf Association, Professional Women's Bowling Association and women's tennis under the Association of Tennis Professional's Tour. The reason for this may be that many women compete in these sports, especially bowling and tennis, at the amateur levels and are on coed teams. Men are used to competing with and against them in these sports and are more inclined to watch other women perform in them live and on television.

This will never really change, because most men feel like sports is the one area where women cannot compete with us. To us, there is no way that women can play basketball better than a man at the highest level. There is no way that a woman can play football with men at any level. There is no way that a woman can play baseball better than a man or hit a slap shot harder. So with this being the case, why should we watch unless there is an attractive woman on the court, field or ice?

The men involved in sports know this as well. This means that they will be less inclined to sink their money into a pro league for women. The only time that these leagues spring up is when interest is created from an event like the Olympics or the World Cup. This was the case with the Women's National Basketball Association and the Women's United Soccer Association. The former has survived, because it is associated with the NBA while the latter died out from lack of interest though other leagues have been formed.

Female boxing had a brief period of interest as well when the daughter of former heavyweight champion Muhammad Ali, Laila, stepped into the ring to become champ in her own right. Though she never fought on network television, Laila Ali was successful when it came to pay per view viewership. Being the daughter of a famous boxer certainly helped, but Laila was very skilled herself. Once she left the scene interest in women's boxing disappeared. With the men struggling as well, there is not much hope for the women to ever gain their niche in the sports landscape.

Women's softball had a short lived league after winning in the Summer Olympics, but found it hard to compete with the major and minor men's leagues and all of the outlets people have for entertainment in the summer.

It has pretty much been established that our lifetime probably won't see any more women's leagues formed which will prosper despite all that has changed.

But the playing arena is not the only place where women have to play by a different set of standards than men. The first and most obvious is in the media.

For years, women were not accepted as equals when it came to covering sports. This began to change when television came along and producers and directors figured out that men would tune in to watch women like Phyllis George and Jayne Kennedy do feature stories on athletes. Soon, women were becoming local sports anchors and writing for newspapers and magazines. Then after quite a struggle, they were allowed access to men's locker rooms. Today, there is not much that women aren't allowed to do in the media, but there are still rules that apply to them which do not for men.

First, if you are going to be a woman on television in sports you had better not age. A woman anchor or reporter had better have a level of attractiveness in the first place or her chances of getting the job decrease no matter how knowledgeable or articulate she is. Even if she is a former player there had better be something to look at. How many times have we seen female anchors go from the local scene to a national network and change physically in front of our eyes? This is because the network is trying to get the maximum sex appeal out of them to increase viewership.

And God forbid a female anchor goes on maternity leave or her looks begin to decline, because of all the makeup she's forced to wear. If on a national network, she will begin to be phased out slowly unless there are cosmetic changes made to her appearance. If she does not make any changes to her body, then the changes must occur in her wardrobe. She had better begin to wear clothing that makes men notice her body more than her face. Men are never asked to do anything more than be clean shaven. They are allowed to age gracefully. Fair or unfair, women are not.

The shelf life of a female sports personality is not as long as their male counterparts. And, unlike actresses, there aren't too many roles on camera that they can transition into.

Women sports reporters are held to a higher standard when it comes to knowledge of the games they cover, also. If one doesn't believe it, just look at the way women sideline reporters are judged compared to men. If a man makes a mistake while reporting he can do a mea culpa and everything is fine. If a woman does, her competence and intelligence is questioned immediately. She is looked upon as nothing more than a glamour girl who got her job, because of her looks. This explains why there are very few women play by play and color commentators on men's sports as well. Men just aren't comfortable with women telling them what's going on and strategy, because we feel like a woman cannot know what the guys playing are thinking and feeling.

Women are almost better off writing sports than talking about them on TV. A writer can go an entire career without anyone really knowing who they are. Though they are still held to a higher standard when it comes to their knowledge of sports a woman can write from a different perspective than a man and it is accepted. Also, today's male athletes are used to having women reporters around which makes them more comfortable in opening up to them. If the sports world is smart there will always be a spot for women journalists.

The ceiling for women in the business of sports isn't much higher than it is in the media. Though there have been female owners in professional sports all of them except Marge Schott have inherited rather than bought their teams. From St. Louis Rams owner Georgia Frontierre to Schott women have been few and far between at the top level of sports. Frontierre and Schott are the only two female owners to win championships in their sport. Neither has been or was completely accepted by their male counterparts.

Frontierre inherited the Rams from her husband Carroll Rosenbloom after his death in 1979. When she became owner, the team resided in Los Angeles and moved to Anaheim in 1980. From there the Rams moved to St. Louis in 1995 where they are now established.

Schott owned the Reds from 1984 to 1999. She was thought to be crude by most and not ownership material by many. Not having known Schott I would say part of the reason for her behavior was because she knew that she was in a man's world and couldn't be thought of as soft. There were definite times where she went too far, but Schott had to come off as gruff in order to gain any respect from her peers.

Once Schott sold her share of the team, baseball was done with female ownership and football will be also when Frontierre passes. And there is no rich female who is going to be allowed to buy a team unless she makes an offer that blows everyone else away. Ownership of a sports team is one of the last bastions of the "old boy" network and every man involved will try to keep it that way to their grave.

Because of this, there will be very few women in front office positions in men's pro sports. The Washington Bullets/Wizards had a female vice president of operations in Susan O'Malley. The Oakland Raiders have a few female front office employees. Not too many other teams do unless the woman is related to the owner in some way. For the most part a woman can't expect to rise much higher in a men's sports organization than cheerleader coach, team trainer or in public relations no matter how qualified she is. That does not mean women should not strive for these jobs. It just means that their chances of being hired are much slimmer than in other professions.

The subject of a female head coach for a men's team in pro sports has to be brought up. Some names have been brought up. University of Tennessee women's basketball coach Pat Summitt's name has come up on occasion and if anyone could do it she can. Basketball is probably the most progressive sport when it comes to minority and gender hiring so most likely to do it first. They have already hired female assistants. Baseball, hockey and basketball probably haven't even given it a thought. First, how would you sell it to the men assistant coaches who have toiled for years to get to the top that a female is going to be their boss? Second, how would you sell it to the players? Third, how much public relations would you have to do to win the fans respect for the new coach? And finally what happens the first time the new female coach makes a call that is open to second guessing or suffers a losing streak? The margin of error would be much smaller for sure.

This is the state of affairs for women in professional sports today. Though it is much better than it has ever been there is still a long way to go. There are too many men set in their ways who rule sports from commissioners to owners, coaches, sports directors and producers, athletic directors and players themselves. They hold the top positions.

And sport is their world.

BOWL CHAMPIONSHIP SERIES VS. BOWLS VS. PLAYOFF

If you are a fan of college football which would you rather have, the current Bowl Championship Series (BCS), the old conference bowl affiliations or a post season or bowl playoff? One would guess that the casual fan has no problem with the BCS while the old school fan who likes tradition wouldn't mind seeing the old conference bowl affiliation system come back. The diehard football fan probably wants to see a playoff. This chapter will try to make a case for all three.

Before going into the pros and cons of each one this much is clear. Division I-A college football will have a playoff system someday. It may include the bowl games or be played afterward. It may be the two teams ranked highest after the bowls or eight teams playing three rounds of games using the bowls. I don't know how it will be done, but a college football playoff will happen as soon as the conferences can figure out the economics of how to split the money. Now let's begin.

The current system for deciding the college football national champion is the Bowl Championship Series or BCS. This system ranks the top 25 teams in the major Division I-A conferences with numbers three through ten getting bids to the four BCS bowls which are the Rose, Fiesta, Sugar and Orange. The top two teams play in a separate game after the bowls called the BCS Championship which is played on a rotating basis among the Rose, Fiesta, Sugar and Orange. The rankings are established by a computer which takes into account each teams overall record, conference record, conference ranking, Associated Press (AP) and United Press International (UPI) ranking, strength of schedule, strength of conference and average margin of victory.

Though most of the time this system does give us the two best teams it has its flaws. For one, it is hard for any team which does not start the season in the top ten of the AP or UPI rankings and is not in one of the conferences considered the strongest to get enough BCS points to earn a spot in the championship game. This means that if you are not in the Southeastern, Big Ten, Big XII, Pacific Ten, Big East or Atlantic Coast Conferences and your name is not Notre Dame your chances of playing for the championship are pretty slim. Or in other words, if you are the champion of the Western Athletic Conference you might get a BCS bowl bid, but you're probably not going to the Bowl Championship Game.

Second, the strength of schedule aspect is suspect, because it's more judgment than fact. Some years the SEC is considered the best conference. Other years it's the Big XII, Pac Ten or Big Ten. This is usually based on which conference has the most teams in the top 25 and with winning records. It is also dependant on how teams do against opponents outside of the conference. The problem is that we really don't know the caliber of the teams in each conference, because they change from year to year. Some years a conference may be very talented and beat each other up causing the best to miss out on a chance to play for the championship. In other years a team may be just pretty good in a weak conference in which the other teams are competitive enough with each other that they make the conference appear stronger than it is. In some seasons the reputation of a conference from previous years may help a team's strength of schedule.

The truth is that we may really not know how strong a conference is until the bowl games. How many times have we heard all year how good a conference is only to see them lose more bowl games than they win? And how many times have we heard how lousy they are only to have them win more bowls than they lose?

Then there is the problem of what to do when more than two teams are undefeated at the end of the season. This does not happen often, but when it does a team that may be worthy of a shot at the championship gets left out. It happened in 2004 when the University of Southern California, Oklahoma, University, and Auburn University all finished undefeated and untied. USC and Oklahoma were ranked in the top ten at the beginning of the season while Auburn was not. USC

Tim Holland

and Oklahoma played in the championship game while Auburn had to take its undefeated record to New Orleans and play in the Sugar Bowl. USC defeated Oklahoma 55-14. Auburn may not have been better than USC. We will never know. What we do know is that Auburn couldn't have done any worse than Oklahoma.

The problem that we get most often with the BCS is when there is one undefeated team and two or more one loss teams. Even worse is when there are no undefeated teams and three or more one loss teams. Unless the undefeated team is from the WAC, they will get a spot in the championship game. Then the debate begins as to which of the one loss teams should play them. It's an either or with no real winner, because there is a 50-50 chance that the wrong team will be picked. The 50-50 is even less when there are no undefeated teams. This is a problem that the BCS will never be able to solve.

As stated earlier, with all of its flaws the BCS may not give us the two best teams but more often than not it gives us the BEST team. There has only been one split national championship since the BCS came into play in 1998. The Louisiana State Tigers won the BCS while USC won the AP championship in 2003. And USC and Auburn both finished undefeated and untied in 2004 with the Trojans taking the crown and the Tigers finishing second. But for the most part every team which has won the BCS national championship was the best over the course of the season.

The traditionalist would rather see the old conference bowl affiliation system come back. This was the system that was in place before the BCS and what most of us grew up with. Simply stated, a conference would affiliate itself with a major bowl and their champion would play in it. The SEC champion got an automatic bid to the Sugar Bowl the old Big Eight went to the Orange Bowl and the old Southwestern Conference the Cotton. The Big Ten and Pac Ten champion played in the Rose. After the conference champions were decided each bowl committee would go out and find a worthy opponent amongst the other conferences and independents and sign them to a contract. The rest of the bowls would take whatever was left with the Fiesta usually getting the best of who was left.

In this system there may not have always been the best matchups, but everyone knew what they were getting and when luck would have it that two top five teams would meet it made the game more meaningful. Also, there was the chance of a team coming into a bowl game with a shot at a championship losing that opportunity after being defeated by an opponent playing for nothing more than school and conference pride. These so called upsets were the equivalent of what we see in the NCAA basketball tournament today. These games helped make college football what it has become as they are a part of the games lore. The BCS championship has eliminated that.

The bowl affiliation is still in effect. The difference between now and before the BCS is that the bowls no longer go out, scout teams and offer them a bid. Instead, they have bowl slots for teams in different conferences based on where they finish in the standings. This is to give the fans a better chance of seeing a game between two evenly matched teams. The problem is that once the BCS takes the cream of the crop all of the other bowls are considered second rate.

The biggest flaw in the old bowl conference affiliation system is that teams are locked into a certain game, because of the conference they play in. This all but eliminated what could have been great matchups like undefeated Alabama vs. undefeated Ohio State in 1979 or undefeated Ohio State vs. undefeated Texas in 1970.

The only way that two undefeated and untied teams could meet was if the Pac Ten and Big Ten champions were unscathed going into the Rose Bowl or an independent like Notre Dame, Pittsburgh, Miami, Penn State or Florida State did the same and took a bid to play against a team with a perfect record in the Orange, Cotton or Sugar.

The landscape changed when the Fiesta Bowl moved to New Years Day starting in 1982. The Fiesta Bowl had no affiliation with any conference and soon began to lure the best teams not going to one of the original Big Four. This led to the first bowl matchup of one vs. two which did not involve the Rose, Sugar, Cotton or Orange, the 1987 matchup between independents Penn State and Miami. The game was so huge that it was moved to January second in prime time. Though it was not the greatest of games Penn State vs. Miami became memorable, because the Nittany Lions came in as underdogs and defeated the Hurricanes.

This strengthened the argument for those who wanted a playoff. It also upset the major conferences and their bowl partners, because they were left on the outside looking in. When the same situation occurred two years later with Notre Dame and West Virginia meeting in the Fiesta, the seeds were planted for a future college championship game where everyone could be involved. The Big Four had been beaten again and vowed that it would be the last time. Thus, we have the BCS.

But the cry for a playoff continues. The scenarios usually given are a four team playoff after the bowl games, an add one playoff between the two top ranked teams after the bowl games, and an eight to sixteen team playoff using the bowl games similar to what the lower divisions in college football do. There are many who feel that college football is headed towards an alliance of 64 teams in a super conference split by region with the top 16 ranked teams earning playoff spots.

The naysayers say to the eight to sixteen team playoffs format that the college football season is long enough. They also say that the young men who play would miss too much class time never mind that most of the games would be played during the break between the fall and winter semesters. Though class time wouldn't be effected time to study and take final exams would and this is a problem, because not all schools take these exams at the same time. However, those for the playoff would say that if it can be done at the lower levels of college football it can be done at the top.

The traditionalist likes having their New Years Day Bowls and a playoff would eliminate this. Even if the bowl games were used as playoff sites they would have to play them before January first and the most games that could be played on New Year's would be two if the semifinals were played that day. New Year's Day would lose a lot of its luster. However, those who are for a playoff say that the bowl games would be more likely to sell out and television would be willing to pay more money to broadcast them. And, since most of the games would be shown independent of each other the ratings would soar.

The third thing is how can one be sure that the eight to 16 teams picked are the best in the land? Just like with basketball picking their

68 team field someone deserving is going to be left out. There is really nothing that can be done about it.

So the more likely playoff would be an additional game or two played after the bowls with the two or four top ranked teams in the country. Most fans would be more likely to agree that the best teams are playing for the championship this way. The only problem with this scenario is that we could have a season in which two teams from the same conference who might have played in the regular season could meet in the championship. Or with four teams in the field there may be a time when only two conferences are represented, because their teams are ranked one through four. And the and one or two game playoff still won't solve the problem of a glut of one-loss teams.

These are the three phases of college football postseason past, present and future. Though none of them are perfect most people would never go back to the bowl affiliation system and don't like the BCS. The majority seems to want a form of playoff sooner rather than later. For what it is worth, they will probably get their wish.

As for me, I'm a traditionalist. I liked the old system of bowl affiliation. I always felt that if a team was good enough to win the national championship they would defeat whomever they played wherever. If they are not, then they won't. I enjoyed seeing a UCLA defeat an undefeated Ohio State team in the 1976 Rose Bowl. The Bruins did it to Michigan State in 1966. Notre Dame pulled the trick and claimed a national championship by beating Texas in the 1978 Cotton Bowl. I miss those games. And I have no problem with the BCS system. Like I said before, they may not always get the two best teams in the championship, but the team which wins is usually the best in the country.

However, if the colleges figure out a way to have a playoff I will be right there front and center watching it with everyone else.

ROLLING THE DICE

Gambling is an important element of sports though it is illegal in every state but Nevada. There are many ways to put money down on a sporting event from friendly wagers between two people to betting the odds. Fantasy leagues came into play in the 1990's where fans picked their own teams from players in a sport and whoever finished with the best record or most points won a percentage of the money earned from entrance fees. Even bowling leagues can be considered a form of gambling as teams pay to play each week and at the end of the season the best get a percentage of whatever is taken in. I have participated in all of these forms and a few more.

Not anymore. I have not gambled on a sporting event except for the office NCAA tournament pool since 2002. I was never a heavy gambler on sports, but did it enough to know that it could become a problem. Football was my game of choice, college and pro, and I played parley cards on a weekly basis. Parleys are cards in which the gambler has to pick at least three games against the point spread in order to play. The point spread is the margin of victory that the odds makers think the winner will win by. The more games that you pick, then the higher the odds. For example, if you pick three games the odds would be five dollars for every dollar that you bet, four would be ten dollars, five would get you fifteen all the way up to twelve at 300 to one. A card with up to nine picks had to be perfect in order to win. Bets of ten to twelve games could not have more than one loss. All ties with the point spread lost.

Another play on the cards is the over-under. That is a total point amount in which the line is set to over a certain amount or under it. To place a bet you had to say that both teams would score under the low number or over the high number. The way that our cards did it was that the under and over would have a five point spread separating them. For example a Giants-Eagles game could have an under of 30 and an over of 35. So if you took 30 the point total for the entire game had to be less than that and if you took 35 it had to be more. A tie or falling in that five point middle and you lost.

So there were two ways to go. You could pick fewer games and dish out more money or play more games and pay less. I picked more and paid less, because I couldn't afford to do it the other way.

I didn't win too often while putting down about thirty dollars a week on three to four cards. Over a ten year period, I finished ahead of the game only once and couldn't break even most of the time. The one year that I had success was winning $1,500 on a great weekend in 1992 where I got ten out of ten. Two years earlier I had gotten a nine out of ten which should have been a perfect card, but the Redskins favored by four on the road in Detroit won by only three in overtime. The 'Skins actually went for the touchdown that would have won for me but quarterback Scott Rutledge overthrew a wide open Ricky Sanders and my money flew with it. That was usually par for the course with me.

My boss at the time used to play the cards also and he was much more successful than me. He always tried to give me advice on how to play them, but it never seemed to work. Tips like if the teams are equal go with the better quarterback. Always take the over and never take the under. Always bet the San Francisco 49ers when they were at home no matter what the point spread. Key certain teams each week instead of playing them all. And never bet both ends against the middle or in other words don't bet the game one way on one card and the other way on another.

All of this worked for him and because he was the boss he could bet on fewer games and put down more money. So he never went with more than four picks and played the same two games on at least three of his four to five cards. He would win, I would go and collect for him and he'd buy me lunch. In a way his buying me lunch allowed me to play my cards the following week.

There was one tip that he gave me that I will never forget. He had told me before, but I didn't really listen until the college football betting scandal at Boston College of 1996 in which 13 BC players were suspended for allegedly betting on sports events. My boss used to always tell me not to bet on the colleges, because they weren't getting paid and it was too easy for the gamblers to pay them off and get them to shave points. He was a New Yorker and knew a lot more about gambling than I did. After I saw what happened at BC my college gambling days were over.

It was during the latter part of the 1990's where I began to bet with a bookie. I didn't know who this person was, because my best friend was placing the bets. And I only did it for one year, though I would do it a few years later for a short stretch, but what a year it was. It was 1997 and he and I would put the money down. I would give him the picks, he would put up the money and I would pay him if we lost. We killed that year. I was hot and couldn't miss. Even when I was wrong most of the time we didn't get our bet in on time and lost nothing. We took it all of the way to the Super Bowl where the Broncos as seven point underdogs beat the Packers outright.

We scored big and everything was alright until his wife found the money in his sock drawer. The thing was that my best friend and I didn't exactly live next door so he was to take care of the money until the end of the season. That way I didn't have to worry about sending him anything to put down, because it was already there. At the end of the season we would split 50-50. I remember telling him to make sure that he put the money somewhere where it couldn't be found by his wife.

Well, she found it. Needless to say she questioned him on it and he had to come clean. I don't believe that he mentioned my name, but it didn't matter. We got our money, but not until his wife got her share. I could have been angry, but wasn't. Hey, easy come, easy go as they say. Any money is better than none. Besides, she was right. We shouldn't have been gambling in the first place and I'm sure some of the money we used may have been hers.

I didn't gamble with a bookie again until my nephew placed a couple of bets for me in 2002. I won the first two weeks then lost the next couple and quit for good. I haven't bet on a football game since.

Not betting on football is harder than one might think, because there are so many ways to do it. Of course, the NFL doesn't want to admit this, but gambling brings just as many fans to the games as anything. Even fans who know absolutely nothing about the game can win money off of it. Some of those people win more than the so called experts.

These are the ways that I remember gambling on football. There were the bookie bets and parley cards that I mentioned earlier. Then there were pick 'em pools in which everyone had to pick the winners of each game that week without a point spread. Each person would put five dollars down on each card that they played and whoever got the most games right won the pot. If there was a tie after the Sunday games then the Monday night game would break it. If those who were tied had the same pick for Monday night then total points came into play. The person who came closest to how many total points were scored between the two teams without going over would win.

Then there is the office block pool which you don't have to be an expert to win. This pool uses ten squares or blocks which go horizontal for the home team and vertical for the visitors. In order to play one must write their name in the block that they want. After the squares are filled they are numbered randomly zero to nine both directions. This is done by shuffling a deck of cards and picking them in the order they come up from top to bottom. Whatever black card comes up that number is placed over the squares in order horizontally and the same thing is done vertically with the red cards. Then the sheets are printed and everyone has two numbers per square, one for each team, that belong to the box where they put their name. So you could end up with a seven on the top for the home team and three vertically for the visitors. At the end of each quarter if the last two digits of the score matched your numbers you won. Just like a lottery more or less. Since there were four quarters there were four chances to win. Very simple and cheap since it was usually only a couple of bucks to play. And if you won a couple of times then you finished ahead of the game at the end of the year.

Our office had a few pools. We played our NCAA tournament pool differently than most. What we did was put the 64 teams in a hat. Anyone who wanted to play had to put up ten dollars each before the first weekend of the tournament. Then those who entered had their names thrown into a hat. If your name was picked first then you got the last pick of the first round and whoever was the last name in the hat got first pick. Then the order was reversed for each round until all 64 teams were assigned. So if you had sixteen people in the pool and 64 teams each person was assigned four teams which they kept for the entire tournament. As long as you had a team in the tournament you put up ten dollars before each weekend of games began. When all of your teams were eliminated then you didn't have to pay. If your four teams won the most games in the tournament, than you won the pool. Another pool where you had to know nothing about the teams in order to win.

Then there was our baseball pool. In that we assigned each person two teams. The team that you were assigned had to fill a line sheet of numbers from zero to thirteen. The way that they did this was that they had to finish one game win or lose with a run total of zero to thirteen until they filled all fourteen squares. The first person whose team did this won the pot. Each person in the pool had to put up five dollars a week until someone won. There was no telling when a team would fill their line so the pool could go on for a couple of weeks or the entire season. Usually, we would get two pools a year out of baseball.

These pools are the only kind of gambling that I will do now. No more point spreads. No betting on the horses which I've never done. No betting on boxing or anything else. And I will only do an NCAA pool if it's in the office.

I have friends who gamble. Some of them win and some lose. I do know guys who have been beaten up for not covering their gambling debts. I know guys who have spent their whole paycheck at the horse or dog track. I know guys who have lost everything from their homes to their marriage. And I know guys that just seem to win no matter who they bet on. Not many, but some. I could have been one of the guys who lost everything, but learned my lesson's early.

When I was a kid I gambled every now and then. Early on I had some success then couldn't win a thing. I lost a bet one time in 1981 when I took a New England Patriots team which would win only two games all year against a Dallas Cowboy team which finished one game short of the Super Bowl. The guy who won wanted me to pay up and I didn't have the money. He wouldn't let up and I can't blame him because I would have done the same so I had to cut a deal. Since lunch at school was a dollar he got my lunch. Hey, it beat being called a welsher.

That same year, a friend and I bet on every Redskin game from one to sixteen at a dollar a week. He took the 'Skins and I had their opponent. This was Joe Gibbs first season as coach and Washington started out 0-5 which made me 5-0. I was five dollars ahead with 13 games to go. The Redskins won eight of the next eleven to finish 8-8. After being up five dollars I broke even.

The final blow which convinced me that gambling on sports would never make me rich was New Year's weekend the end of that season. A friend and I bet on ten football games at one dollar apiece. We bet on the two NFL wildcard games the weekend before the bowl games and eight college bowls. He let me pick each team and I went more with my heart than with logic. I lost all ten games. Every one. That was it for me. Sure I would gamble on something here or there, but never to the point where I couldn't afford to pay it. And if I felt like luck was not on my side I would quit right then and there. I would take my losses and go home.

Another reason why I gave up gambling on sports was that I couldn't enjoy the games with money riding on them. I was thinking more about the point spread than the actual playing of the game. I found myself checking the scoreboard updates of other games than paying attention to the one that I was watching. And most important, even if my team won if they didn't cover the spread I was unhappy and if they lost and covered I was. I like watching football too much to not enjoy it, because there is money on the line.

So the advice that I give anyone who asks me about gambling is not to do it. The odds are against you. Though I do think that there are people with inside information most gamblers don't have access to this kind of source. The bookmakers will always be a step ahead, because they have to in order to make money. If you do gamble do it like we did in the office. Block and pick 'em pools. They usually don't cost much and with many of them one doesn't have to know much about the teams to win. Heck, we had one employee who would bet all home teams and all road teams each week and win at least once a year.

But there will always be people out there who put their money down. They do it for the challenge. They do it for the rush of adrenaline that they get while watching the event knowing that there is something at stake for them. They do it, because they think that their system is full proof and they can't lose. They do it, because they are addicted.

I don't do it, because I'm smart enough to know that the competitor in me would not take losing well and would want to keep playing until I broke even or got ahead. I would probably end up getting deeper and deeper into debt, because of it. I don't want that to happen to me or anyone else.

But as long as sports are played there will be gambling. And as much as the leagues don't want to admit it they know that it's good for them, because it boosts interest. Take away gambling and you take away a lot of fans.

You can bet on that.

WHICH SPORT HAS THE BEST ATHLETES

I'm not one to proclaim a certain player, team or coach as the greatest. And I'm not one to proclaim a certain player or coach the best at any given time. I've always felt that there were too many variables involved to do this. But there is one thing that I will weigh in on when it comes to who's the best and it's this.

Which sport has the best athletes?

This is not an easy task either as each sport's athletes has a unique set of skills necessary to be successful. In basketball, you have to be able to run, jump and have the depth perception necessary for putting the ball in the basket. In football, you need speed, quickness and strength. In hockey, you need agility, quickness and good hand eye coordination. In baseball, you need quickness, good hand eye coordination, good footwork, good depth perception and super quick reflexes. In soccer you need stamina and good foot eye coordination. The Olympic decathlon incorporates just about every athletic skill imaginable among its ten events. So with so many different skill sets and the specialization of each sport there may be no definitive answer as to which sport has the best athletes. But I will make my case for the one that has the best to me.

First let's take into account what the athletes in each sport need to be successful and how much of this translates to other sports.

In football you first must be able to take the pounding that the game dishes out. So anyone whose body cannot take the punishment will not succeed. This means that NFL players have to be bigger and stronger than their counterparts in other team sports. They need to be strong enough to move opponents, break away from them and pull them down when tackling. And they have to do this over and over again. Enduring play after play, game after game takes its toll on the body so football players are never one hundred percent during the season. It's the ones who can produce at less than peak physical condition who make it. The strength factor is what football has on other sports.

The other thing that a football player needs is usable speed and quickness. There are many athletes who can run fast and do agility drills, but that doesn't translate into being a good football player. The good football player knows how to control his speed and quickness. He doesn't run up his blockers back he waits for the block and then makes his move. He runs his pass routes under control until it's time to make the move which gets him open. Everything is done under control.

Then there is the explosion factor. The great football player is able to coil his body in such a way that he can explode into his opponent when making a block or tackle. This creates maximum impact and allows him to move or stop their opponent. This explosion can also be used by the ball carrier to break a tackle or get through the line.

These are the skills that a football player must have to be successful. All of them can transfer to other sports. Of these skills the one that may be detrimental in other sports is size. Football player muscles don't always translate to other sports. A football player's arms may be too thick to swing a baseball bat, shoot a basketball or swing a hockey stick. And their weight can definitely be a disadvantage in other sports as the more one bulks up the less speed and agility they have. Because of the specialization by position football player's ability to play other sports decreases.

Then there is the hockey player. He must be a very good athlete in order to skate at top speed from one end of the rink to the other while holding a stick and controlling a little round puck from time to time. He must be strong enough to take the pounding that is dished out from being checked in the open and against the boards. He must have the quickness to start and stop on a dime in order to shoot, pass and transition from offense to defense. And he must have the hand eye coordination to catch the puck on their stick, skate with it, pass it and shoot it. All of this while under the duress of an opponent.

All of these skills can be translated to other sports. The only thing with hockey is, like football, it is a game of specialist. Not that the defensive hockey player does not have offensive skills they just aren't as efficient as the men who score the goals and hand out the assist. The most specialized position on the ice is goalie and they have to have a unique set of skills all of their own the main one being the ability to stop a speeding puck coming at them from point blank range. The only way that they can do this is with super quick reflexes. The only athletes that I can think of who can match a hockey goalies reflexes are baseball players and lacrosse goalies. But hockey goalies are not asked to do anything else but protect the net. This is very important, but limits the number of skills a goalie needs to play.

Soccer is the worlds' game and maybe that's because the only real skills needed are the ability to dribble the ball, pass it or shoot it with your feet and head and the stamina to run up and down the field. The stamina part translates to any sport. The foot eye coordination does also though I think that soccer players have to adjust more in sports where hand eye coordination is important. But when it comes to strength soccer players are lacking. And with the exception of the goalie who has to try and block shots, soccer players don't need super quick hand eye reflexes.

There are those who say that decathletes are the best. They have to compete in so many events that every skill level is tested. They have to have strength in order to throw the shot put and javelin. They must have speed to run the 100 meters. They have to be able to jump for the pole vault. And they have to have stamina for the distance running. The only thing that decathlon athletes are not tested on is their quickness. So as much as they are good all around athletes this may not make them the best. I'll give an example when making my case for the sport which I think has the best athletes.

The case for basketball players has been made for years. They are quick and agile. They have great depth perception when shooting the ball. They are great when it comes to total body control. Basketball players make their game look so easy that people naturally assume it's because they are the most natural athletes in sports.

They are great athletes and all of their skills translate to other sports. The only thing is that the height which is an advantage in basketball is a disadvantage in other sports. The taller an athlete, the longer his limbs are. This translates to less strength in the arms and legs and longer movements to accomplish getting to where one is going which cuts down on their reflexes. How many successful athletes in other sports have you seen with basketball bodies, especially tall athletes with slim builds and sinewy muscles?

Before getting to the two sports that I have narrowed it down to let me give a quick read on a few others. Wrestlers and weightlifters are too muscle bound. Boxers may have the most stamina of all athletes considering the fact they have to execute while getting pounded on. And their reflexes are uncanny. But boxers do not need to be fast of foot in order to succeed. Tennis players don't need to jump high or at all. And golfers don't have to run at all.

So which sports do I think have the best athletes? I'll give you the one that I think has the best first then what may be a surprise runner up.

To me, the best athletes are baseball players. Every quality that an athlete has to have comes into play in baseball. And they all have to be performed at a high level.

The baseball player must be agile and quick with good hand eye coordination and footwork in order to get to a ball and field it. If it is on the ground he has track it with his eyes, move his feet in order to get to the spot, move his hands in position to field it cleanly then set his feet and make an accurate throw. Along the way he has to react to any bad hop which may come before the ball gets to him. All of this while the ball is headed towards him at a high rate of speed.

If it is in the air, he has to track it with his eyes, get to it with his feet and get the glove in place in order to catch it. He has to get a read on the ball from the moment the hitter makes contact sometimes more than 300 feet away so that he can beat it to the spot where it will land. If there are runners on base then he has to catch it and set himself to make an accurate throw. In order to get the ball in quickly the fielder has to have a strong arm.

A catcher must catch pitches traveling on an average of 90 miles per hour coming right at him without flinching even if the batter swings. If a runner tries to steal a base the catcher has to catch the ball rise and make an accurate throw to the base. In order to do this the catcher has to have a strong arm just as the outfielder does.

Then, because almost all baseball players have to play offense and defense, there is the aspect of hitting. A hitter has to be able to read the direction that a pitch going 90 miles per hour is going in a split second. They have to get their bat moving fast enough to be able to make solid contact. They have to have the strength in their arms and legs to hit it solidly. And they have to be able to tell whether the ball is in the strike zone or not. All of this in the blink of an eye.

To me, the baseball player has to have every skill that athletes in every other sports have along with fast twitch muscles. And more of their skills translate over to other sports. It was my time in college which convinced me of this.

Like most schools, we had an intramural sports program which everyone participated in. The sports for men were volleyball, flag football, basketball and softball. Everyone in the school could participate, even the varsity athletes of which our major sports were basketball and baseball. Of course, the basketball players couldn't play that in intramurals, because it was during their season, but they did compete in the other sports.

Baseball would enter a team in each sport. They had the best football team, volleyball team and softball team. And they had the best basketball team. My sophomore year the baseball team won the championship in every sport. And they won them easily. That was all the proof I needed.

Think of all the players who are great athletes who struggled at baseball. Deion Sanders of football and Michael Jordan of basketball immediately come to mind. And the man considered the greatest athlete of the first half of the twentieth century, Jim Thorpe, struggled at baseball. For the decathletes let's not forget that Thorpe won the decathlon and pentathlon at the 1912 Stockholm Olympics.

Then think of all the men who played baseball growing up who succeeded at other sports. How many times have you read about an athlete who started out with baseball as their first love then switched over to the sport in which they became successful? The stories are numerous.

Now the sport which I think has the second best athletes is lacrosse. I have had the experience of playing many sports against lacrosse players having grown up in Maryland. Whether it's basketball, baseball, football, soccer or whatever they were more than worthy opponents. They could run, jump, throw and catch. They had very good footwork and hand eye coordination. They had strength to go along with this. And they had quick, sharp reflexes. As you can tell I was impressed.

The lacrosse player is a very good athlete. In fact one of the most dominant lacrosse players of all-time is considered by many to be the best athlete at his position to ever play his sport if not the best overall player period. He is also considered by many to be one of the top five athletes of all time. His position was fullback. His sport was football.

And his name is Jim Brown.

WHO LOST OUT IN INTEGRATION

First off, let us start by saying that a segregated society though it may be productive can never reach its full potential. In order for any society to maximize its potential everyone must contribute in some way. Ideas have to be discussed by all people not just a few in order to come up with the best plan of action in making things better for society. Also, all cultures should be celebrated not dismissed in order to learn from them and promote the self esteem of its people. An integrated society which works together is best for all involved.

American history shows that this has not always been the case. We tend to forget that segregation was in place for many years in our country and that it has not been fifty years since the first civil rights bill was passed. Though things are much better than they were before, we still grapple with the issue of race. As long as America is made up of different races and nationalities this will always be the case.

Since this book is about sports, this chapter will deal with race in those terms. Though the games are better off with everyone being a part of them there are still things which need to be worked out. There is a distinct lack of minority front office personnel and ownership in sports and that's a problem which won't easily be solved. And there are still sports which are predominant by race in the number of people who play them especially the "elitist" ones like golf and tennis.

There was a time where African-Americans could not participate in professional or college sports with whites, because of segregation. The only place where one might find an integrated team would be at a northern college or two and they never fielded more than a couple of African-Americans. So if African-Americans wanted to play sports they had only one choice. That choice was to form professional leagues and college conferences of their own which they did.

The first sport in which this was done was baseball. Though blacks had played ball professionally as far back as the 1870's the Negro National League was not formed until 1920 by Andrew "Rube" Foster and black baseball lasted until the early part of the 1960's. Posey organized the league and was its de facto commissioner until his death. Along the way, he made Negro League baseball the number one African-American business in the country and everyone benefitted from it.

Though the life was hard on them with travel, the players benefitted, because they got to show off their skills. The owners benefitted, because they had a talent pool that no one else was willing to touch. African-American businesses around the country benefitted, because when games were played in their cities the fans who came out would stop by their stores, hotels and bars to do business. And the white major league owners benefitted by renting their ballparks to the Negro Leagues while the big league team was on the road.

What Negro League baseball did is what former football player and activist Jim Brown has been striving for since his retirement from the game. It put African-American money into the black community and kept it there. Though it may not have been as much as what white people had it stayed in the community. Negro League baseball was responsible for the empowerment of black communities.

Another sport in which African-Americans were able to form their own professional league was basketball. Though it was not as widespread as baseball, pro basketball was very popular amongst blacks in the north during the time of the Harlem Renaissance(c. 1918-37). Teams would play games on hotel ballroom floors where afterwards the floor would be cleared so that the fans could dance. They would also travel to other cities to play as well. It was in 1927 that the Harlem Globetrotters were born. Though they originated in Chicago, the Globetrotters Jewish owner Abe Saperstien took the name Harlem, because he knew that more fans would relate to it. He was right.

Though African-Americans excelled in the individual sports of boxing and horse racing as jockeys there were no other opportunities besides baseball and basketball to play team sports in a professional league. Truth be told, there weren't too many sports leagues around at that time. Baseball had been around the longest. Football and basketball were still in their infancy. There were only six professional hockey teams and soccer was an afterthought having been replaced by football.

The one place where African-Americans could put teams on the field in any sport that they wanted was at historically black colleges and universities (HBCU's). Though they may not have had the big money that the Big Ten, Pacific Coast and Southeastern Conferences had these schools got by with what they could and made it work. They bought their own uniforms, built their own stadiums and paid their own way when traveling. And they formed their own conferences.

Most of these HBCU's were located in the south from Maryland to Texas. They were good for African-American business just as baseball was and for a longer period of time since most colleges in the south did not integrate their sports teams until the 1960's while baseball did it starting in 1947. And though they did not get all of the best African-American talent once the northern and pacific schools started to recruit it, the HBCU's got most of it and was able to let them showcase their talents for the pros. Even when southern colleges did begin to integrate there was still plenty of talent available to HBCU's up into the middle point of the 1980's.

Here are just a few names of the men who played football for HBCU's in the 1970's and 80's. Hall of fame running back Walter Payton played at Jackson State where he had fellow hall of fame tackle Jackie Slater blocking for him. The first black quarterback to play in a Super Bowl, Doug Williams went to Grambling. For that matter the second one played at an HBCU also as Steve McNair went to Alcorn State in the 1990's. The most prolific wide receiver in pro football history, Jerry Rice, went to Mississippi Valley State. Defensive end Michael Strahan went to Texas Southern University. Defensive back Everson Walls attended Grambling. Offensive lineman Nate Newton played at Florida A@M. Linebacker Greg Lloyd went to Fort Valley State. And hall of fame wide receiver John Stallworth went to Alabama A@M.

Not a bad group and we didn't mention legendary coaches such as Grambling's Eddie Robinson who retired with more victories than any other coach. Then there was Alonzo Smith "Jake" Gaither who coached at Florida A@M and William "Billy" Nicks at Prairie View A@M.

Basketball had its fair share of talent at HBCU's as well. This includes Earl "The Pearl" Monroe of Winston-Salem State, who played for legendary coach Clarence "Big House" Gaines, Willis Reed of Grambling and Dick Barnett of Tennessee State A@I.

All of these great players and coaches along with their baseball counterparts like Leroy "Satchel" Paige, Buck Leonard, Judy Johnson, Josh Gibson, James "Cool Papa" Bell and Martin Dihigo performed in front of big crowds in black communities. Their exploits were documented by black news outlets such as the Pittsburgh Courier, Washington Afro-American, Baltimore Afro-American, Chicago Defender, Ebony magazine and Jet magazine. I can remember reading about HBCU football and basketball in Ebony and Jet while growing up. It was usually the only source in which one could find anything about HBCU sports.

And black American cities and towns who had teams benefitted from the business which came with them.

Then major league baseball integrated with the signing of Jackie Robinson by the Brooklyn Dodgers and the domino effect began. The domino effect was not taking place on the field as baseball and all pro sports would have a quota system in place until well into the 1960's. No, the effect was felt in the stands as fans who would normally attend Negro League baseball games began to go watch their brothers in the major leagues. This brought down the attendance in the Negro Leagues and was devastating to them and black business. With very little compensation in return for players lost and nothing to fall back on Negro League baseball suffered a slow death until by the early sixties it was gone.

As mentioned earlier black college sports were born around the same time as Negro League baseball and when the latter integrated the former had to pick up the slack. This was done throughout the south as HBCU athletic talent was second to none. However, in the north where there were very few HBCU's, nothing could replace Negro League baseball.

The HBCU's were able to hold their own with black sports fans even though integration of southern white colleges began in the late 1960's. Of course these colleges did not immediately run out and sign all of the black high school talent in football and basketball which made a difference. And the alumni factor helped with those who attended HBCU's returning to watch their teams and following them in the press. But once the quota system was dropped and every major Division-I basketball and football school began to recruit black talent everywhere more African-Americans began to follow the big schools. And once again, everyone whose businesses had benefitted from black college sports suffered along with the schools, their teams and the athletic departments.

The point being made here is that segregation is not the way to go, but when desegregation takes place it's always to the benefit culturally and financially of the majority which makes it a detriment to the minority. It is a benefit to the majority culturally, because their way of life remains while the minorities has to blend in. Usually this is not the case as the minority is not allowed to totally integrate, but must assimilate or blend in. And it is not the case financially, because businesses owned by the majority, which usually has more capital to begin with, profit off of the minority while businesses owned by minorities lose customers. This will never change.

The only African-American business that I can think of today which may rival what Negro baseball and HBCU sports did for black America is the music industry. However with fewer musicians performing concerts and more of them focused on compact disc sales the music industry cannot have the same effect on black America as sports did, because tickets aren't sold, event employees aren't needed and local businesses don't make money.

The money is being spread around now among the wealthy businesses which own and run sports almost all of which are owned by white Americans. We know who lost out in integration.

The Negro Leagues, Historically Black Colleges and Universities and local black business.

IF YOU CAN PLAY, YOU CAN PLAY

We hear it a lot. Today's athletes are better than their predecessors. They are bigger, stronger and faster. They train better with modern methods and take better care of themselves physically. They practice harder and longer with sport as their main job year round. Advances in medicine have allowed them to come back quicker and more effective from injury allowing them to play longer. And the use of modern visual technology allows them to gain advantages on their opponents which athletes of the past could not. This has led to sports being better than they were twenty, thirty, forty and one hundred years ago.

Then we hear the flipside. The athletes of yesteryear were better. They were more fundamentally sound than today's athlete. They may have practiced less, but more efficiently. Because there was limited substitution and most players had to play the whole game they were more well rounded in their skills. They, also, had more stamina and played with more injuries. The athletes of the past didn't have as much modern technology as today's so did their scouting through personal experience and made most, if not all, of the on field decisions. And they cared about the game more. To those in this camp, sports were better when the old timers played.

Not to take anything away from the old timers, but I fall into the former camp. I think that sport, like most things that have evolved in America is better now than it has ever been. We get the best athletes in their best condition. We get them put into the best positions to succeed by coaches who evaluate their players and thoroughly scout the opponent. Because today's games have almost unlimited substitution and more specialization, there is a better chance we have the best athletes on the field at all times. The playing fields and arenas are better taken care of which allows athletes to perform and cuts down on injury. This is just the evolution of sports.

But the real argument is whether or not today's players could have played yesterday and vice versa. I have heard from many athletes of today who say that the players of the past could not play with them for all of the reasons already mentioned in the first chapter. I've heard players and fans who won't even acknowledge the players of the past especially in basketball and football. The game has changed and is much better they say. What those guys did and what today's players are doing is like the Wright brothers flying the first plane and man going to the moon. They were too small and too slow. If they played today, they would get killed.

Then the old timers chime in. Guys today are too soft, they say. Today's athlete is so coddled that they get by more on talent then skill. None of them are willing to hone a variety of offensive and defensive skills just enough to get them playing time. They are not willing to play hurt and lack stamina. They lack fundamentals. The money has made them less hungry. And worst of all, today's athlete only cares about him and putting on a show for the fans.

I think that both sides make good points. However, I am one who feels that if a player can make it in one era than they can make it in another. If you take an old timer and transpose him into today's athletic climate they would make the adjustments necessary to compete. And I think that if you take today's athlete back in time they would hone all of the skills necessary to compete. Everyone is a product of their era.

The old timers were smaller and slower than today's athlete. There was not as much emphasis put on speed and strength as it is today. Scouts and coaches evaluated talent on the fundamental skills necessary for their sport so that's what the athletes focused on improving. Though there was not as much specialization during their era as is today, each position had different skill sets. For example, backfield men had to know how to handle the ball in football while lineman did not just as is the case today. Catchers didn't have to learn how to field hard hit ground balls in baseball and second basemen weren't taught how to throw from a crouch. Centers in basketball weren't taught to dribble the ball up the court and guards weren't asked to back their defenders in. Specialization has always been a part of sports.

Substitution rules were different in the old timer's day. If you started a baseball or basketball game you finished it. The substitution rules in baseball haven't changed much. They have in basketball, but the game was played at a much slower pace when first invented. Then the fast paced, fast break game came into play in the 1950's and lasted until the mid 1990's. Today's game, as good as it is, has slowed down at the pro and college levels.

The sport where substitution has changed the most is football. Before World War II, football players were asked to play offense and defense. Substitutions could only be made at the end of a quarter or for injury and once a player came out, he had to remain on the bench until the quarter or half ended. So players had to play the full sixty minutes.

After the war, substitution rules were relaxed and two-platoon football came into play with teams now assigning players to either offense or defense. Now the quarterback did not have to risk injury by playing safety on defense and the slow lineman who could move a man while blocking, but couldn't shed him to make a tackle could be replaced. This led to the specialization that we see today and the grumbling by the old timers that theirs was a better game and they were tougher. Well, not all of them. Hall of fame quarterback Sammy Baugh was adamant that today's game was better, because of free substitution and specialization. Baugh said that in his era the players were so tired from playing both ways that by the fourth quarter all they could do was lean on each other.

However, if the old timers were given the advantage of focusing on one position there is no reason to believe that they could not have perfected it.

Specialization has made our games better, but has it made the athletes better? We've already made a case for today's athlete being better physically. Are they better all around?

One could make an argument for the old timers on this one. Today's athlete is more inclined to focus on one sport at a much earlier age than they did years ago. Even when I was in high school, it was a point of pride to be an all around athlete. You were not considered to be in the elite of your school playing just one sport. The more varsity pins on your jacket the better. The old timers had the four- letterman, who would earn a varsity letter in four different sports. We didn't have any four-lettermen but a lot of three. Two at the least.

Now, athletes are all but forced to concentrate on one sport by their parents and coaches which cuts down on them reaching their full athletic potential. This, in turn, cuts down on them reaching their full potential in the sport in which they decide to play. The old timers were able to take the skills that they learned in other sports and translate them to their primary sport. And by playing more than one sport they were able to find the one which they liked the most. Athletics was not thought of as a means to an end like it is today so things were more laid back.

By the same token, if the athlete of today was sent back to the past with the genetics of the old timer and brought up the same way, there is no reason to believe that he couldn't be a four-letterman too. And he would probably have more fun doing it.

The changes in training methods and modern medicine without question give today's athlete an advantage. So do the better playing field conditions. The athlete of the past would thrive under these circumstances. Though the old timers don't think so, today's athlete would have made the adjustments necessary to compete with playing in pain and on the poor playing surfaces of the past.

The use of modern technology for scouting purposes would also help the old timer. In fact, football has been using film study for years. Now all sports do. Knowing what your opponent is likely to do at a given moment is a huge advantage.

Today's athlete would have to learn how to beat an opponent without visual aid. More of the thinking would be on the field during the actual game. Quarterback's would have to call their plays. I think that they would do just fine. For one, everyone would be on a level playing field, because there would be fewer people doing the scouting, and less information to decipher. And thinking would be done more on a one on one basis rather than say five on five. Necessity is the mother of invention and if forced to today's athlete could be just as creative as the old timer.

Then there is the biggest sore spot between today's players and those of the past. The money aspect. The fact that today's players make so much more money than those of the past and play less. This, to me, is the reason why so many old timers have problems with today's athletes. This is the reason why they say today's athletes are selfish and only care about putting on a show for the fans. This is the reason why they say today's athlete doesn't respect the game. And this is the reason why they say that today's athletes are soft and wouldn't make it in their era.

Well, it's not the athlete's of today's fault they are paid large sums of money. They only get what the market says they deserve. And despite what is said all of them have earned a chance to make it. No matter how much talent a person has they have to put in the work for a chance to earn the money. The old timers were just born at the wrong time.

As for selfishness, it's been around since the beginning of sport. Baseball players have always cared about their numbers. Basketball players have always wanted to score. Football players have always wanted to carry the ball. Not everyone volunteers to play goalie in hockey or catcher in baseball. This is why it is so hard to win championships in sport. The hardest part is getting a group of people from different backgrounds to pull together for a common goal. Today's athlete is no more selfish than his ancestors.

The difference is that he has a bigger forum to showcase it. Sure there are players who showboat. But didn't Babe Ruth stand and watch some of his homers? Didn't Dizzy Dean play to the crowd? The truth is that once you turn on a camera you are asking the person being filmed to put on a show. It sells tickets and commercial air time. It fills highlight reels. It brings out the casual fan. It may not be necessary, but it is effective in promoting the sport whether we like it or not. Turn those cameras off and we are more likely to get good behavior.

The money has changed the game. It has made it more of a business. The old timer may begrudge today's athlete for what he makes, but wouldn't have turned it down if it had been given to him. And today's athlete would have played for what the old timer did, because he didn't have a choice.

The bottom line is that athletes are products of their eras. They make do with what they have. We always hear that the great athletes transcend eras. This means that they could play at any time under any conditions.

I think that ALL athletes can transcend any era. Some of today's athletes would not be able to play in the old timer's era, because there were fewer jobs, but that doesn't mean they couldn't. If anything some of the old timers may not make it, because the talent pool of athletes is bigger than it was in their day. That's a debate for another day.

For my money every athlete who played in the past could be transformed into a good player today and vice versa. One, elite athletes are genetic freaks. They are built differently than the normal human being. Their hands are bigger, their legs thicker. They are taller than most. Athletes of all eras are born with the genes necessary to become successful. And two they would still be willing to put in the work to succeed. All elite athletes have the burning desire to be the best. That never changes. These two things trump everything else in my book.

Young or old, if you can play, you can play.

WHO IS THE CHAMP?

Of all the sporting events that I've wanted to attend a championship heavyweight boxing match top's the last. I would settle for a championship match at any weight class if the fighters are worth it. The fight could be in Atlantic City, New Jersey or Las Vegas, Nevada though I would prefer the latter. Sad to say, I will probably never get to do this. Even if I had a chance to, I probably wouldn't. That is because boxing isn't what it used to be. I mean who is the champ?

I haven't followed the heavyweight class of boxers since Lenox Lewis retired as the champion in 2003. Occasionally, one of the lower weight classes will catch my attention, but the days of ordering pay per view or going to someone's house to watch are becoming few and far between. I haven't done either in more than a decade. If the fight doesn't come on cable or network, then I probably won't go out of my way to watch. It's hard enough staying awake until almost midnight for the main event much less driving home after it.

Boxing has lost me and I'm sure it's lost many other fans. The younger generation is being brought up on Mixed Martial Arts and Ultimate Fighting Championships neither of which excites me. Almost every championship fight is on pay per view and most just aren't worth paying for. And the main reason why boxing is losing fans is that there is no new blood. No one wants to box anymore. We get the same old warriors who fight into their forties and refuse to meet each other unless the money is too good to pass on.

Though I came along after the golden age when boxing was one of the big four sports along with baseball, college football and horse racing it was still in the top five during the decade of the seventies.

The sport had so many advantages when it came to bringing in fans. With so many different weight classes there was the potential for a championship fight every week. Three television networks vying for the rights to televise boxing made it easy to promote. Because there is no offseason in boxing, fights can be shown year around on any day of the week. And there were plenty of poor, young men in America and other parts of the world without many options which turned to boxing supplying the sport with new blood on a regular basis.

The money wasn't as much as it is today. A fighter had to work his way up in order to get the big payday and that still wasn't much unless you were a heavyweight. This kept boxers in the ring frequently. It was nothing for a champion to have three or four title defenses in a year. Challengers fought more in order to move up in the rankings and keep themselves in the public eye so their managers could promote them. And there was no ducking of an opponent in your weight class. The rankings may have been rigged from time to time, but if a fighter was good enough he got a shot at the title or the champ had to relinquish his belt.

This created a natural order of things which boxing fans got used to. A fighter would begin in the amateur ranks, usually boxing in Golden Gloves tournaments. Some would get the chance to fight in the Olympics where winning a medal pretty much guaranteed a pro career. Then they would make their pro debut in a couple of club fights before appearing on the undercard of a big fight card. Once they moved up in the rankings it was time to showcase their talents on television. This was usually when the national buzz began.

I can remember friends telling me about certain fighters they had seen on television. You had to see Aaron Pryor, or Tommy Hearns, or Hector "Macho" Camacho. The good thing was that with sports programming like ABC's "Wide World of Sports", CBS's "Sports Spectacular" and NBC's "Sports World" one didn't have to wait long to see them. The "Friday Night Fights" may not have been around, but Saturday and Sunday afternoon ones were. Especially after football season ended and the networks had to fill that air time. I can remember guys literally clearing their schedules so that they could watch whatever fights were on that weekend. This wasn't hard, because fights never last more than an hour so one could get things done, take a break to watch then get on with their day.

The big fights were promoted by the fighters themselves more than the promoters. When boxers signed contracts to meet each other for a title they would usually fight a practice or "tune up" match before. There was always the danger of the champion losing, but most of the time the opponent was handpicked by the manager and wasn't a real threat. These fights were more for showing off the two opponents who would meet shortly thereafter and drum up interest. The better they looked in disposing their opponent, the more interest from the fans for the big fight.

Before cable television and pay per view became the norm, championship fights were shown on network television in prime time any day of the week. I recall a 1980 Monday night lineup in which Sugar Ray Leonard defended his welterweight title, John Tate his half of the heavyweight and Larry Holmes the other half in different parts of the country all on ABC. Every fight was a good one with Leonard knocking out his opponent, Holmes holding on to his title and Tate getting knocked out in the fifteenth round by Mike Weaver. Can you imagine a lineup of fights like that on network television today? ESPN would be showing it as an "Instant Classic" for two years.

I think that I can safely say that I saw every heavyweight champion from my birth in 1967 up to Larry Holmes in the mid 1980's fight live on network television. The fighters at the lower weights, also. Aaron Pryor, Ray Leonard, Tommy Hearns, Roberto Duran, Alexis Arguello, Danny "Little Red" Lopez and Marvin Hagler all defended their titles on network TV. They had no choice in the seventies. To me, this was good for boxing and good for the fans. You could buy "Ring" magazine and know the fighters they were ranking. That's not the case today.

Boxing began to lose its steam in the early 1990's. The fight game was starting to move more towards cable and pay per view. First it was just championship fights then everyone started to box on ESPN, HBO and Showtime. The money became more prevalent and boxers began to fight less. The tune up fight has been all but eliminated. Networks now have plenty of sports programming to fill the void on weekends. With no network TV, the Saturday and Sunday afternoon fights which helped fans to get acquainted with new fighters are a thing of the past. So is the prime time championship fights shown on weeknights. Boxing is basically a Friday night ESPN staple or cable and pay per view Saturday night event. Because of the lack of network TV, the casual boxing fan may not even know that a championship match or big fight is even on the horizon.

By going exclusively to cable and pay per view, boxing opened the door for another sport to come along and take its place and that was mixed martial arts. The younger generation of today which was not weaned on boxing was looking for a sport to call their own. They found it in mixed martial arts and ultimate fighting. These sports mix boxing with wrestling and karate. When it first began it was very violent, but rules were put into place for safety and the sport has grown in popularity. MMA and UFC are considered too violent for network TV though one can find it from time to time. Their bread and butter are pay per view. They charge less than boxing and to its fans is more action packed. I've talked to many young people who think that boxing is boring compared to MMA and UFC. Like boxing, there aren't that many fighters, but the ones who do fight have a loyal following.

Another reason why boxing began to decline is that athletes who used to turn to boxing began to play other sports. Once the colleges, not the pros, began to integrate their basketball and football teams elite African-American athletes began to move towards them and away from boxing. Basketball was much safer and football had more positions which meant more chances to succeed. Both could lead to a college education which was a much better fallback plan than what was available if they failed at boxing.

But the biggest reason for the decline of boxing is the fact that minorities who made up most of the work force don't need the sport as much as they used to. Before civil rights and affirmative action most of the men who boxed were poor minorities who knew that their best ticket out of the ghetto was by boxing. Many of them were steered towards the ring in order to keep them off of the streets and out of trouble. They were not going to get the same education as the majority so their chances of going on to college were slim. Boxing was the lottery ticket of their time just as basketball and football is today.

Then the government stepped in during the 1960's and '70s and gave minorities a chance to get jobs and education that had been denied to them. Affirmative action opened doors for minorities which had been closed for years. It took a couple of decades for the full effect to take place, but minorities are now able to make it in society without having to step into a ring and get their heads knocked off. Now, parents and adults can tell their children that education and job opportunities are available that once were not. To me, this is a good thing. For boxing it is bad.

And I don't see boxing making a comeback anytime soon. The heavyweight championship of the world which had almost always been the property of the United States is now in the Soviet Union. We get the same fighters growing older with no new blood in the pipeline. Society doesn't tolerate boxing the way that it once did. It is thought too violent and corrupt. I think that boxing has gotten to the point where not even a "Great White Hope" could save it.

And if that's the case it may not be dead, but it's on life support.

WITH A LITTLE LUCK (OR A BREAK OR TWO)

Luck plays a major part in sports just as it does in life. Every player and team that has ever won anything has had a bit of luck along the way. To me, when the team or athlete makes the play it is not luck. So you won't see the Pittsburgh Steelers "Immaculate Reception" of 1972 or the Dallas Cowboys "Hail Mary" pass of 1975 or Lorenzo Charles of North Carolina State's dunk to win the NCAA championship in 1983 or Derek Jeter's cutoff and throw to the plate to get Jeremy Giambi in the 2001 American League Divisional Series. No this is about plays that the other team didn't make which may have saved a team or the bounce of a ball or an official's call or non call. Even weather can bring a team good or bad luck. They say that the breaks even up. In a few instances that may be the case. Let's take a look.

The first and most recent one that comes to mind for me is when the New England Patriots made their run at an undefeated season on 2007. In order for the Patriots to become the first team in NFL history to go 19-0 they would need a break or two along the way. As good as they were playing that season in order for them to lose their opponent would need one also. The Patriots did finish the regular season 16-0, but not without a break in game number 12 which was given to them on a Monday night in Baltimore by the Ravens.

Trailing 24-20 late in the game, New England faced a fourth and one at the Ravens 30. Quarterback Tom Brady tried a sneak and was stuffed. The game and undefeated season seemed over. But as the Ravens defense celebrated an official ran in signaling that the play did not count. The Ravens sideline had called time out before the ball was snapped. Though the Patriots were flagged for a false start which moved them back five yards, because the timeout had given them a second chance they picked up the first down when Brady ran for it. New England went on to score a touchdown and win the game 27-24.

The Patriots went into Super Bowl XLII with a perfect 18-0 record where they faced the 13-6 New York Giants. Most fans remember the play which ruined New England's perfect season as the miracle catch made by Giants wide receiver David Tyree where he caught it with one hand on his helmet. Truthfully, that play should have never happened, because the Patriots should have had the ball. On the play before Tyree's catch, Giants quarterback Eli Manning threw a perfect pass right into the hands of Patriots cornerback Asante Samuel. If Samuel intercepts, the Patriots run out the clock and the 1972 Miami Dolphins are all but forgotten. Samuel dropped the ball and the rest is history. 18 and 1.

So, one could make a case that the Patriots shouldn't have been undefeated going into the Super Bowl anyway, because they got a lucky break against the Ravens. And Samuel dropping the interception was just the breaks evening out.

Everyone remembers Villanova beating Georgetown in the 1985 NCAA basketball championship game. I remember Georgetown being shorthanded in that game as guard Reggie Williams sprained his ankle in the semifinals against St. Johns two nights earlier. In going back and looking at tapes of the game one will find that when Williams played Georgetown led most of the game. When Williams' ankle could not take it anymore and coach John Thompson had to bench him Villanova made their move and won the game. There is nothing to say that Villanova would not have won if Williams had played the whole game, but it definitely was a break for them that he didn't.

The Oakland Raiders have been in these situations a few times. Raider Nation will growl about the "Immaculate Reception" when Pittsburgh's Franco Harris caught a deflected pass that Oakland says they never touched and ran it in for the winning touchdown during a 1972 AFC playoff game. At that time, the rules said that one offensive player could not catch a pass which was tipped directly to him by a teammate. But, the Raiders say "Just win, baby," whenever the "Holy Roller" in 1978 against the San Diego Chargers comes up. On that play, Raider quarterback Ken Stabler actually flipped the ball forward and it ended up in the end zone where Oakland tight end Dave Casper recovered it for a touchdown. So what should have been an incomplete pass was ruled a fumble and resulted in the winning score for Oakland. Though one was a playoff game and the other was not, a case can be made that these breaks even out.

The breaks evening out may take a while. It did in another case with the Raiders. This time the opponent was New England and both plays helped the winner go on to win the world's championship.

The first came in a divisional playoff game in 1976. Oakland trailed New England 21-17 late in the fourth quarter when Stabler threw deep and incomplete on third down. But the officials called roughing the passer on New England and Oakland got new life. Though the league had been very lenient in calling blows to the head at that time and the hit had been a glancing blow, Oakland got the call. They took advantage of it and drove downfield for the winning score. Three weeks later they were holding their first Lombardi Trophy.

It took 25 years, but the Patriots got their revenge. It came in the final game at New England's Foxboro Stadium in a driving snowstorm. And just as in 1976 a seldom if any called penalty saved them.

This time it was New England which had the ball and quarterback Tom Brady dropped back to pass. He was hit by Oakland's Charles Woodson after faking a throw and putting both hands back on the ball. Brady fumbled, the Raiders recovered and the game was thought to be over. But the officials went to the replay booth and overturned the call saying that since Brady had started a throwing motion before tucking the ball back into his hands the ruling was an incomplete pass. This is the "tuck rule" which no one had ever heard of.

New England scored to tie the game then won it in overtime on a field goal. Three weeks later, they were holding up their first Lombardi Trophy.

The Los Angeles Dodgers got an offseason break which helped them to win the 1988 World Series. Though free agency had been around for a little more than a decade in 1987 baseball's owners decided that they would do something about the escalating salaries in their sport. So they colluded by not signing free agents like Andre Dawson and

Kirk Gibson. Dawson ended up having to go to the Chicago Cubs for far less than he would have made in a normal free agent bidding year. He signed a one year contract then went on to win National League most valuable player.

Gibson ended up with the Los Angeles Dodgers, because the Detroit Tigers did not offer him a new contract. This seemed odd, because Gibson was still a young man in the prime of his career. Gibson went on to lead the Dodgers to the World Series and hit a dramatic two run homer to win game one before bowing out due to injury. There is no question that without Gibson, the Dodgers do not win the championship and without collusion, which the courts ruled that baseball owners were a part of, he would not have been on the team.

The New York Mets got two breaks in game six of the 1986 World Series against the Boston Red Sox. This is the game in which New York's Mookie Wilson hit a slow roller threw the legs of Boston first baseman Bill Buckner with two outs in the bottom of the tenth which led to Ray Knight scoring the winning run.

The first break that the Mets got was when Boston pitcher Roger Clemens was removed for a pinch hitter in the top of the eighth while holding a 3-2 lead, because of a blister on his index finger. If Clemens, who was the American League Cy Young Award winner that year, had stayed in the game for maybe one more inning Boston might have won.

The second break came courtesy of Boston manager John MacNamara who let Buckner stay in the game instead of replacing him for defensive purposes with Dave Stapleton as he had done all year. MacNamara wanted to reward Buckner for all he had done that season by letting him be on the field for the final out when the Red Sox won the series. Unfortunately, that final out never came.

The Southern Cal Trojans won a share of the football national championship in 1978 with a little help from the Alabama Crimson Tide and a lot of help from the officials in the Rose Bowl. The Trojans went into their bowl game ranked number two in the country with a record of 10-1. Alabama was ranked number three with an identical 10-1 record. The number one team in the country was the Penn State

Nittany Lions with a perfect 11-0 record who just happened to be Alabama's opponent in the Sugar Bowl.

Southern Cal had given Alabama its only loss that season, but could not play Penn State because of their contractual obligation to the Rose Bowl. So the only way that Southern Cal could have any shot at winning the championship was if Alabama defeated Penn State. The Crimson Tide defeated Penn State 14-7 opening the door for Southern Cal if they could beat Michigan later in the day.

Southern Cal did beat Michigan 17-10, but not without controversy. Late in the first half, Southern Cal Tailback Charles White dove over the Michigan goal line for an apparent touchdown. The officials gave the signal for six points, but Michigan came out of the pile with the ball. Replay clearly showed that White fumbled before he crossed the goal line, but it couldn't be used to overturn the call and the touchdown stood. Thus, Southern Cal won a share of the national championship. The other half went to Alabama which would have won it outright if White's touchdown had not counted.

Pittsburgh Pirates second baseman Bill Mazeroski became a household name in 1960 when he blasted a game seven, bottom of the ninth home run to beat the New York Yankees in the World Series. The home run wasn't luck, but the circumstances which led up to it were very lucky for the Pirates.

The Yankees went into the eighth inning with a 7-5 lead. With nobody out and a runner on first, Pittsburgh's Bill Virdon hit a ground ball to shortstop Tony Kubek which looked like a sure double play. The ball took a wicked hop and hit Kubek in the throat. The Pirates went on to score four runs in the inning and take a 9-7 lead. If Kubek had been able to turn the double play, Pittsburgh may have gotten nothing in the eighth and New York would have gone into the ninth ahead instead of tied. That one bad bounce changed the course of baseball history.

This wasn't the only famous bad bounce in World Series history. In 1924, the Washington Senators won their only World Series by defeating the New York Giants four games to three. Washington won with the help of not just one bad hop, but two and a dropped foul ball by an all star catcher. Both bad hops came off of grounders hit toward third base.

The first bad hop came with the Senators down 3-1 in the bottom of the eighth, the same inning in which Kubek was struck 36 years later. Senators second baseman Bucky Harris hit a ground ball right at Giants third baseman Freddie Lindstrom which hit a pebble and bounced over his head. Two runs scored on the play tying the score at three.

In the bottom of the twelfth with the score still tied at three and one out the Senators Muddy Ruel hit a foul ball that Giants catcher Hank Gowdy circled under for what seemed like the second out. But Gowdy tripped over his mask and dropped the ball. Ruel then doubled and two batters later Earl McNeely stepped to the plate. Just as Harris had in the eighth, McNeely hit a grounder to third which hit a pebble and skipped over Lindstrom's head. Ruel scored from second and the Senators were world champions. That's Lady Luck if she ever was.

In the 1954 World Series between the Cleveland Indians and New York Giants, Giant outfielder Willie Mays made his famous over the shoulder catch in center field of a long fly ball by Cleveland's Vic Wertz. Wertz ball traveled 460 feet for an out. In the bottom of the tenth with the score tied at five, Giants pinch hitter Dusty Rhodes lofted a fly ball down the right field line which fell into the bleachers for a game winning three run homer. Rhodes hit traveled a grand total of 260 feet. The Giants won the game and the series in four straight.

The breaks evened up in a way for the Giants when after moving to San Francisco in 1958 they faced the Yankees in game seven of the 1962 World Series. Trailing 1-0 with two out and runners on second and third in the bottom of the ninth San Francisco first baseman Willie MCCovey scorched a line drive that was hit much harder than the home run Rhodes hit in 1954. The only problem was that it went straight to Yankee second baseman Bobby Richardson who caught it for the final out of the game and series. Ironically, the pitcher for the Yankees was Bill Terry. He was the man who gave up the home run to Bill Mazeroski two years earlier. The breaks definitely evened out for him.

Former football coach Marty Schottenheimer definitely had his fair share of bad luck while coaching the Cleveland Browns, Kansas City Chiefs and San Diego Chargers. The breaks never evened out for him. Whether it was John Elway and the Broncos beating him with "The Drive" in 1986 or "The Fumble" in 1987 or the Jets beating him in a playoff game on a missed field goal in 2004 Schottenheimer's teams just couldn't get over the hump. But his last playoff loss had to be the most bitter and was no fault of his own.

With his Chargers leading New England (yes, the Patriots again) 21-13 in the fourth quarter all San Diego had to do was stop the Patriots on fourth down and the game was over. New England quarterback Tom Brady threw a pass which headed towards San Diego's Marlon McRee. Instead of knocking the ball down, McRee intercepted and tried to run with it. New England wide receiver Troy Brown went in stripped the ball from McRee and the Patriots recovered giving them a first down. Brady took the Patriots downfield for the tying touchdown and two point conversion. Then he led them to the winning field goal on the next series. This loss cost Schottenheimer his job and it could have been avoided if McRee had simply knocked the ball down. This is the fragile life of an NFL head coach.

The Patriots aren't the only dynasty which has gotten a break or two. The Green Bay Packers of head coach Vince Lombardi are the only team to win three consecutive NFL titles in the modern era having done it from 1965-67. This cemented Lombardi's place for many as the greatest coach in pro football history. But the Packers probably should not have won the first of those titles in 1965.

Forced to play a Baltimore Colts team without a quarterback in a Western Conference championship game, Green Bay trailed 10-7 with time running out. This was the game where Baltimore halfback Tom Matte had to play quarterback for the injured John Unitas and Gary Cuozzo. Though Matte had not led the Colts to any touchdowns (the defense scored on a fumble recovery by Don Shinnick), he did have them in the lead. If the Colts defense could hold one more time, the game would be theirs.

The Colts forced Green Bay to try a game tying field goal late in the fourth quarter. Packer kicker Don Chandler swung his foot into the ball, looked up and grimaced in agony as it swung wide right. However, the official under the goal post called the kick good. Baltimore protested, but the ruling stood and the game went into overtime. Chandler got another chance in the extra frame and kicked it cleanly through the uprights for a 13-10 Packers victory. The Colts and Matte were denied history while Green Bay was on the way to accomplishing the first step in making their own.

There is such a thin line between winning and losing in sports. I've only covered a few situations in this chapter, but there are many more. Sometimes we forget how hard it is to win a championship at any level. So many things have to go right just to have the chance. First a team must assemble the coaches and players. Then everyone has to stay healthy and reach their potential. Then they have to be able to put personal agendas aside for the good of the team. And they have to execute the game plan almost flawlessly and consistently.

Even with all of that there is still one element that is needed in order to win a championship.

Luck.

WHY DO SPORTS MOVIES OVERDO IT?

For the most part, I don't watch sports movies. Let me correct myself. I don't go out of my way to watch sports movies. One reason is that I'm not a movie watcher anyway. I would much rather read the book than watch the movie. I love "The Godfather", but read the book before watching the movie. If the movie has no book, than there is a good chance that I won't watch it. That doesn't mean I'm not entertained when watching a sports movie. It's just that the game scenes don't impress me most of the time.

When it comes to sports movies everything seems to be overdone. Every dramatic home run is hit in the bottom of the ninth and goes 500 feet. Every football movie seems to end with a game winning touchdown shown in slow motion. Every basketball game ends with the winning basket being scored with no time on the clock and in slow motion. The only good sports movies are usually comedies like "Slapshot", "Major League" or the first "Longest Yard". The ones that are based on a true story are usually just that, because they take dramatic license to tell a story rather than the truth. Let me give you some examples of what I've seen in sports movies that just seemed over the top dramatic.

Football movies always seem to take it too far. The tackling is always vicious. Someone is always getting somersaulted like the players Jefferson tackled in "Fast Times at Ridgemont High." There always seems to be a helmet flying off, usually the ball carriers or the quarterback. There is always a guy on defense who leaves his feet in a headfirst dive into the ball carrier (which is illegal by the way). And the blockers always lift their men off their feet and slam them to the ground. Whenever a game is played in bad weather it is always a muddy monsoon or blizzard up to the players knees, usually the former.

Though I did find Adam Sandler's "The Water Boy" funny, his launching himself at the ball carrier did nothing for me. "Any Given Sunday" was a good film in my book, but they took it too far for me with the player losing his eye after being hit. I thought that "Varsity Blues" was pretty close to being realistic until they started launching tacklers at ball carriers. In one scene, the defensive player dove completely over the blocker and hit the quarterback on the way down with his helmet right in the face which is a personal foul. I haven't seen "The Blindside," but from watching clips it seems as every block by the star of the movie has his man ending up in the third row of bleachers.

Red Grange did a movie back in the 1920's called "Ten Seconds to Play." As far as Hollywood goes, this should be the title of every football movie. "The Longest Yard" ended with the hero, Burt Reynolds, scoring on the last play. So did "Varsity Blues", "Any Given Sunday", "Remember the Titans", "Semi Tough" and "Wildcats". The Robin Williams movie "The Best of Times" got it right, because they basically told us up front that the game would come down to the last play. Even though "The Water Boy" was about a defensive player it came down to the last ten seconds. At least "North Dallas Forty" changed it up by having a goat at the end instead of a hero when the holder of the extra point fumbles the snap and the Bulls lose the game. Then again, "North Dallas Forty" is actually a football movie that I like.

Let's talk about the weather. Honestly, I can't remember weather being involved in a football movie until I watched "Semi Tough". Probably, because it was too hard to stage a rainstorm. In that movie, the conference championship game was played in the mud. That's realistic enough.

Then the directors of "All the Right Moves" about a high school team starring Tom Cruise were able to use fire trucks with hoses to make it rain on the big game late in the second half. The field turned into a quagmire with ankle deep mud and water. This led to a fumble in the end zone on the last play of the game in which Cruise's team loses. This may happen in some places, but where I come from if it rains that hard in high school the game is stopped.

"The Last Boy Scout" with Bruce Willis and Damon Wayans had the opening game played in a rainstorm with fists flying, players kicking one another and guys beating each other over the head with their helmets. The scene ends with the star running back pulling out a gun and shooting the men trying to tackle him on his way to scoring the winning touchdown. Then he turns the gun on himself in the end zone and commits suicide. If that's not over the top then I don't know what is.

"Any Given Sunday" has a scene in which quarterback Willie Beamon, played by Jamie Fox, loses the respect of his teammates in a game played during a thunderstorm. Time after time, Beamon is slammed into the mud losing his helmet along the way, of course. You would think the man would have drowned after swallowing so much mud and water. But he makes it through and so do both teams even though we know that football games haven't been played in thunderstorms since the early seventies.

The movies have not been able to find a way to incorporate snow yet. The only snow scene that I can remember is from "Everybody's All-American" starring Dennis Quaid. The sideline clips are of Quaid on the sideline standing in the snow, but the game clips are provided by NFL Films. The movies will get there someday. Then they will overdramatize it as with everything else.

Turning to baseball, the game in the movies is pretty simple. The story is either about a hitter or pitcher with superhuman powers or a team which can't get out of its way all of a sudden becoming the 1927 Yankees and winning the pennant. Or it is based on a true story with the truth stretched a little.

"The Scout" is about a pitching phenom who signs with the California Angels after being scouted by a longtime baseball man who finally hits the jackpot. He goes out and dominates in his first appearance and signs a big time contract at the end of the movie. Along the way, the scout who was a lifelong minor leaguer, sneaks into the game to catch him for one inning without anyone knowing it. That part of it was cool.

"It Happens Every Spring" is a comedy about a science teacher who invents a chemical which is wood repellent. He bottles it and goes to pitch in the majors in order to earn some money to get married. Of course, he puts the wood repellent on the ball and no one can hit him. It is just ridiculous watching the special effects of the time as the ball made its way to the plate and the batter swung. The funniest part was that the ball never got by the catcher.

Even in "Bull Durham" the on field struggle was between the teams rising star pitcher and its power hitting catcher. The star pitcher ends up going to the big leagues while the catcher ends up getting the girl that they are both courting.

Where do we start with hitters? "Damn Yankees" in which a fan of the Washington Senators sells his soul to the Devil in order to become a young ballplayer with exceptional skills in order to beat the Yankees out of the pennant. Shoeless Joe he is called and he does lead Washington to the pennant, but not until after he finds out that the Devil wants him to sign with the Yankees the next year. He refuses and the Devil makes him an old man again just as he catches the final out to win the pennant. Yes, I read the book that the movie was based on. It's called "The Year the Yankees Lost the Pennant."

"The Natural" had Robert Redford starring as Roy Hobbs and helping his team win the pennant by hitting and fielding like Joe DiMaggio. In the climactic scene he hits a pennant winning home run that explodes in the stadium light tower. I read Cedric Malamud's book and it definitely didn't end like that.

The worst to first thing has been done forever. "Angels in the Outfield" was done twice with the first one in 1951 seeing the lowly Pittsburgh Pirates winning the pennant with the help of a team full of angels helping them. In the 1990's the California Angels were used with the same premise.

"Damn Yankees", which was mentioned earlier, was about the lowly Washington Senators defeating the lordly New York Yankees for the pennant.

"Major League" was about a Cleveland Indian team whose new owner wanted to move them to Florida by having the worst team in baseball in order to keep attendance down. The team finds out and, inspired, goes on to win the pennant. The game winner comes after the star reliever comes in and strikes out the opponents best hitter with a 100 mile per hour fastball in the top of the ninth and the winning run is scored when the fastest runner on the team gallops home from second on a bunt single. In slow motion, of course.

Even at the Little League level we see a bad team become good with "The Bad News Bears." This crew became so good that they never aged and went to Houston, Texas and Tokyo, Japan.

Baseball does change up the ending from time to time. I mentioned the end of "Damn Yankees" and "Major League." In "Major League II" it is the pitcher who gets the final out with another 100 mile per hour heater, this time earning a trip to the World Series. The pitcher is the hero in the first "Angels in the Outfield" as well. And it's not always in slow motion.

But truth told, just like with football, if you've seen one baseball movie, you've seen them all.

Basketball uses the same premise as football and baseball with a little more cool put into it. Whether it's "The Fish that Saved "Pittsburgh", "White Men Can't Jump" or "Semi Pro" the athletes are always way cool. Except for "Hoosiers" which is based on a true story. Maybe that's why everyone likes it so much. The movie is good, but the scene before the state finals of the team which was favored to win dunking in their layup line was total fiction. I wasn't born then, but think that there is a rule in high school basketball against dunking during warm ups.

Then we get the last second shot in slow motion. Did we not know that Woody Harrelson would dunk at the end of "White Men Can't Jump"?

The only hockey movie that I've watched is "Slap Shot" and it's one of my favorites. Just having the Hanson brothers is enough to make it worth watching and honestly I can't say that they go too far with the fighting scenes. Anyone who saw the "Broad Street Bully" Philadelphia Flyers of the 1970's would agree.

Then there are the Rocky movies with the fights to end all fights. Of course, all boxing movies are continuous action with one minute rounds, nonstop punching and no defense. But the Rocky films take it way over the top. Besides Apollo Creed in Rocky and Rocky II, I can't recall anyone throwing a jab. The hits that these fighters take are bombs from beginning to end. Heck, if Joe Frazier and Muhammad Ali are any indication of what boxing does to a man then Rocky Balboa would have been dead after the second fight just as his manager Mickey told him in Rocky III. And Apollo Creed wouldn't have fared much better. The Rocky movies had me until IV in which he goes into the Soviet Union already washed up and beats a young Russian fighter on steroids. Now, the only scenes I watch are when he loses to Clubber Lang in Rocky III and beats up Tommy Gunn in the street in Rocky V.

Like I said earlier, it's not that sports movies don't entertain me. When I do watch, I look at them as I would any other form of entertainment. Some of my favorite movies are sports related. "North Dallas Forty", "Bang the Drum Slowly" and "Brian's Song" are a few of them.

And I know that the men who act in these movies are not always the best athletes. Heck, it's hard enough to find amateur, semi pro or minor league players who can perform as the pros would. That's why the pros are elite athletes. What they do cannot be duplicated by normal humans like you and I.

I just get tired of the same old dramatics time after time. Most of all, I get tired of the movies making these actors do things that only pros on performance enhancing drugs would do.

I get tired of them overdoing it.

IN ALL FAIRNESS

I like a little unfairness in sports. Life is not fair so why should we expect anything less from the sporting events we watch? Besides, as long as the human element and Mother Nature come into play, sports can never be totally fair. Rules can be put into place to make the games fair as possible, but some intangible will always be out there to tip the scales. I don't mind at all.

I don't just say this when it happens to some other team than the one I'm rooting for. I will say it even if it happens to my team. It wasn't fair that Baltimore Colts defensive tackle Joe Ehrman drove both of his knees into Pittsburgh Steelers running back Franco Harris' ribs late in a 1976 AFC playoff game which caused Harris to miss the championship the next week against Oakland. It may have cost the Steelers a trip to Super Bowl XI, as Oakland defeated them, and a chance to become the first team to win three consecutive Super Bowls. So what? It's the breaks of the game.

Here are some other "unfair" moments that I have seen.

It's wasn't fair when Reggie Jackson of the New York Yankees blatantly stuck out his hip to deflect a sure double play relay to first in game four of the 1978 World Series against the Los Angeles Dodgers. Everyone knows that it was interference and the runner at first should have been called out, but the umpires didn't see it that way. It was a bad break for the Dodgers and may have cost them the game. Sure what Jackson did broke the rules and was unfair to the Dodgers, but it was a smart move on his part for it kept the inning alive. But the series was still tied at two games apiece afterwards and if the Dodgers couldn't recover, so be it.

It was unfair when Michael Jordan, in his last game as a Chicago Bull, put his hand on the hip of Utah Jazz forward Bryon Russell and pushed him out of the way before taking the game and series winning shot of the 1998 NBA Finals. No question Jordan's push helped create the room he needed to take the winning shot. And nine times out of ten it would have been called a foul especially with the Bulls being on the road. Jordan was the one out of ten that it wouldn't be called on. Well, if the Jazz and Karl Malone had been able to protect the basketball better down the stretch, Jordan would not have gotten the opportunity to win the game fair or not.

Indiana Pacer guard Reggie Miller scored nine points in 15 seconds to beat the New York Knicks in a 1995 NBA playoff game. With a little help from the officials. After scoring a three pointer to cut the lead to three, Miller and the Pacers pressed the inbounds pass in order to steal the ball. Just as the Knicks inbounded the ball, Miller pushed guard Greg Anthony to the floor. The inbounds pass which was intended for Anthony went straight to Miller who stepped back from the three point line and sank the tying basket. Indiana went on to win the game and the series.

Was what Miller did unfair? No question. But if the Knicks couldn't overcome it in a seven game series, then so be it.

I recall a really unfair moment in a 1975 NFL game between the Washington Redskins and St. Louis Cardinals. With it fourth down late in the game the hometown Cardinals trailed 17-10. St. Louis quarterback Jim Hart threw a pass into the end zone for wide receiver Mel Gray who got his hands on it before having it knocked away by Washington's Pat Fischer. Gray never possessed the ball and lost it before getting either foot on the ground. Under today's rules, it would be an incomplete pass without question. But in 1975 one official called it incomplete while another who was not on the goal line called it a touchdown. After a long discussion without instant replay the officials ruled touchdown. The Cardinals kicked the tying extra point, got the ball back in overtime and won it on a field goal 20-17. St. Louis went on to win the division and the Redskins missed the playoffs.

Everyone who saw it knows that Gray never had two hands on the ball with both feet down at anytime. It should have been an incomplete pass. As Redskin fans we were livid at the time and those who saw it still remember. It was unfair to the Redskins. They should have won the game. These things happen. The world did not come to an end as this game was played 35 years ago.

Same as in 1979 when the Houston Oilers lost a touchdown in the AFC championship game against Pittsburgh that would have tied the score. Houston receiver Mike Renfro was clearly inbounds with possession of the ball in the end zone, but the officials did not see it or called it wrong. The Oilers had to settle for a field goal and ended up losing the game. Who says that they would have won anyway as the touchdown would have only tied the score? But it was not fair that officials missed the call. If they had gotten it right then there could have been a Houston upset to talk about or a dramatic Steelers fourth quarter victory. In that way we were all cheated. Boo hoo.

The New York Yankee dynasty of the late 1990's got its kick from a blatant unfair act in game one of the 1996 American League Championship Series. Trailing the Baltimore Orioles, New York shortstop Derek Jeter hit a line drive towards the right field bleachers. Orioles' right fielder Tony Tarasco went back to the fence and put his glove up to make the catch only to have it taken away by a fan who reached over the wall. It was fan interference for sure, but the umpires gave Jeter a home run. The Orioles protested to no avail and the call stood. New York went on to win the game and the series on their way to four world championships in five years. The Orioles are still looking for their first championship since 1983. It was unfair what the fan did, but what could the Orioles do? And the Yankees didn't ask for the help they just got it.

Sure it was a shame that the University of Maryland's men's basketball team missed out on the NCAA tournament in 1974 after losing the Atlantic Coast Conference championship game to the North Carolina State Wolfpack in what many call the "greatest college basketball game of all time." The Terrapins were probably one of the three best teams in college basketball that year, but because only the league tournament champion got to go to the NCAA tournament they were left out. This was thought to be so unfair that the NCAA began to expand the tournament field the next year until they got to the current 68 we have today. The allowing of more than one team from a conference to make the NCAA tournament became called the "Maryland Rule." Maryland wasn't the first good team to not make the NCAA tournament. South Carolina had gone undefeated in the ACC four years earlier only to lose in the conference championship game and miss the NCAA tournament, but Maryland's loss was more high profile. So even though their loss was no more unfair to them as the one South Carolina had suffered it was thought to be enough of an injustice to expand the tournament field.

I still feel no remorse for any team that does not make the NCAA field of 68 no matter what conference they are from. If you can't make a clear cut case for being added to a field of 68 teams, than there is none. Try harder the next time and hope that the breaks go your way. If they don't, go to class. Isn't that the other half of being a student athlete? If not having the experience of playing in the NCAA tournament is the worst thing to happen to a young adult than they will live a pretty good life.

The same with college football teams who are left out of the BCS championship game or not invited to one of its bowls. Every year we hear that this team or that should be in a certain bowl while one of the teams who will be competing should not. Then the case is made about how these poor young men's lives are so bad, because they won't get a chance to win a championship or play on New Year's Day. My feeling is that every day the good Lord gives them a chance to compete is a good day no matter when or where it is. And if they finish undefeated without getting a share of the National title, then so be it. For me they are still a worthy team. If the title is split I have no problem with that either especially if they are both undefeated. To me, if two students in a class get a perfect score on an exam then one is not better than the other. They should be rewarded with the same score of one hundred per cent. Why should we feel any different if two teams from major conferences run the table? But we cry too much for the team who is supposedly done wrong in these situations.

What is so unfair about a football team which plays its home games in a dome having to play outdoors for the right to go to the Super Bowl? Football has been played in bad weather since its inception and the good teams structure themselves in a way that they can handle all situations. If a team which plays in a dome and passes the ball all of the time suddenly can't move it in the snow and wind of Foxboro, Massachusetts or Pittsburgh, Pennsylvania, than it's their fault for not developing a running game not the weather's or the team which earned home field advantage. The weather has never been unfair in football. It can't be controlled, but how you build your team and where they end up in the standings can. Like Pittsburgh Steelers head coach Mike Tomlin says, "No excuses. No explanations."

Then there is the 1972 Men's Olympic Gold Medal basketball game between the United States and Soviet Union. This is the game in which the Soviets got three chances by the officials before finally winning the game with a last second shot in which the shooter knocked down two Americans before scoring. The United States protested vehemently, as they should have, but the officials let the game stand. In protest, the U.S. men did not take the medal stand to accept the silver medal for second place and still have not taken their medals. I understand that they were done wrong and it hurt, but time moves on. Most of them have gone on to success in their lives and maybe it's time to let it go. Sometimes you have to be a bigger man and accept defeat even though an injustice may have been done.

Boxing has always had its share of unfair scoring. One that immediately comes to mind is the Sugar Ray Leonard- Marvin Hagler middleweight title fight in 1987. Leonard, the challenger, had not fought in three years and defeated the favorite champion Hagler in a twelve round split decision. Almost everyone who has seen the fight believes that Hagler won. Hagler thought the decision so unfair that he retired from boxing. A champion should never lose his belt on a split decision we heard. He should be clearly beaten.

Well it is true that Leonard did not clearly beat Hagler, but he didn't lose the fight either. He didn't lose, because he told Hagler and everyone else exactly what he was going to do in the ring before he did it. Leonard told them that he would flurry at the end of rounds to impress the judges and steal rounds. This was the only way that he could win and he knew it. And he did.

Hagler had two options. Go out and fight Leonard's style or press the issue and try to knock out a man who hadn't been in a boxing ring in three years. Hagler chose the former and it cost him. The decision wasn't unfair, because Hagler should have erased all doubt and knocked Leonard out.

In the 1986 World Cup, Argentina's Diego Maradona scored the winning goal against West Germany when he deflected the ball into the net with his hand which is illegal. The West Germans complained bitterly, but the call stood and Maradona's "Hand of God" goal became world famous. Sure it was unfair and couldn't have happened at a worse time for West Germany. But it did and nothing could change it then or now.

Golfers deal with the unfairness of sport every time that they tee it up. The game is designed that way with sand traps, water hazards and tree lined fairways. How a golfer handles these things decides his fate. And he has to do all of this while walking a course as big as a cattle ranch. He has no one to blame but himself if he loses. Though there may be some grumbling from time to time most golfers accept this as the way the game is played and I commend them.

These are just a few examples of teams and men getting the short end of the stick. It happens in sports on a weekly basis around the world. It's just that the more high profile the event, the more people watching and see the injustice. I've been on both sides of it as a player and coach. It happens. And life goes on. Even with better rules and technology to govern the game, unfair things are going to happen. Nothing is perfect. Not life or sports. And you know what? I wouldn't want it any other way.

What doesn't kill you makes you stronger.

TRIED AND TRUE

I am no general manager or owner of a sports team. I don't pretend to be the world's greatest talent scout. I have missed on evaluating talent from afar just as those who have up close. I have missed on whole teams in their ascension to greatness. I have waited for teams that I thought had talent to become something only to see it never happen.

Having said that, if I were to become the general manager, because I don't want to be an owner, of a team in each of the three sports that I know (football, baseball, and basketball), this is how I would build my teams. The steps that I would take are nothing special or new. They have been around since the beginning of time. So long that I call them "The Tried and True."

First, no matter what the sport, I would have to hire a coach or manager who has the same philosophy in building a team that I do. He can have his own style on the field, but when it comes to the personnel needed to fill out the roster we have to be on the same page. He will hire all of his assistant coaches and the scouts would be hired jointly. And whoever I hire must have a plan for success. If there is no planning then there is no success. There will be no on the job training under my watch. Once we get our staff and scouts together, it's time to build a team.

Let's start with football. We always hear what teams must do in the draft in order to win. Some teams believe in the philosophy that you draft the best player on the board regardless of position. Others think that you have to draft at the position where you need the most help. Then there are those who draft in order to stockpile at different positions. Using the draft and free agency here is how I would build.

The most important position on a football field is quarterback. He handles the ball on every offensive play and must know what every man on the field is doing. Since a team cannot win without scoring, the quarterback must find ways to put points on the board. He has to be able to lead men by word and most important performance. He must be tough enough to take punishment and durable enough to play game after game. He must be able to manage a game when ahead and bring his team from behind to win. A team can win a championship with a good one, but for long term success they need a great one.

But a quarterback should not be drafted with the number one pick or in the first round unless there is no doubt he will be great. If there is any doubt, pass on him and pick another position. A bad choice at quarterback can hurt a team for years. One should always do their homework on a quarterback before drafting him or signing him as a free agent. One must find out about his personal and psychological makeup as well as his athletic skills. The position of quarterback is way too important for a team not to be diligent in their homework. If you are going to miss don't have it be because every stone was not turned.

The quarterback is the most important position, but the offensive line is the most important unit with the defensive front seven running a close second. The offensive line must be built before any other unit, because they protect the quarterback and control the tempo of the game. Without a great offensive line the quarterbacks can't throw, the running backs run or the receivers catch. Most people feel as though the second most important position on a team is the tackle which protects the quarterback's blindside. That may be true, but an offensive line's strength has to come up the middle. This consists of the center and two guards.

Defenses know that the easiest and shortest way to the quarterback is up the middle so they want to collapse the pass pocket and get in his face. They also know that the shortest distance between two points is a straight line so if an offense can run the ball up the middle this exposes the outsides and opens up the passing game, because the defense has to put more players near the line of scrimmage to stop them. So offensive lineman must be able to keep the vision and sight lines of the quarterback clear and open holes inside for the runners. Teams want to run the ball inside the tackles first and then outside. This helps to slow down the outside pass rush, because they have to account for the inside run. If they go wide to get around the offensive tackle then they are taking themselves out of the running play. If the guys up the middle don't control this space than they can neither run nor pass no matter what the tackles do.

The offensive line controls the tempo of the game, because they allow a team to hold onto the ball. The longer a team can control the ball, the easier they make it on their defense which will be on the field for fewer plays and is more rested late in the game. By the same token they wear down the opponent by making them play more plays. And they put more pressure on the opponent's offense to score, because possessions are cut to a minimum. The offensive line is truly the heart and soul of a football team.

The defensive front seven of linemen and linebackers is next. Once again, most people feel as though the most important position in this group is the defensive end, because he has to be able to get to the quarterback. This may be true, but just as on offense the defense must be strong up the middle. The triangle of linemen and linebackers inside must find a way to collapse the pocket on pass plays and shut down the run on running plays. If they can rush the passer up the middle, they can cut off the sight lines to his receivers and stop him from stepping up towards the line of scrimmage. This allows the fast, quick defensive end or linebacker the time to come around the corner and get to the quarterback. If they shut down the inside run, they force a team to try to get outside where they can string them towards the sideline and use it as an extra defender. By shutting down the running game, they force teams into predictable passing downs, which once again, increases the value of the defensive end or outside linebacker.

Now that I've gotten my offensive and defensive lines and hopefully my quarterback it is time to find a good, solid running back on offense and two cornerbacks who can play man to man in defensive pass coverage.

Even though it is the passing game which allows an offense to reach its full potential it is the versatile running back which complements the quarterback best. The running back who can do everything that his position asks him to do. He must be able to move the chains by running the ball, get out of the backfield and catch it and block for the quarterback on passing downs. Those who can run it are somewhat easy to find. Same with those who can catch. But the ones who can run, catch and block are the jewels, because they don't have to be replaced in any situation and defenses can't key on them.

If a defense knows that all a man can do is run then they will set up to stop it. If they know that he is only in to catch the ball then they will defense him that way. If they know that he is a blocker then they won't account for him in the running or passing game. But if the running back can do all three, the defense has to play straight up in order to account for the passing and running games. This opens up everything for the receivers and quarterback in the passing game. And it helps the offensive line, because the defense doesn't know if they are going to pass or run block. And once again, it strengthens the middle of your offense.

The cornerbacks on defense are important, because if they can play man to man on the offenses receivers this allows everyone in the front seven more time to get to the quarterback on passing plays and more freedom to play the run on running plays knowing that if it is a fake the deep pass will be covered. In other words, it shrinks the field for what the offense can do. With less field to work with, the offense can't create holes in the defense and it becomes harder for them to move the ball.

Then I move to the safety positions on defense where I have to find a big strong one to cover the tight end and help out in playing the run and a quick athletic one who can roam the deep part of the field, read the offense, knock the crap out of a receiver and come up with the big turnover. The free safety should be one of the best athletes, if not the best, on the field. Once the safeties are put into play, my strength up the middle is total and it's going to be hard for a team to run on me.

The last positions I would look for are the receivers not because they aren't important. They are. It is because they are so reliant on everyone else offensively that they would be my last pick. Don't get me wrong, if there is a Randy Moss or Andre Johnson out there I am going to grab him if my offensive and defensive lines are set. But if I don't have my quarterback or offensive line then my receivers cannot be used to their full potential.

The special teams would be far from neglected. Anyone who doesn't start or play quarterback would have to be able to play special teams. The argument can be made that it is a third of the game for these two reasons. No one play in football decides field position more than punts and kickoffs. And the only unit that can score in every way possible (field goal, safety, touchdown, extra point) is the specialty unit.

Any championship team must have a solid reliable field goal kicker. The talent on most pro football teams is pretty evenly matched. The more evenly matched the teams the more important the field goal kicker, because points are going to be at a premium. A good field goal kicker can be good for three to four wins a year and a bad one can cost you a season.

And a punter who can pin the opposition deep is a defenses best friend. As much as we give credit to the New York Giants defense in their victory over the New England Patriots in Super Bowl XLII, punter Jeff Feagles was just as important. He changed field position every time and instead of New England starting out around their own thirty or forty yard line where they could open up the playbook, they were starting inside the twenty where they had to be more conservative.

There is my football team.

Baseball is next. The old adage that pitching and defense is the way to go in baseball is true. The teams with the best pitching staffs and defenses usually win, because these two things come to the ballpark even when hitting does not.

For a while during the 1990's and early 2000's this notion was starting to be challenged. Because of players using performance enhancing drugs, it was the hitters who took control of the game and teams with lineups full of guys who could hit began to win more and more. Pitchers were becoming less effective and relievers were becoming just as important, if not more so, than starters. Defense didn't mean as much because guys were hitting balls out of the park in record numbers. There is no defense for a ball which goes over the fence.

Now that the major and minor leagues have finally implemented drug testing, the game will go back to its natural order of pitching and defense. And that's where we will start.

First, you can never have too much good pitching. The more good arms that you have, the better your chances of sustaining success through an entire season or decade. Even during the PED era the New York Yankees, Atlanta Braves and Boston Red Sox had the bulk of good pitching and won regularly. The good thing about having a lot of talented pitchers is that you can weed out the ones you don't need or want and they are good trade bait for bringing in the position players that you need to back them up. So bring on the pitchers.

Then I shore up my defensive middle. I get a solid catcher who can handle pitchers, has good mechanics around the plate, can throw out base stealers and run the show on defense. The second baseman has to be able to cover ground left and right, especially to the left to take up the slack for whoever my first baseman might be. He must be able to turn the double play and make all of the routine plays. The shortstop must be able to do the same and must be the best athlete on the field. He must be able to range left and right. He must have a very good if not great arm for the long throws in the hole and making the cutoff throws from the outfielder to each base. He must be able to turn the double play. He must make the routine look easy. He must help the catcher with calling the infield signals. He must know every hitter's tendencies as well as the pitcher and catcher. And the center fielder must have the speed to cover ground left, right, in front and behind him. He must be able to back up the left and right fielders if balls get behind them. He doesn't have to have the best arm in the outfield, because his range is more important, but it must be above average. And, like the shortstop, catcher and pitcher he must know every hitter's tendencies.

Then we move to the outsides. I've got to have a right fielder who can throw the ball from the outfield fence to the plate on the fly. He must be able to field his position and handle balls in the corner. He must be able to field balls hit in front and behind him especially sinking line drives hit by right handed hitters. For my money, he must be able to hit the ball with some power and steal a base or two.

The third baseman would be next. He has to be able to field the hot shots sent his way and the slow rollers which dribble towards him. He has to be able to range to his right, turn and throw a runner out going to first base. He has to be able to field a bunt. He has to know how to field a ball in foul territory. And he has to be able to start the 5-4-3 double play with a clean pick of the ball and good throw to second.

The left fielder has to be solid in fielding, because with most hitters being right handed, he will get more fly balls hit to him than the right fielder. Like the right fielder, he needs to know how to play balls in the corners and caroms off of the wall. He doesn't have to have the greatest arm, because most of the bases he throws to are right in front of him and runners will be coming towards him at second and third base. All of the outfielders should know where to throw the ball in every situation and who the cutoff man is. And the infielders should know who the cutoff man is and what base they are covering on every play.

First base would be the last position to fill. I would like to have a good smart fielder who can hit like former all-star Keith Hernandez. At first base, I would sacrifice a little bit of range on defense for offense, but he had better be good with the glove. I would prefer a left hander, because he won't have to backhand as many throws as a righty and has an easier time throwing to each base.

All of my fielders would have to know the fundamentals or they don't play. They need to know the situation and what they must do with the ball if it is hit to them or where to go if it's not. They must know how to field their position and make throws in the simplest form. They must know where everyone is supposed to be and what form of communication to use on plays such as pop ups between two fielders. Physical errors will be tolerated. Mental ones will not.

For my batting order, I would like to have a center fielder with great speed leading off. This puts pressure on the defense if he gets on. Then my second best hitter comes up in order to get him into scoring position and get on himself, because I don't like to waste early outs. Then my best hitter bats third so that I can get him to the plate in the first inning and maximize his times at bat. My best power hitter bats fourth and then I must have some power in the fifth and sixth spots to protect him. The seventh, eighth and ninth spots are filled by the two guys, usually shortstop and catcher, who are more important to me on defense than offense and of course if I'm in the National League the pitcher bats last. If the American League, the designated hitter is one of my top four in the batting order and the second baseman more than likely falls into that seven, eight, nine category.

My bench would be stocked with three utility infielders, a backup catcher, three backup outfielders and a designated or pinch hitter. All of my backups should be able to pinch hit and the outfielders pinch run. That's 16 everyday players and nine pitchers of which five would be left handed and four right. It's a start.

Basketball is a little easier than football and baseball, but more complicated, because the key player is the hardest to find. The center is the most important player on a basketball five, but it is a position that is dying out. The teams that win big in basketball have a good, if not great, center in their lineup. The only two championship teams that I would say did not were the second three peat Chicago Bulls of 1996-98 and the Detroit Pistons in 2004. Even with that being said they got enough points in the paint to offset this.

To me, basketball is pretty simple. It is about defending the paint and scoring in the paint. The teams which can get easy field goals and prevent them win. If I have big men who can get me points in the paint every night I've got a better chance than if I rely on jump shooters. A lot of purists don't like the dunk shot, but if I were a coach I'd be happy if all of my team's points came via the dunk, because it's the easiest way to score. Scoring inside also helps a team sustain when the jump shooters are off their mark in a game also. By keeping pace with steady scoring inside a team can stay within range until their shooters find their touch. And by working the ball inside it frees up the jump shooters to do their thing, because the defense has to collapse inside to protect the basket leaving the perimeter open.

Defensively, the paint has to be off limits. No layups or dunks. They must be altered or blocked. No one can post up and get to the rim. No drives to the basket. And no second chance points. If a shot goes up from the opposition, then my defense had better get it if it misses. Defensively we won't be able to stop them from scoring every time, but will try to make them take the lowest percentage shot.

So my center is first and foremost. Strength up the middle again. He must be able to play in the post facing the basket or with his back to it. He must have a go to move when the shot clock is running down. He must have the ability to get separation from the man guarding him when he shoots. He must be an excellent passer out of the post able to see double teams and get the ball to the open man and hit teammates cutting to the basket. He must be able to rebound missed shots and or tap them in. And he must be a good free throw shooter, because the offense will go through him.

On defense, he has to be able to stop the other team's center from finding his spot in the post. He has to help out with the guards on the pick and roll play. This is when the center takes a pass from the guard, then the guard breaks past him to the basket. If the guard loses his man and the defensive center doesn't stop him than the offensive center passes to him for a layup. If the defensive center goes with the guard then the offensive center shoots a short set shot. The defensive center must be smart enough to recognize this and know what to do. The center must stop anyone who drives to the basket by altering or blocking their shot. And he must be able to get defensive rebound position to take away the second chance shot. Back in the day, the center had to be able to trigger the fast break by getting the ball into the hands of the guards as quickly as possible, but the fast break is a dying art. If the center takes away the paint on defense, then the offense will take more low percentage shots.

Then we need a point guard who can run the show. He has to be able to dribble and pass with shooting being an added bonus and more necessary in today's half court game. He must know where each player on the floor is most effective with the ball on offense. He must know when to speed up and slow down the tempo of a game. He must be able to get proper spacing between his teammates. And he must be able to find the cracks in a defense and penetrate into the lane in order to score or open things up for teammates. On defense he must be able to stop the opponents point guard from penetrating and help with double teams on the low blocks. A good ball theft who can steal it from the opposition and translate it into easy baskets makes life easier also.

Now, we need a scorer. I would like for it to be a guard, but it can be a small forward. Whoever it is, he must be able to get to the rim and score no matter what the defense. If the defense stops him from penetrating then he must be able to hit the pull up jumper or shoot the three. He has to be able to score with either hand and do it under duress. He has to be able to get to the free throw line and score when he gets there. He has to be the most creative offensive player on the floor. This is the guy who gets me 25 points a night. This is the guy that, along with the center, defenses have to account for. The one thing that he has to be able to do is let the game come to him. Trust that his teammates will get him the ball when and where he needs it and be ready when they do. He is either the first or second scoring option depending on how good my center is. On defense, I will give up a little as long as he's scoring. He is more of a help defender than one on one guy, but he had better be able to get to loose balls and long rebounds.

My power forward is next. He brings the toughness to my team. He rebounds on both ends of the floor. He plays defense on the opponent's power forward and helps out with the center when the ball goes into the post. He cuts off the lane from opponents who try to drive into it. And he scores his baskets on put backs from missed offensive shots

My small forward, if he is not the scorer has to be able to defend the other team's best offensive player who is not the center. He has to be able to clean up the loose balls and get rebounds. He must be able to score in the paint and make the fifteen foot jump shot. He must be able to run the floor along with the guards on the fast break.

Let me say this. With the exception of power forward, any basketball team that I build will be based around offense. To me, the more scorers that you can put on the floor the better your chances of winning. It is harder to stop a team with five guys who can put the ball in the hoop than three. They will space you out more and though defense is easier to teach than offense, it's hard for anyone to guard a man 24 seconds at a time for an entire game without getting tired. The defense may be able to stay with my team for three quarters, but by the fourth I've got them.

My first player off of the bench would be a scorer if I can help it. Then a center and a point guard. To me, you can't have enough good centers and point guards. Then I would need someone to spell my forwards. There would always be at least three players on the floor who could score. Of course, this is easier said than done in today's basketball, because of the emphasis on the half court game. But I would want the other team to know that we can score on every trip down the floor.

So there you have it. Nothing special. No magic potions. It has pretty much been the blueprint for winning teams since their sports began. The organizations who follow it and have a plan win and the ones who don't lose. But there is one more thing that every general manager and the coaching staff need to address before their season starts.

What do we do if we lose our best player? A contingency plan must be formed before anything else takes place in case the best player on the team goes down due to injury. Hopefully, it will never have to be used. But a lot of times it does. Most teams never think about this going into a season, they just worry about it when the time comes. I say that every team and coach should ask this question in their first meeting before practices start, then coach from there. Because if you can solve that problem, the others will be much easier to handle.

I'D RATHER LIVE IN THE PAST

As a Pittsburgh Steelers fan, I have seen wide receiver Santonio Holmes' game winning catch in Super Bowl XLIII about 500 times. I saw it 150 times in the first week after it happened. I am pretty sure that I will see it again. As a University of Southern California football fan, I have changed the channel when they show Texas University quarterback Vince Young running into the end zone to defeat USC and win the National championship in 2005 about 500 times. I changed it 150 times in the first week after it happened. I am pretty sure that I will change the channel again.

Today, we are bombarded with sports highlights. It used to be that the only highlights we got were of the local team on the six and eleven o'clock news. Then we would get a clip of whatever the game of the week was. This was because they were the only games shown on local TV and, since satellite dishes were not prevalent, the only ones that could be taped. National highlights were only shown in small clips for football after the Sunday games were over and at halftime of the Monday night game. Not every game was covered. Baseball and basketball didn't even give you that. In order to see all of the teams, one had to hope that there was a weekly highlight show shown in their area like "Pro Football Weekly" or "This Week in Baseball."

Then a local Washington D.C. station gave a sports anchor by the name of George Michael a half hour Sunday night highlight show in which he had the use of satellite technology and the landscape changed. A fledgling sports station called ESPN took the idea one step further with their "SportsCenter" and the highlight boom was on.

I have already stated that there are way too much sports programming on television. Networks have to fill air time so we will get anything from beach volleyball to poker. We even get old highlights of beach volleyball and poker. Every sports network shows highlights of the days sporting events on the hour so that they are impossible to miss. Then they show the best of them at the end of the week and month. Then they show them again at the end of the year. Who needs a newspaper or magazine anymore? If we want to see how it happened all that we have to do is go on the internet and look it up in the archives. A lot of times we can go to a game then come home and watch the whole thing on television. It is a little much in my opinion.

I do watch the highlight shows in order to see what I've missed. And the replay shows from time to time. Then I will watch NFL Films version of a pro football game in order to hear what it was like down on the field. But after 24 hours, I don't want to see them for a while. It's time to move on to the next game. As a kid I wouldn't have been able to get enough of it. One of my dreams was a 24 hour football channel and now I have it. But now I've had too much. It's like having Christmas every day.

What I want to see are not highlights and game replays of today. I want to go into the archives. I want to watch highlights from events that happened during my youth and before my lifetime. I want to watch the classics.

When the original Classic Sports Network was born, they were a niche network that showed old highlights of everything. Baseball, college and pro football, basketball, hockey, boxing and sports talk and game shows were their staple. I can remember them showing Alabama football coach Bear Bryant's show. Old World Series highlights and NFL Films that I had never seen were broadcast on a regular basis. The network built itself on theme oriented programming with nights set aside for boxing, baseball, pro football, hockey and basketball. Not everyone could get Classic Sports Network and I did only on occasion. Those who couldn't really missed out.

Then ESPN bought them out and the gig was up. My personal reaction when I heard of the new ESPN Classic was a groan. I knew that Classic would never be the same. It took some time, but all of these classic highlights were replaced by ESPN programming. I said then and will say it now, they may as well call it ESPN3.

The replacements for Classic Sports are the individual networks each league has now. When Classic Sports was born the only pro sport which had its own network was golf. Then the NBA created its own network. Now all of the major sports and the Big Ten conference in college have their own television networks. They have the rights to their programming, thus the vault to the classics. Every now and then we will get something from the past, but most of the highlights are vintage 2000 and beyond. Haven't we seen enough of them?

I like to watch the old highlights and game replays for many reasons. A lot of times, if it's not a championship game or series highlight reel I will see something that I haven't seen before. Most of the highlights weren't shown more than once or twice at the time they happened so got lost. Many of them were never kept. Believe it or not, there is no known copy of the original broadcast of Super Bowls I and II, nor a full one of Super Bowl V. It just wasn't thought to be that important at the time, especially if it didn't happen in New York.

Another reason that I like to watch is hearing names of players I've never heard of or, if they played in my lifetime, had forgotten. We always get highlights of the hall of famers. What about the guys who were good players and didn't get the recognition? Or even marginal players that put together solid careers. How can you not like hearing names like Kiko Garcia, Bubba Bean, Nick Witherspoon, I.M. Hipp, Craig Baynham, George "Boomer" Scott, Bobby Stein, and heck even Phil Jackson when he was with the New York Knicks? For that matter, it's neat seeing highlights of any man who is a coach or general manager during their playing days.

Highlight reels from the past will show players flaws, also. Baseball historians and former players will have you believe that no one before 1970 ever committed an error or struck out. Then you turn on a World Series or All-Star game highlight film and see hall of famers booting grounders and misplaying fly balls. You see great hitters striking out to pitchers no one has heard from since. You see pitchers who are in the hall of fame giving up home runs.

In football you have to look more closely to see the great ones fail. The league does not like to promote their star players losing. The way to see great players fail is to look at highlight films that are not about them. One man's highlight is another's lowlight. While looking at a highlight of Green Bay Packer hall of famer Herb Adderley intercepting a pass against the Baltimore Colts you will notice that it was the great quarterback John Unitas who threw it. You might see a couple of hall of fame defenders miss tackles on a great run by Chicago Bear halfback Gale Sayers. You might see a good offensive lineman like Baltimore's Jim Parker get beat for a quarterback sack. You might see Cleveland Brown great Jim Brown get tackled for a loss.

Basketball is the same. Just watch and every now and then you will see a clip of Wilt Chamberlain dunking on Bill Russell and Russell blocking Chamberlains shot. Or the clip of Russell hitting the wire above the basket on the inbound before the famous play in which John Havlicek stole the ball for Boston in the 1966 playoff against Philadelphia. Or the look on the faces of Chamberlain, Jerry West, Elgin Baylor and the rest of the Los Angeles Lakers when injured Knicks center Willis Reed walked onto the court for game seven of the 1970 NBA Finals.

I'm not looking for these flaws, but don't mind seeing them. It shows that these players were not Gods. They were flawed human beings just like the players of today. I wish that we had more of them from the early part of the 20th century.

Seeing the old arenas and stadiums is nice. Today's venues look so much alike that it's hard to tell who the home team is anymore. In the old highlight films, you can almost tell immediately where the game was being played even with the indoor arenas. Many of them are gone now. They were heralded as great venues while being used, but were nothing compared to todays. It's still neat to see them on film.

Most people don't like to watch original television broadcasts of old games, but I do. Highlight films and written media can only give you so much because they have to be compressed for time and space. By watching the original broadcast one can get more of a sense of what the moment was really like and how the game was played. It's nice to see how a great pitcher like Sandy Koufax or Bob Gibson operated from the first inning to the last. Or how Joe Namath orchestrated the

New York Jets offense in their Super Bowl III victory over the Baltimore Colts. Or find out that Willis Reed only scored the first two baskets of that game against the Lakers and didn't play much afterwards. It's neat seeing hockey goalies wearing masks which didn't cover much and players with no helmets.

You also see plays and moments that aren't talked about that if maybe had been called differently could have changed the outcome. For example, there is a play in the third quarter of Super Bowl III in which New York receiver George Sauer catches a pass and clearly fumbles, but the referees called it complete and blew it dead. In a game in which Baltimore was struggling, that play could have turned things around. Things like this can only be seen by watching the actual game.

Another thing that I've noticed while watching these old games is the amount of extracurricular stuff which was allowed. Today if a pitcher hits a batter he gets a warning and is tossed if it happens again. In the 1971 World Series, Pittsburgh Pirates pitcher Bruce Kison hits three Baltimore Orioles and the umpires did nothing. He was just considered wild. Grab an old NFL football game and somewhere down the line there will be a fight between two players or the whole team with both benches clearing at times. Same with basketball and hockey. These things were accepted as part of the game back then.

In watching these old games you can see how rules changes have had an effect on what we see today. A lot of people don't know that offensive holding in football used to be a fifteen yard penalty not ten. This was basically a drive killer, because once an offense got moved back they had to go almost one quarter of the field in order to get a first down. Many forget that the goal posts used to be on the goal line. We've gotten used to seeing the three point line on basketball courts, but it wasn't there during the 1950's, 60's and most of the 70's, except for in the old ABA. The crease in hockey used to be a square not an arc. And the light used to be over the glass which protected the fans not on top of the net. Baseball players used to be allowed to take their batting helmets off once they got on base. They also left their gloves out in the field when coming in to bat. Boxing matches used to go 15 rounds. You won't see any of this today.

The old television graphics and replays are priceless. You didn't get nearly as many statistics as today. The score was not kept on the screen and only shown while going to a commercial break. Scores of other games were literally rolled onto the screen by hand. You might get one or two replays, many shown at actual speed and from only a couple of angles. Some of the replays may be in black and white even though the game was being shown in color. Then we got the old split screen with action on two parts of the field being shown at the same time.

The announcers were very vanilla. The play by play man gave you the facts and the analyst told you what happened on the last play or what to look for on the next. Everything was low key. I have a clip of the New Orleans Saints Tom Dempsey's 63 yard record setting field goal in 1970 which defeated the Detroit Lions. Don Criqui was the announcer. He never got excited until the ball went through the uprights and that was only because he didn't think it would happen. It was par for the course at that time. Actually, I miss it.

And I guess that's one of the reasons why I'd like to see more of the old highlights and less of the new. I've seen everything in the last two decades a hundred times. Even meaningless plays from meaningless games. It's too much. Sometimes new gets old.

And sometimes old is as good as new.

LET IT PLAY OUT

We have a tendency of wanting to be right. We always think that we know what the outcome of something will be before it happens. All of us want to anoint this team or athlete as a future champion. All of us want to feel as though we know which players or coaches will succeed or fail. This leads us to use a word that we never should. Never.

How many times have we heard that so and so athlete will never make it? How many times have we heard that so and so coach doesn't have the stuff to be successful? How many times have we heard that so and so player, coach or team will never win a title? We hear it all of the time. We hear it with records too. This one will never be broken or that. But this chapter is more about human beings than teams or records.

I try to keep an open mind. It doesn't happen all of the time, but I do. I would rather defend so and so coach or player than say that they will never do something even if I don't think they will. To me, as long as they have the opportunity, there is always a chance to succeed. But I still fall into the trap myself. Most of the time, I'm right, but miss on more than a few.

The first time that I can remember saying that someone would never do something was with Dallas Cowboy quarterback Danny White who replaced Roger Staubach in 1980. Being the Cowboy hater that I was, Staubach's retirement made me very happy. I felt that Dallas hadn't won anything before Staubach and wouldn't win anything afterwards. So I told everyone who would listen, that Danny White would never win a Super Bowl. There were a few close calls, but I was right.

On the flipside, I can remember when people were saying that Julius "Dr. J" Erving of the Philadelphia 76'ers would never win an NBA championship, especially after Magic Johnson joined the Lakers and Larry Bird the Celtics. I was a big fan of The Doctor so felt like he would win it eventually. He did in 1983 with the help of center Moses Malone.

Come to think of it, many of my decisions were made based on personal feelings towards teams and players. I wasn't a big fan of the "Air Coryell" San Diego Chargers of the late seventies and early eighties. I thought head coach Don Coryell relied too much on offense to win so felt he'd never get a title. I liked the California Angels so thought that their manager during the 1980's, Gene Mauch would eventually win a World Series which he never did. Neither did outfielder Fred Lynn who was one of my favorite players. That was just my thought process growing up.

That changed when I became an adult. I became more jaded and looked at sports much differently than I did as a kid. Now, I kept out my personal feelings and dealt with everything individually.

I can remember people asking if Michael Jordan would ever win a championship for the Chicago Bulls. Believe it or not, there was the feeling that Jordan was too selfish and didn't trust his teammates enough to give them the ball. It was felt that he would win lots of scoring titles, but no championships. I wasn't buying it. I felt like all the Bulls had to do was get Jordan some players around him and a coach who could get him to trust them. The Bulls got Horace Grant, Scottie Pippen and Bill Cartwright to help on the court and Phil Jackson to coach them. It took Jackson a while to get Jordan on board, but once he did the rest was history. Today, it's almost laughable to think that people actually thought Jordan would never win a title.

Before Jordan helped him win a championship, there were those who thought that University of North Carolina Tar Heel coach Dean Smith would never win it all. Smith had been coaching the Tar Heels since 1961 with seven Final Four appearances and three trips to the NCAA championship game losing them all. When Jordan arrived as a freshman in 1981 there were those who felt this was Smith's best chance. He won it all that season and got his second in 1993. With these titles, Smith is considered one of the best coaches of all time. Without them, he would be the considered the greatest to never win a title.

Just the opposite of Jordan and Smith, heavyweight champion of the world Mike Tyson was thought to be unbeatable. Tyson mowed through his opponents one after the other on his way to becoming the youngest heavyweight champion of all time. After knocking out Michael Spinks 91 seconds into their bout in 1988 to become the undisputed champion, there were those who said Tyson was already the greatest of all time and would never be beaten. Then life got in the way. Tyson married and got caught up in celebrity. This led to him losing his title to journeyman Buster Douglass in 1990 by knockout in Tokyo, Japan. This did lead to something we thought we'd never see. "Iron Mike" Tyson on his hands and knees in the ring with his mouthpiece in backwards as the referee counted to ten.

There were those in New York who felt that the Giants would never win a Super Bowl with Phil Simms at quarterback. In his first few seasons in New York, Simms took a beating and was benched more than once by coaches Ray Perkins and Bill Parcells, but he hung in there. In a 1984 playoff game against the eventual champion San Francisco 49'ers Simms had a terrible game. I thought that he was the reason the Giants lost. But something in that game told me Simms had the stuff to get it done. Two years later he did as he led the Giants to victory in Super Bowl XXI.

This same scenario played out six years later when Washington Redskins quarterback Mark Rypien was maligned after losing a 1990 playoff game to the Niners. Even his own teammates didn't think that Rypien had the goods. One local radio station played an April fool's joke in early 1991 in which the Redskins had supposedly traded Rypien for Miami's Dan Marino and people actually fell for it. I told everyone that Rypien would bounce back and win league most valuable player while Washington won the Super Bowl the next year. He did, they did and I was right.

So they moved on from Rypien to San Francisco quarterback Steve Young. Just as Danny White had taken over for Roger Staubach and people like me felt he'd never win, when Young took over for Joe Montana there was the feeling that he couldn't lead his team to a title. He was good, but no Joe Montana. I didn't want to take a chance of being wrong, because never means never so sided with Young. I wasn't a big 49'ers fan, but felt that Young winning a championship was inevitable. The team was too good and so was he. He got his "monkey" off of his back in 1994.

One would think that people would learn, but John Elway became next. He was getting up in age and many felt that he would never win a championship. There were those who thought that one of his contemporaries, Marino, had a better chance than he did. I thought that it was Elway who would win, not Marino. I didn't say outright that Marino would never win a Super Bowl, but felt as though he wouldn't. Elway, on the other hand, just needed a better team around him. He had taken three average teams to the big game so why couldn't he win it with a good one? Eventually, he did and people started to realize that maybe we should wait before saying never.

I got away with one in the 1990's, but barely. When the New York Knicks let forward Xavier McDaniel leave and go to the Boston Celtics, I immediately told everyone that center Patrick Ewing's title went with him. They tried to tell me that it was too early to make that judgment and were right. But as a Ewing fan, I was upset that the Knicks hadn't kept McDaniel and this was my way of expressing it. New York lost to the Chicago Bulls again in the 1993 playoffs then won the East barely the next year. I was on the spot when they played the Houston Rockets in the 1994 NBA Finals, but was bailed out when New York guard John Starks had a terrible shooting night and the Knicks lost. Ewing never got his title. Though I'm not into the whole athletes deserving titles thing, this was one I wish I'd been wrong on.

Shaquille O'Neal and Kobe Bryant had to deal with the never winning a championship label also. It was thought that the two of them could not share the basketball enough for the Lakers to succeed. The fact that reports said they didn't get along fueled the fire. So Lakers general manager Jerry West went out and hired Phil Jackson. Jackson worked his magic and O'Neal and Bryant bought in. Now Bryant has five championship rings getting all of his as a Laker and O'Neal has four winning three in Los Angeles and one in Miami.

I think that I, for one, have finally learned my lesson. The man who got me was Giants head coach Tom Coughlin.

When Coughlin was head coach of the Jacksonville Jaguars, I thought he would win a Super Bowl with Mark Brunell as his quarterback. The

Jaguars best chance came in 1999 when they went 14-2 in the regular season and made it to the AFC championship game. The only team which defeated them in the regular season was the Tennessee Titans who did it twice. The Jaguars defeated the Dolphins 62-7 in their first round playoff game and waited to host the Titans in the championship. Tennessee defeated the Jaguars again and easily. During the game, I saw Coughlin lose his cool and thought to myself that he was done in Jacksonville. He would never win there. Or anywhere else for that matter.

When the Giants hired him I thought it was a mistake. I didn't think that he handled Brunell correctly and was not the right coach for Eli Manning. I thought that he was too much of a disciplinarian and wasn't good at connecting with his players. He was all of these things when first getting to the Giants and I was going to be right. But something happened at the end of the 2007 season. Coughlin began to relax. With his job on the line, Coughlin's Giants barely made the playoffs that year and with nothing to lose as the sixth seed, he became more relaxed. There were still moments of fire on the sidelines, but Coughlin didn't let them effect his coaching. The Giants went on to become the second team in as many years to win the Super Bowl as a sixth seed, never playing a playoff game at home. They defeated the undefeated New England Patriots in the Super Bowl and Coughlin had his title.

And I ate humble pie and deserved it. Of all people, I should have been the one to never say never. I will never say never again, I don't care if I feel that way or not.

Who are the teams and players who are at the never win stage today? Well, there is quarterback Donovan McNabb who didn't win a championship with the Philadelphia Eagles before being traded to the Washington Redskins. There are those who feel that if he couldn't win in Philly, he won't win in Washington. If Marty Schottenheimer ever comes back to coach, there are those who say not to hire him, because he can't get his team to the Super Bowl. In baseball, the Chicago Cubs have gone 101 years without winning a championship and there are fans of the team who think that they never will. Baltimore Oriole fans feel as though they will never get to a World Series as long as Peter Angelos owns the team. Basketball has Dallas Mavericks forward Dirk Nowitzki and Phoenix Suns guard Steve Nash who are great players at the end of their careers. Neither has won a championship and many feel that time will run out on them. Utah Jazz head coach Jerry Sloan is the elder statesmen of the NBA and has yet to win it all. Even though he is only 25 NHL great Alex Ovechkin of the Washington Capitals is already starting to hear whispers that he may not have the stuff to be a champion.

Who knows? Maybe one day all of these men will be able to walk around with a championship ring on their finger. Maybe a few of them will. And maybe none of them will. The one thing that we do know is as long as they are part of a team they have a chance to win it all. As we know, many players and coaches of lesser talent have done it.

Until they no longer compete, let's keep an open mind on anyone who is involved in sports when it comes to winning a championship. Let's wait until the book closes on their careers. Let's never say never or we take the risk of getting burned.

Let's let it play out.

DRAFT DAY: I WILL SEE YOU WHEN THE SEASON STARTS

How has the drafting of players in the major sports become such a big event? I mean think about it. All we are doing is watching teams do the same thing that we did growing up on the playground. Choose sides. The differences are that there are more than two people picking, a bigger talent pool, more money at stake and no guarantee that the player picked will play at all. Is this enough to give it two and three days of live television? There are no games going on. Most of the players drafted no one knows, even with all of the access we have to college and high school players today. Most of the broadcast is nothing more than a bunch of draft experts talking in order to fill time between picks.

I know that the draft is where teams are built. I know that draft day is a day when hope is renewed for the fans. I know that this is the moment that the young men who are drafted have worked for their entire lives. I know that the draft is where we find out where they are going to play at the beginning of their careers. But is it worth all of the coverage it gets?

I went to the MCI Center in Washington, D.C. for the 1999 NBA draft. It was a big production with the TNT announcers and their guests. There were contests between picks to keep the crowd interested. There were live look-ins at the VIP room where the players waited to be drafted. We didn't have to pay for our ticket and I'm happy for that. The best moment was seeing University of Maryland basketball coach Gary Williams give his former player Steve Francis the stare down after Francis walked slowly on stage to show his disappointment at not only being picked number two, but going to the Vancouver Grizzlies. If looks could kill Williams would have stretched Francis out. We left before the first round ended.

I have gone to FedEx Field in Landover, MD to watch the NFL draft. This was 2004 and the Redskins had a chance to draft Miami University safety Sean Taylor. I can remember when the Redskins pick came up everyone began chanting, "Sean Taylor! Sean Taylor! Sean Taylor! Sean Taylor!" When it was announced that Taylor was drafted, the fans went crazy. For once Washington had done something right.

Actually, it was a pretty good day at FedEx Field even for a Steelers fan like me. We got to watch Eli Manning get drafted number one by the Chargers even though he said that he didn't want to play for them. The fans loved that one as well. Then the Chargers traded Manning to the New York Giants for their first round pick quarterback Phillip Rivers. We hung around long enough to see the return of hall of fame Redskin coach Joe Gibbs who made his first public appearance since retaking the job. And on the way out, I heard that the Steelers had drafted quarterback Ben Roethlisberger from the University of Miami of Ohio. I remember walking out and telling the guy I was with how I wanted Phillip Rivers, but had no problem with Roethlisberger. However, I had never seen Roethlisberger play so didn't do any back flips.

That's because to me the draft is a crapshoot. No one knows who is going to pan out and who isn't. It's nice to see who is the first pick overall. For me, the football draft begins with the first pick goes until the Heisman Trophy winner, if he is available, is taken and finishes when my team makes their first pick. In basketball it begins and ends with the first pick. I have never watched the baseball or hockey drafts, because most of those players won't be up for two or three years anyway.

After that, I'll check in to get updates on local players who are in the draft and when my team is on the clock again. When the draft is over I will look to see who my team drafted and at what positions. For the Steelers, I don't need to know the positions just the names. They always drat offensive linemen, linebackers and defensive lineman. Every year.

No, the draft is not where I make my assumptions on how a team or player will do, unless it's a quarterback who gets drafted by a terrible team. When that happens, I know almost instantly we will probably never hear from him again. No matter how good he may have become, it won't happen on a bad and poorly managed team.

I make my assumptions on players after they take the field or court. I'm not one to go to training camp and watch my team. I want to see how the rookies perform on stage. Sometimes you can tell right away, other times you can't. I knew that Roethlisberger had the goods the first time I saw him in a pre season game against Detroit. The Redskins Brian Mitchell ran the first kickoff that he had ever fielded in a game back for a touchdown during his first preseason game. Lebron James was better than advertised in his NBA debut with the Cleveland Cavaliers. Recently, Washington Nationals pitcher Steven Strasburg wowed the fans with a seven inning fourteen strikeout performance in his first major league start.

On the other side, how many quarterbacks have we seen who couldn't win with their first teams, that went to others and became stars? How many defensive backs have we seen get lit up their first season and turn into all-pros? How many hitters have started out going a whole week before getting their first hit on the way to hall of fame careers? How many basketball players have gotten better in the pros than they were in college? And how many players have started out great only to fizzle after one season?

We don't know any of this on draft day. Anything can happen before a player puts on the uniform for the first time. Contracts have to be finalized and players have to get acclimated to their new surroundings. Players have to stay healthy long enough to get on the field in a game. They must avoid injury. Then they must be able to learn their teams system in order to succeed. All of this means nothing if they don't have the talent in the first place which many don't.

The experts want to tell us that this pick was a good one or that one bad. They tell us that this player will fit and that one won't. They will tell us that this player was drafted too high and that one too low. They will give us each player's background as to their position, what school they played for, their college statistics and how they fared at the scouting combines or player tryouts. They will tell us which team is having a good draft and which bad. All of it is speculation.

Talk is cheap. It is performance that matters and we don't get to know about that until the season starts. Every year we hear how the number one overall pick will be the savior for the franchise choosing them. Every team gets their man with their first pick. "This is the guy we wanted all along," we hear. Then when he doesn't pan out it's never the organizations fault. They were right by picking him. It's the players fault for not working hard enough or being unable to grasp the playbook or not being fundamentally sound or having an attitude which makes him not coachable. It's his fault if he is injury prone and can't stay on the field. Management is never wrong when it comes to drafting and evaluating talent.

Despite the fact that we have no idea how a player will pan out the draft still interests us. There are mock drafts done all of the time by experts and sports fans. Radio and television shows try to predict who will be drafted first overall and where all of the other opening picks will end up. The rumor mill is hot with reports on players coming in minute by minute. Who is going to go first? Will the pick be traded? If this player gets picked will his team be able to sign him? Player's agents are sought out also in order to find out where they want their clients to go and who has shown interest. College coaches are brought in to tell us how good their players are and how every team should want to draft them. Players are followed on their way to interviews with teams that are interested in them. It's just overkill.

Sports teams are built through the draft, no question. The better a team drafts, the better their chances of success. But no one knows on draft day how it's going to pan out. Not the teams. Not the players. Not the experts. Not the fans. No one knows. Everything is hype, until the player actually steps on the field and plays.

That's when we all find out the truth.

CELEBRATE!

As a sports fan, if you are lucky your team will win a championship in your lifetime. Some people, like New York Yankee fan, are lucky enough to see this happen very early in life. Others, like Chicago Cub fan, have been waiting for what seems like forever and may never see their team win it all. Most fans will only see their team win a championship once. Others, maybe twice. The chance of seeing them win back to back titles is slim. Most fans never see their team reach dynasty status, but do enjoy an era when they win a lot.

If you like sports as much as me, there will come a time when you get to celebrate a championship. Since I am a fan of football, baseball and basketball and live in an area with teams in all of those sports I've been lucky enough to see the locals win championships. I saw the Washington Wizards win the NBA championship as the Bullets in 1978. The Redskins won the Super Bowl in the 1982, 1987 and 1991 seasons. And the Baltimore Orioles won the World Series in 1970 and 1983. I'm not a Baltimore Ravens fan, but they won the Super Bowl in 2000 and their predecessors, the Colts, won it in 1970. I have seen two college basketball teams win the NCAA tournament with Georgetown University doing it in 1984 and the University of Maryland in 2002. The only professional sport that hasn't seen a title in the Baltimore-Washington D.C. area is hockey.

Before I go on, let me get one thing straight. Baltimore and Washington are not one and the same. Baltimore fans have a chip on their shoulder and are blue collar. They feel as though the city of Washington along with Philadelphia and New York look down on them. They can't stand any of them, especially Washington D.C. No one in

Baltimore roots for Washington. When the Colts left Baltimore their fans did not convert to the Redskins.

On the flip side, Washington acts like Baltimore doesn't exist. Washington is a more elite city with it being the center of national government and more transient. Most Washington fans come from outer suburbs or other parts of the country and really have no ties to the city. Washington fans will go looking for entertainment so will travel to Baltimore. When the Senators moved to Texas, Washington fans began to make the trip to Baltimore's Memorial Stadium to watch the Orioles. Even with the Montreal Expos move to Washington as the Nationals in 2005, there is a generation of D.C. fans who root for the Orioles. Heck, the Washington sports radio station still carries Oriole games.

The only thing that Baltimore and Washington fans agree on is Maryland University basketball and we all celebrated like crazy when they won the title. A little too much.

When Maryland University wins a big basketball game, the students on campus go nuts. Inside the arena, they immediately rush the floor which everyone does. It's outside where things are different. They burn objects on the campus lawn and run into the streets. They drink and get a little rowdy. And it spills off campus which is not good. The first time I really remember them doing this was when the team defeated Indiana to win the championship in 2002. It was a victory that every Maryland fan thought they would never see so emotions ran high. There was no doubt that when the final buzzer sounded the students were going to tear down the campus. I set my VCR to record it and still have it on tape.

The students started a bonfire with furniture from the dorms. They did all of the things I mentioned before turning the city of College Park and nearby Hyattsville into a mini riot zone. Local businessmen and home owners had to go out and protect their homes from the fans. It was not a pretty sight, but typical of what goes on around the country when fans celebrate a championship especially if it is the first one. As a Maryland fan I saw it coming, but wasn't happy with the conduct of the students or anyone else who was involved. That celebration has become a campus tradition with Terps fans celebrating this way every time the basketball team wins a big game, the rushing of the floor then the rush to the campus and streets. I wish that they would save it for the next national championship the team wins, but would rather they not do it at all.

So what would be my rules for fans celebrating a big win? Most team's fans take to the streets immediately after the win, then the team stages a public celebration through town a couple of days later. Then things settle down and everyone basks in the glow of victory until the next season.

The immediate reaction celebrations are the ones which can get out of hand, because they are spontaneous and no one knows what is going to happen. Many of the fans have been drinking while watching the event so feel a little more emboldened. There usually are not enough police on staff to handle the crowds and the area they encompass. If the fans are celebrating a championship which is a first or long time coming, then the years of frustration and grief are released in a more intense celebration. The more a team wins, supposedly the less celebrating is done, because it becomes old hat. But it always gets a little crazy, because the fans feel that the team's victory is theirs as well and they are entitled to celebrate just as hard as the players and coaches who won it.

The planned celebrations are more organized so less likely to have anything bad happen. The worst that one may get is the fans crowding the street and slowing down the team motorcade in order to get close to the players. But with these celebrations happening a couple of days after the game most people have had time to calm down and are more apt to just enjoy the moment. Also, with the team involved most fans are more focused on getting glimpses of their heroes and seeing the championship trophy than causing trouble.

I'm not one to celebrate either way. When my team plays for the championship I'm more apt to watch the game by myself. That way if they lose, I can suffer in peace. If they win then I can celebrate the way that I want. I yell just as loud as anyone else. I raise my hands to the sky and whoop it up. And I get cocky and tell the opponent to get outta town. Nice try, but you lose. However, I stop short of patting myself on the back. Why? I didn't win anything, the team did. If anything I'm relieved that I don't have to face people the next day as the fan on the losing side. As great as winning a championship game is, losing hurts even more.

I lived on campus when our basketball team won the conference championship and had no idea what was going on outside until I saw the news that night. Our school was very small, but there were students running around on campus and toilet paper streaming from dorm room windows. One guy who I played rugby with was filmed hanging from a lamp post drinking out of a shoe. The next morning on the way to the cafeteria you could see toilet paper hanging from the trees. It was a tame celebration compared to most schools.

You won't see me out in the streets celebrating a championship, especially if the Steelers win it, because I don't live in Pittsburgh and I'm more into watching the post game victory ceremonies and highlights. But I don't have a problem with people who do. Nothing in life is guaranteed, not even tomorrow. If a team wins a championship there is no guarantee that they will win it again so their fans are entitled and should celebrate. And the longer the wait, the bigger the celebration. If the Chicago Cubs finally win a World Series after more than 100 years than their fans can celebrate for a week as far as I'm concerned. Championships bring joy to the fans as well as the players and should be celebrated. To me, one of the worst things that a sports fan can do is not celebrate a championship, because it shows arrogance and entitlement.

But there is a right way to celebrate and a wrong way. A spontaneous celebration should not involve burning and looting on college campuses or in the streets. It should not wreck businesses and spill into people's homes. There should be no violence and things done in an orderly way. Anyone who fires a gun should be put under the jail, because they are endangering the lives of so many people. If New York Giant wide receiver Plaxico Burress has to serve time for toting a gun in public, than so should a fan. Fans can scream and shout all that they want, but not destroy property. No fireworks, firecrackers or flares. And when law enforcement gives a fan an order then they have to listen.

The main thing that fans should remember is have a good time, but safety first. Make sure everyone who is celebrating is able to have a good time. Don't destroy property, because you are only damaging the neighborhood and costing everyone money. Make all of the noise that you want, but know that everyone is not as excited as you. This is easier said than done in the moment, especially with alcohol involved. In spontaneous celebrations really all one can do is hope for the best.

These victory celebrations have been around for a long time and will never go away nor should they. There will be burning and looting on college campuses and in cities from time to time when the home team wins a championship. Things will get broken and property destroyed. It's sad, but that's the way it is and most people accept it as the joy of sports fans. If a city doesn't celebrate a title this way, especially the first one, than they are perceived to not be a good sports town. How can anyone win a championship and not celebrate? It's the way of the world despite the fact that the world is full of champions.

So when my team wins a championship, I will celebrate it the way that I want and people can do it their way. Whether that be at home, in a bar, at someone else's house or in the streets. The thing is that we must try to do it in a responsible way.

So that everyone involved will be able to celebrate the next championship.

RELEASING ONESELF

People are passionate in their feelings towards athletes showing emotion. Some feel that sports cannot be played without it so athletes should express themselves any way that they want as long as it doesn't show up an opponent. Others feel as though showing too much emotion is showboating and disrespectful to the game and one's opponent. Then there are those like myself who feel that we should allow athletes to be themselves. If that means playing with a lot of emotion or a little, they should do what's best for them as long as it doesn't show disrespect to the game or an opponent.

Things have changed in sports since I grew up. When I played no one danced after scoring a touchdown, stood at home plate and watched a ball sail over the fence or hung off of the rim after dunking a basketball not even on the playground. There were rules against showboating in organized football and basketball and still are. In baseball if you did it the other team would make you pay the price eventually. If they didn't, the manager would make you pay by running sprints after the game.

I took after the pros even when playing by myself in the backyard. Sure there were football players like Billy "White Shoes" Johnson and Elmo Wright who did dances in the end zone after scoring, but no one on the Redskins or Steelers did it and they were the teams I liked so I didn't. I do remember spiking the ball after scoring a touchdown early in my boy's club career, but was told it was illegal and never gave it a thought again. When I hit the baseball I ran to first base. When it went over the fence then I slowed down to a jog. I couldn't dunk a basketball so never had to worry about hanging of off the rim, but wasn't a trash talker on the court either.

That was just my way. If I played against someone who did showboat it really didn't bother me unless it was directed my way. There was way too much going on in the game to focus on the antics of someone on the other team. If anything, I wanted a chance to shove it back in their face. The best way to beat a showboat is to stop them, outplay them and outscore them. The scoreboard is always the deciding factor.

If a teammate of mine did something after making a play, I gave him his space and let him do it. In football, you had to get over to them and shut it down before the flag was thrown for unsportsmanlike conduct. In basketball there wasn't much you could do, because the game doesn't stop. In baseball, you just shook the guys hand after he was done.

As a coach, I didn't allow it. For one it was against the rules. Second, I thought that the kids who did it were only doing what they see on television and trying to bring attention to them. Third, I thought that it distracted them from the task at hand. And fourth, where I come from showboating can escalate into bitterness between opponents which can lead to dirty play and fisticuffs.

But what we used to tell the kids was this. I'll never forget when I was an assistant high school coach at a predominantly black high school where the head coach was white and from Western Pennsylvania. He was as old school as it gets. One day in a meeting he told the players that if they scored a touchdown in a game they were to give the ball to the referee, because in high school it was a 15 yard penalty for celebrating and he didn't condone it anyway. Then he said that if they scored a touchdown in college that they should show some class and give the ball to the referee. Then he paused for a second and I'll never forget what he said next.

"If you make it to the pros and score a touchdown, than you can sing, dance and get totally naked if you want, because if you get into the end zone at that level you deserve it." He said it with a smile and everyone in the room laughed.

That's what we told them. Get to the pros and you can do what you want. There are very few people in this world who get to perform at the highest level and when the goal is accomplished, then what the heck, celebrate. Mind you that does not mean celebrating a five yard gain, but a touchdown.

Nowadays celebrating in sports is tolerated at all levels as today's youth have more video to watch and emulate and their coaches and parents who grew up with celebrations are more lenient in letting them do it. Rules are still in place against it at all levels, but the higher one goes the fewer there are. That is because, the higher one goes in sports, the more cameras are involved and the more it becomes entertainment. When fans come to be entertained the game itself won't do the trick. They have to see the same thing in person that is on television especially with the price of admission.

The athletes of yesterday who didn't have TV around don't understand it. They feel as though players should just play the game. If they do show emotion, it should be after doing something truly great or for a teammate. They feel as though athletes should not bring attention to themselves, but the team should be the focus. But there were athletes who showboated years ago with Babe Ruth, Satchel Paige and Dizzy Dean coming to mind.

Today's athlete feels as though celebrations are a part of the game. If you do something good there is nothing wrong with showing some emotion. If the opponent beats you than to the victor goes the spoils. If you don't want the opponent celebrating then stop them.

I fall on both sides. I feel as though the old timers are right in this respect. You don't celebrate something mundane like a layup in basketball, a five yard gain or tackle in football, or striking someone out in the first inning in baseball. Also, you don't celebrate when your team is way ahead or behind, especially if you are losing big. This just shows total selfishness.

On the other side, I feel that if you get an Alley Oop dunk on a fast break during a key run in a basketball game, or score the go ahead touchdown in football, or hit a game winning home run in baseball, or the winning goal in hockey you can do what you want. If a golfer wants to pump his fist after a big putt more power to him.

Professional athletes are putting on a performance. They work hard to get to and stay at the pro level and their careers are short. What's wrong with having a little fun while they are there? Especially the ones who understand the team concept first. If these guys are willing to put the team first, when their moment comes to shine and they produce than they can express themselves.

And despite what people on the networks say, they know that it is good for their broadcasts. They know that fans tune in to see what Cincinnati Bengals wide receiver Chad Ochocinco is going to do if he scores a touchdown. They know that fans are going to tune in to see Los Angeles Dodgers outfielder Manny Ramirez do his slow walk from home plate before going into his home run trot. They know that the fans are going to tune in to see Lebron James throw baby powder into the air before taking the court. They know that the fans tune in to see Tiger Woods pump his fist after sinking an important putt. If they don't want to show something, than they won't. And if they don't show it, than they will lose some of the casual fans. Broadcast networks know that sport is show business. If it wasn't we wouldn't have thirty minute halftimes at the Super Bowl and pomp and circumstance when two boxers enter the ring.

And everyone had better get used to it if they aren't already. As long as there are television cameras, cell phone cameras, highlight shows and the internet celebrations will take place. I can remember an older friend of mine telling me that if you wanted to attract a group of young women, just break out a video camera and start filming. They will strut and pose for that camera until you run out of film.

In this sense, athletes on the playing field or in the arena are the same. They know that the cameras are on them and will milk it for all it is worth.

At the highest level, more power to them.

THE GAMES NEED CHARACTERS

Sports are nothing more than childish games. They are made so that people can get exercise and have fun. Sports and games were not invented to be watched, but played. Every sport that we watch today began on some vacant lot or gymnasium with no one around, but the people who were playing it, then grew into the entertainment that we see now. They have grown, because of our interest in who wins and who loses. They have grown, because we like to watch people perform. And they have grown, because of the personalities involved.

There are many types of people who make up sports. There are the intellectuals who outsmart people on and off of the field. There are the strong willed who take every game and play as a life or death situation. There are the quiet, lead by example type who do their job and go home. There are the outspoken that always have something to say. There are the hard workers who are thankful for every minute that they get to play.

And then there are the characters. The men and women who make us laugh and entertain us. The athletes who do things that just make you shake your head and say, "What was that?" They are the people who pull practical jokes on their teammates. They are the ones who say things that make us pause and think, "What?" They are the people who make the game fun.

Sport has always had characters. Baseball has been known to be full of them. As great a player as Babe Ruth was, he is also known for being a character. From standing at the plate to admire his home runs to gorging on hot dogs and beer the Babe is reported to have done everything that he could to excess. Who else could get away with claiming that he called his own home run shot in the 1932 World Series?

Pitcher Dizzy Dean of the St. Louis Cardinals was another. In fact, he and his teammates called themselves the "Gashouse Gang" on their way to winning the 1934 World Series. Dean was well known for butchering the English language and carried this into the broadcast booth after he retired. There he was considered a bad influence to the youth of America for saying things like, "He slud into third base." So much so that there were some who wanted him taken off of the air. But the public sided with Dean as we are wont to do with characters and Dean remained on the air for many years.

Pitcher Leroy "Satchel" Paige was one of many characters in Negro League baseball. He pitched professionally well into his fifties. No one knows for sure, because only Paige knew when he was born. Paige was a showman who would sell himself to the highest bidder, because he could. There are many stories about him calling in the infield and outfield before striking out the side. Paige was a legend in his time just as Ruth and they still are today.

There were many other characters in baseball before my time. Names like Casey Stengel, Babe Herman, Yogi Berra (who really wasn't a character, but a man with many sayings), and Moe Drabowsky. Any baseball fan has heard stories about these men.

Football has had its share as well. The most famous of the old timers was 1920's and 30's halfback Johnny McNally, known to many as Johnny Blood. The story goes that while on his way to play as a ringer in a pro game McNally and a partner were trying to come up with aliases to use so not to disclose their true identity. They passed a marquee for the movie "Blood and Sand" and opted to use those two words as their last names. Does anyone know who the guy was that used the last name Sand? Probably not, but we do know who Johnny Blood was. He was the man who while coaching the Pittsburgh Pirates went to Green Bay to watch a game by himself thinking that his team had the day off only to hear the score of the Pittsburgh game announced over the loudspeaker. Something like that would never happen today for sure.

The great Notre Dame halfback of "win one for the Gipper" fame, George Gipp, was also a legendary character. Despite the image that his death bed speech may depict, it was reported that Gipp was no choirboy. He smoked, drank and gambled all while playing for legendary coach Knute Rockne. There were those who say he gambled on Notre Dame games while he played. For Gipp, class was supposedly not an option. He died young, but definitely lived fast from what we are led to believe.

Then there was and is Arthur Donovan who played for the Baltimore Colts in the 1950's and 60's. Donovan was known to eat hot dogs while sitting on the bench during games. One of my favorite stories is one that Donovan tells about a chicken eating contest between teammates Don Joyce and Gino Marchetti in which Arthur and two other guys bet on Joyce. According to Donovan, Joyce ate 36 pieces of chicken to Marchetti's 25 which made Artie and his pals the winners. The funny part is when Donovan says Joyce ate mashed potatoes and peas along with it. Then when Joyce went to wash down the food with some iced tea, he added two packs of saccharin. Just classic stuff.

Other football characters from that time were Alex Karras, Paul Hornung, Max McGee, Paul McGuire and Joe Don Looney. Looney is said to have once told a coach who wanted him to send in a play, "If you want a messenger, call Western Union." Today, he would be killed on every media outlet from coast to coast for weeks.

The only characters that I have read about from the early days of basketball were the Harlem Globetrotters of Meadowlark Lemon, Curly Neal, Marques Haynes and Geese Tatum.

Professional wrestling may not be considered a sport, but it has had many characters from Gorgeous George Wagner to Duane "The Rock" Johnson. Wrestling has had too many characters to list. But the reason that I bring wrestling up is because many of the athletes who are characters today emulate the wrestlers of yesterday. It is well known that heavyweight champion Muhammad Ali modeled his persona after Gorgeous George. Ali went to a wrestling match and saw all of the attention that Gorgeous George was getting from the fans and figured that if it was good enough for him it was good enough for Muhammad. Imitation is the sincerest form of flattery and all of the athletes who take after Ali must thank Gorgeous George as well.

I was a young pup when Ali was the champ and remember it well. I remember the rhymes in which he would predict which round he was going to knock out his opponent. I remember the interviews with Howard Cosell in which Ali would proclaim himself "The Greatest". Regrettably, I remember him beating up the toy gorilla and calling it Joe Frazier. Any time that Ali was on it was must see TV. Boxing has not been the same since. People have tried to emulate Ali and failed. Even his successor as champion Larry Holmes tried to rhyme like Ali.

The television age brought characters to light. Sonny Jurgensen who quarterbacked the Washington Redskins when I was a kid is a local and national legend. Everyone seems to have a Sonny story and so do I. While at the Bobby Mitchell Golf Classic, I was getting Jurgensen's autograph when someone yelled out, "Sonny you were the best!" To which Jurgensen replied while chewing on a cigar, "Mister, you have a very good memory." It cracked the place up. I was told by a man and his wife who were members of the Redskin choir while Jurgensen played that their sons would have to go down and wake Sonny and his teammates up on Sunday mornings so that they would not be late for the game. From what I was told, they would be tired from hanging out the night before and if the young man didn't awaken them than they wouldn't wake up themselves.

I don't know if that's true. Jurgensen, who still does Redskin games on radio and is beloved by the fans, will probably tell you that it is.

Joe Namath was a character too, but the difference between he and Jurgenson was that Namath's exploits were reported on so often you wondered if some of them were publicity stunts. With Jurgensen it was all spontaneous.

Namath's teammate running back John Riggins was a different story. He was, and still is, the genuine item. When first seeing Riggins while growing up we thought that he was black, because he had basically an afro before shaving it into the first Mohawk any of us had seen. When Riggins became a member of the Redskins he became known as "The Diesel" and Washington fans loved him and hearing about his antics. After his retirement, the Redskins had a ceremony to put him in their "ring of Honor" during halftime of a game against the Philadelphia Eagles along with a few other athletes including former quarterback

Joe Thiesmann. While everyone else took the field in suits and ties we waited for Riggins not knowing if he was even in the stadium. Suddenly a diesel horn sounded and out of the dugout came Riggins in full uniform. RFK Stadium went nuts.

Riggins played for the 1982 Redskins who won Super Bowl XVII with a cast of characters. People talk about the 1985 Chicago Bears and their characters, but the Redskins were the Bears before Chicago. Washington had Riggins, of course, who was to the Redskins what quarterback Jim McMahon became to the Bears. Then the 'Skins had their offensive line known as the "Hogs", the wide receivers known as the "Fun Bunch" and the defensive secondary which was named the "Pearl Harbor Crew" though I think the name was given to them in 1983. The Bears had nothing on the Redskins when it came to characters. And to appreciate how much fans love characters in sports, the Bears victory over the New England Patriots in Super Bowl XX was the highest rated football game up to that point even though it was a total blowout. This was, because people had tuned in to see what McMahon, William "The Refrigerator" Perry, the Bears defense, defensive coordinator Buddy Ryan and head coach Mike Ditka were going to do. After all, this was a team which made a video called "The Super Bowl Shuffle" weeks before even making it to the playoffs.

Bill "Spaceman" Lee who pitched in the majors back in the 1970's, was known for his antics too. The one that I know happened was that rainbow pitch he threw to Cincinnati Reds first baseman Tony Perez in game seven of the 1975 World Series which ended up being deposited over the Green Monster at Fenway Park. I was eight years old at the time and remember thinking, "If a guy can throw a pitch like that to Tony Perez in game seven of the World Series, he must be a different breed of cat."

Thomas "Hollywood" Henderson played linebacker for the Dallas Cowboys from 1975 to 1979. He was probably the best athlete on the team and would let you know. Everyone knows my distain for the Cowboys, but I liked Henderson. I liked him, because he didn't fit the Cowboy mold. He was willing to take chances on the field unlike many other Cowboys and did it from day one. He also wasn't afraid to speak his mind which was a no-no in Dallas. His most famous quote came before Super Bowl XIII when he said that Steelers quarterback Terry

Bradshaw was so dumb he couldn't spell cat if you spotted him the C and the A. Henderson's problem was drugs and it ended up getting him cut from the Cowboys and shortened what could have been a great career.

The NBA began to see its share of characters during this time. I remember a guard for the Philadelphia 76ers named Lloyd Free. He could shoot with the best of them. Just like his name, he was a free spirit. So much so that he changed his name from Lloyd to World B. As in World B. Free. Now that's a shooting guards name if ever there were.

Then there was his teammate, center Darryl Dawkins who nicknamed himself "Chocolate Thunder" for his dunking prowess. Dawkins said that he hailed from the planet "Lovetron." No one, not even Ali, has ever come up with a better name for something they have done than Dawkins when he shattered a backboard to pieces with a dunk. He called it, "The Chocolate-Thunder-Flying, Robinzine-Crying, Teeth-Shaking, Glass-Breaking, Rump Roasting, Bun-Toasting, Wham-Bam, Glass-Breaker-I-Am-Jam." It is Dawkins who is responsible for the unbreakable rims of today.

Walt Frazier of the New York Knicks was a character of a different sort. He was the coolest dude in the NBA. Nicknamed "Clyde", Frazier was known for his smooth moves on the court and his smooth dress off of it. There were many smooth dressers at that time, but Frazier was considered a standard bearer. He was also very glib and today does Knicks games on radio and television.

Bill Walton played center for the Portland Trailblazers during the seventies after four years at UCLA under head coach John Wooden. Walton was known as a free spirit before coming to the NBA as he and Wooden clashed over issues such as how long Walton's hair could grow. Walton was known to participate in campus movements which Wooden did not agree with. Walton was and is a fan of the rock group the Grateful Dead. He has matured over the years, but still has some character in him.

I remember being at a gas station listening to Walton speak while filling my car up. He was going on and on talking about traveling with the Grateful Dead and it was very funny. The guy at the next pump looked at me and said, "Who is that and what station is he on?" I told him and he said, "Bill Walton?" I said yes and we both began to laugh. We stood there and listened until Walton was finished, because it was that funny.

Everyone is a Charles Barkley fan. How can you not be? He is funny, bright and not afraid to speak his mind. The same Barkley that we see on television is the one that played for the Philadelphia 76ers and Phoenix Suns. Barkley is such a character we forget how good a player he was. The clip of Barkley mocking teammate Rick Mahorn's butt by walking around with two basketballs down his shorts is a classic. And the prank that he and Mahorn pulled on Manute Bol is high on the list of gags in my book.

While at a hotel, Barkley ushered Bol to the buffet and steered him to a covered dish. When Bol lifted the lid, Mahorn's head popped out from the table scaring the wits out of Manute. The look on Bol's face is priceless. I still laugh at Charles Barkley.

Former Steelers quarterback Terry Bradshaw became a character while in the broadcast booth and studio more than on the field. He was always a fun loving guy, but the game made him have to curtail it a little in order to be successful. Once he retired and got into television, the old Bradshaw came back. His stories on Fox NFL Sunday are the only reason why I watch it.

Bradshaw isn't the only character in broadcasting. There was John Madden who gave us so much good stuff they named a video game after him. The late Phil Rizzuto made Yankee fans laugh for years. The late Pittsburgh sports announcer Myron Cope would do and say things that would make my nephew look at me and say, "What is up with your boy?" ESPN's Craig Kilborn and Kenny Mayne always made me laugh. Mayne is still there and still funny.

How about major league outfielder Manny Ramirez? Man Ram has done things on the field that just can't be explained. While playing for the Red Sox, he once went into the Green Monster during a pitching change at Fenway Park. Fly balls are always an adventure when Ramirez is in left field. His home run trot is so slow and low that my nephew and I call him "Pokey." But the kicker was when he literally stretched out to cut off a throw from center fielder Johnny Damon during a game against the Baltimore Orioles which allowed the batter an inside the park home run. Ramirez is the only outfielder I've ever seen who thought that he was the cutoff man. To this day, I crack up when seeing it. And for those who say that Ramirez is a clown and detriment to his time, I say the man has two World Series rings which trump everything.

Shannon Sharpe was a great tight end and is an even better character which is saying a lot for a future hall of famer. Who can forget him pretending to call the National Guard and telling them his Broncos were killing the Patriots? Then answering the call back and telling Patriot fans that help was on the way. Or wearing the Bronco mascot head in the locker room after the team won the AFC championship in 1998. But the best Shannon Sharpe moment was when the rookie in training camp impersonated him during the talent show on HBO's "Hard Knocks." I have it on tape and it is hilarious, especially watching Sharpe laughing at himself.

Cincinnati Bengal Chad Ochocinco just got done doing "Dancing with the Stars." He didn't win and that is a surprise to those who watch his end zone antics on Sunday afternoons. From the river dance to salsa, Ochocinco will try anything. And he is a man of his word. Ochocinco said that if he scored a touchdown at Green Bay's Lambeau Field last year he'd do the leap into the stands and did. Just as he went into Cleveland's Dawg Pound after scoring against the Browns.

But the guys who are characters today don't have it as easy as their predecessors. With so many media outlets, it's hard to do anything without being criticized for it. If an athlete looks like he is having too much fun than it is said he doesn't take his sport seriously, especially if he hasn't won a championship. If he does get serious and says or does something worthwhile people don't take him seriously or tell him to stick to sports. If his team wins, they do it in spite of him. For some people, sports would be better off if everyone showed up, played and went home until the next game. Anyone who does something outside of that is considered a nuisance.

We need characters like these men in sports. How could we watch without them? What fun would it be? What stories would we have to tell? I know that there are many more characters than the men I've mentioned and more stories that I could write or don't know about. Everyone has their favorites.

Sport is not corporate America to the fan. They were invented as an escape from the mundane work life. We don't turn on the TV simply for X's and O's. We don't go to games just to watch the teams. We don't want athletes to say and do the same things over and over. We want people who are different. We want people who look like they are having fun being an athlete, because that's what it is supposed to be. We want characters.

Without them the game may as well be played by robots.

BETTER KNOWN AS

Another reason why we need characters is because we don't have nicknames anymore. Growing up I can remember nicknames were common among athletes. Sometimes the nickname would replace an athlete's real name. Quick what is soccer great Pele's real name? How about former New York Mets outfielder Mookie Wilson? Or former Baltimore Colt defensive end Bubba Smith? What do the L and the C stand for in former Pittsburgh Steelers defensive end L.C. Greenwood? What are Harlem Globetrotters Goose Tatum and Curly Neal's real first names? No one outside of their families know their names.

Well they are in order: Edson Arantes de Nascimento, William Hayward, Charles Aaron, L.C. Henderson (that's right), Reece and Fred.

Even I had a nickname growing up. Two or three, which I will not tell. Only my family knows what they are and let's leave it at that. Everyone in my family had a nickname growing up. Even today, we know if a family member is talking to us, because they will call us by our nickname. Outside of the family our friends had nicknames as well. I grew up with guys named Buck, Moose, Batman, Bird, Moo Moo, B.B., and Gazoo just to name a few. The girls had nicknames too, but I won't give them out for fear of running into them one day.

Let's see? What are the nicknames we have for today's athletes? The most well known is pro golfer Eldrick Woods whom we know as Tiger. NBA guard Alan Iverson is known by his friends and family as Bubba Chuck, but no one calls him that on the court. Besides, Bubba Chuck Iverson doesn't sound right to me. On the court he is better known as "The Answer." All star forward Lebron James is known as The

366

King. Every now and then an announcer will call him King James and it actually sounds pretty good. Alex Ovechkin of the NHL's Washington Capitals is called the Great Eight or Ovie. That's all I can think of off the top of my head. Tiger is the only one which has replaced the athlete's first name, and second for that matter, but King might replace Lebron down the road.

Today's athletes do have nicknames, but they are usually kept inside the team. Most of them are so well known nowadays that they don't need a nickname to separate them from everyone else like David "Deacon" Jones said he needed to do when he played for the Los Angeles Rams in the 1960's. Jones came up with his own name to drum up press. So did Thomas "Hollywood" Henderson of the Dallas Cowboys in the 1970's. As mentioned in another chapter, NBA guard Lloyd Free changed his name legally to World B.

But athletes giving themselves nicknames was, and is, rare. Most nicknames are given to them by someone else, often the press. Years ago, the press would think up a catchy nickname to give an athlete in order to drum up interest in them. Thus, Illinois halfback Harold Grange, better known as "Red" to his friends and teammates, became the "Galloping Ghost" or "Wheaton Iceman" to the public. George Herman Ruth nicknamed "Babe" as a young pitcher for the Red Sox, became "The Great Bambino" and "The Sultan of Swat" to his fans. The Notre Dame backfield quartet of Harry Stuhldreher, Elmer Layden, Fred Miller, and Don Miller became known as "The Four Horseman" and their lineman "The Seven Mules." Wisconsin and Michigan halfback Elroy Hirsch became known as "Crazy Legs." You get the picture.

Boxing has always been big on nicknames from "The Manassa Mauler " Jack Dempsey, to "The Brown Bomber" Joe Louis, to "Jersey" Joe Walcott to a bunch of guys name Rocky, Sugar and Kid.

Some guys have nicknames, like Tiger, that are so good that it replaces their first and second names. Say Dr. J and everyone knows that you are talking about former ABA and NBA hall of fame forward Julius Erving. The name Magic belongs exclusively to Los Angeles Lakers point guard Ervin Johnson. Prime, short for Prime Time, is NFL cornerback Deion Sanders. Former two sport star Vincent Jackson is simply known as Bo. Say Air and the next name that comes out of a person's mouth is Jordan, as in Michael. In Washington D.C. and football circles there is only one Sonny and that' Jurgensen. And of course everyone knows who Babe is. In order to be among this group, you have to be someone who transcends sports and every man mentioned has. That doesn't mean there haven't been other good nicknames, but most of them are shared or didn't totally replace the player's real name.

Before television, the fans got a lot of good nicknames. Baseball gave us Ted Williams, known by "Teddy Ballgame" or "The Splendid Splinter." Joe DiMaggio was "The Yankee Clipper." Lawrence Berra was and is "Yogi." Leroy Paige was known as "Satchel." There is Stan "The Man" Musial, "Hammerin'" Hank Aaron, "Say Hey" Willie Mays and Edwin "Duke" Snider.

Football brought out Dick "Night Train" Lane, Bob "Hunchy" Hoernschmeyer, "Jaguar" Jon Arnett, "Deacon" Dan Towler. Hugh McIHenny was known as "The King" before Lebron James. Lenny Moore was "Spats" for the way he taped his shoes.

Basketball had the one and only "Dipper" in Wilt Chamberlain, Nat "Sweetwater" Clifton, Earl "The Pearl" Monroe, John "Hondo" Havlicek and "Pistol" Pete Maravich.

Sure some of these men played after television was invented. In fact all of them. But they played in an era where most of their deeds were more word of mouth than seen. The game and players had to be promoted more to sell tickets, because that's where the revenue was at that time. And nicknames looked better in print than names like John Smith, Tom Jones and Charles Brown.

Growing up guys would take the nickname of their favorite players or have them given to them by opponents or teammates. There was a pair who fancied themselves as Magic and "The Iceman" on the basketball court for Ervin Johnson and George Gervin. A teammate of mine who got the number 34 in boy's club football took the name "Sweetness", because it belonged to Walter Payton of the Chicago Bears. Our star pitcher in high school wore the number 22, because it belonged to Baltimore Oriole Jim Palmer whose nickname was "Cakes" and we called our teammate that from time to time. If we wanted to be a little cruel, a player who was thought to be overworking himself to impress the coaches was called "Charlie Hustle" after Pete Rose.

Nicknames are fun and nice to have. Here are some favorites from my lifetime:

In the NBA there was Charles "Sir Charles" Barkley. Karl "The Mailman" Malone, Cedric "Cornbread" Maxwell", Darryl "Chocolate Thunder" Dawkins, Robert "The Chief" Parrish, Dominique "The Human Highlight Reel" Wilkins, Kenny "The Jet" Smith, Hakeem "The Dream" Olajuwon, Eric "Sleepy" Floyd, Nate "Tiny" Archibald", "Big Game" James Worthy and every nickname that Shaquille O'Neal has given to himself.

In Major League Baseball I like "Mr. October" Reggie Jackson, "El Presidente" Louis Tiant, Nate "Blue Moon" Odom, George "Boomer" Scott, Larry "Chipper" Jones, Greg "The Bull" Luzinski, Gary "The Sarge" Matthews, Fred "Crime Dog" McGriff, Arnold "Bake" McBride, John "Dusty" Baker, John "Boog" Powell, Lee "The Big Bopper" May, Dave "Hindu" Henderson and Rich "Goose" Gossage.

And football nicknames to remember are Billy "White Shoes" Johnson, "Broadway" Joe Namath, O.J "Juice" Simpson, John "The Diesel" Riggins, "Mad Dog" Mike Curtis, Eugene "Mercury" Morris, Jack "The Assassin" Tatum, "Bullet" Bob Hayes, Bill "Whiskey" Kilmer, Junious "Buck" Buchanon, Willie "Contact" Lanier, Otis "Duck" Taylor, Carl "Moose" Eller, John "Frenchy" Fuqua and Jerome "The Bus" Bettis. I remember every nickname for the members of the Pittsburgh Steelers who made up their famous "Steel Curtain" front four. They were "Mean" Joe Greene, Ernie "Fats" Holmes, L.C. "Hollywood Bags" Greenwood and Dwight" Mad Dog" White.

Speaking of the "Steel Curtain", it's not just individual nicknames that are disappearing, but team ones as well. If there are any they are few and far between. Football brought us defenses with nicknames like "The Fearsome Foursome", "Doomsday", "The Purple People Eaters", "The Gold Rush", "The No Names" and "The Grits Blitz". There were even a couple of offenses with nicknames in "Air Coryell" and "Ground Chuck." The Chicago Bears are still called "The Monsters of the Midway" from time to time.

Baseball had "The Big Red Machine", "The Bash Brothers", "The Swinging A's", "The Bronx Bombers" (which is still used from time to time), "Harvey's Wall Bangers" and "The Lumber Company."

Pro basketball had the "Showtime" Los Angeles Lakers, Run TMC in Golden State for Tim Hardaway, Mitch Richmond and Cris Mullin and the "Bad Boy" Detroit Pistons while the college game had Michigan Universities "Fab Five."

Now we have........nothing.

Like other forms of creativity, nicknames are becoming a thing of the past. Maybe we think that they are too childish. Maybe the athletes just aren't colorful enough to warrant a nickname. Maybe people like the names that they already have.

Or maybe we just don't want to work our brains too hard to come up with them.

KNOW YOUR HISTORY

We as fans don't know our sports history. That doesn't stop us from arguing our point. I've been at parties, sporting events, picnics and jobs where people, including myself, have just butchered sports history. If I'm not involved in the conversation and hear people doing this, I don't butt in for fear of sounding like a know it all. I just listen in to hear what they are saying. If the people talking know who I am, they will usually ask me to help them, because of my love for sports and only then will I join in. If I don't know the answer then I'll look it up so as not to get it wrong. Either way, it is interesting to hear people's accounts of sports history.

For example, just recently while refereeing a flag football tournament the discussion turned to how many Super Bowls certain teams had won. Almost everyone involved has lived through most of the Super Bowl era dating back to the 1966 AFL-NFL season and January, 1967 Super Bowl. The conversation started as a discussion between Dallas Cowboy, Pittsburgh Steelers and Washington Redskin fans. Steelers fans were bragging about how they had whipped up on Dallas and Washington during the 2008 season on their way to becoming the first team to win six Super Bowls. This went on for a few minutes before Dallas fans had enough. They chipped in that their team had five Super Bowl rings themselves. Redskin fans really didn't say anything until one of the Steelers fans asked how many Washington had won. When Redskin fan answered three, the argument began.

First, Steelers and Cowboy fan disputed Redskin fans number. Both said that Washington had only won two. Redskin fan said no, it was three. So everyone got their heads together to try and figure when and how many the Redskins had won. Redskin fan remembered the years their team had won as 1982, 1987 and 1991. Steelers and Cowboy fans argument was that the Redskins had never won a Super Bowl in a season not torn by a players strike. Since the only two seasons where in season player strikes occurred were 1982 and '87, Washington had only two Super Bowl rings. They may have been off a year or two as some said 1983 and others '88, but everyone agreed that the Redskins had won two Super Bowls during strike torn years.

No one asked, so I didn't answer, but the Redskins fans were right. Washington has won three Super Bowls doing it in 1982, '87 and '91. Both sides were right that the Redskins won two of them during strike torn seasons, which Cowboy and Steelers fan were quick to point out. To them the Redskins only legitimate title was 1991. The Cowboys and Steelers titles were legit, because they were won in full seasons, but not Washington's championships of '82 and '87. This went on until we took the field again. What makes all of this crazy is every person involved grew up in Washington D.C. or its suburbs, lived Redskin history, and are avid football fans. If these guys didn't know Redskin history than who would?

Conversations like this go on all of the time. My friends text message me to settle bar room arguments or ask sports related questions. They know that if I don't have the answers, I've got resources at hand to find them. Most people just agree to disagree or get it wrong.

Why is it that avid sports fans don't know their history? Is it because we are today people and don't really care about the past? Let's face it, not too many people list history as their favorite school subject. Heck, even the men involved in sports aren't interested in its past. Is it because as we get older the responsibilities of life become more important than knowing the starting lineup of the 1975 Cincinnati Reds? Is it because today's news becomes yesterday's by midnight? Is it that with so many teams and sports to follow it's hard to keep up? Is it because we have other things to entertain us? Is it because to find the answers all we have to do is log on to the internet no matter how inaccurate it may be? All of this is probably true.

Or maybe it is the fact that when sports history is documented it is not always accurate. Everyone who reads a sports book will come across a factual error eventually. There probably are a couple in this one. Sometimes it is the fault of the author. Other times their fact checker and editor. If it is an autobiography, the subject may report the facts wrong as not everyone has the best memory. In any book where people are told to give an account versions will vary as no two people see things the same. Still it bothers me to read inaccuracies in a history book, hear them on TV and radio or see them visually.

I love NFL Films, especially the older clips. There are times when I would rather watch an old NFL Films highlight show than the game which is on that Sunday. However, there are times when they drive me nuts. They will take a clip and use it just to have a highlight for a particular story despite the fact it doesn't pertain to it. Years ago, when team highlight films weren't really shown nationwide, they would use clips from past seasons for the current one. They would even do this for games if the teams played twice in the same season. The 1969 AFL championship film of the Kansas City Chiefs and Oakland Raiders has a few clips from their regular season finale. I've seen them use a clip of a player who has the same number and played for the same team as the subject they are talking about. With things like this no wonder our perception of history gets blurred.

I know why NFL Films does it and they aren't the only ones. Sometimes you just can't find a highlight of the actual event you are talking about. Other times another highlight is more dramatic or shot from a better angle. Highlight films are just that. Highlights of events that happened, not true accounts of history. This is no different from a movie based on a true story. And I still enjoy watching them.

The problem with sports books is that the more time passes and the people who experienced it get older or pass away, the less accurate account is given. Everyone sees their life and experiences through his own eyes and athletes, coaches and media people are no different. Because of this one can get five different accounts documented of the same story. Some are true and some false with the truth usually falling somewhere in between. In this way, sports are no different than a court of law in which every witness has their own version of what they saw.

Another thing about sports books is many times the writer will try to make the subject look better or worse than they really are. If a legend is trying to be built than there is a good chance that some falsehoods will be written. Thus, we get Babe Ruth calling his shot. If a legend is trying to be torn down, then we get accounts disputing the deeds of supposed legends.

All of this information from books, magazines and media eventually filters to the internet on websites like Wikipedia. Just like with the accounts given by the people who lived it, wrote about it, broadcast it and watched it, internet posters get and give inaccurate reports as well. These reports become considered fact and history is rewritten again.

Most people don't care enough to find out the facts. Especially if it happened before their lifetime. I don't know how many times I've talked to younger sports fans who tell me, "I don't care what happened back then. All I care about is what I've seen." And many of us feel as though the Golden Age of sports occurred in our childhood, was never better before and will never be as good again. Hero and legend worship usually begins and ends with childhood.

Some of us do and I'm one. I keep old magazines and newspapers of important sporting events. I do record sporting events from time to time. I have a library of old books and encyclopedias which are used to confirm or deny something, just as a lawyer would with law. I watch original broadcasts of old sporting events to see what it was really like at the moment and how it was reported. Though some of the stories written and reported at the time have some inaccuracies they are pretty closer to the truth than what we read later and give us a better account of what happened. The quotes are written in the moment while the people involved have a shorter period of time to forget and events are still fresh in their memory.

If I didn't have what I wanted handy, than it was off to the library and microfilm. Though many of the reels had seen better days, they were still quite useful whether it be newspaper or magazine. Now, many of these periodicals can be found on the internet and are must reading for any historian. One won't get much of what the athletes did off of the field, but most sports arguments aren't about that. What they do give is the who, what, where, when, why and how of the event at the moment it happened. That's all we really need to know.

That is if we cared enough to look which most of us don't. We would rather be right than accurate, especially if our favorite player or team is involved. Even if the history occurred before our lifetime and we didn't witness it, we like to think that we are right. Even the people involved would rather tell their version than be accurate, because to them it sounds better.

The truth is people don't like to admit that they are wrong. We don't like to lose at anything especially an argument. And if a legend sounds better than the truth people will make fiction into fact.

This shouldn't matter, because when it comes to anything in life the main thing is to get the facts right being wrong and legends be damned. If we don't than everything that is recorded means nothing.

All we have left are tall tales.

IT IS OUR GAME

We complain about a lot of things. We complain about our jobs. We complain about traffic. We complain about how much money we make. We complain about the weather. We complain about politicians. And we complain about sports.

Is there anyone who thinks that professional athletes are worth what they are being paid? Those who think they are, say that if they weren't worth their salaries than the owners wouldn't give them the money. But even these fans believe that the money pro athletes are getting is rather ridiculous. How can one justify a person getting millions of dollars for playing a game?

Is there anyone who does not think that ticket prices to sporting events are too high? It costs the same now just to get into the last row of seats as four front row seats used to. Not only that, one has to pay the same price for a preseason game as for the regular season. If they buy a season ticket package it has to include the preseason games.

Is there anyone who doesn't think that parking and concessions at sporting events are too high? Where I live, it costs almost as much money as it does to fill your gas tank in order to park in a stadium lot. And I can buy lunch for a week for the amount of money it costs to buy food at a sporting event.

Is there anyone who doesn't think that television broadcasts sporting events way too late on weeknights for people to stay up and watch, especially kids? A nine o'clock start on the east coast usually means a midnight finish at best. There are many who want to watch, but just can't because they have to get up in the morning. With more people choosing to work earlier hours, this makes it even tougher on the fans.

Is there any of us who think that building a new stadium or arena with city funds is more important than rebuilding schools, roads, and hospitals or funding police and fire departments? Most would agree that though in the short term it would create new jobs, the city will never recoup the funds necessary to build.

There are those who are tired of listening to announcers that seem to make the event about them and not the game. There are those who are tired of hearing this agent and that say their client, not player, is underpaid. There are those of us who are tired of not having a college football championship playoff. There are those of us who are tired of watching players not give full effort. All of us are tired of something.

The problem is that we do nothing to stop any of this. If the team raises ticket prices, we renew our season package anyway. If the price of parking is raised, we pay it anyway. If concessions go up, we buy the food and drink anyway. If television puts the game on at ten o'clock at night, we watch anyway. If the owner says he needs a new place to play or will move to another city, we give him a new stadium or arena. We do all of this even if the product stinks. We do all of this even though we are in a recession. Because we do, we have no right to complain about anything. It's obvious that nothing is going to change, because apparently we don't want them to.

The thing of it is we CAN change the way sports treats us fans if we wanted. We as fans have more power than we think. We could get ticket prices to go down. We could get parking prices to go down. We could get concession prices to come down. We could get the television networks to show games at a reasonable hour. We could get players salaries to come down. We could do all of this very easily.

All we have to do is stop paying the price of admission and watching on television.

The business of sport is unique. Most businesses success is based on supply and demand. If supply is greater than demand, than the price goes and stays down. If demand is greater than the supply, then the price goes up. In sports it doesn't matter what the demand is, because the supply always stays the same unless a new stadium or arena is built. Because, the supply doesn't change, the only way owners can make money is by raising ticket prices on a regular basis. They will do this whether the demand increases or decreases as long as people are willing to buy season or single game tickets.

Here is another fact. The owners don't really care who buys tickets or what they do with them. Well, they care about what scalpers do with them, because no owner likes to see someone else make a profit off of their product. And scalpers help set the bar for the next price hike, because owners know there is a market for their product. Besides that, owners don't really care if fans of the home team or an out of town one buys a ticket as long as it's sold. They don't even care if the fan shows up, because the money is already in their pocket. Players are businessmen too and feel the same despite what they say about home field advantage.

That's why I say in order to bring the price down, don't pay the admission. If fans stopped buying season and single game tickets, than owners would have no choice, but to bring the price down. However, this will not work if just one or two cities did this, because the teams would still make money from their road games along with television. And the owners of the teams in those cities could simply threaten to move them. No, this would have to be a nationwide move. Every fan base in every city would have to boycott their teams whether they are winners or losers. Don't renew the season ticket package. Don't walk up to the window on game day and spend fifty dollars for a nosebleed seat. Just stay at home.

This would get the television networks attention as well. Pro football has the rule in which if the home team does not sell out 72 hours before game time than it is blacked out in that teams market. The fan not buying a ticket in football is a double whammy in that it makes for an empty stadium and hurts promotion of the team, because those nearest to the stadium can't watch on television. It hurts nationally, because no network wants to show a team's games across the country if there is little interest locally. And it hurts the team when it comes to revenue from advertisements, because businesses will not attach themselves to live programming that doesn't exist.

Other sports don't have this rule for regular season games so fans could still watch on sports cable networks. As for the post season, I know that the NBA has the home blackout rule for their games. This doesn't mean that not buying tickets wouldn't hurt the teams. It would hurt, because of the trickle-down effect. No fans coming to the stadium means no parking revenue. No fans buying tickets means no concessions sold. No fans in the stadium means no revenue from souvenirs. No fans means no money. This hurts both of the teams which are competing, because ticket sales are shared revenue. Business is built on income. Without income, it cannot survive.

While it is true that professional sports teams make a lot of money from television revenue, they cannot sustain on this alone. Most of that money would be gone by the time everyone's salary is paid. The teams need a strong season ticket base along with their TV money to survive. They need the money from parking, concessions and souvenirs. Then they need to earn extra money from luxury boxes and club level seating, which most owners don't have to share, in order to make a profit. Teams also make money away from the stadium with the sale of merchandise in stores and online along with meet and greet functions for the fans.

Think about how much money everyone in sports would lose if we simply decided enough is enough and stopped going to games. Think about how much they would lose if we stopped watching them on television and listening on radio. Think about how much they would lose if we stopped buying team merchandise. The amount would be in the billions not only at the pro level, but college as well. The NCAA has already set up a pod system of bracketing in which local teams stay close to home for their basketball tournament, because of lack of interest in certain regional sites By losing billions of dollars those in sports would have no choice but to acquiesce to whatever the fans wanted.

The truth is many of us have already stopped going to sporting events, because we can't afford them. However, if many of us could we would, because there is nothing like actually witnessing an event live. Others, who can afford them with cash or credit card, buy season tickets and, if the team is really bad, sell them. Some sell them no matter how good or bad the team is. Who can blame them?

I go to one or two games a year in basketball, football and baseball. Ninety percent of the time the ticket is given to me. I will not pay for it. Why when I can watch the same game at home on TV? If I do go to a sporting event I won't spend a thing there. I will eat before or afterwards. If I can avoid paying for parking by taking public transportation I will. I refuse to buy any merchandise. I go to the stadium, watch the game and go home. That's it.

The only time that I will pay for a ticket to a sporting event is if the team gives me a reason to. What I mean by that is they or someone there had better be worth seeing. If the team stinks, I'm not paying. If the owner doesn't seem like he's trying to put a winner on the field, I'm not going. If both teams stink, I'm not going.

Now, if the team is a winner or trying to win, then I'll think about going AND buying a ticket. If the team has a superstar worth seeing, I'll think about it. If the opponent is a great team, than I might think about it. If the opponent has a superstar like Lebron James, Kobe Bryant, Michael Jordan or Shaquille O'Neal (I have seen all of them for free at the arena) than I will definitely think about it, because I might see something special. If it is a playoff or championship game, I'll think about. Other than that, it's home in front of the TV. I'll let the teams get my money that way. Besides, why should I go watch an NFL game in person when I can get every one of them on DirecTV? Call me cheap, but I haven't missed anything that I've wanted to see happen in sports over the last twenty years.

I have a lot of Pittsburgh Steelers merchandise. The only thing that I bought myself was a terrible towel and tee shirt after they won Super Bowl XL. Everything else has been bought for me. The team may be getting my families money, but they aren't getting mine. Same with all of my favorite teams. Again, call me cheap, but I have all of the Steelers stuff that I need.

In America, we are lucky in that we are free to make choices. If we don't like a certain radio or television show, than we can change the station. If we don't like a certain newspaper or magazine, than we don't have to read it. If we don't like a movie, than we don't have to watch it. If we don't like a song, than we don't have to listen to it. If we don't like a book, than we don't have to read it. All of these things are critiqued and rated with the ratings being reported to the public. And what happens when people stop listening to radio, watching television and movies, reading newspapers and magazines, listening to songs and reading books?

The stations either go off of the air or change their format, shows are canceled, movie theaters stop showing the movie, newspapers and magazines go out of business, songs drop out of the top twenty and books come off of the shelf. Everyone involved loses money. The one thing that all of them have in common is that they will LOWER THEIR PRICES before removing the product. And all of them will try to come up with a better product next time, because the public through their actions has held them accountable. Why shouldn't sports have to do the same?

So instead of complaining about the salaries of the players and coaches, the price of going to an event, the late television starting times, the cost of buying merchandise and everything else financially in sports think about who is at fault. It's not the people involved in sports. It is us, because we feel as though we can't live without it and we can. And until we figure this out and act we are nothing more than willing sheep led to slaughter.

To which I say, "BAAAAAAAAH!"

RECRUITING

I only buy two college football preview magazines annually, "The Sporting News" and "Sports Illustrated. I buy the latter, because it usually comes out just before the season starts which makes it up to date. I buy the former, because they cover the lower levels of college football meaning Division I-AA, II and III. I, also, buy "The Sporting News", because it used to be "Street and Smith's". "The Sporting News" and "Street and Smith's" merged a couple of years ago. When I was a big college basketball fan, their "Sports Illustrated" and "Street and Smith's" annuals were favorites as well.

Both magazines are good, but I like "The Sporting News" better, because it has a high school preview section as well. In it, they give the top 50 recruits, the top senior recruits, the 100 top junior recruits and the top 25 high school teams in the country. I read all of the names in search of local players in order to track them during the season. I also want to know who the best players are in the state of Florida since I went to college in that state. And, of course, I want to know who the top recruits in the country are and what colleges they are looking at.

Having said this, I am not one to buy into the recruiting hype which accompanies these athletes. Almost all of them I have never seen play. Everything that I hear about them is word of mouth. Many of them that are in the honorable mention section are just names coaches, and sometimes the players themselves, have sent in to the magazine. I know this, because a kid that I once coached did this. All of it means nothing to me until I actually see the kid play at the college level. Then I'll judge.

I keep all of these magazines and every year pull out the ones from five and ten years earlier. I do this for many reasons. One, I want to see who made it to the pro level. Two, I want to see who made it to the college level. Three, I want to see who didn't make it at all. Four, I want to see if I remember the local recruits and what happened to them. And five, I want to see who the magazines and recruiters thought were the best players and what was being said about them at the time.

Every time that I do this, I find out how inexact a science recruiting is. Many of the top 50 recruits go on to college, but never really make it big. A handful of them make it to the pros. A very small percentage of the honorable mentions do well in college and make the pros. Most of the players mentioned are hardly heard from again. Meanwhile, many of the players who make it to the pros and become stars aren't even mentioned. So if you are a young man in high school who plays football or basketball and doesn't see your name in "The Sporting News College Football Preview" relax. It doesn't mean that you can't play and aren't as good as the young men mentioned. It just means that you haven't made a name for yourself yet.

One would think that with all of the evidence stating that most top recruits don't pan out, people wouldn't get so excited over the recruiting process and national letter of intent day, but they do. It has gotten to the point where fans track players from the time they enter high school until the time that they sign their letter of intent. When a top notch player is ready to commit, schools around the country hold their breath waiting to see if he will choose dear old Whassamatta U. If he does, everyone is thrilled. If he does not, they are disappointed at the kid, his high school coach and their coach for not going after him hard enough. While it is true that many coaches future success depends on recruiting, who signs and doesn't on letter of intent day does not determine victory or defeat. What happens after they sign does. This doesn't stop people from dreaming big dreams.

Fans of college basketball and football know the recruiting process. They know their schools and what they need to be successful. They know what local and national talent is available. They know who their schools are recruiting. They know who their rival schools are recruiting as well. They know that recruits are rated on a five star scale in which the higher a recruits number the better he is supposed to be. The top players are called "blue chippers". Supposedly, the more a school gets, the better they will be. So national letter of intent day means something to fans and we don't care how our school gets the player as long as they do and our rival does not. We have all heard stories of recruiting violations some big and some small. There are way too many to list here and this chapter is more about the way recruiting begins and how it usually ends for the athlete and those around him.

All of us have seen or been involved in the recruiting process in some way. We have not only been involved in college but at the high school and even the youth sports levels. Free agency in professional sports has brought recruiting to it as well. How many of us have kids who have been asked to play for travel teams in sports like baseball, basketball and soccer? That's recruiting. How many of us have kids who have been asked to attend a certain high school, public or private, to play a sport? That's recruiting. How many are coaches who have asked kids to come and play for their teams? That's recruiting. All of this has been going on since organized sports began and has been out of hand for a while.

I can remember being 14 years old when a coach of a rival baseball team came up to me after a game and asked if I wanted to play for his team. He told me that I would start and get more exposure playing for him than playing for my current team. He told me how he was rounding up talent from other teams to build his. And he did all of this right in front of my coach who just smiled, because he knew that I wasn't going anywhere.

Compared to what goes on elsewhere, that was small potatoes recruiting. I have known high schools who have told groups of kids to go and play for a certain youth program, even if they did not reside in its boundaries, in order to be coached by an assistant of the school. This way, they could learn the system that they would use in high school together. This is out and out recruiting. I know of schools which will let certain youth league talents come to their games and hang out on the sideline in order to persuade them that their school is the one for them.

True story. While in my first year as an assistant coach at a certain public high school (where recruiting is illegal) we had what was called a football jamboree in which every public school in the county would meet at the local college and teams would play a half hour scrimmage. After the half hour scrimmage was over they would leave and the next two teams would take the field. Since the scrimmages cut into practice time, most teams would put in their half hour and send the kids home. The bad teams, which included us, would hop on the bus and leave en masse meaning coaches and players. The good teams would leave too, but without their head coach. Head coaches would stay behind and watch the other teams scrimmage. They weren't doing this to scout them, because most of us were just putting our plays in. They were there to recruit good players on bad teams to come to their school. Since they couldn't talk or approach them, they would lean against the fence which led to the bus parking lot. As a kid that they were interested in walked by they would make eye contact with them. Everyone knew what they were doing, but how could we prove it. As coaches we talked about it at the school and waited to see what would happen. Sure enough, we lost three starters to rival schools the next day.

Some high schools and colleges recruit by inviting kids to offseason camps. In high school, they do it by opening the camp to the public since schools cannot practice until a certain date. By bringing kids in from different areas coaches can pinpoint the ones that they want and keep an eye on them through middle school. If a public school gets the kid to commit and he does not live in the school district, a simple address change solves the whole problem.

I have known parents to recruit schools. They take their kid from school to school until they find the coach who will let them play the position that they want. If the coach says that the kid will be moved to another position or won't start, then it's off to the next school. This happens more than one would think.

All of this is done in order to get the kids name in "The Sporting News College Football/Basketball Preview Issue", Fox Sports "Future Phenoms" and all of the recruiting websites from coast to coast. The more exposure that a kid can get, the better their chances of not only getting a college scholarship, but choosing the school they want to attend. Thus parents, kids, coaches, media and colleges work the hype machine. And the fans buy into it.

In recruiting, everyone has an agenda. The parent wants their kid to get a scholarship and in many cases have a shot at the pros. The kid wants to play for the best team while growing up then choose the college that he wants with hopes that it gives him the best chance to make it to the pros. The youth coach just wants to win. The high school coach wants to win and send kids off to college in order t o recruit other players. The college coach wants to win in order to make money and pad his resume. And the colleges simply want to win in order to bring notoriety and revenue to their schools.

Sometimes everyone does end up benefitting, but often times they don't. Many times the parent does get their kid into the high school they want them to attend only to find it wasn't the right fit after all. Or the kid just isn't as good as everyone thinks. If things do pan out in high school then it's off to college. There they find that the competition is even tougher and all of the sweet talking done during recruiting is history. Their sport becomes work and they must be able to put forth extra time to be successful. If they are lucky the coach stays all four years. Some aren't cut out for college academically and never adjust. Some aren't cut out for college socially and can't handle it. Others enter with big man on campus syndrome and think that they are untouchable which leads them into off the field trouble. Some, unfortunately, suffer injuries which hamper their play or end careers. All of these things weed the names out that are in the magazines and those that are not.

So that explains why I don't get too wrapped up in recruiting. I like to see local kids get a chance at college and hope that they do well. As a former football coach and present referee, I get to see a lot of the top recruited players in my state play. And I can tell you that most of us know which ones are going to make it and which ones won't. There is no better tool in recruiting or scouting than to see a player perform close up.

While looking at the old magazines, I sometimes wonder what happened to the ones who didn't make it. I hope that most of them got something out of the recruiting process, but don't know if they did. If they got nothing more than an education it was a success. I mean that's the whole point of the recruiting process and going to college isn't it?

Well, isn't it?

73-0 (AND OTHER THOUGHTS)

This chapter is basically nothing more than a few random thoughts that are too small to make a single chapter out of. It is just a few tidbits for the reader to think about. Starting with:

The 1940 NFL Championship Game:

The 1940 NFL Championship game was played in Washington D.C. on December 8th. It pitted the hometown Redskins against the Chicago Bears. It is one of the most famous games in NFL and sports history in that the Bears crushed the Redskins 73-0. The Bears victory helped to usher in the T- formation as the standard set used by all football teams today. It is said that the T-formations was the reason why the score was so lopsided. I have a different opinion as to why Chicago beat Washington so badly.

Maybe, just maybe, the Redskins took a dive. Maybe they didn't want to win the game.

Now, hear me out before calling this crazy. First, I am not saying that the game was fixed. There is nothing that indicates a fix, because a team doesn't have to win or lose by 73 points in order to cover any point spread. No, the gamblers had nothing to do with this one. And fixing a game and taking a dive are two different things. A fix means that the outcome has been determined by people who are gambling and playing. Taking a dive is done on one's own. Heavyweight champion Buster Douglas took a dive when he got knocked out by Evander Holyfield in 1991. Why else would he lie on the mat and check his nose for blood while the referee counted to ten?

The Redskins did this on their own accord, which makes it a dive. It is well documented that the Washington players were none too happy with the way their owner, George Preston Marshall, treated them. They were not happy with their salaries and felt that Marshall had made a promise to them that they would get a raise for making it to the championship game only to renege. Once the players found out that Marshall was not going to pay them they may have figured, "Why win a championship for a guy who doesn't care about us?" Before you say anything, this situation is very similar to the one faced by the Dallas Cowboys in the late sixties who felt as though they were underpaid and always seemed to lose the big game. With no incentive, the Redskins went out and laid an egg.

The thing that got me thinking about this was a look back at past postseason performances before and after the 1940 NFL championship. Before the 1940 game no NFL championship had seen both teams score 73 points much less one. To this day, the Bears 73-0 win is the largest margin of victory in NFL history. The Bears scored 21 points in the first quarter. It would be 23 years before another team equaled that feat when the San Diego Chargers did it in the 1963 AFL championship game. Three weeks earlier, the Bears had been able to muster only three points for an entire game to these same Redskins.

After the 1940 game, it would be 14 years before another team scored 50 points or more in a championship game when the Cleveland Browns defeated the Detroit Lions 59-14. It would take 59 years after the 1940 game before another team scored sixty or more points in a postseason game when the Jacksonville Jaguars scored 62 against the Miami Dolphins. The Bears and Jaguars are the only two teams to score over sixty pints in a postseason game. In the history of pro football there have only been two other games where a team scored 70 or more points. The Los Angeles Rams scored 70 against the Dallas Texans in 1950 and, ironically, the Redskins scored 72 in a regular season win over the New York Giants in 1966. In postseason play, the winning team has scored fifty or more points only nine times since the 1940 championship game.

The Bears are the only road team to score more than fifty points in a postseason game. Seven of the nine who did it after them won at home and two did it in the Super Bowl which is played at a neutral site as the San Francisco 49ers scored 55 against Denver in Super Bowl XXIV and Dallas score 52 against the Buffalo Bills in Super Bowl XXVII. And the Bears had to travel halfway around the country by train to get to Washington while the Redskins got to sleep in their own beds. Chicago, also, only had one week to prepare for their game. Teams just don't dominate on the road to that extent in postseason play, T-formation or not.

Offensive football has evolved to the point where it is much more common to see teams score 50 points in a game. In 1940, the passing game was nowhere near what it has become. But with all of the advances and rules changes no one has scored more than the Bears 73. Is this, because the Bears on that day were the greatest team of all time? Or is it because the Redskins just didn't care and took a dive?

I'm just saying.

Abe Pollin and Michael Jordan

When the late Washington Wizards owner Abe Pollin told Michael Jordan that he would not give back part ownership of the team which Jordan had relinquished to make a second comeback as a player, there were those who said Pollin had done Jordan wrong. I said that Jordan had done himself wrong.

When Jordan first signed on as part owner of the Wizards in 2000 it was huge news in our area. Everyone was abuzz with excitement, because His Airness was coming to D.C. I wasn't. I said that the only way I would get excited was if he put on a Wizards uniform. Apparently, Pollin thought the same because he mentioned many times that it would be nice to see Jordan in a Wizards uniform. It was not Pollin's idea to bring Jordan into the fold, but minority owner Ted Leonsis. Jordan and Pollin had been adversaries for years with a recent shouting match during labor negotiations just a couple of years ealrier and there was no reason to believe they could be partners in anything.

Eventually Jordan decided that he still wanted to play and Pollin was more than happy to let him. Never mind the fact that Jordan would have to give up his small percentage of the team as league rules state that no one can play if they have a stake in the franchise. Jordan, naively, was led to believe that once he stopped playing his stake would still be there. Pollin never promised him this. All Pollin was thinking about was the revenue he could make from Jordan playing.

So Jordan went back to the court in 2001, the fans cheered, arenas were packed and everyone was happy. The King was back. I didn't see it that way. Not because Jordan was past his prime and I didn't want to see him hurt his legacy. No, I thought that Jordan had made a mistake by giving up his ownership interest in the team and wasn't afraid to say it. There just didn't seem to be any reason why Pollin would give back the title of general manager to Jordan or his percentage of the team when Jordan's contract ran out in 2003. Pollin saw a two year cash cow and he was going to milk it for all he could. Once Jordan retired for good, Pollin would cut him a check and let him go, because he could no longer make a profit off of him and wasn't about to share his team with a man he didn't get along with.

Sure enough, all of this came to pass. And people were outraged. "How could Pollin do that to Jordan?" they asked. After all Michael had done for him and the Wizards. I heard this from everyone, especially my buddies in the barbershop. They were all over Abe with nothing complimentary to say. Jordan was the victim in their eyes, bottom line.

Being the pain in the butt I am sometimes, I asked them if they remembered what I said when Jordan decided to make another come back. They asked me what I had said. I told them exactly what I had said two years earlier. You don't give up ownership once you get it. For any reason, especially to go back to work. It was Jordan's fault that he no longer was a part of the Wizards organization because he had gave back all of his leverage by playing. Once he retired, he was no longer the general manager or part owner, he was unemployed. Since his track record as a GM was nothing special Pollin had every right to not take him back. The mistake that Jordan made was that he was thinking of basketball as a game and M.J. never losses when it comes to playing the game. Pollin was thinking of it as a business. Jordan learned this lesson the hard way.

And so did the men in the barbershop.

Tom Landry should have trusted his players more:

Dallas Cowboy hall of fame coach Tom Landry was one of the greatest football minds of all time. He coached for 27 years from the Cowboys first season of 1960 to 1987. Along the way, Landry led his team to 18 playoff appearances, five NFC championships and two Super Bowl victories. The Cowboys won more regular season and playoff games than any team during the decade of the seventies. Landry coached the offense and defense for Dallas and is considered the father of the modern 4-3 defensive alignment most teams use today. In short, he deserved every honor that he got.

As great as Landry was, I think that he and the Cowboys could have been much better. All that Landry needed to do was trust his player's abilities a little more than he did. I think that if he had Dallas would have won more Super Bowls than they did. If Landry, with his football acumen, had trusted his players in the same manner that Dallas head coach Jimmy Johnson did in the 1990's when he won his two Super Bowls the Cowboys could well be considered the greatest team of all time.

The Cowboys of the seventies had a lot of talent, maybe not as close as what the Pittsburgh Steelers of that era had, but close. The teams met in two of the best Super Bowls ever played. Pittsburgh won them both. They won, because they had more talent. And they won, because their head coach Chuck Noll trusted that talent and let it perform. Landry felt that each play was designed to be run a certain way with little deviation. Noll felt as though his players could figure out things on the fly and make adjustments accordingly. Landry did not like for his players to color outside the lines which hampered such men as Tony Dorsett, Thomas Henderson, Drew Pearson and even Roger Staubach. Noll let his players color outside the lines quite often. To me, this is why Noll beat Landry every time they played a game that mattered.

There are many who think that Landry was the most important person in Dallas Cowboy history and to some extent, he was. But to me, the man who made Dallas the so called "America's Team" was quarterback Roger Staubach. Staubach was the one player who wasn't afraid to color outside the lines. Landry being the controller that he was preferred to have his quarterbacks stick to the game plan. This was one of the reasons why Don Meredith did not win a championship. Landry would not let Meredith improvise.

With Staubach, it was different. Landry hated running quarterbacks. It was one of the reasons it took Staubach a while to win the starting job from Craig Morton. It almost cost him Staubach as Roger asked to be traded early in his career. But Staubach would not change his style and continued to run if he had to, because he knew it would help the team win. It was Staubach and wide receiver Drew Pearson who brought the Cowboys back time after time from certain defeat, because they would work on situations in practice and use them to bail out Landry in the fourth quarter. To me many of Staubach's foruth quarter comebacks would not have been necessary if Landry had simply let Roger and the offense do their thing from the first quarter on. I don't think that it is coincidence at all that the Cowboys never won a championship under Landry before Roger Staubach and didn't win one after he left. Because after Staubach, Landry went back to his old ways. The Cowboys players stayed inside the lines.

And never won another championship under Landry.

The Atlantic Coast Conference should not have expanded:

The Atlantic Coast Conference (ACC) was the premiere college basketball league in the country. Going into the 2004 season it consisted of nine teams along the eastern seaboard from Maryland to Florida. Four of those teams had won national championships in Duke, Maryland, North Carolina and North Carolina State. Duke had won it as recently as 2001 and Maryland in 2002. Every member of the ACC at that time except Clemson had played in at least one Final Four. With nine teams, the league played a 16 game home and home schedule which meant everyone played each other twice and fans got to see every team annually. This made for some of the most intense rivalries in all of sports.

Then the ACC decided that it was more important to be a football conference than basketball and asked Miami University and Virginia Tech to leave their conference, the Big East, to join them in 2004. Then they went above the Mason-Dixon Line for the first time and added Boston College in 2005. This brought membership to 12 and allowed the conference to split into two divisions. It was supposed to be great for the conference, because they had brought in three of the best football schools in the Big East hurting that rival and strengthening them. And it would mean more revenue for everyone in the form of television and bowl dollars. As far as the tradition of the conference, well the new schools would bring in new traditions.

Five years later, that is not the case. The ACC, which was never known as a football conference, still can't compete with their neighbors in the Southeastern Conference. The SEC is considered the premiere conference in college football and gets all of the top southern recruits, leaving the ACC to take what's left. Couple that with the fact, Florida State, Miami, Boston College and Virginia Tech have not been as competitive nationally in football as the conference thought and the expansion would have to be considered a disappointment up to now.

Even basketball has suffered. There is no longer the 16 games home and home schedule as with 12 teams the conference does not want to play 22 league games. This means that teams that are not in the same division play each other once a year which has cut into rivalries like Maryland-North Carolina. And because ACC fans really don't know much about Miami, Boston College and Virginia Tech basketball they are less inclined to build up any animosity towards them or even consider them to be a part of the conference. I can recall never seeing an empty seat at Maryland University for an ACC game. Now I do quite a bit.

The ACC was a basketball conference. But basketball is not the sport which brings in the revenue on college campuses its football. So football decisions trump everything.

Tradition be damned.

The United States Football League should have stayed with a spring schedule:

The United States Football League (USFL) began as a spring alternative to the NFL in February of 1983. It was a twelve team league which played an eighteen game schedule. Its games were broadcast on ABC and ESPN. During its inaugural season the league featured such stars as 1982 Heisman Trophy winner Herschel Walker and Kelvin Bryant.

After its initial season, the league expanded to 18 teams and saw an influx of new talent in another Heisman Trophy winner in Mike Rozier, Steve Young, Jim Kelly and Reggie White. While the quality of play wasn't the greatest, the USFL brought professional football to cities such as Memphis, Birmingham, San Antonio, Jacksonville and Orlando. And with a TV contract the owners had guaranteed money coming in. The only thing that could stop the league from being a success was trying to outbid the NFL for talent. Or moving to the fall and trying to compete head to head with them.

Which is what the league decided to do in 1985. The USFL would play the 1985 season during the spring then transition over to the fall in 1986. This was a major mistake. The league was not established enough to challenge the older NFL. They did not have a big enough fan base, their television contract with ABC would be in conflict with the NFL's. And it didn't have the finances to compete with the NFL teams. And by not playing a spring schedule in 1986 the league left too much down time for the players which forced them to sign with NFL teams. Once the players started to leave, the league was done.

There are those who say that New Jersey Generals owner Donald Trump was the one responsible for moving the league to the fall and challenging the NFL. There are those who say that Trump bought the Generals, because he wanted to own and NFL team and couldn't get one. By buying the Generals and moving to the fall, he could broker a deal with the NFL and get his team accepted into their league.

Whoever came up with the idea made a mistake. It had already been established that a market for spring football existed. All the USFL had to do was spend within its means, not challenge the NFL for players, keep their TV contract and continue to play in the spring. The possibility of the league growing was there as it was just being born at the same time as cable television. If the USFL had stayed the course until the big TV sports boom of the 1990's than everyone would have cashed in. Think about it. We had NFL Europe for years and the Arena Football League has been around every year but one since 1987. If they could do it then why not the USFL?

Silly me. Because they decided to move to the fall, that's why.

Baseball needs to contract:

This has nothing to do with the talent pool. I've said it once. I'll say it again. As long as scouts travel around the world there is an endless supply of athletic talent. This has to do with fan attendance, economics and organizational skills.

First, there are not enough cities interested in baseball to warrant thirty teams. If you don't believe me just look at the attendance figures in cities like Miami, Tampa, Toronto and even where I live Baltimore-Washington. This is the reason why Washington has a team after 33 years without one. The Montreal Expos moved to Washington, because there was no fan support there and the league had no place else to put them. All of their leverage cities had teams. And since folding the franchise meant having to fight the players union over lost jobs, the league went to a city which had already lost two franchises through no fault of their own. But you can bet that if the higher ups in baseball could have gotten rid of the Expos all together they would have.

Then there is the economics. Many baseball cities fans just don't have the money to go to games and won't if the team stinks. With free agency and no salary cap player movement is constant and the small market teams can't afford to keep young talent or bring in high priced superstars. This leads to competitive imbalance. With little chance of having a competitive team fans in cities such as Pittsburgh, Kansas City, Miami and Milwaukee lose interest and attendance drops. Contraction would not solve this problem, only a salary cap would, but having non competitive teams is not good for any sport.

And finally, there just aren't enough quality owners, front office personnel, managers, coaches and scouts for 30 teams. The talent is there, but it has to be mined, developed and allowed to play. If an organization can't find the people to do this it will suffer. Many teams don't have the people who can find the diamond in the rough which help a team save money and stay competitive. This is the case in all sports not just baseball. So to me it would be better to contract than have incompetent people running a franchise.

Baseball should not have expanded in 1994 or '98 in my book. If anything it should have stayed the same or cut back.

Hockey would cut out fighting if more African-Americans played:

In hockey, players can fight. In basketball and every other pro team sport they cannot. If you fight in hockey it's off to the penalty box to calm down. If you fight in every other team sport, you get kicked out of the game even football where there is contact on every play. There is a place in hockey for fighting and it is encouraged, while in other sports fans look at fisticuffs as detrimental.

I would place a bet that if more African-Americans played hockey, fans would not be as inclined to accept the fighting. There is nothing more volatile in our country than seeing white and black men fight. Anywhere. It divides the races like nothing other than interracial dating and marriage. Blacks side with blacks, whites side with whites. All you have to do is look at professional boxing for proof of that.

If African-Americans began to be more prevalent in hockey and scrapped with their white counterparts you'd see some changes to the rules in a hurry. Whites would say that blacks are bringing a thug element to the game. Blacks would say that the thug element was already there, but hockey just called their bad boys goons. Both sides would have people of influence complain that fighting should be removed from the game. And I think that it would in today's politically correct society.

If you don't think so go back and look at how much fighting was done in football, baseball and basketball before integration. There was a lot, but it wasn't reported. Even the fights reported were considered a boys being boys thing just like with hockey today. Basketball used to have fights all of the time until Los Angeles Lakers forward Kermit Washington hit Houston Rockets forward Rudy Tomjonavich with a right that caved his face in. Fights happened, but were thought to be not a part of the game so were legislated against.

This won't happen in hockey until two men of different shades square off on a regular basis. God forbid it's more men than that or we will have a problem on our hands. One similar to the brawl which occurred in the Palace at Auburn Hills between the NBA's Indiana Pacers and Detroit Pistons in 2004.

I think that it would put a stop to all of it.

The NFL does not need Los Angeles

The National Football League had at least one team in Los Angeles from 1946 to 1995. The Cleveland Rams moved out to L.A. in 1946 and stayed until moving to St. Louis in 1995. The Oakland Raiders moved to L.A. in 1982 and stayed until moving back to Oakland in 1995. The NFL has not had a team in L.A. since and some in the league think that's a problem since it's the number two TV market in America. I don't think it's a problem at all.

The NFL has enough teams with 32. They have two 16 team conferences split into four divisions and play a 16 game schedule. Every team plays the other at least once every four years. If there was ever a perfect setup, the NFL has it. So, why the fuss over L.A.?

If the league gives L.A. an expansion franchise, than they have to add another taking the league to 34. This would break up all the symmetry of the regular season. If a team moves to L.A. that means some city which already supports a team would lose out. There are those who say that the Jacksonville Jaguars may be that team. Or the Minnesota Vikings.

But what evidence is there that says Los Angeles will support an NFL team any better than the cities which already exist? And there is no evidence which says they will support an expansion team. Los Angeles does not support losers and an expansion team would be a loser. Even if the team wins, it had better be exciting or the fans will find other things to do. In L.A. there are lots of things to do.

And despite what the NFL may think, Los Angeles is not going to beat the door down to get back into the league. They are perfectly content with watching USC football, Dodger baseball and Lakers basketball. If they want the NFL, than they turn on their television and watch someone else play. No tickets to buy, no traffic to fight, no boorish fan behavior. And most of the time they get whatever the game of the week may be. Nothing wrong with that.

And there is nothing wrong with the NFL either. They are doing just fine without Los Angeles. I don't think too many fans miss the Rams or Raiders being in Los Angeles. I don't even think that they care. So why should the NFL? They care because of the money, that's why?

I think that they already have plenty of it.

Each sport needs something unique:

We are attracted to sports in hopes of seeing something that we've never seen before. Often times we don't. Usually we have to settle for seeing a great performance by someone, but nothing that sets it apart. This will keep people coming back for a while, but the casual fan will get tired quickly and move on. In order to keep them a sport has to have something that is unique to it. Some do and some don't. Some did and now don't. Let me explain.

Though we don't like it, Division I college football is unique in that it does not have a true championship game to crown its king. Not only that, but it doesn't even have a playoff. The champion is determined by team rankings which are voted on by coaches and media then fed into a computer. The only way to guarantee a spot in the championship game is to finish the season undefeated and untied and even this might not get you in. Because of this, every college football game means something. A team can be undefeated going into the last game of the season and still have a say in who will meet for the title if they play a team in the running. This gives the players on the losing team continued incentive to play. What other sport can say that? And at the end of the year there is always a debate over who should and shouldn't be in the title game. The fact that college football has no championship game keeps it in the news longer than it would if there were a playoff. All you have to do is look at NCAA basketball to see this. In that sport, no one cares about the regular season and when the NCAA tournament is over talk of college basketball ends as well.

Major League Baseball used to have two unique situations in the race for the regular season pennant and lack of interleague play. Before expansion and wildcards, baseball always had the most climactic finishes to their regular season. There was nothing like watching two or three teams fight for one playoff spot over the course of two months. Usually, the teams involved would make their move in August and battle it out through September. Because they didn't play each other all of the time each team had to rely on others to help them which led to scoreboard watching around the country. When they did play, the rest of the sports world stopped to watch. There was nothing like seeing a team get hot and make their move up the standings while the team in first began to tighten up as their lead shrunk. There was nothing like seeing a player carry a team on his back to a pennant. That all disappeared with the addition of the wildcard and, for me, postseason baseball can't make up for it.

At the same time baseball took away the uniqueness of the All-Star game and World Series with interleague play. I know that the fans should be able to see every team in a league play in their city, but it was nice watching the World Series and wondering how one team would fair playing the others style. And it was nice watching the All-Star game in order to find out how each team's stars fared against their counterparts in the other league. Now baseball is no different than any other sport with the exception of the game having no time clock.

Pro football is unique in that it's the only professional sport with a one and done postseason. Every other sport plays a best of so teams can have bad games and still win the series. If a team has a bad game in the NFL playoffs, chances are they go home. That's why the leagues playoff and Super Bowl TV ratings are so high. Each game has a week's buildup and the fans know that if their team loses the season is over. How can you top that kind of drama?

Boxing is unique in that it has a set time frame, but can end at any moment. A boxing match can be scheduled for 12 three minute rounds and go the distance or it can end on the first punch of the fight. The fans pay for twelve rounds, but may only get three thus the need for preliminary fights leading up to the main event. The boxers can decide the issue themselves by knocking out their opponent or leave it up to judges to score their performance. So fans have to stay involved, because the end can come at any time.

This is what I'm talking about. Give us something unique. Give us something that separates your sport from the rest. Give us a reason to talk about it.

**Why shouldn't athletes speak out and act
on social and political issues?**

There are those who think that professional athletes should play and
not talk or get involved in social or political issues. They think that
athletes are nothing more than entertainers who get paid handsomely,
for which they should be thankful, and leave social and political issues
to others who are "more intelligent." I don't agree. I believe that as long
as an athlete has done their homework and know what they are talking
about than they should speak out just like everyone else.

Think of all of the athletes who have made stands which have
affected the course of history? Major league baseball hall of famer Jackie
Robinson broke the color line in 1947. Before and after he accomplished
this, Robinson worked tirelessly for equal rights in and out of baseball
until his death in 1972. Then there are hall of fame football player Jim
Brown, hall of fame basketball player Bill Russell and heavyweight
champion Muhammad Ali. Those are just a small few.

Think of the athletes who have gone on to careers in justice and
politics. Hall of fame football player Alan Page is a judge as was Byron
"Whizzer" White who made it all of the way to the Supreme Court. Hall
of fame basketball player Bill Bradley and baseball pitcher Jim Bunning
became Senators along with former NFL quarterback Heath Shuler. Hall
of fame basketball player Dave Bing became Mayor of Detroit. These
are all intelligent men who happened to be talented athletes.

There are many athletes who are as intelligent as the men I've
mentioned. And they should be heard just as the newsman, doctor,
lawyer, businessman, professor AND politicians are. Believe it or not,
there are athletes who are smarter than some newsmen, doctors,
lawyers, businessmen, professors and politicians. No one who does
their homework and has something to say should be muzzled. Athletes
should not be labeled as unintelligent and put into a box, because those
days are long gone. We need input from everyone not just a select few.
Part of the problem with our society is that when things are going bad
or being done wrong people say and do nothing. The more intelligent
people we have speaking out and acting in all walks of life the better
off we are.

Why shouldn't athletes speak out on social and political issues? Aren't they human beings with brains and thoughts like everyone else? Not all of them are smart enough to know what is going on, but there are a lot of newsmen, doctors, lawyers, businessmen, professors and politicians who don't either. Yes, the ones who know what they are talking about should be allowed to speak and act.

Those who don't think so are either being elitist or not seeing the whole picture.

Perspective:

We hear it all of the time when a human interest story is told or something tragic happens. "This puts everything into perspective," the anchor will tell us.

Well here is the truth.

We shouldn't need to open a newspaper or magazine, listen to a radio or turn on a television in order to get perspective. We should have it every day that God wakes us up and gives us another 24 hours to live.

This chapter is over. Thank you for your time.

DAMN ITS GREAT ISN'T IT

I stole that line from hall of fame football player Ronnie Lott who said it to his San Francisco 49er teammates in the locker room after their victory in Super Bowl XXIII. I hope that he hasn't patented it and doesn't mind me using it. It's just that when Lott said this, he hit the nail on the head as to what sports are supposed to be about. Sports are supposed to be great in that they should be fun. We should enjoy participating, watching and talking about them. There shouldn't be anger when it comes to the actual games and events, but joy. Joy in the fact that the Good Lord gave us another day to celebrate and participate in something that we love.

So this final chapter is about moments pertaining to sports that have occurred in many of our lives that were great, unforgettable and brought joy starting with childhood.

Wasn't it great getting that first baseball glove, basketball or football? Remember the moment, whether you or your dad bought, that you got it from the store. The baseball glove had to be broken in and molded to fit your hand. When it did, it was distinctly yours and no one else. The basketball and football had to be pumped up with an air hose and needle then they were taken outside and beaten up. The good ones would last, but the bad ones would get a big knot in the bladder before bursting.

Wasn't it great finally learning how to catch and throw a baseball or football and being able to put the basketball through the hoop? Better yet was being able to hit a baseball. After seeing the big boys make it look easy you thought that you could do it too only to find out that your hands were too small and the basket too high. Then one day one of them threw the ball to you and you caught it. Then you cocked your arm and fired a strike back to them. After that it was off to the basketball court to shoot at the ten foot rim. Once that ball went in the first time you were hooked. And hitting that first line drive in baseball? What a feeling. It was a feeling that you could do just about anything.

Then, isn't it great when you become an adult and pass on the things that you have learned to young children? Whether it is coaching a child of your own, a group of children on a playground or in a classroom or an organized team, there is nothing like teaching youth. Seeing their faces light up as they learn a fundamental skill for the first time. Seeing them become better and gain confidence in their abilities. Watching them as they go from youth league to high school and then adulthood. Watching as they learn to trust their teammates and coaches and put the team above themselves. Then years later, seeing them as adults with families of their own and having them tell you how influential you were in their lives.

Wasn't it great when the big boys picked you to play with them for the first time? It was like a rite of passage. There was nothing like having the people you looked up to accept you as an equal or close to it. The only thing that they would say is no crying. If you were going to play with the big boys than tough it out and prove you belong. Then you would go up the pecking order from the last pick to one of the first. That was all of the motivation one needed to be good.

Wasn't it great to make the team for the first time in organized sports? To have the coach tell you that you're good enough and belong on the squad is such a confidence boost. Then going to your first practice and meeting your teammates. Just as with the big boys you had to prove that you could play. When you did, they accepted and counted on you. The first uniform is always the one you remember. You remember the team name stitched on it and the number. It was the first time that you really felt like a pro.

Wasn't it great hitting your first home run or scoring your first touchdown? Swinging the bat and seeing that ball sail over the fence was almost surreal, because it felt like you barely hit it. Being so focused that when the pitcher let go of the ball you could actually see the laces as it seemed to travel in slow motion. Then rounding the bases and meeting your teammates at home plate. Scoring that first touchdown and seeing your teammates come to hug you and hearing the crowd cheer, say your name and call out your number. Seeing the sheer joy of your teammates, the coaches and the cheerleaders on the sidelines. Feeling almost invincible. And wanting to do it again.

Wasn't it great when your dad came to see you play for the first time? Especially in the time that I grew up in, because most of our parents were just way too busy trying to support their families to make time for watching a ball game. As kids we accepted this, because it wasn't that they didn't care. But when they did come to a game and you did something special it was great hearing your father cheering for you from the stands or any family member for that matter. It was always nice to have other people see that your family cared about you. And it was great watching your siblings play and do well also. I was proud of all my brothers and sisters growing up as well as my cousins. Because I was one of the youngest, they set the bar for me and all I ever really wanted was for them to say that I was pretty good.

Wasn't it great when you went to your first baseball game with your father? Just the two of you, no one else. Walking up to the ticket booth and getting great seats behind home plate (try that today). The tickets cost eight bucks apiece. Then walking into the stadium and seeing how green everything was unlike the black and white of television and newspaper. Having your dad explain to you the little nuances of the game and which players to watch and learn from. Just spending the day together talking and having a good time.

Wasn't it great seeing your favorite team win the championship for the first time? If you were a kid it meant bragging rights with your friends for an entire year. But the sooner your team wins a championship, the less you appreciate it and the more entitlement one feels. They should repeat for sure and win it all of the time. The best championships are the ones which come after years of waiting and near miss disappointments. When it does finally happen it's almost as if you're dreaming. This can't be? They never win. Ah, but it is true. And what a thrill.

Wasn't it great being on a championship team of your own? Getting together with a group of guys at the beginning of a season with high expectations and one goal. Then going through the season winning game after game in so many different ways until, by the end of the year, everyone expects it to happen. Winning in the playoffs, having the pressure ratchet up with each game and not feeling it one bit. Finally, winning a chance to play for the championship by beating your opponent in the semifinals. The anticipation leading up to the championship game. Then playing in it and winning it. An unbelievable feeling of joy and accomplishment. Leaving the field smiling so hard until your jaw hurts. And knowing that as long as you live once in your life you were one of the best.

Wasn't it just as great to win a game or beat an opponent when no one thought you would, maybe not even yourself? To be told all day or week that you or your team had no chance of victory. To be told that so and so was going to strike you out or block your shot or score four touchdowns against you. To be told that you may as well not even show up. Then getting into the game and finding out that the other team is human. That they can be beaten. And seeing the look on their faces as you hang in there with them throughout the game. The look of confidence turning into surprise, then self doubt as something happens during the course of the game which tells them you can beat them and they can lose. Then you take the lead, they panic and the game is over with the wrong team winning. They may call you lucky and the fans may call it an upset, but you can just way, "We won."

Isn't it great when your team is down and makes an unbelievable comeback or pulls a game out as time expires? The games when your team seems all but finished only to storm back and win are always better than the ones in which they lead from wire to wire. These comebacks are even better when they come against a rival or happen in post season. These are the games when we cuss and fuss while vowing to give up on our teams only to have them bring us back by coming back. And there is nothing like seeing the faces of the other team's fans as their lead slips away. I don't know too many people who don't like saying, "It's not over 'til it's over," to the other team's fans. And we all live for that buzzer beater in basketball that just sends the place into hysterics at home or silences the crowd on the road. Or the walk off home run with two outs and your team down in the last inning. Or the "Hail Mary" pass that actually clicks for a touchdown as time runs. We love these moments, because they are so rare for our team and unexpected that they bring on a spontaneous explosion of emotion. There is no reality show or video game that can match that.

I don't condone gambling, but isn't it great when you beat the bookmakers and win a huge bet? You put your money down on an athlete, animal or team knowing that the odds are not in your favor. So many things have to go right in order for you to win that when it happens there is almost a feeling of disbelief. Did my team really win? Is this the ticket that has the trifecta? Did I really win that much money? It is almost as if you don't believe it until the money is put in your hands. You know that you're not really that smart, but it doesn't stop you from feeling like the smartest man on the planet. And everyone who lost is a sucker. It is such a high that you can't wait to feel it again, because everyone loves to win money. You may end up being the sucker more often than not, but the times when you beat the house are worth every cent. The key part of that last sentence was the beginning so no matter how great it may be I still recommend not gambling at all.

Isn't it great getting together with a group of friends or fans at someone's home, in a public place or at the stadium to cheer on your favorite team? There you are with a group of people from different ages, races, backgrounds, education, income, religions and political beliefs all sharing a common bond. Everyone is united in the love of their team and nothing else matters at that moment. You cheer together. You laugh together. You get angry and swear together. You commiserate together. You may not like the person next to you and they may feel likewise, but for those few minutes all of that is put aside, because your team needs you. Everyone can forget about their troubles and cares for a while and just have a good time.

These moments are made even better when someone you love is competing. As great as it is to watch your favorite team it can't beat watching a parent, sibling, relative, son, daughter, niece or nephew compete. Getting together with the other adults in the community to get them to the games and cheer for them. Seeing them do something really well and hearing people cheer for them. If it is a child, having other parents and coaches come up and tell you how impressed they are with them on and off the field. Seeing them grow in confidence. And just watching them have a good time. Everyone should take a personal snapshot of these moments, because they happen fast and are gone before you know it.

And isn't that what sports and life is about? Shared moments of love between people that create lasting memories? Good times which unite people break down walls and bring them closer together. There is nothing outside of a national disaster or war which brings people of all walks of life closer together like sports does whether we like it or not. And it is the people who make sports and life what it is. Whether it's the owners, management, players, officials, fans or media all of us make up the sporting landscape. And all of us are drawn to it, because it is supposed to be fun. Of all the things written in this book this last chapter is the most important. Sport is not life and death. In the end, its importance is that it makes us fit human beings, help develop life skills, brings us closer together as people and gives joy to those who participate in them and have fun if they allow it to. That's it.

If we are in it for any other reason, than watching and participating is a waste of time.